D0941217

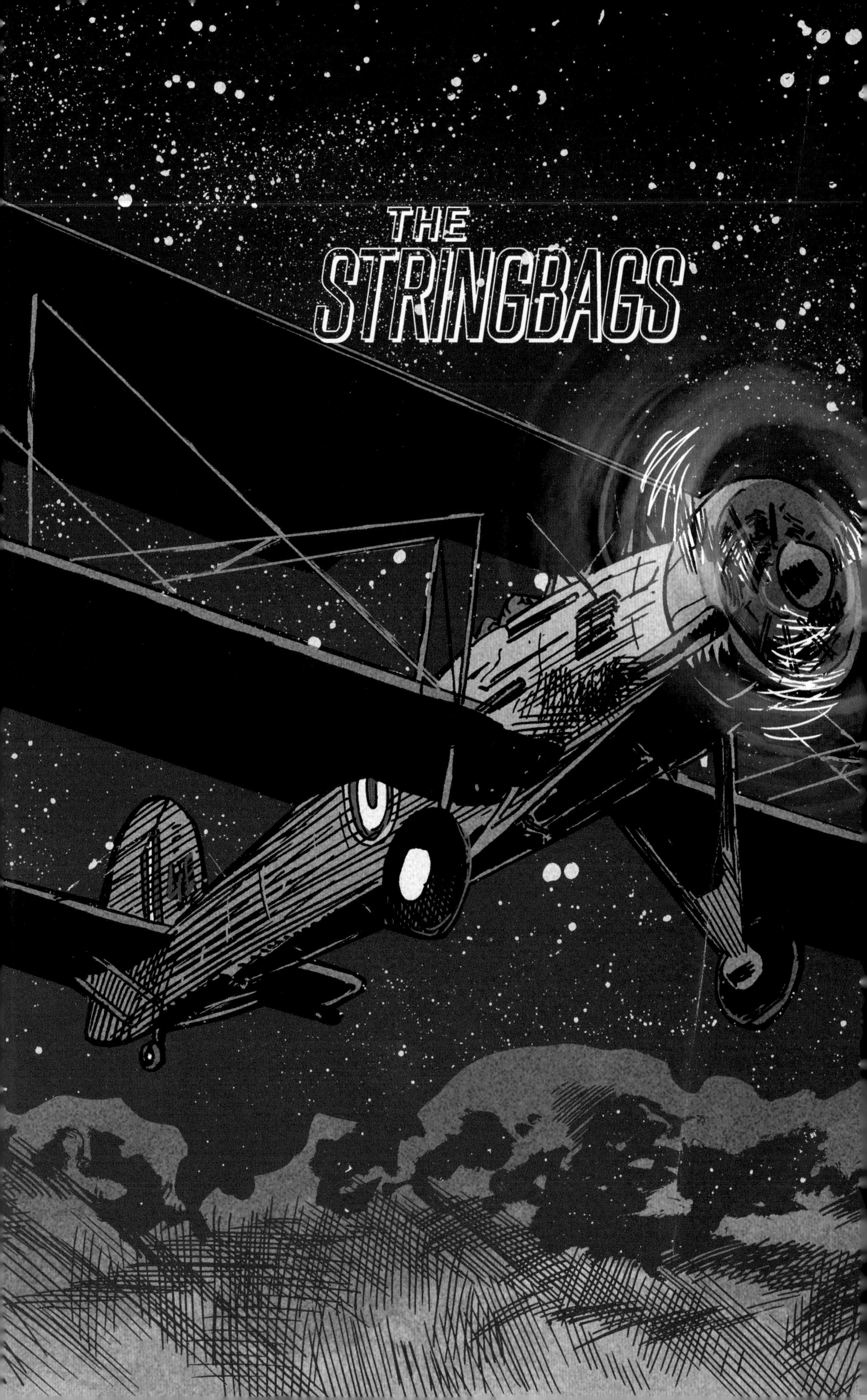
THE
STRINGBAGS

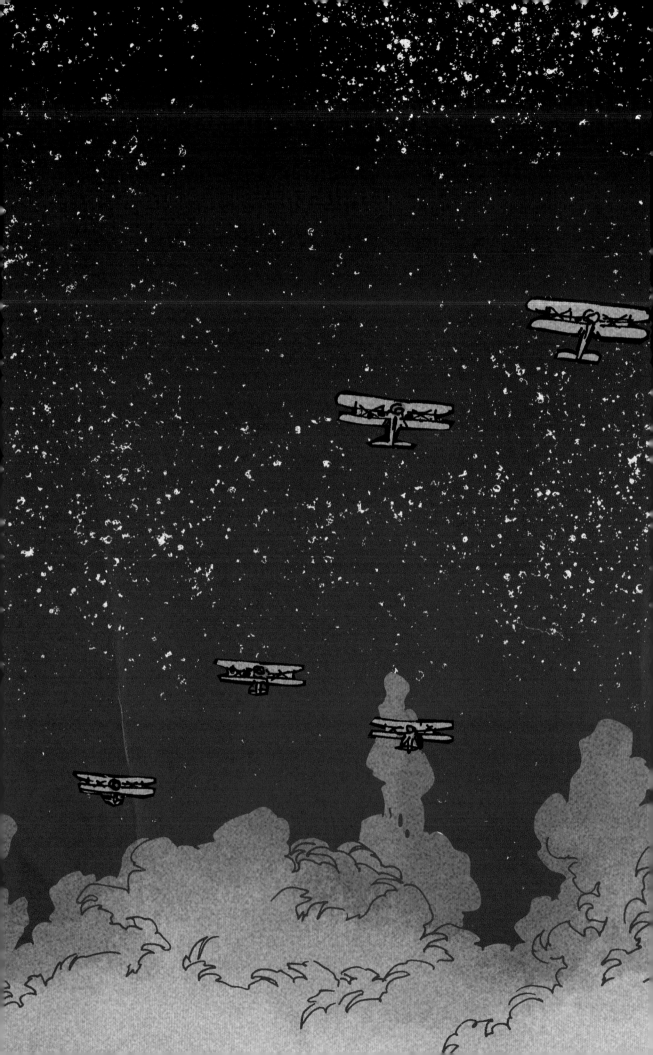

THE STRINGBAGS

Written by Garth ENNIS

Drawn by PJ HOLDEN

Colored by Kelly FITZPATRICK

Lettered by Rob STEEN

DEAD RECKONING

Annapolis, Maryland

Published by Dead Reckoning
291 Wood Road
Annapolis, MD 21402

Library of Congress Cataloging-in-Publication Data
Names: Ennis, Garth, writer. | Holden, P. J., illustrator. | Fitzpatrick, Kelly,
    date, colourist. | Steen, Rob, date, letterer.
Title: The Stringbags / written by Garth Ennis; drawn by PJ Holden; colored
    by Kelly Fitzpatrick ; lettered by Rob Steen.
Description: Annapolis, Maryland : Dead Reckoning, [2020]
Identifiers: LCCN 2019043247 (print) | LCCN 2019043248 (ebook) |
    ISBN 9781682475034 (hardcover) | ISBN 9781682475232 (pdf) |
    ISBN 9781682475232 (epub)
Subjects: LCSH: Great Britain. Royal Navy—Aviation—Comic books, strips, etc. |
    Great Britain. Royal Navy. Fleet Air Arm—Comic books, strips, etc. | Swordfish
    (Torpedo bomber)—History—Comic books, strips, etc. | World War, 1939–
    1945—Aerial operations, British—Comic books, strips, etc. | Graphic novels.
Classification: LCC PN6727.E56 S77 2020 (print) | LCC PN6727.E56 (ebook) |
    DDC 741.5/973—dc23
LC record available at https://lccn.loc.gov/2019043247
LC ebook record available at https://lccn.loc.gov/2019043248

♾ Print editions meet the requirements of ANSI/NISO z39.48-1992.
(Permanence of Paper).
Printed in the United States of America.

28 27 26 25 24 23 22 21 20   9 8 7 6 5 4 3 2 1
First printing

Contents

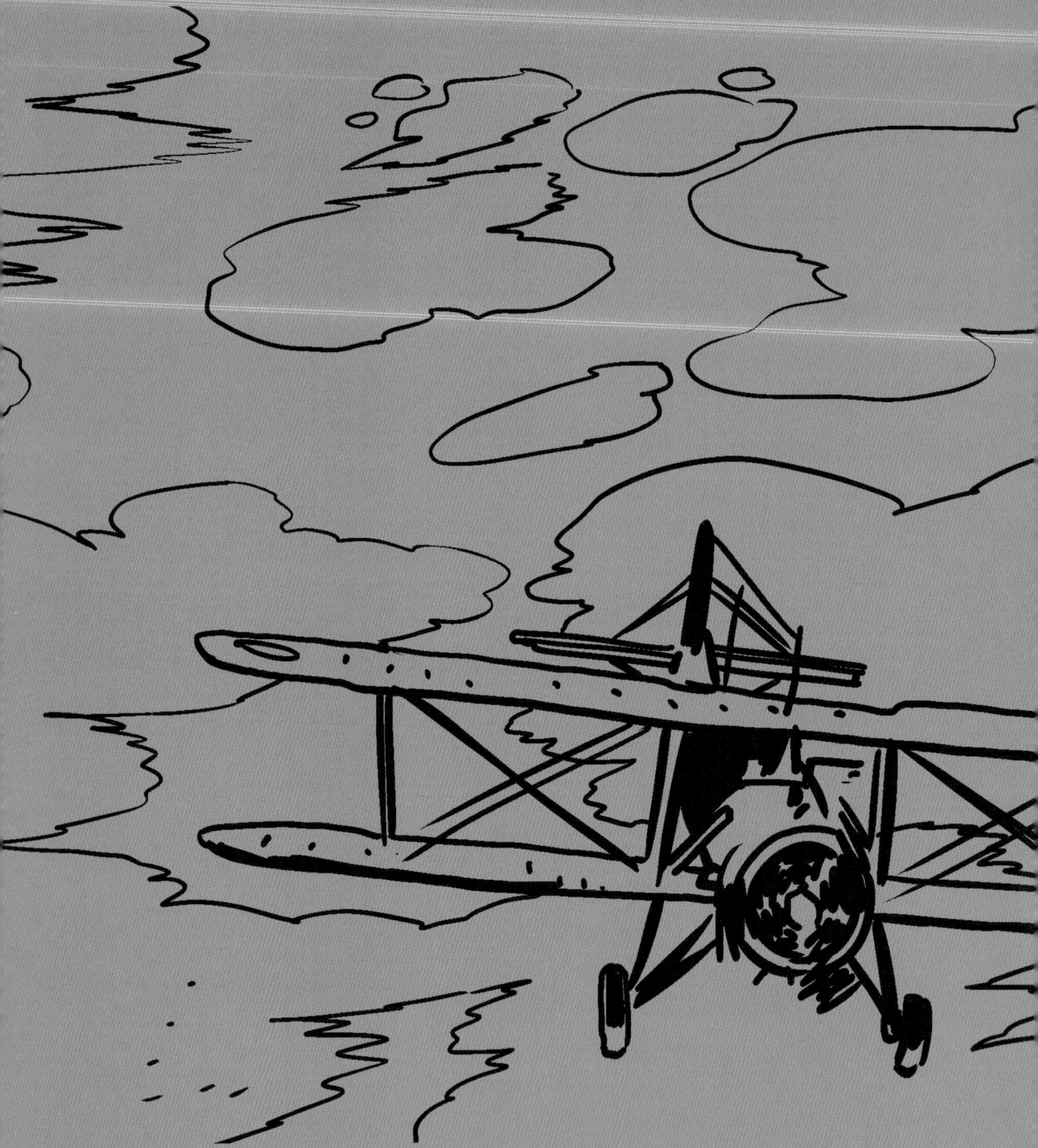

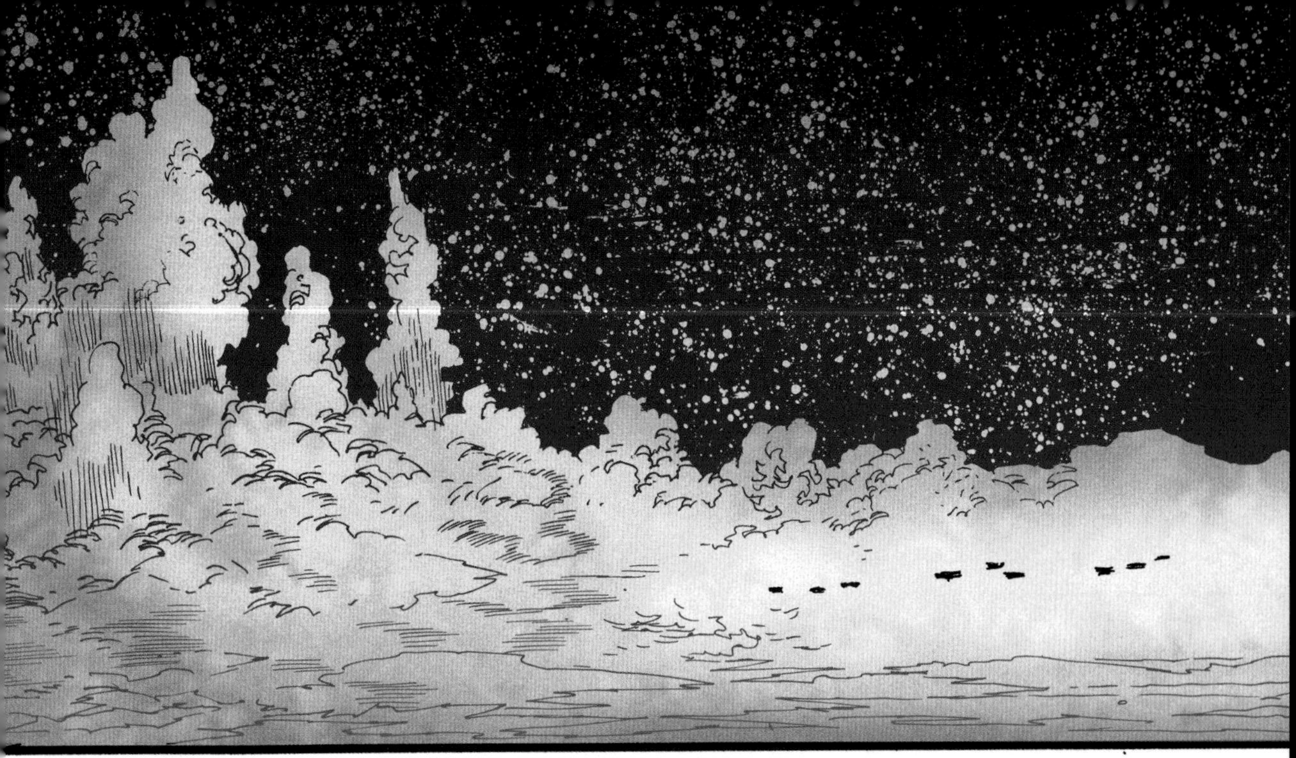

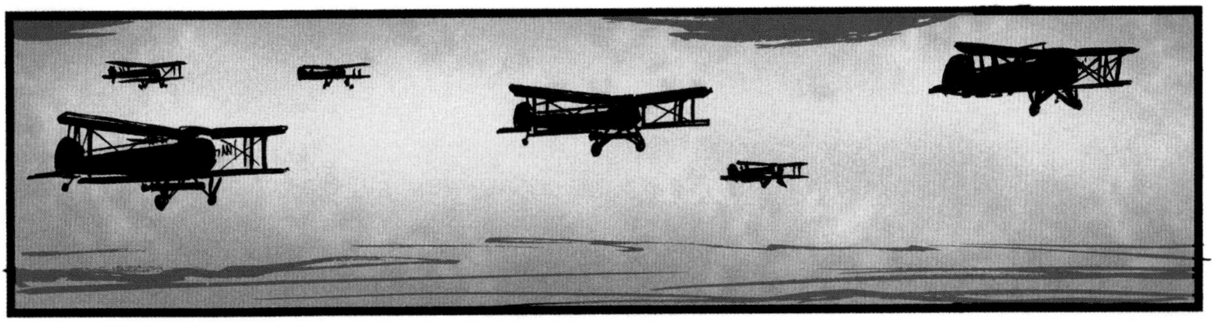

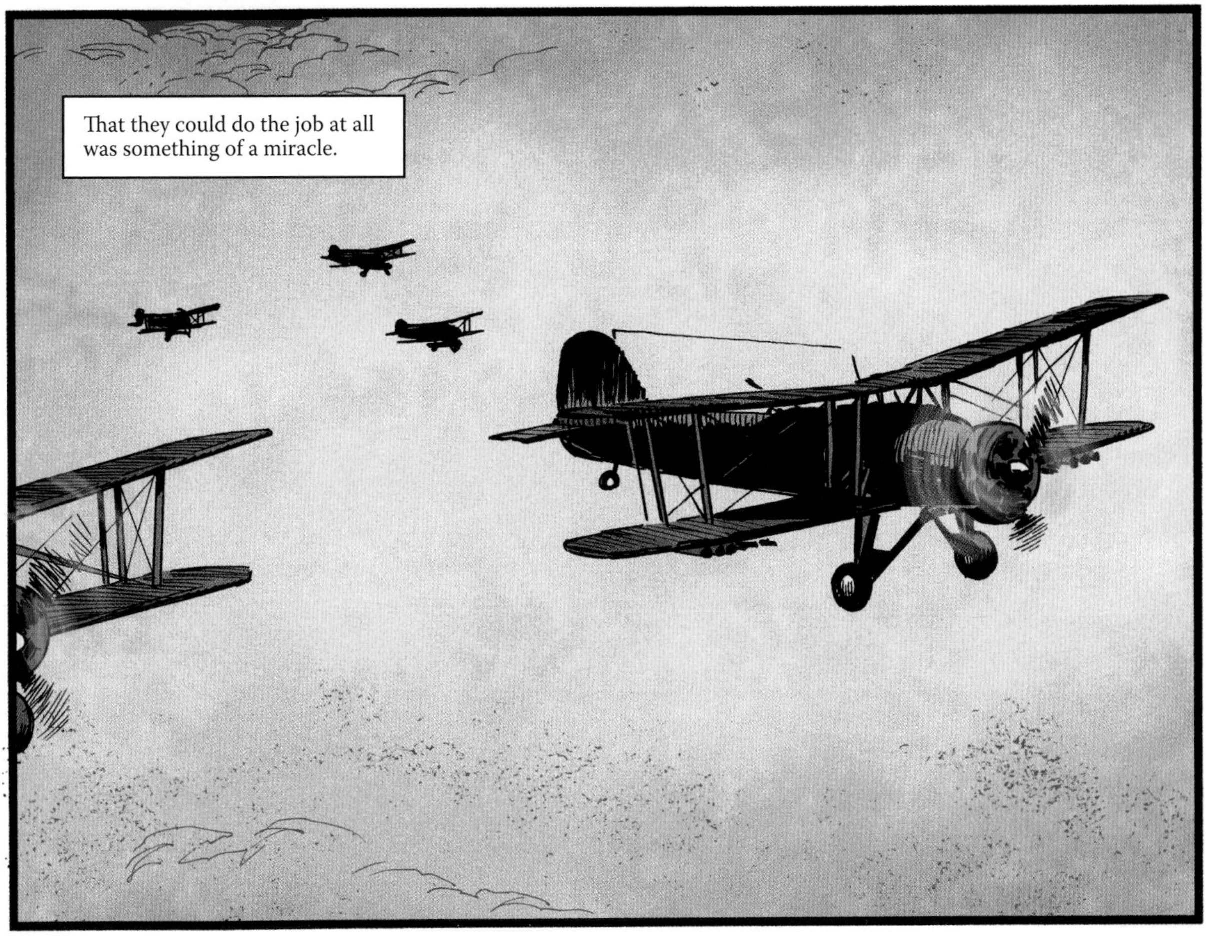
That they could do the job at all was something of a miracle.

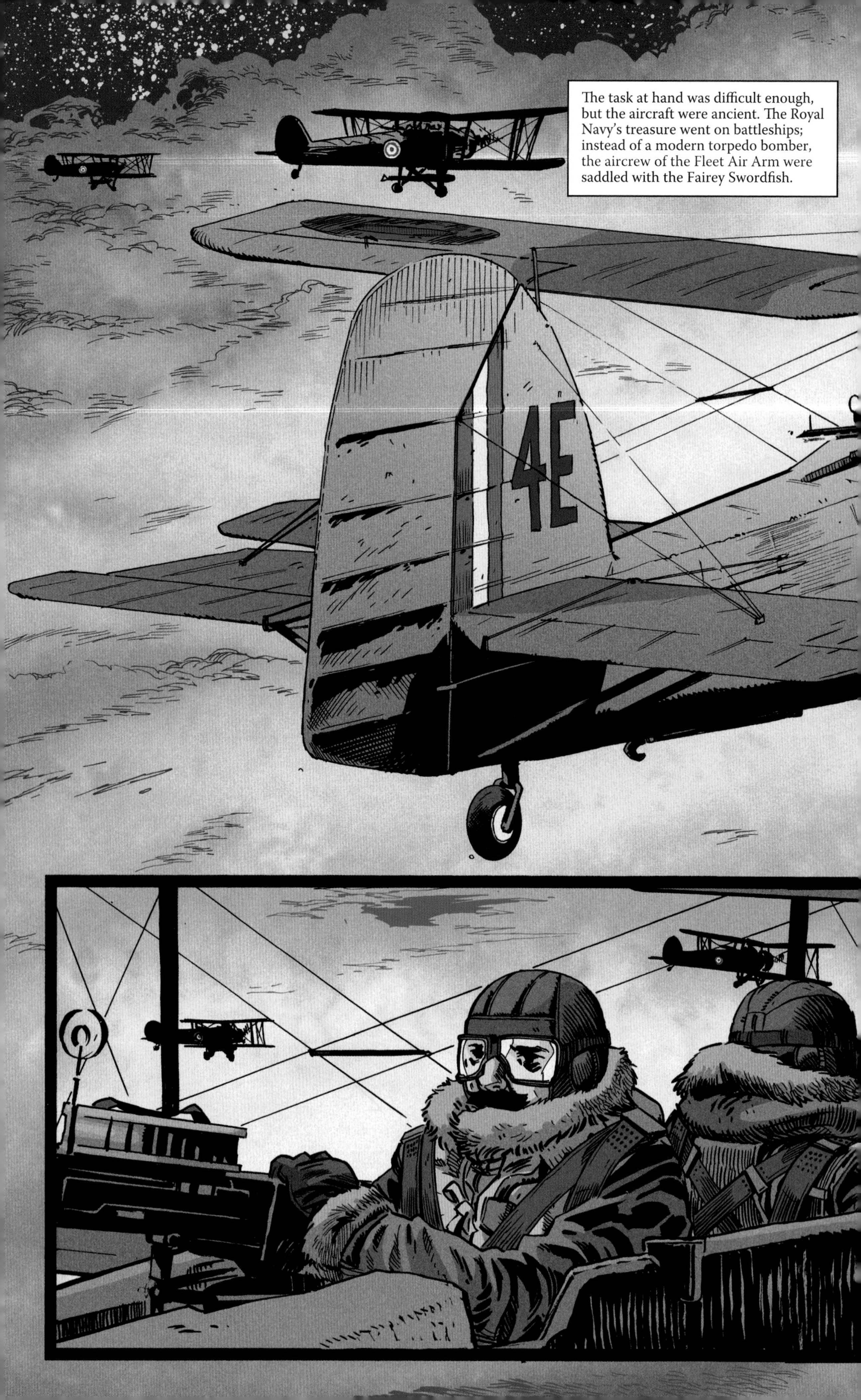
The task at hand was difficult enough, but the aircraft were ancient. The Royal Navy's treasure went on battleships; instead of a modern torpedo bomber, the aircrew of the Fleet Air Arm were saddled with the Fairey Swordfish.
4E

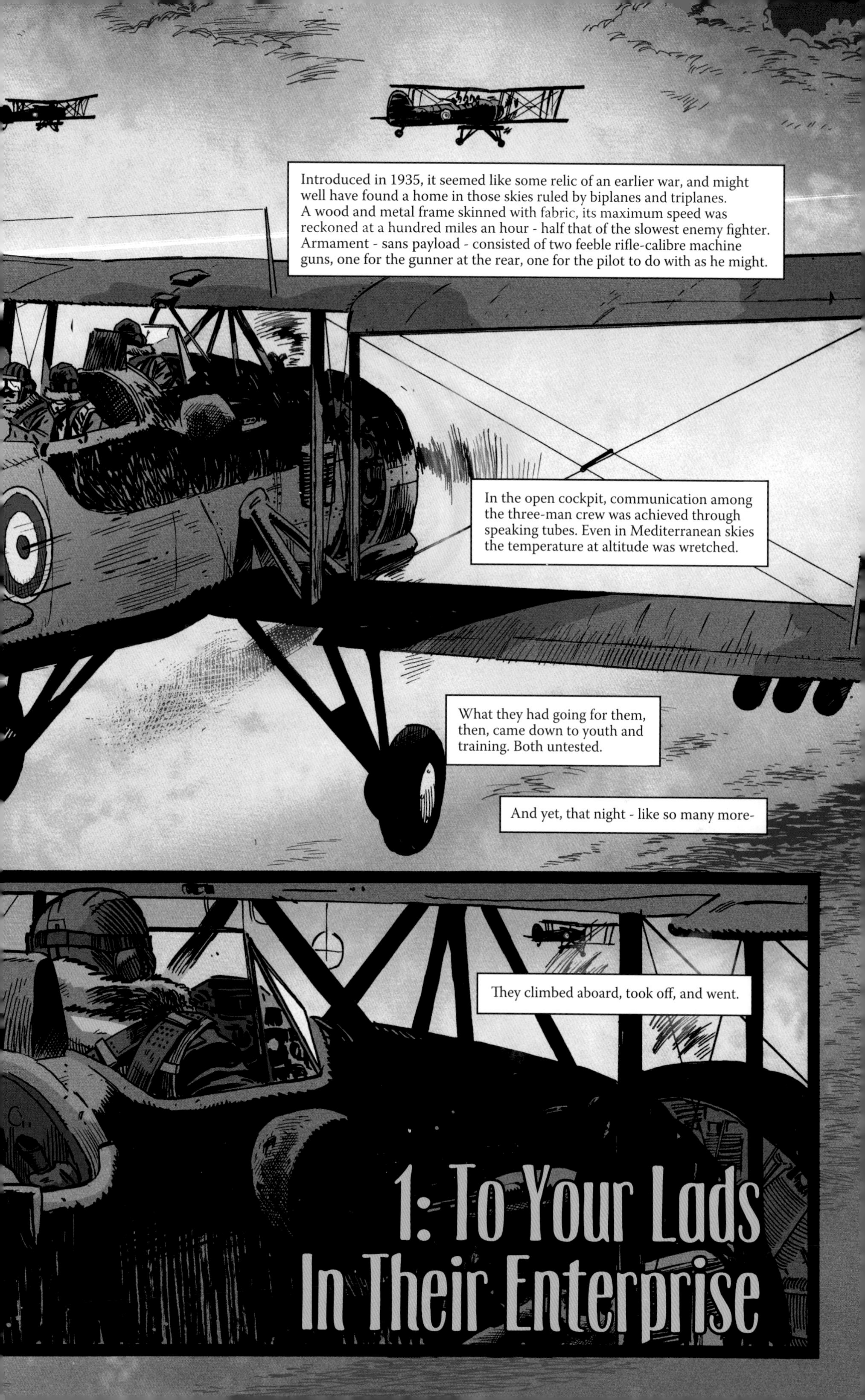
Introduced in 1935, it seemed like some relic of an earlier war, and might well have found a home in those skies ruled by biplanes and triplanes. A wood and metal frame skinned with fabric, its maximum speed was reckoned at a hundred miles an hour - half that of the slowest enemy fighter. Armament - sans payload - consisted of two feeble rifle-calibre machine guns, one for the gunner at the rear, one for the pilot to do with as he might.
In the open cockpit, communication among the three-man crew was achieved through speaking tubes. Even in Mediterranean skies the temperature at altitude was wretched.
What they had going for them, then, came down to youth and training. Both untested.
And yet, that night - like so many more-
They climbed aboard, took off, and went.
1: To Your Lads In Their Enterprise

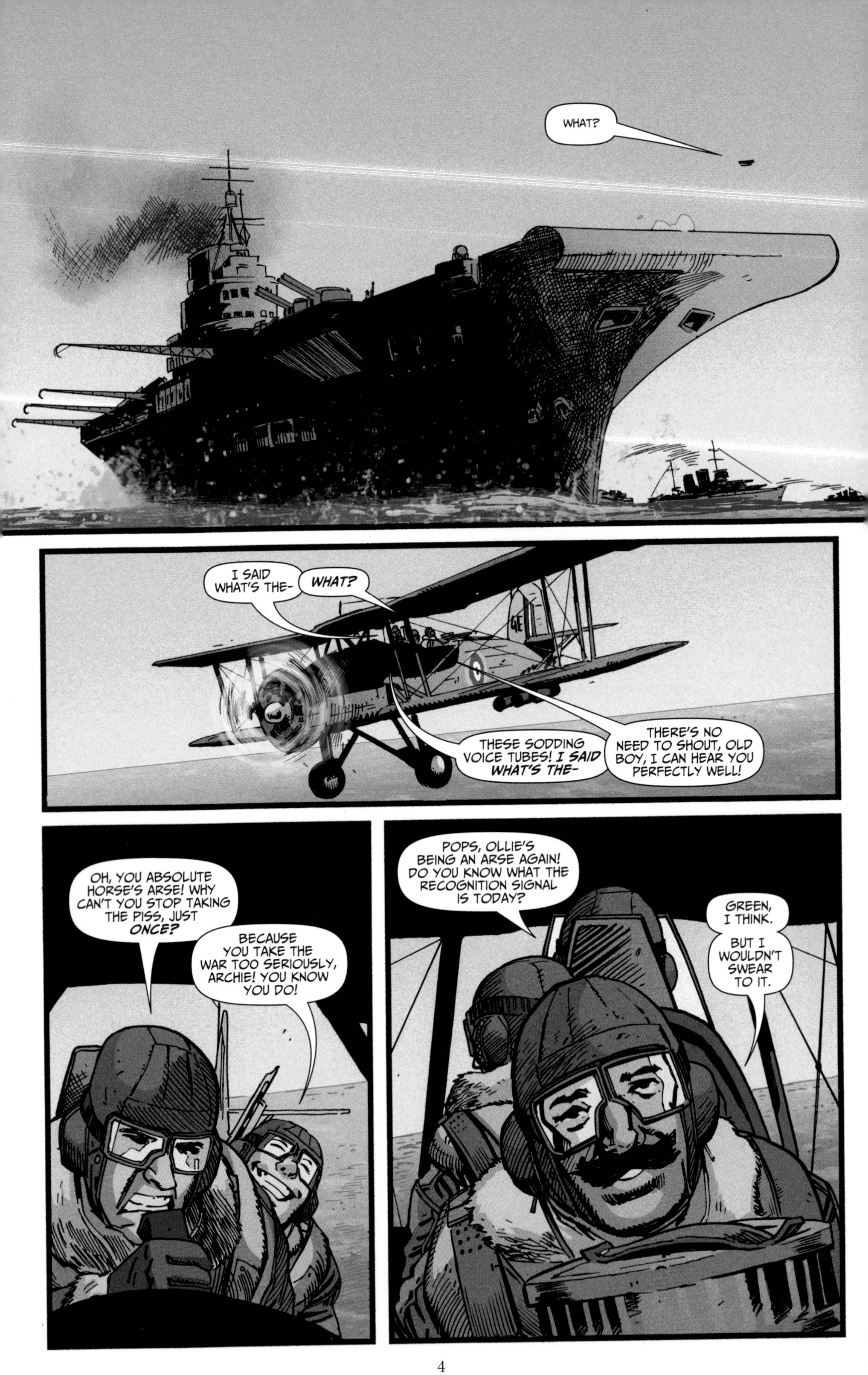
WHAT?
I SAID WHAT'S THE-
WHAT?
THESE SODDING VOICE TUBES! I SAID WHAT'S THE-
THERE'S NO NEED TO SHOUT, OLD BOY, I CAN HEAR YOU PERFECTLY WELL!
OH, YOU ABSOLUTE HORSE'S ARSE! WHY CAN'T YOU STOP TAKING THE PISS, JUST ONCE?
BECAUSE YOU TAKE THE WAR TOO SERIOUSLY, ARCHIE! YOU KNOW YOU DO!
POPS, OLLIE'S BEING AN ARSE AGAIN! DO YOU KNOW WHAT THE RECOGNITION SIGNAL IS TODAY?
GREEN, I THINK.
BUT I WOULDN'T SWEAR TO IT.

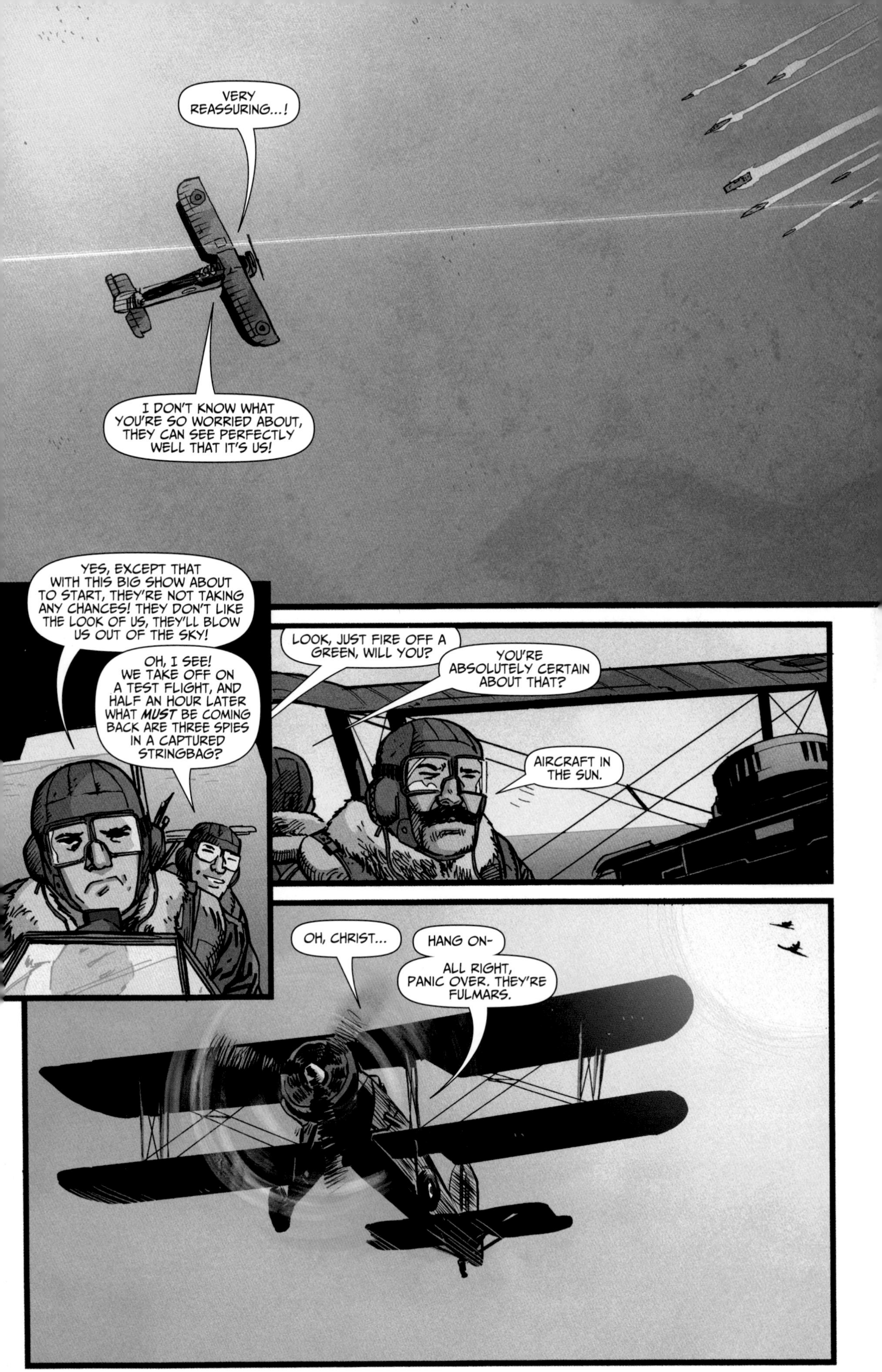
VERY REASSURING...!
I DON'T KNOW WHAT YOU'RE SO WORRIED ABOUT, THEY CAN SEE PERFECTLY WELL THAT IT'S US!
YES, EXCEPT THAT WITH THIS BIG SHOW ABOUT TO START, THEY'RE NOT TAKING ANY CHANCES! THEY DON'T LIKE THE LOOK OF US, THEY'LL BLOW US OUT OF THE SKY!
OH, I SEE! WE TAKE OFF ON A TEST FLIGHT, AND HALF AN HOUR LATER WHAT *MUST* BE COMING BACK ARE THREE SPIES IN A CAPTURED STRINGBAG?
LOOK, JUST FIRE OFF A GREEN, WILL YOU?
YOU'RE ABSOLUTELY CERTAIN ABOUT THAT?
AIRCRAFT IN THE SUN.
OH, CHRIST...
HANG ON-
ALL RIGHT, PANIC OVER. THEY'RE FULMARS.

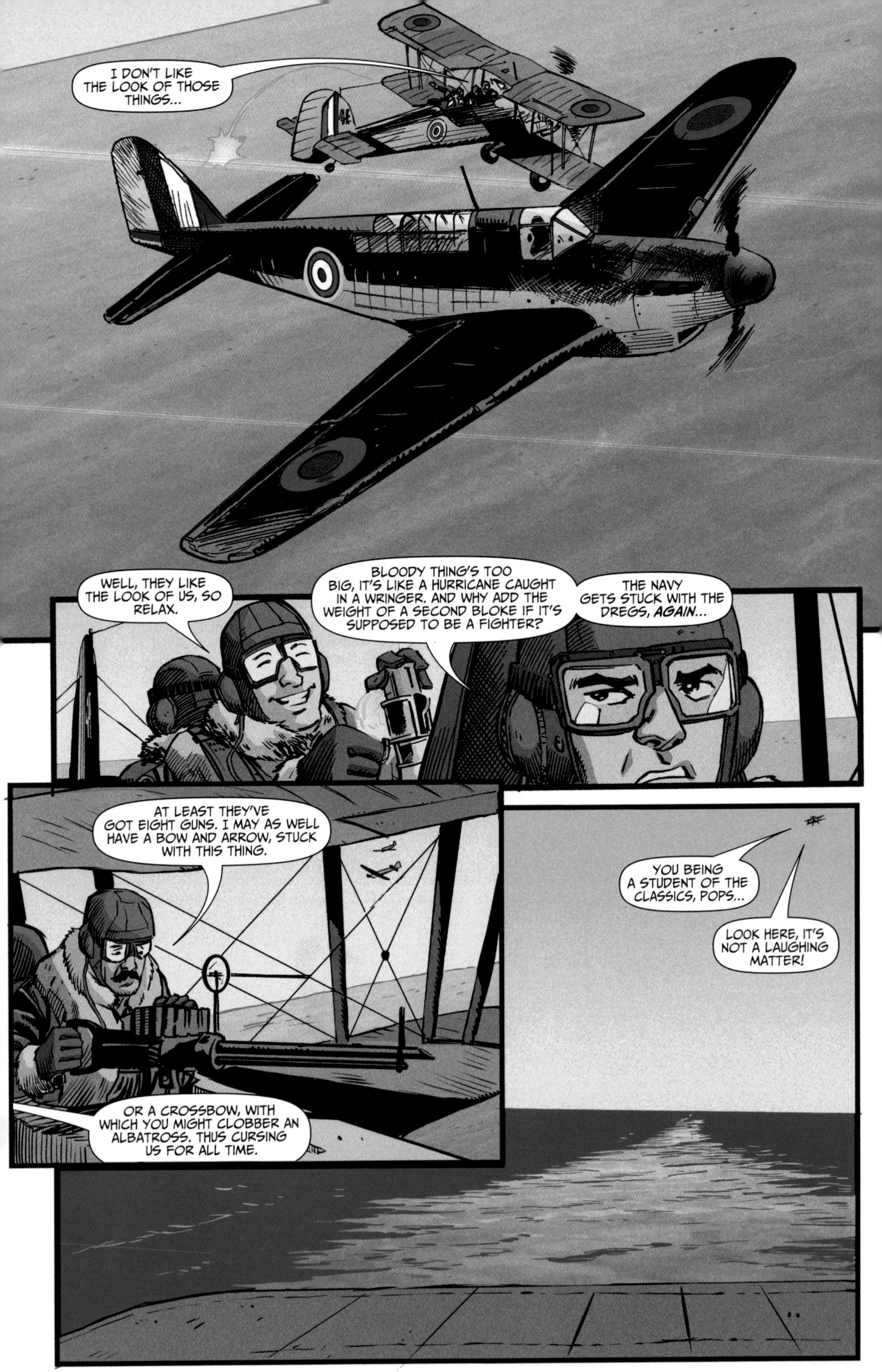
I DON'T LIKE THE LOOK OF THOSE THINGS...
WELL, THEY LIKE THE LOOK OF US, SO RELAX.
BLOODY THING'S TOO BIG, IT'S LIKE A HURRICANE CAUGHT IN A WRINGER. AND WHY ADD THE WEIGHT OF A SECOND BLOKE IF IT'S SUPPOSED TO BE A FIGHTER?
THE NAVY GETS STUCK WITH THE DREGS, AGAIN...
AT LEAST THEY'VE GOT EIGHT GUNS. I MAY AS WELL HAVE A BOW AND ARROW, STUCK WITH THIS THING.
OR A CROSSBOW, WITH WHICH YOU MIGHT CLOBBER AN ALBATROSS. THUS CURSING US FOR ALL TIME.
YOU BEING A STUDENT OF THE CLASSICS, POPS...
LOOK HERE, IT'S NOT A LAUGHING MATTER!

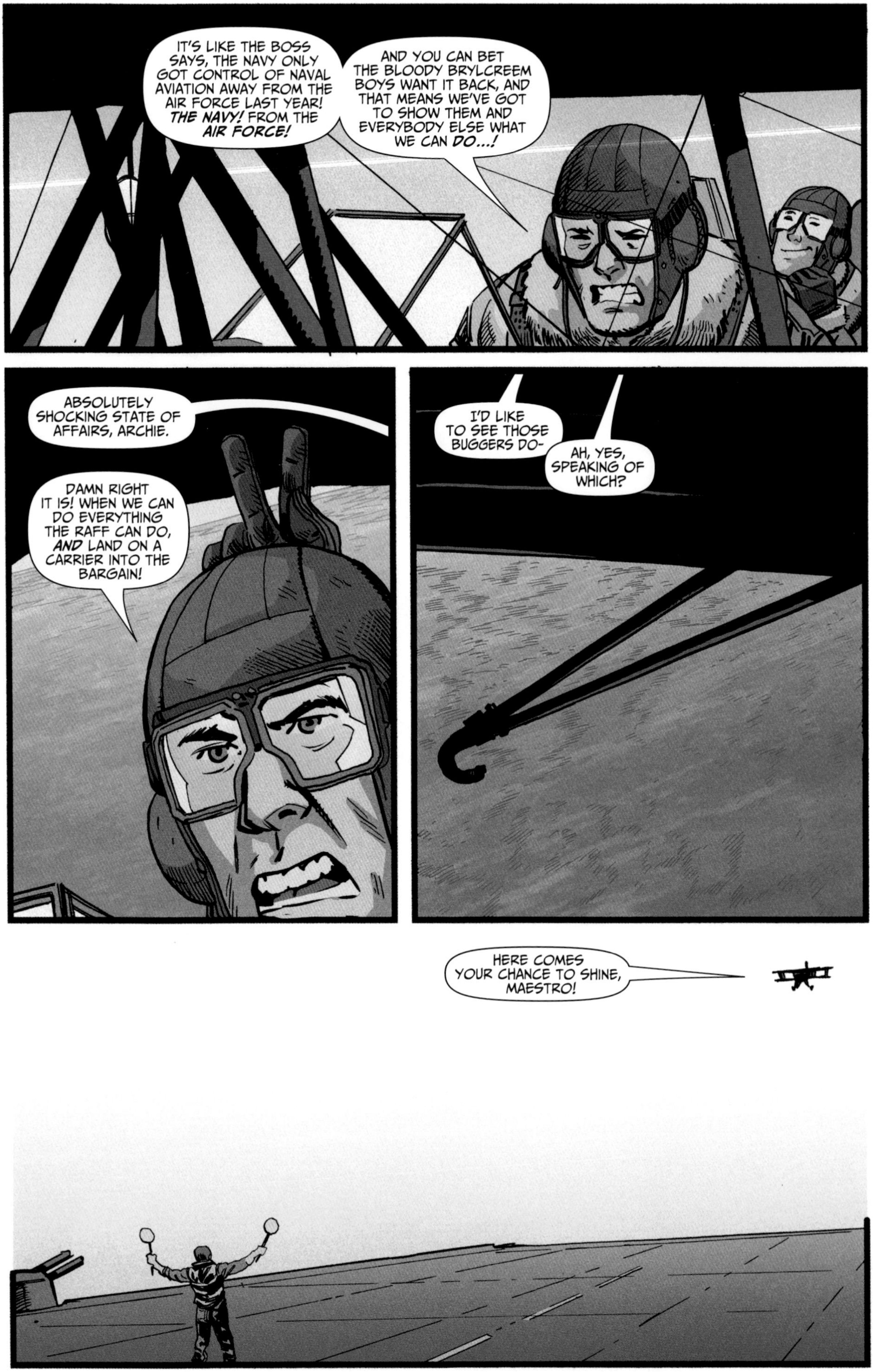
IT'S LIKE THE BOSS SAYS, THE NAVY ONLY GOT CONTROL OF NAVAL AVIATION AWAY FROM THE AIR FORCE LAST YEAR! *THE NAVY!* FROM THE *AIR FORCE!*
AND YOU CAN BET THE BLOODY BRYLCREEM BOYS WANT IT BACK, AND THAT MEANS WE'VE GOT TO SHOW THEM AND EVERYBODY ELSE WHAT WE CAN *DO...!*
ABSOLUTELY SHOCKING STATE OF AFFAIRS, ARCHIE.
DAMN RIGHT IT IS! WHEN WE CAN DO EVERYTHING THE RAFF CAN DO, *AND* LAND ON A CARRIER INTO THE BARGAIN!
I'D LIKE TO SEE THOSE BUGGERS DO-
AH, YES, SPEAKING OF WHICH?
HERE COMES YOUR CHANCE TO SHINE, MAESTRO!

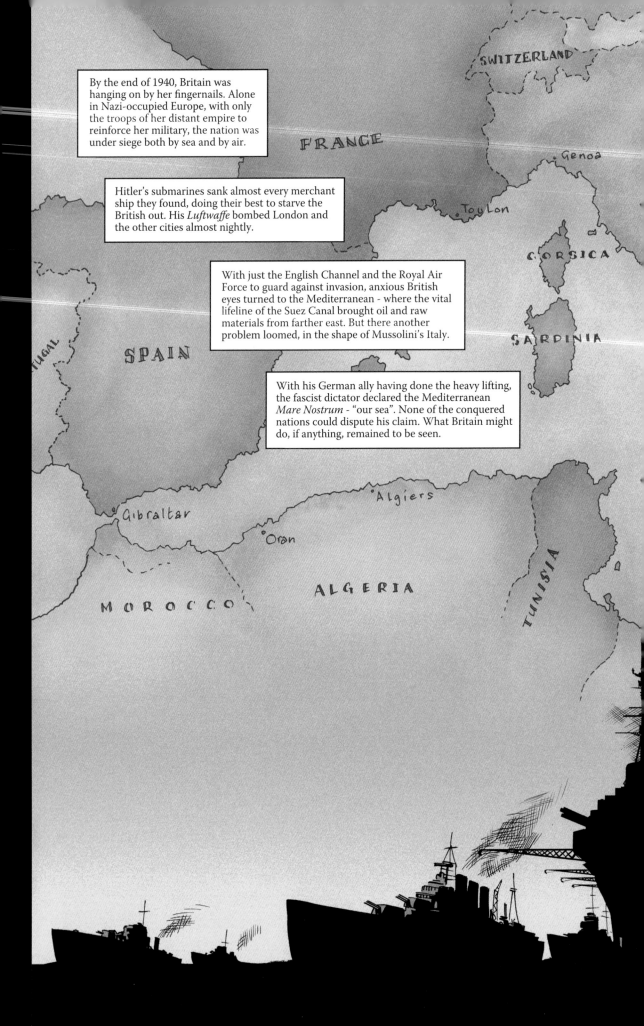

By the end of 1940, Britain was hanging on by her fingernails. Alone in Nazi-occupied Europe, with only the troops of her distant empire to reinforce her military, the nation was under siege both by sea and by air.

Hitler's submarines sank almost every merchant ship they found, doing their best to starve the British out. His *Luftwaffe* bombed London and the other cities almost nightly.

With just the English Channel and the Royal Air Force to guard against invasion, anxious British eyes turned to the Mediterranean - where the vital lifeline of the Suez Canal brought oil and raw materials from farther east. But there another problem loomed, in the shape of Mussolini's Italy.

With his German ally having done the heavy lifting, the fascist dictator declared the Mediterranean *Mare Nostrum* - "our sea". None of the conquered nations could dispute his claim. What Britain might do, if anything, remained to be seen.

SWITZERLAND

FRANCE

Genoa

Toulon

CORSICA

SARDINIA

SPAIN

PORTUGAL

Gibraltar

Oran

Algiers

MOROCCO

ALGERIA

TUNISIA

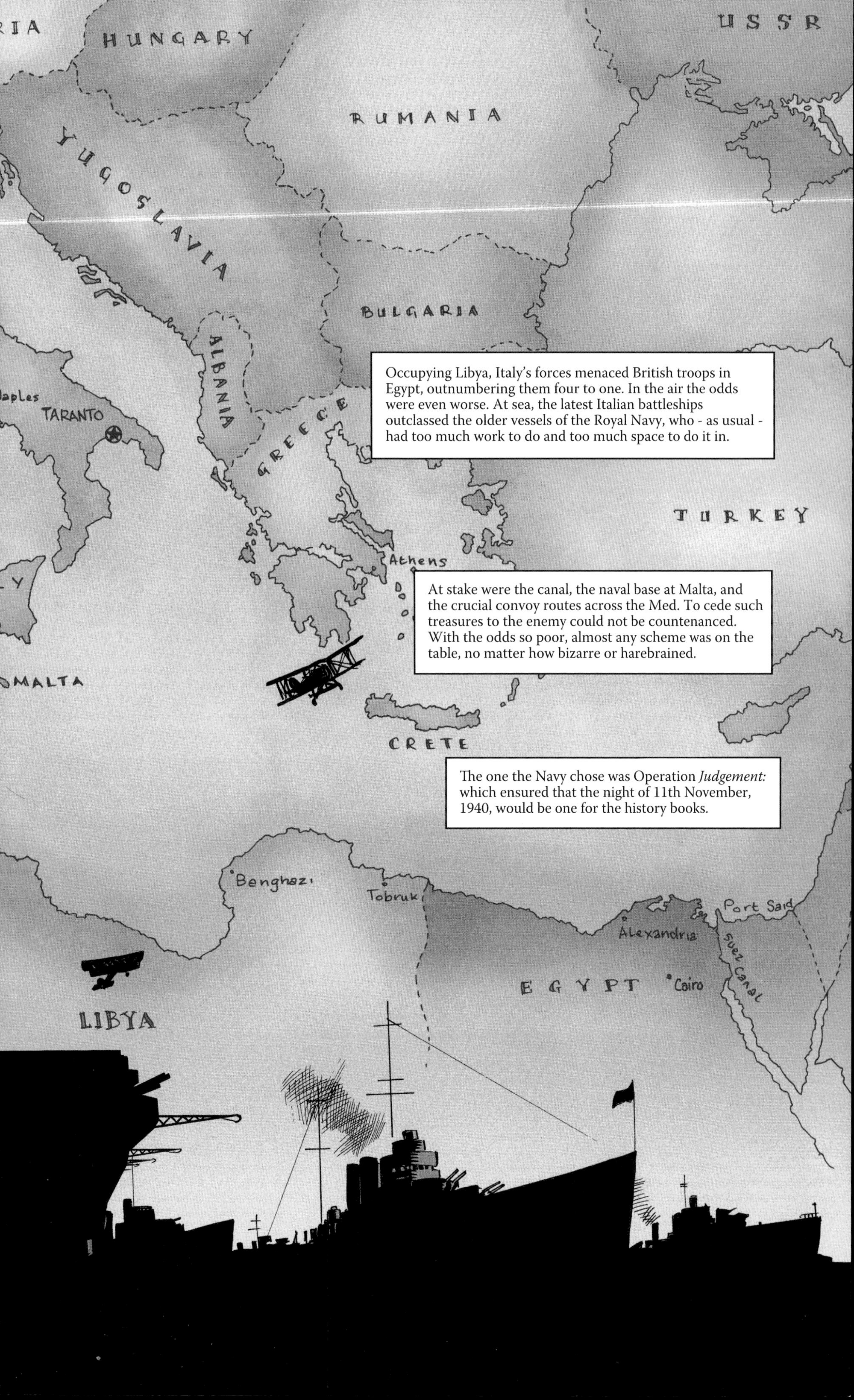

HUNGARY
USSR
RUMANIA
YUGOSLAVIA
BULGARIA
ALBANIA
TARANTO
GREECE
Occupying Libya, Italy's forces menaced British troops in Egypt, outnumbering them four to one. In the air the odds were even worse. At sea, the latest Italian battleships outclassed the older vessels of the Royal Navy, who - as usual - had too much work to do and too much space to do it in.
TURKEY
Athens
At stake were the canal, the naval base at Malta, and the crucial convoy routes across the Med. To cede such treasures to the enemy could not be countenanced. With the odds so poor, almost any scheme was on the table, no matter how bizarre or harebrained.
MALTA
CRETE
The one the Navy chose was Operation *Judgement:* which ensured that the night of 11th November, 1940, would be one for the history books.
Benghazi
Tobruk
Port Said
Alexandria
Suez Canal
EGYPT
Cairo
LIBYA

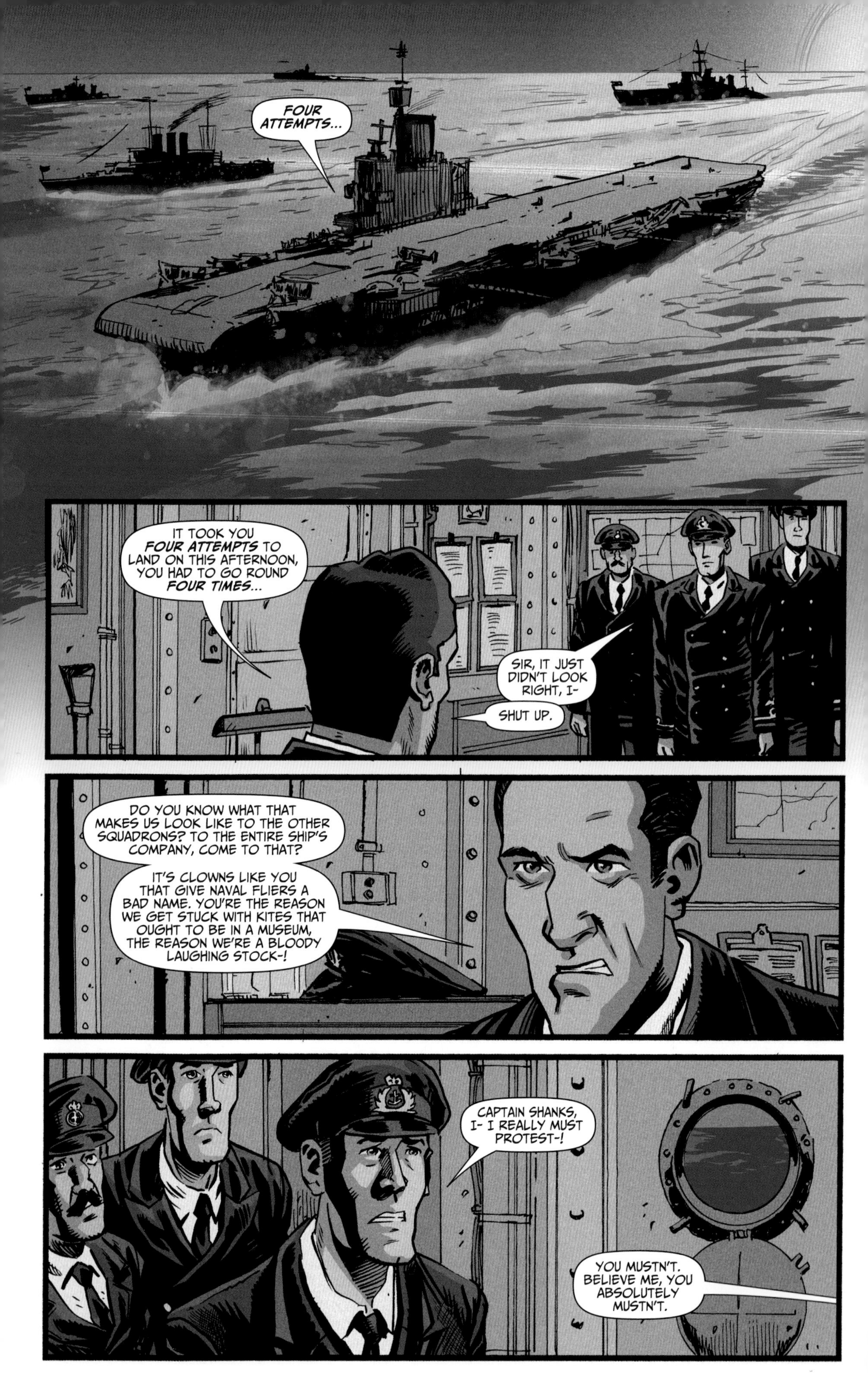
FOUR ATTEMPTS...
IT TOOK YOU FOUR ATTEMPTS TO LAND ON THIS AFTERNOON, YOU HAD TO GO ROUND FOUR TIMES...
SIR, IT JUST DIDN'T LOOK RIGHT, I-
SHUT UP.
DO YOU KNOW WHAT THAT MAKES US LOOK LIKE TO THE OTHER SQUADRONS? TO THE ENTIRE SHIP'S COMPANY, COME TO THAT?
IT'S CLOWNS LIKE YOU THAT GIVE NAVAL FLIERS A BAD NAME. YOU'RE THE REASON WE GET STUCK WITH KITES THAT OUGHT TO BE IN A MUSEUM, THE REASON WE'RE A BLOODY LAUGHING STOCK-!
CAPTAIN SHANKS, I- I REALLY MUST PROTEST-!
YOU MUSTN'T. BELIEVE ME, YOU ABSOLUTELY MUSTN'T.

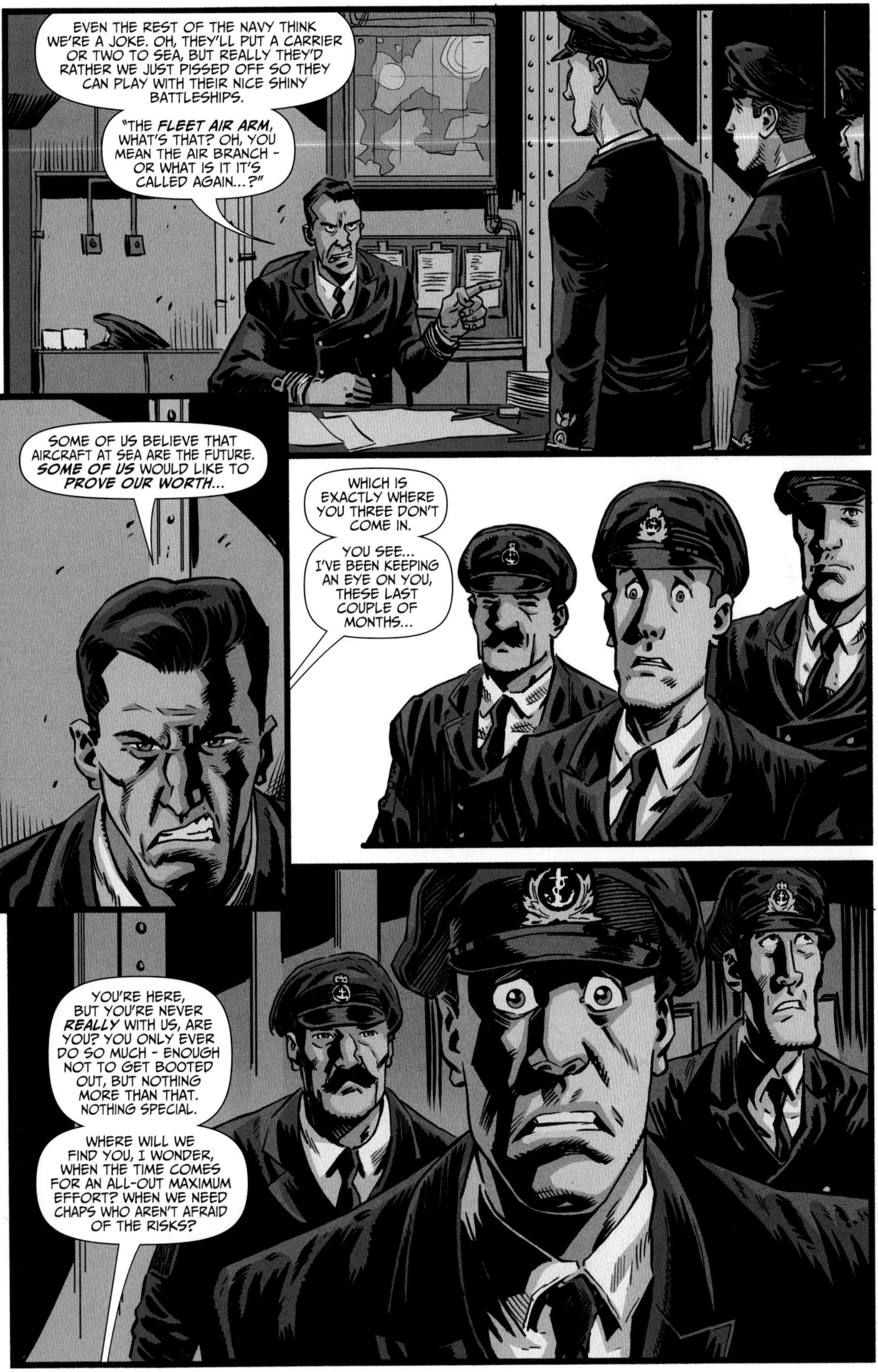
EVEN THE REST OF THE NAVY THINK WE'RE A JOKE. OH, THEY'LL PUT A CARRIER OR TWO TO SEA, BUT REALLY THEY'D RATHER WE JUST PISSED OFF SO THEY CAN PLAY WITH THEIR NICE SHINY BATTLESHIPS.
"THE FLEET AIR ARM, WHAT'S THAT? OH, YOU MEAN THE AIR BRANCH - OR WHAT IS IT IT'S CALLED AGAIN...?"
SOME OF US BELIEVE THAT AIRCRAFT AT SEA ARE THE FUTURE. SOME OF US WOULD LIKE TO PROVE OUR WORTH...
WHICH IS EXACTLY WHERE YOU THREE DON'T COME IN.
YOU SEE... I'VE BEEN KEEPING AN EYE ON YOU, THESE LAST COUPLE OF MONTHS...
YOU'RE HERE, BUT YOU'RE NEVER REALLY WITH US, ARE YOU? YOU ONLY EVER DO SO MUCH - ENOUGH NOT TO GET BOOTED OUT, BUT NOTHING MORE THAN THAT. NOTHING SPECIAL.
WHERE WILL WE FIND YOU, I WONDER, WHEN THE TIME COMES FOR AN ALL-OUT MAXIMUM EFFORT? WHEN WE NEED CHAPS WHO AREN'T AFRAID OF THE RISKS?

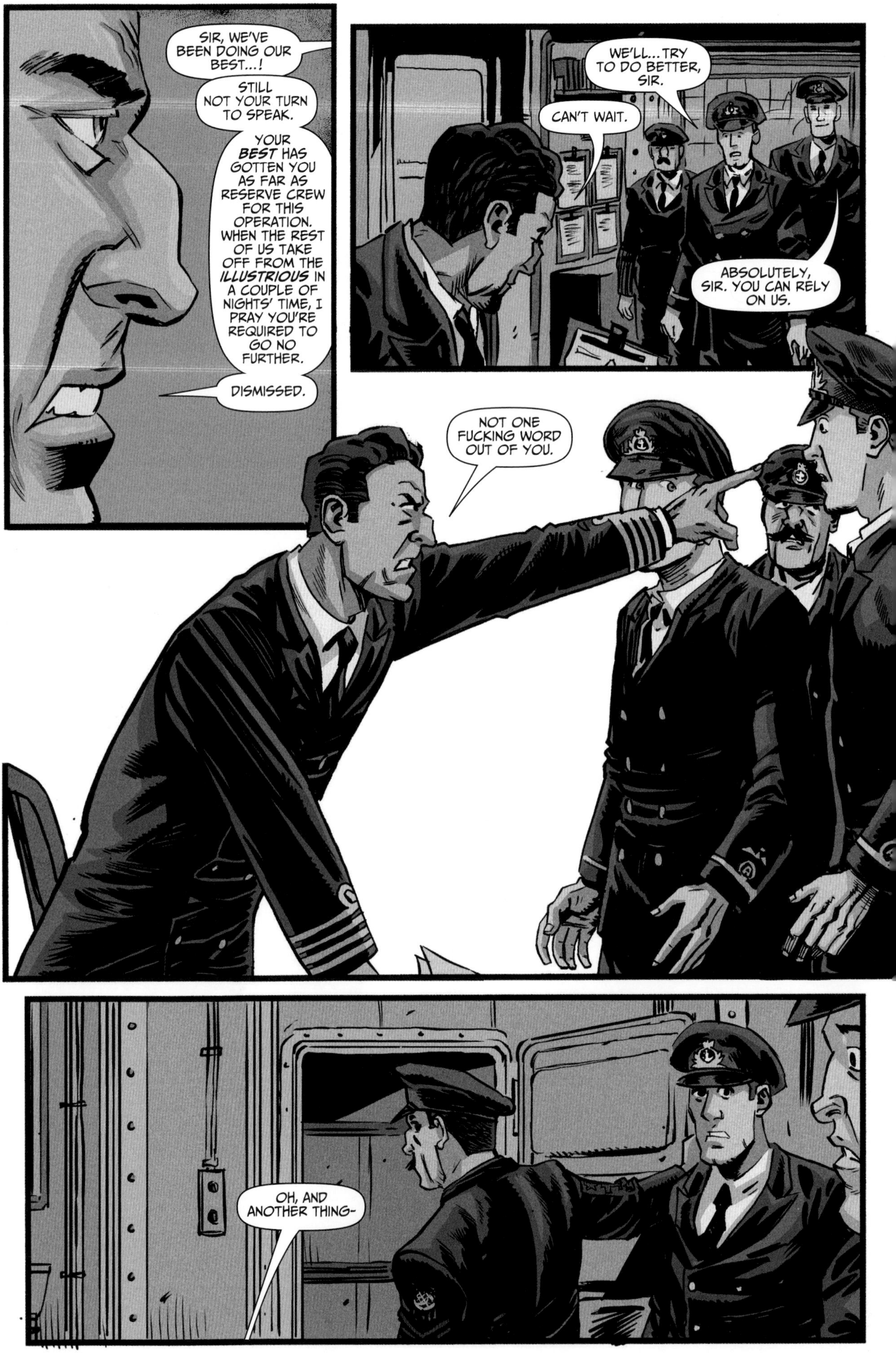
SIR, WE'VE BEEN DOING OUR BEST...!
STILL NOT YOUR TURN TO SPEAK.
YOUR **BEST** HAS GOTTEN YOU AS FAR AS RESERVE CREW FOR THIS OPERATION. WHEN THE REST OF US TAKE OFF FROM THE ***ILLUSTRIOUS*** IN A COUPLE OF NIGHTS' TIME, I PRAY YOU'RE REQUIRED TO GO NO FURTHER.
DISMISSED.
WE'LL...TRY TO DO BETTER, SIR.
CAN'T WAIT.
ABSOLUTELY, SIR. YOU CAN RELY ON US.
NOT ONE FUCKING WORD OUT OF YOU.
OH, AND ANOTHER THING-

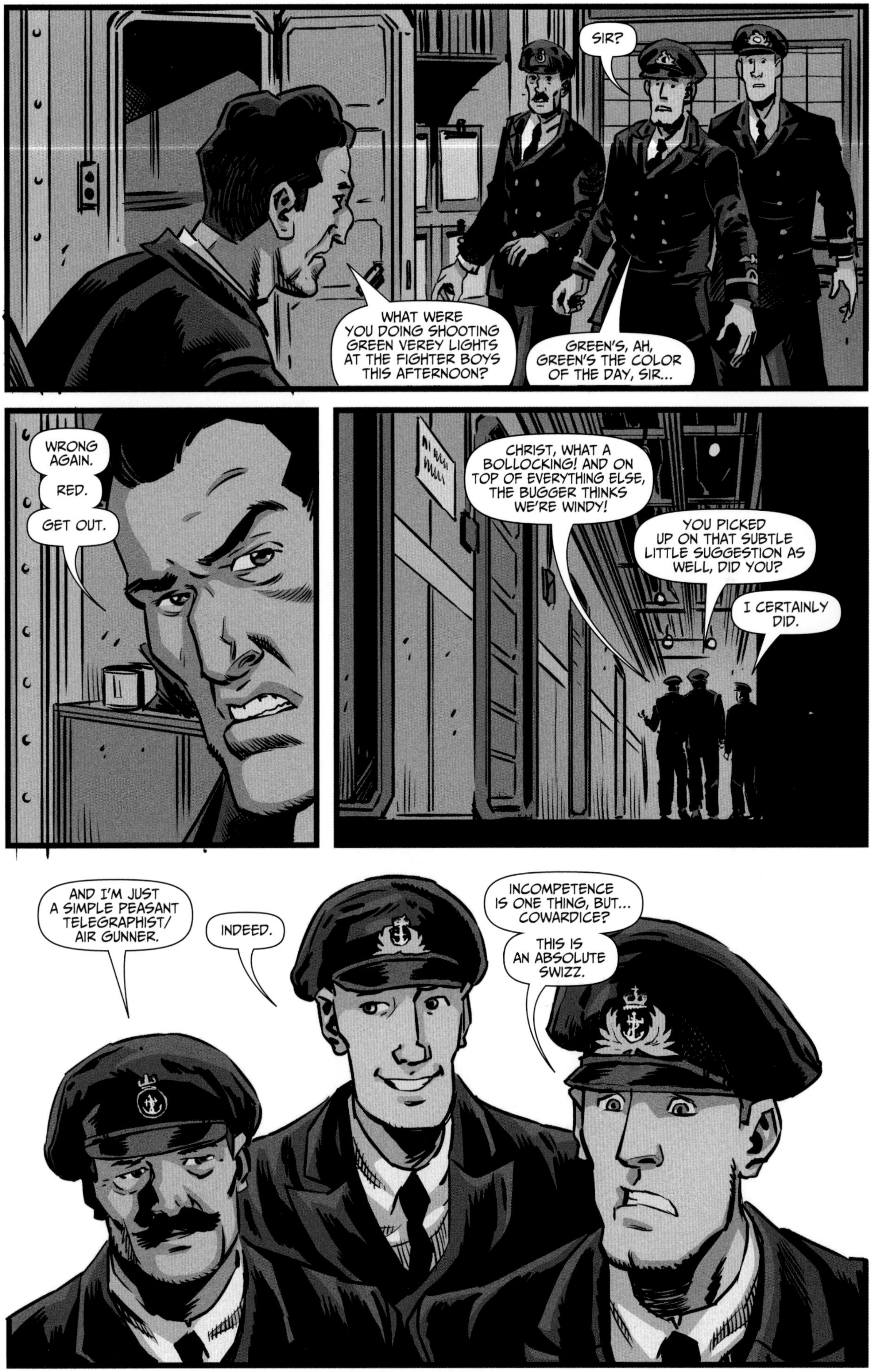
SIR?
WHAT WERE YOU DOING SHOOTING GREEN VEREY LIGHTS AT THE FIGHTER BOYS THIS AFTERNOON?
GREEN'S, AH, GREEN'S THE COLOR OF THE DAY, SIR...
WRONG AGAIN.
RED.
GET OUT.
CHRIST, WHAT A BOLLOCKING! AND ON TOP OF EVERYTHING ELSE, THE BUGGER THINKS WE'RE WINDY!
YOU PICKED UP ON THAT SUBTLE LITTLE SUGGESTION AS WELL, DID YOU?
I CERTAINLY DID.
AND I'M JUST A SIMPLE PEASANT TELEGRAPHIST/ AIR GUNNER.
INDEED.
INCOMPETENCE IS ONE THING, BUT... COWARDICE?
THIS IS AN ABSOLUTE SWIZZ.

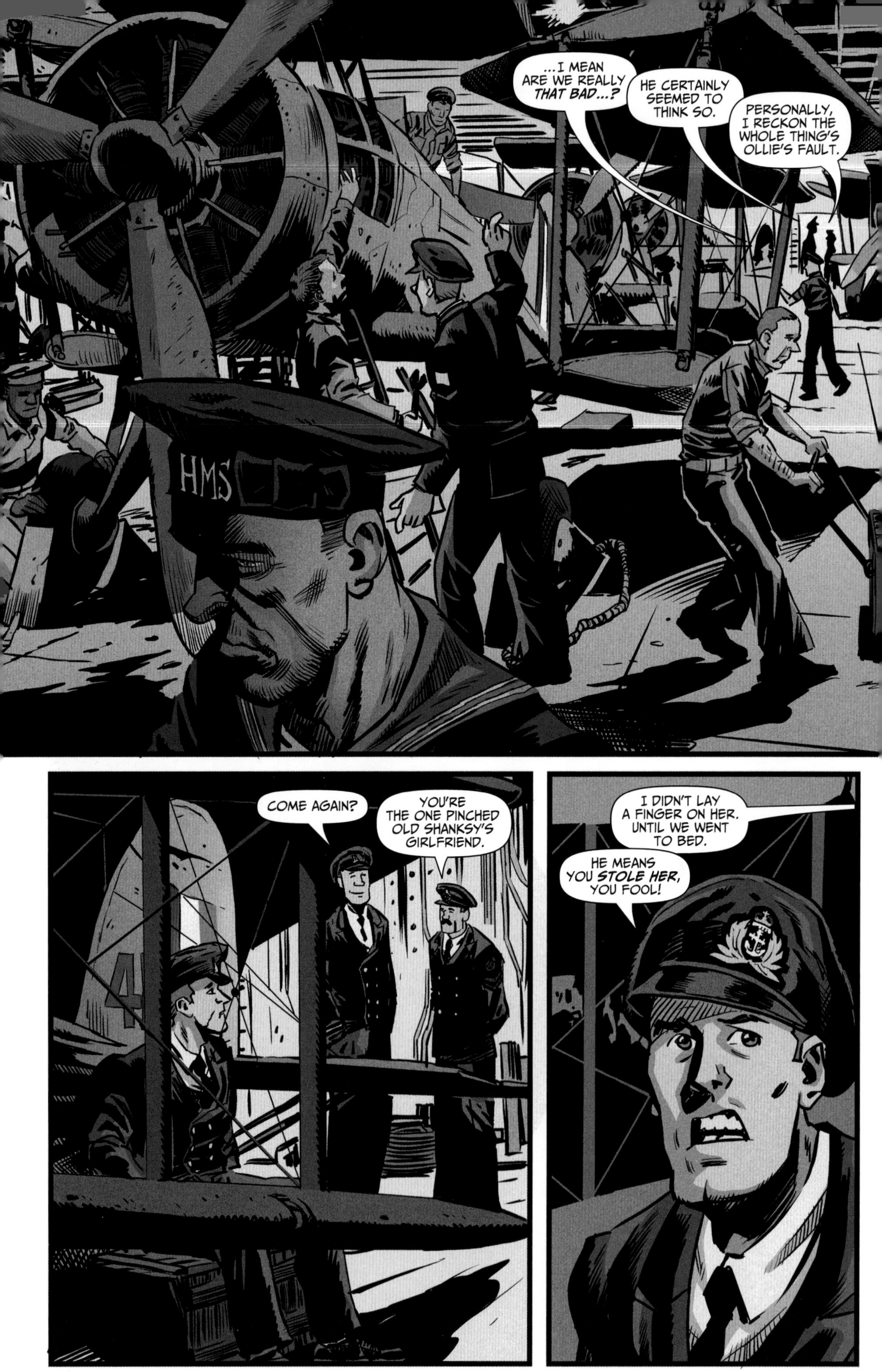
...I MEAN ARE WE REALLY *THAT BAD...?*
HE CERTAINLY SEEMED TO THINK SO.
PERSONALLY, I RECKON THE WHOLE THING'S OLLIE'S FAULT.
HMS
COME AGAIN?
YOU'RE THE ONE PINCHED OLD SHANKSY'S GIRLFRIEND.
I DIDN'T LAY A FINGER ON HER. UNTIL WE WENT TO BED.
HE MEANS YOU ***STOLE HER***, YOU FOOL!

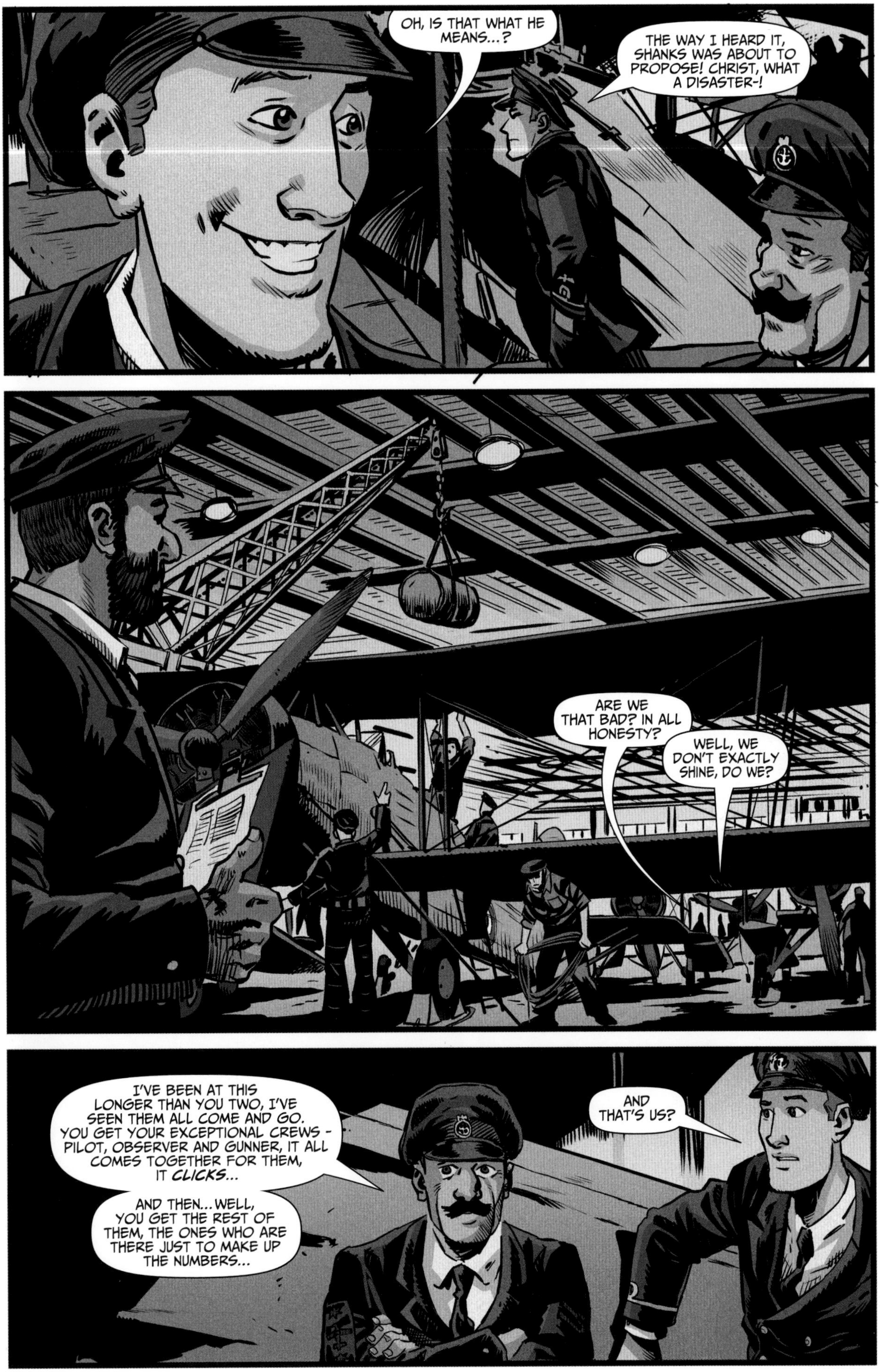
OH, IS THAT WHAT HE MEANS...?
THE WAY I HEARD IT, SHANKS WAS ABOUT TO PROPOSE! CHRIST, WHAT A DISASTER-!
ARE WE THAT BAD? IN ALL HONESTY?
WELL, WE DON'T EXACTLY SHINE, DO WE?
I'VE BEEN AT THIS LONGER THAN YOU TWO, I'VE SEEN THEM ALL COME AND GO. YOU GET YOUR EXCEPTIONAL CREWS - PILOT, OBSERVER AND GUNNER, IT ALL COMES TOGETHER FOR THEM, IT *CLICKS*...
AND THEN... WELL, YOU GET THE REST OF THEM, THE ONES WHO ARE THERE JUST TO MAKE UP THE NUMBERS...
AND THAT'S US?

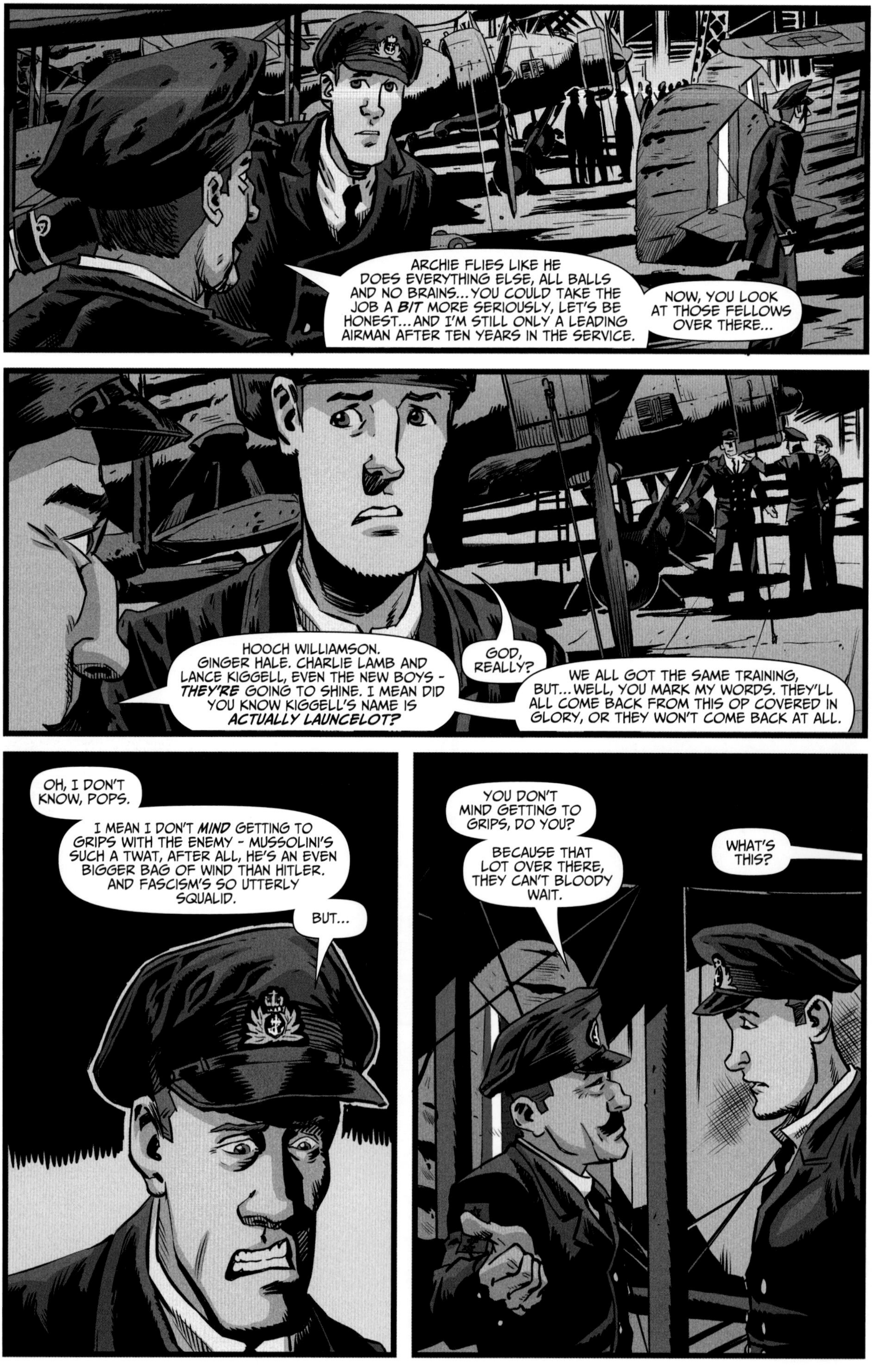
ARCHIE FLIES LIKE HE DOES EVERYTHING ELSE, ALL BALLS AND NO BRAINS... YOU COULD TAKE THE JOB A *BIT* MORE SERIOUSLY, LET'S BE HONEST... AND I'M STILL ONLY A LEADING AIRMAN AFTER TEN YEARS IN THE SERVICE.
NOW, YOU LOOK AT THOSE FELLOWS OVER THERE...
HOOCH WILLIAMSON. GINGER HALE. CHARLIE LAMB AND LANCE KIGGELL, EVEN THE NEW BOYS - *THEY'RE* GOING TO SHINE. I MEAN DID YOU KNOW KIGGELL'S NAME IS *ACTUALLY LAUNCELOT?*
GOD, REALLY?
WE ALL GOT THE SAME TRAINING, BUT... WELL, YOU MARK MY WORDS. THEY'LL ALL COME BACK FROM THIS OP COVERED IN GLORY, OR THEY WON'T COME BACK AT ALL.
OH, I DON'T KNOW, POPS.
I MEAN I DON'T *MIND* GETTING TO GRIPS WITH THE ENEMY - MUSSOLINI'S SUCH A TWAT, AFTER ALL, HE'S AN EVEN BIGGER BAG OF WIND THAN HITLER. AND FASCISM'S SO UTTERLY SQUALID.
BUT...
YOU DON'T MIND GETTING TO GRIPS, DO YOU?
BECAUSE THAT LOT OVER THERE, THEY CAN'T BLOODY WAIT.
WHAT'S THIS?

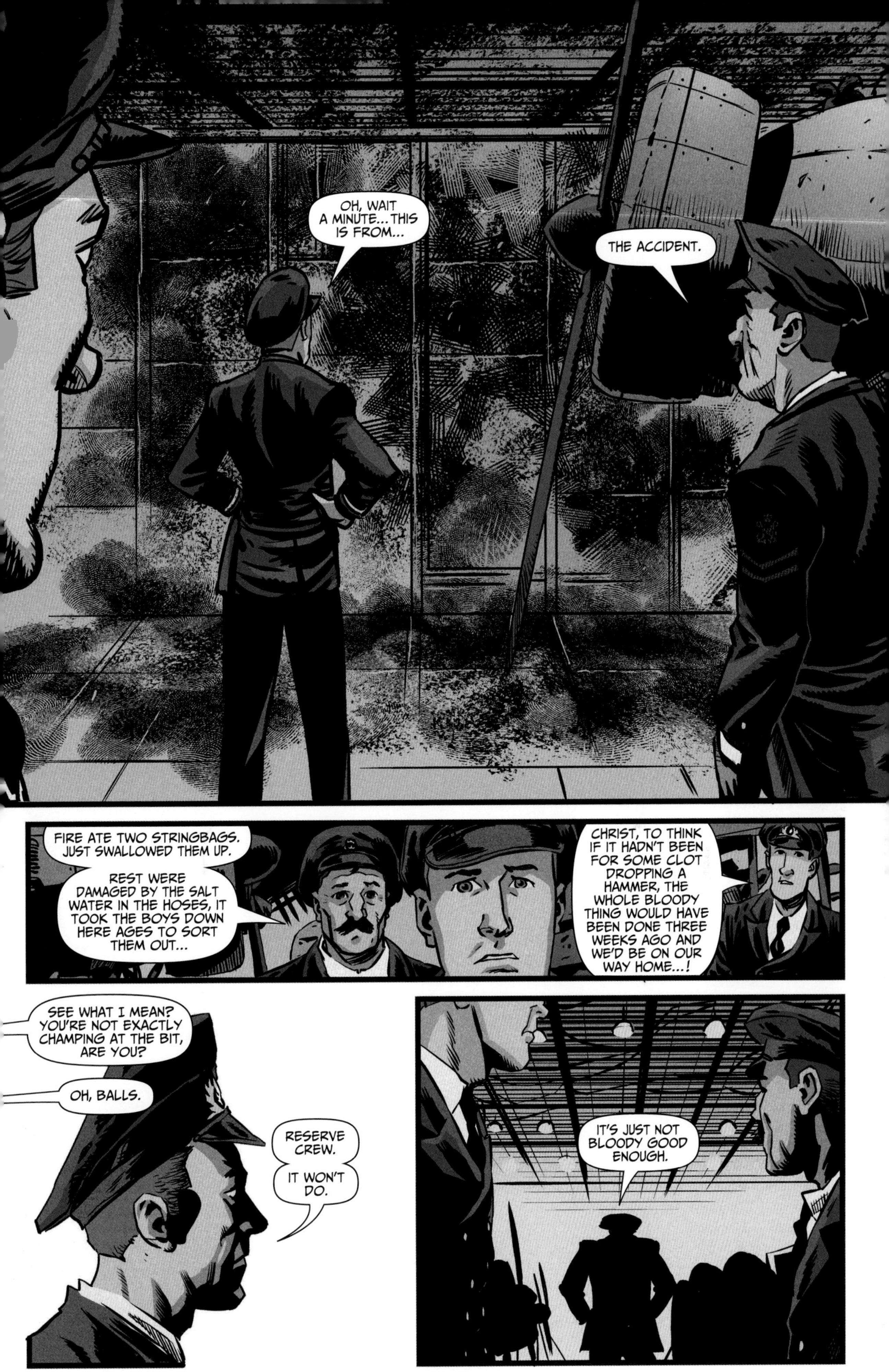
OH, WAIT A MINUTE... THIS IS FROM...
THE ACCIDENT.
FIRE ATE TWO STRINGBAGS. JUST SWALLOWED THEM UP.
REST WERE DAMAGED BY THE SALT WATER IN THE HOSES, IT TOOK THE BOYS DOWN HERE AGES TO SORT THEM OUT...
CHRIST, TO THINK IF IT HADN'T BEEN FOR SOME CLOT DROPPING A HAMMER, THE WHOLE BLOODY THING WOULD HAVE BEEN DONE THREE WEEKS AGO AND WE'D BE ON OUR WAY HOME...!
SEE WHAT I MEAN? YOU'RE NOT EXACTLY CHAMPING AT THE BIT, ARE YOU?
OH, BALLS.
RESERVE CREW.
IT WON'T DO.
IT'S JUST NOT BLOODY GOOD ENOUGH.

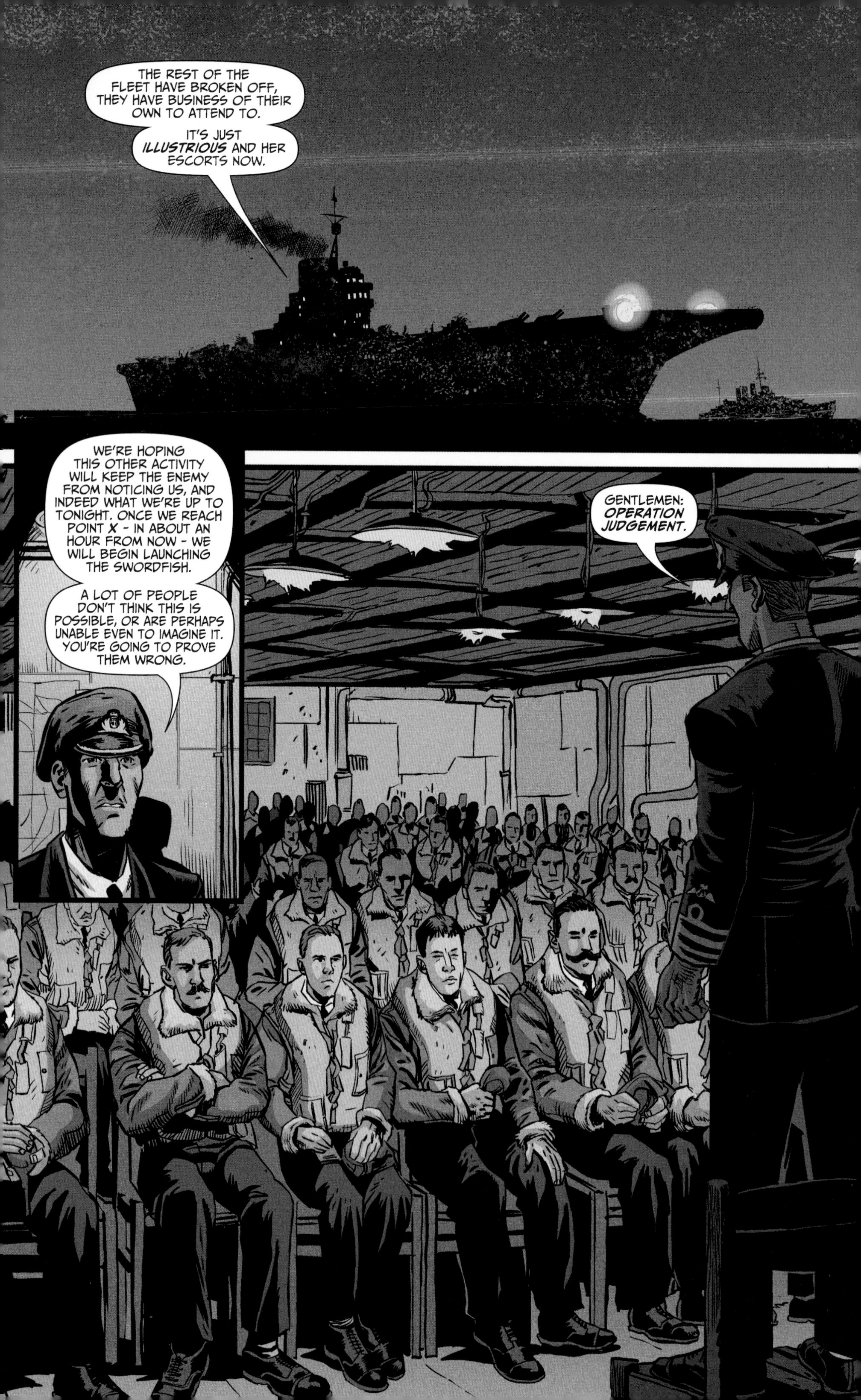
THE REST OF THE FLEET HAVE BROKEN OFF, THEY HAVE BUSINESS OF THEIR OWN TO ATTEND TO.
IT'S JUST *ILLUSTRIOUS* AND HER ESCORTS NOW.
WE'RE HOPING THIS OTHER ACTIVITY WILL KEEP THE ENEMY FROM NOTICING US, AND INDEED WHAT WE'RE UP TO TONIGHT. ONCE WE REACH POINT *X* - IN ABOUT AN HOUR FROM NOW - WE WILL BEGIN LAUNCHING THE SWORDFISH.
A LOT OF PEOPLE DON'T THINK THIS IS POSSIBLE, OR ARE PERHAPS UNABLE EVEN TO IMAGINE IT. YOU'RE GOING TO PROVE THEM WRONG.
GENTLEMEN: *OPERATION JUDGEMENT*.

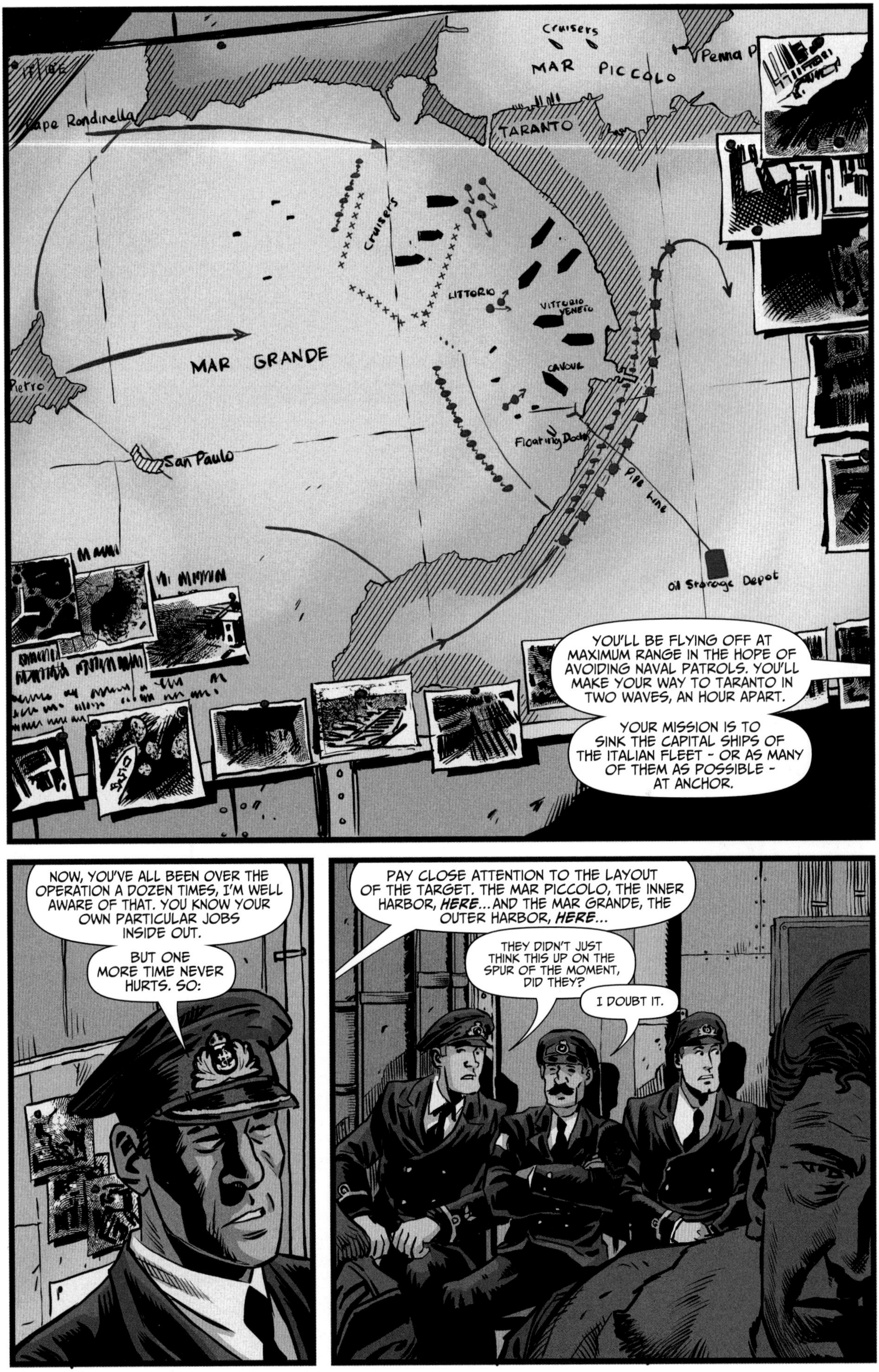
Cruisers
MAR PICCOLO
Penna P
ape Rondinella
TARANTO
Cruisers
LITTORIO
VITTORIO VENETO
MAR GRANDE
CAVOUR
ietro
Floating Docks
San Paulo
Pipe Line
Oil Storage Depot
YOU'LL BE FLYING OFF AT MAXIMUM RANGE IN THE HOPE OF AVOIDING NAVAL PATROLS. YOU'LL MAKE YOUR WAY TO TARANTO IN TWO WAVES, AN HOUR APART.
YOUR MISSION IS TO SINK THE CAPITAL SHIPS OF THE ITALIAN FLEET - OR AS MANY OF THEM AS POSSIBLE - AT ANCHOR.
NOW, YOU'VE ALL BEEN OVER THE OPERATION A DOZEN TIMES, I'M WELL AWARE OF THAT. YOU KNOW YOUR OWN PARTICULAR JOBS INSIDE OUT.
BUT ONE MORE TIME NEVER HURTS. SO:
PAY CLOSE ATTENTION TO THE LAYOUT OF THE TARGET. THE MAR PICCOLO, THE INNER HARBOR, ***HERE***... AND THE MAR GRANDE, THE OUTER HARBOR, ***HERE***...
THEY DIDN'T JUST THINK THIS UP ON THE SPUR OF THE MOMENT, DID THEY?
I DOUBT IT.

...AND REMEMBER: NOT THE DESTROYERS, NOT THE CRUISERS...

IT'S THE OBVIOUS WAY TO SCUPPER THE EYETIES IN THE MED, THEY PROBABLY STARTED PLANNING IT BEFORE THE WAR...

WHERE'S SHANKS?

IT'S THE BATTLEWAGONS WE WANT.

THE *LITTORIO*. THE *VITTORIO VENETO*. THE *CAIO DUILIO*, THE *ANDREA DORIA*, THE *GIULIO CESARE*. AND THE *CONTE DI CAVOUR*.

AS MANY OF THEM AS YOU CAN MANAGE, PLEASE. ALL OF THEM WOULD BE VERY NICE INDEED.

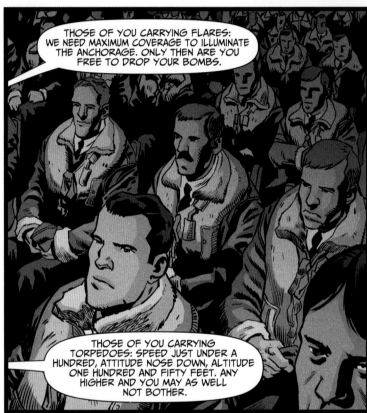

THOSE OF YOU CARRYING FLARES: WE NEED MAXIMUM COVERAGE TO ILLUMINATE THE ANCHORAGE. ONLY THEN ARE YOU FREE TO DROP YOUR BOMBS.

THOSE OF YOU CARRYING TORPEDOES: SPEED JUST UNDER A HUNDRED, ATTITUDE NOSE DOWN, ALTITUDE ONE HUNDRED AND FIFTY FEET. ANY HIGHER AND YOU MAY AS WELL NOT BOTHER.

WHAT ELSE...OH YES, DEFENSES...

OH YES. DEFENSES.

LISTENING DEVICES, FLAK, BARRAGE BALLOONS.

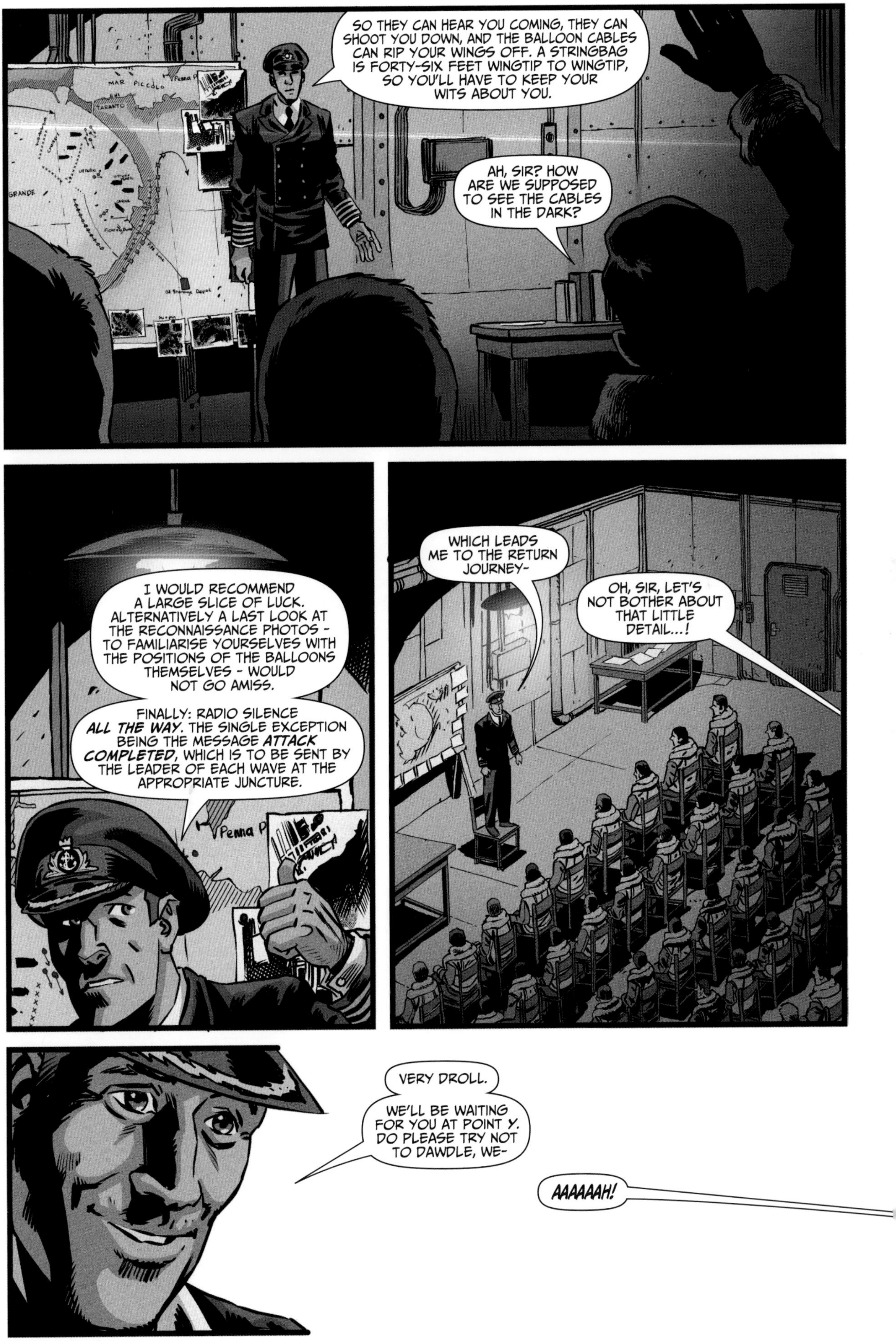
SO THEY CAN HEAR YOU COMING, THEY CAN SHOOT YOU DOWN, AND THE BALLOON CABLES CAN RIP YOUR WINGS OFF. A STRINGBAG IS FORTY-SIX FEET WINGTIP TO WINGTIP, SO YOU'LL HAVE TO KEEP YOUR WITS ABOUT YOU.
AH, SIR? HOW ARE WE SUPPOSED TO SEE THE CABLES IN THE DARK?
I WOULD RECOMMEND A LARGE SLICE OF LUCK. ALTERNATIVELY A LAST LOOK AT THE RECONNAISSANCE PHOTOS - TO FAMILIARISE YOURSELVES WITH THE POSITIONS OF THE BALLOONS THEMSELVES - WOULD NOT GO AMISS.
FINALLY: RADIO SILENCE *ALL THE WAY*. THE SINGLE EXCEPTION BEING THE MESSAGE *ATTACK COMPLETED*, WHICH IS TO BE SENT BY THE LEADER OF EACH WAVE AT THE APPROPRIATE JUNCTURE.
WHICH LEADS ME TO THE RETURN JOURNEY-
OH, SIR, LET'S NOT BOTHER ABOUT THAT LITTLE DETAIL...!
VERY DROLL.
WE'LL BE WAITING FOR YOU AT POINT *Y*. DO PLEASE TRY NOT TO DAWDLE, WE-
AAAAAAH!

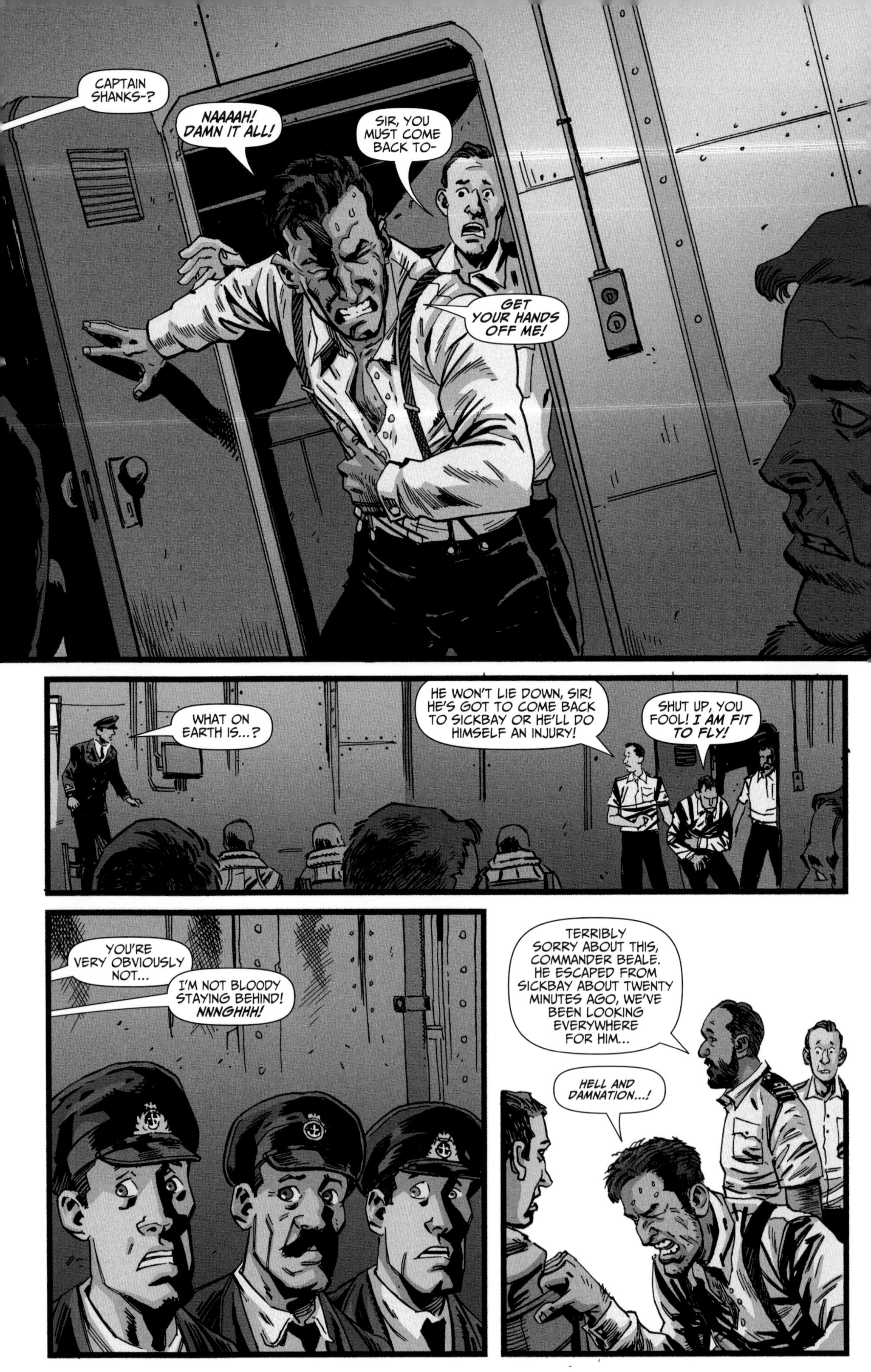
CAPTAIN SHANKS-?
NAAAAH! DAMN IT ALL!
SIR, YOU MUST COME BACK TO-
GET YOUR HANDS OFF ME!
WHAT ON EARTH IS...?
HE WON'T LIE DOWN, SIR! HE'S GOT TO COME BACK TO SICKBAY OR HE'LL DO HIMSELF AN INJURY!
SHUT UP, YOU FOOL! I AM FIT TO FLY!
YOU'RE VERY OBVIOUSLY NOT...
I'M NOT BLOODY STAYING BEHIND! NNNGHHH!
TERRIBLY SORRY ABOUT THIS, COMMANDER BEALE. HE ESCAPED FROM SICKBAY ABOUT TWENTY MINUTES AGO, WE'VE BEEN LOOKING EVERYWHERE FOR HIM...
HELL AND DAMNATION...!

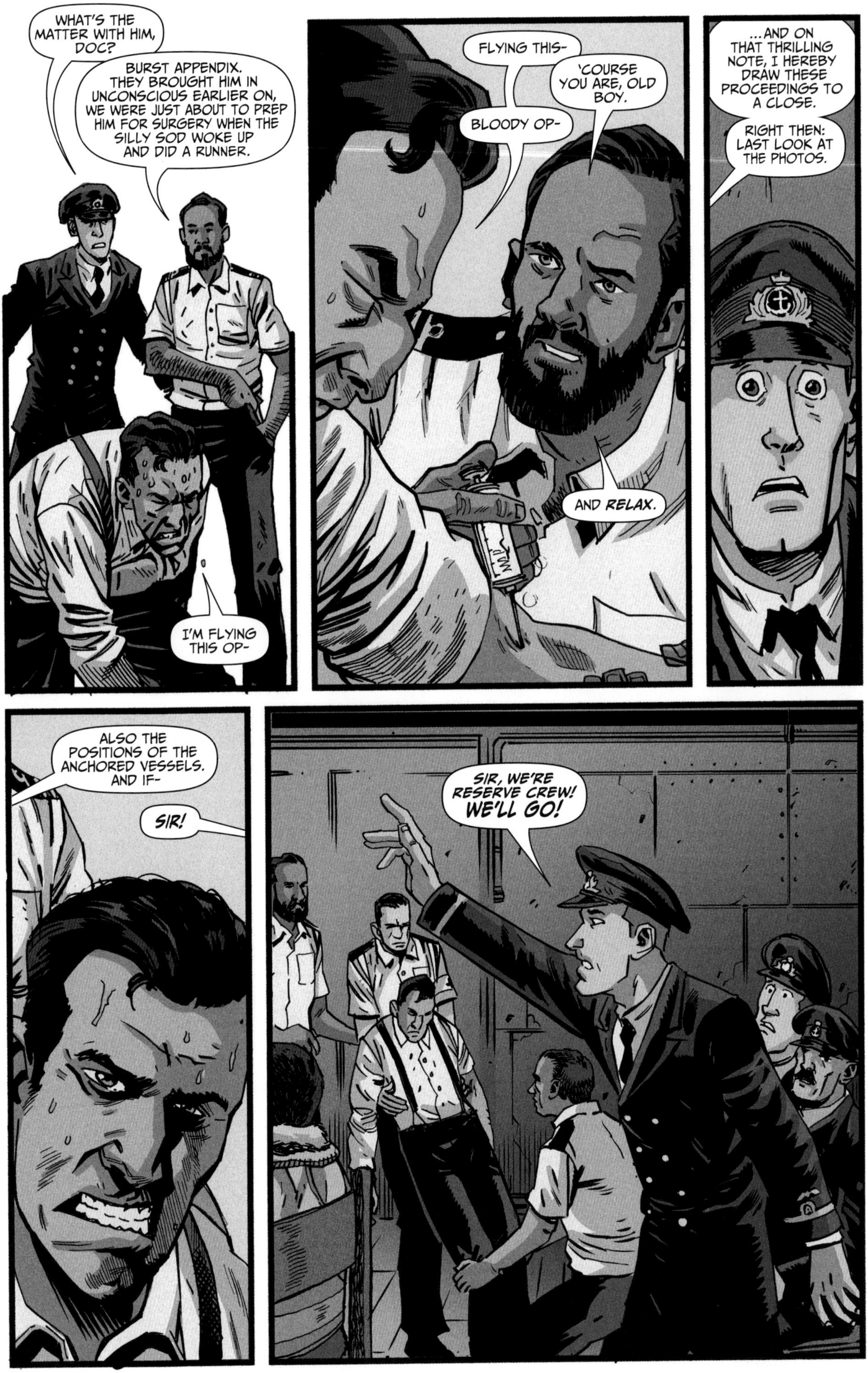
WHAT'S THE MATTER WITH HIM, DOC?
BURST APPENDIX. THEY BROUGHT HIM IN UNCONSCIOUS EARLIER ON, WE WERE JUST ABOUT TO PREP HIM FOR SURGERY WHEN THE SILLY SOD WOKE UP AND DID A RUNNER.
I'M FLYING THIS OP-
FLYING THIS-
BLOODY OP-
'COURSE YOU ARE, OLD BOY.
AND RELAX.
...AND ON THAT THRILLING NOTE, I HEREBY DRAW THESE PROCEEDINGS TO A CLOSE.
RIGHT THEN: LAST LOOK AT THE PHOTOS.
ALSO THE POSITIONS OF THE ANCHORED VESSELS. AND IF-
SIR!
SIR, WE'RE RESERVE CREW! WE'LL GO!

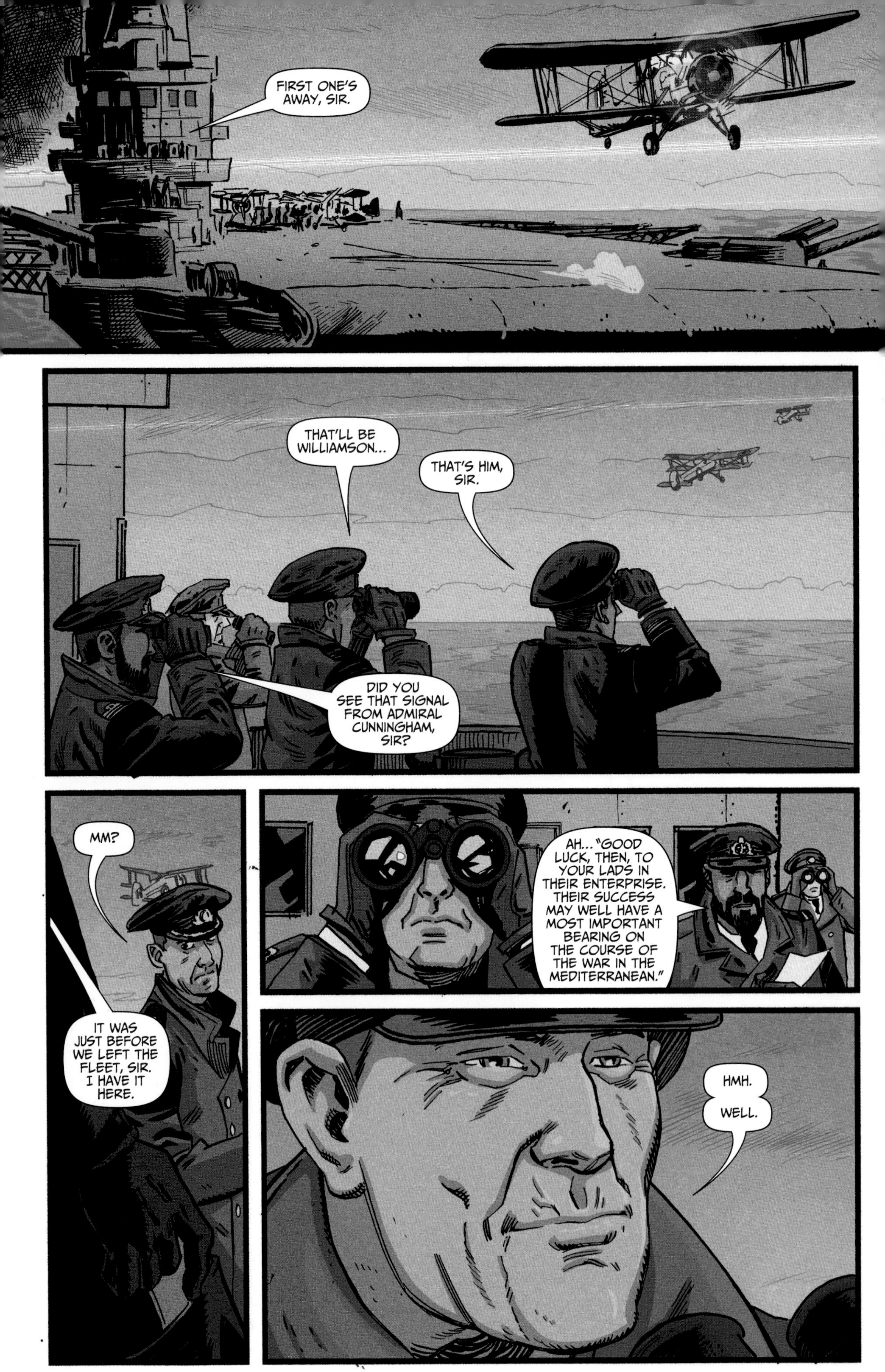
FIRST ONE'S AWAY, SIR.
THAT'LL BE WILLIAMSON...
THAT'S HIM, SIR.
DID YOU SEE THAT SIGNAL FROM ADMIRAL CUNNINGHAM, SIR?
MM?
IT WAS JUST BEFORE WE LEFT THE FLEET, SIR. I HAVE IT HERE.
AH... "GOOD LUCK, THEN, TO YOUR LADS IN THEIR ENTERPRISE. THEIR SUCCESS MAY WELL HAVE A MOST IMPORTANT BEARING ON THE COURSE OF THE WAR IN THE MEDITERRANEAN."
HMH.
WELL.

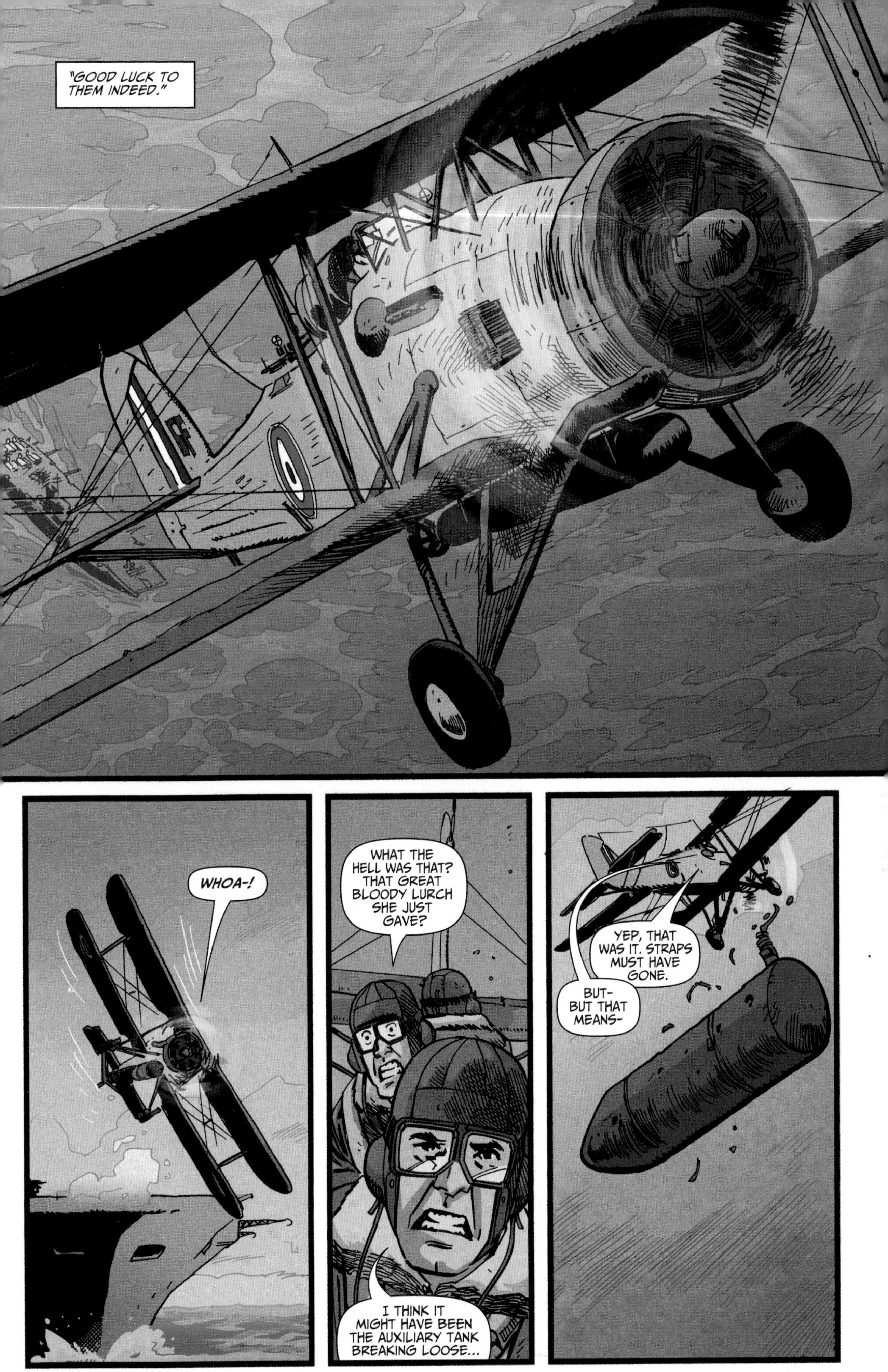
"GOOD LUCK TO THEM INDEED."
WHOA-!
WHAT THE HELL WAS THAT? THAT GREAT BLOODY LURCH SHE JUST GAVE?
I THINK IT MIGHT HAVE BEEN THE AUXILIARY TANK BREAKING LOOSE...
YEP, THAT WAS IT. STRAPS MUST HAVE GONE.
BUT- BUT THAT MEANS-

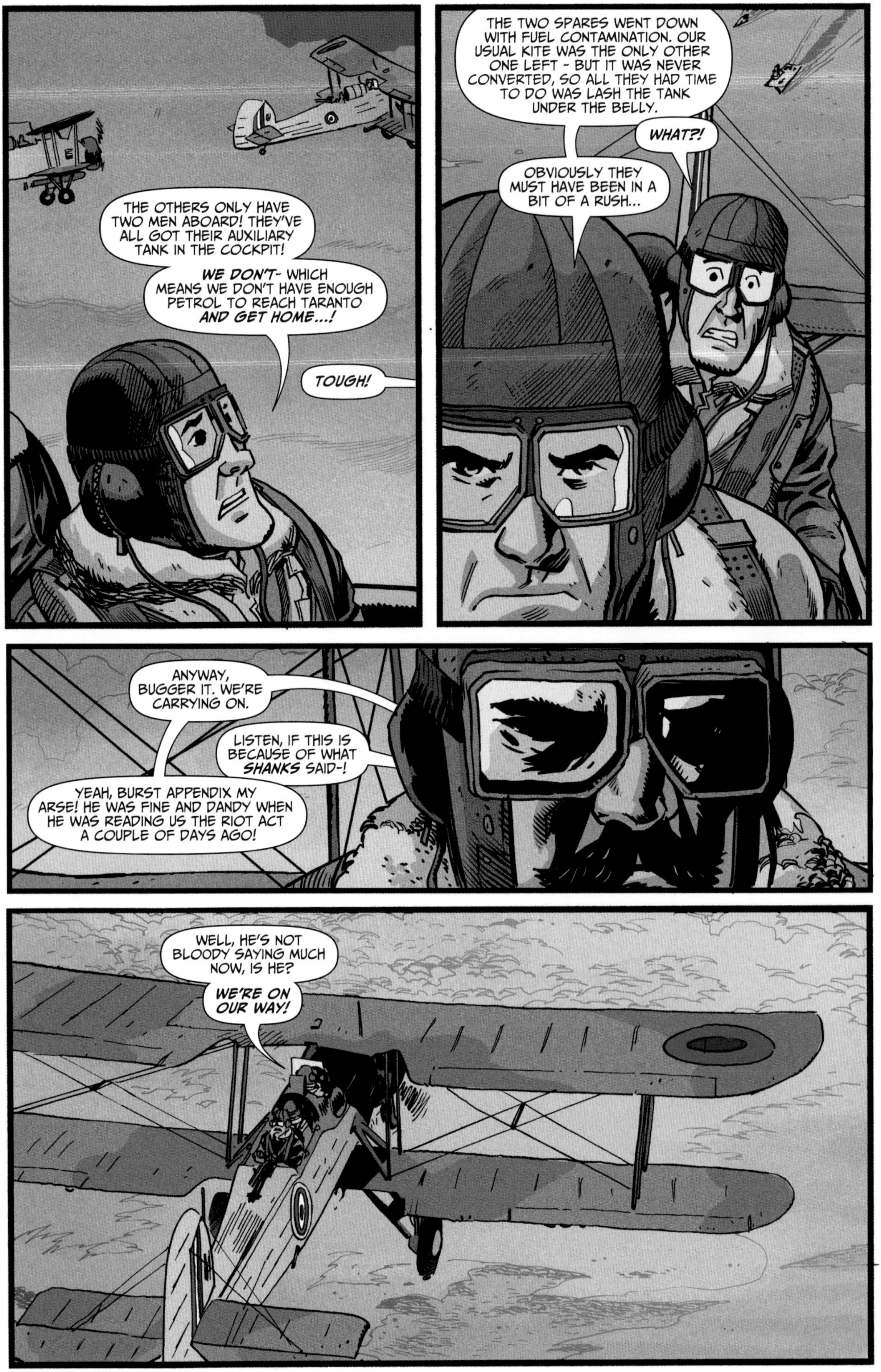
THE OTHERS ONLY HAVE TWO MEN ABOARD! THEY'VE ALL GOT THEIR AUXILIARY TANK IN THE COCKPIT!
WE DON'T- WHICH MEANS WE DON'T HAVE ENOUGH PETROL TO REACH TARANTO AND GET HOME...!
TOUGH!
THE TWO SPARES WENT DOWN WITH FUEL CONTAMINATION. OUR USUAL KITE WAS THE ONLY OTHER ONE LEFT - BUT IT WAS NEVER CONVERTED, SO ALL THEY HAD TIME TO DO WAS LASH THE TANK UNDER THE BELLY.
WHAT?!
OBVIOUSLY THEY MUST HAVE BEEN IN A BIT OF A RUSH...
ANYWAY, BUGGER IT. WE'RE CARRYING ON.
LISTEN, IF THIS IS BECAUSE OF WHAT SHANKS SAID-!
YEAH, BURST APPENDIX MY ARSE! HE WAS FINE AND DANDY WHEN HE WAS READING US THE RIOT ACT A COUPLE OF DAYS AGO!
WELL, HE'S NOT BLOODY SAYING MUCH NOW, IS HE?
WE'RE ON OUR WAY!

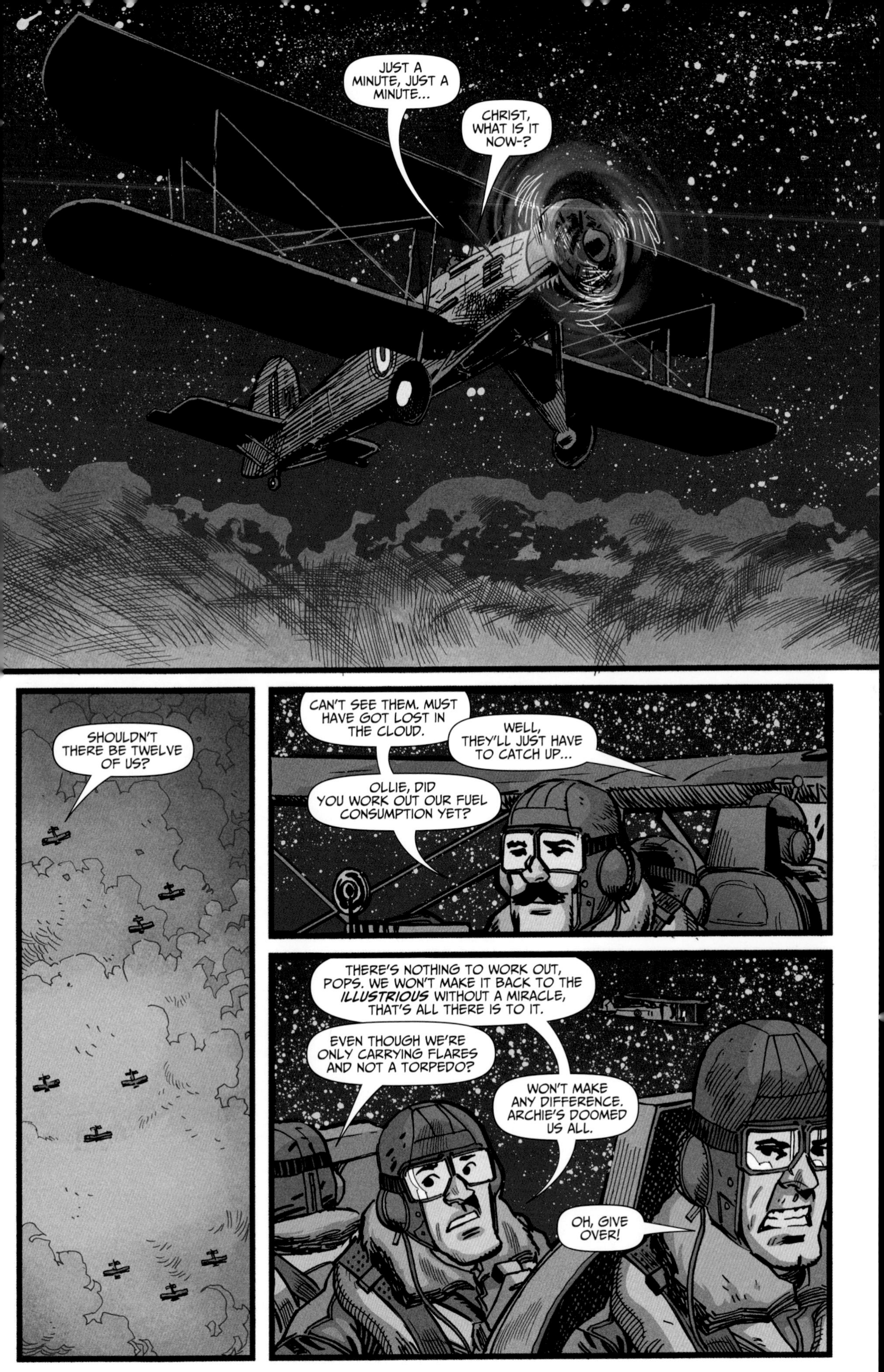
JUST A MINUTE, JUST A MINUTE...
CHRIST, WHAT IS IT NOW-?
SHOULDN'T THERE BE TWELVE OF US?
CAN'T SEE THEM. MUST HAVE GOT LOST IN THE CLOUD.
WELL, THEY'LL JUST HAVE TO CATCH UP...
OLLIE, DID YOU WORK OUT OUR FUEL CONSUMPTION YET?
THERE'S NOTHING TO WORK OUT, POPS. WE WON'T MAKE IT BACK TO THE *ILLUSTRIOUS* WITHOUT A MIRACLE, THAT'S ALL THERE IS TO IT.
EVEN THOUGH WE'RE ONLY CARRYING FLARES AND NOT A TORPEDO?
WON'T MAKE ANY DIFFERENCE. ARCHIE'S DOOMED US ALL.
OH, GIVE OVER!

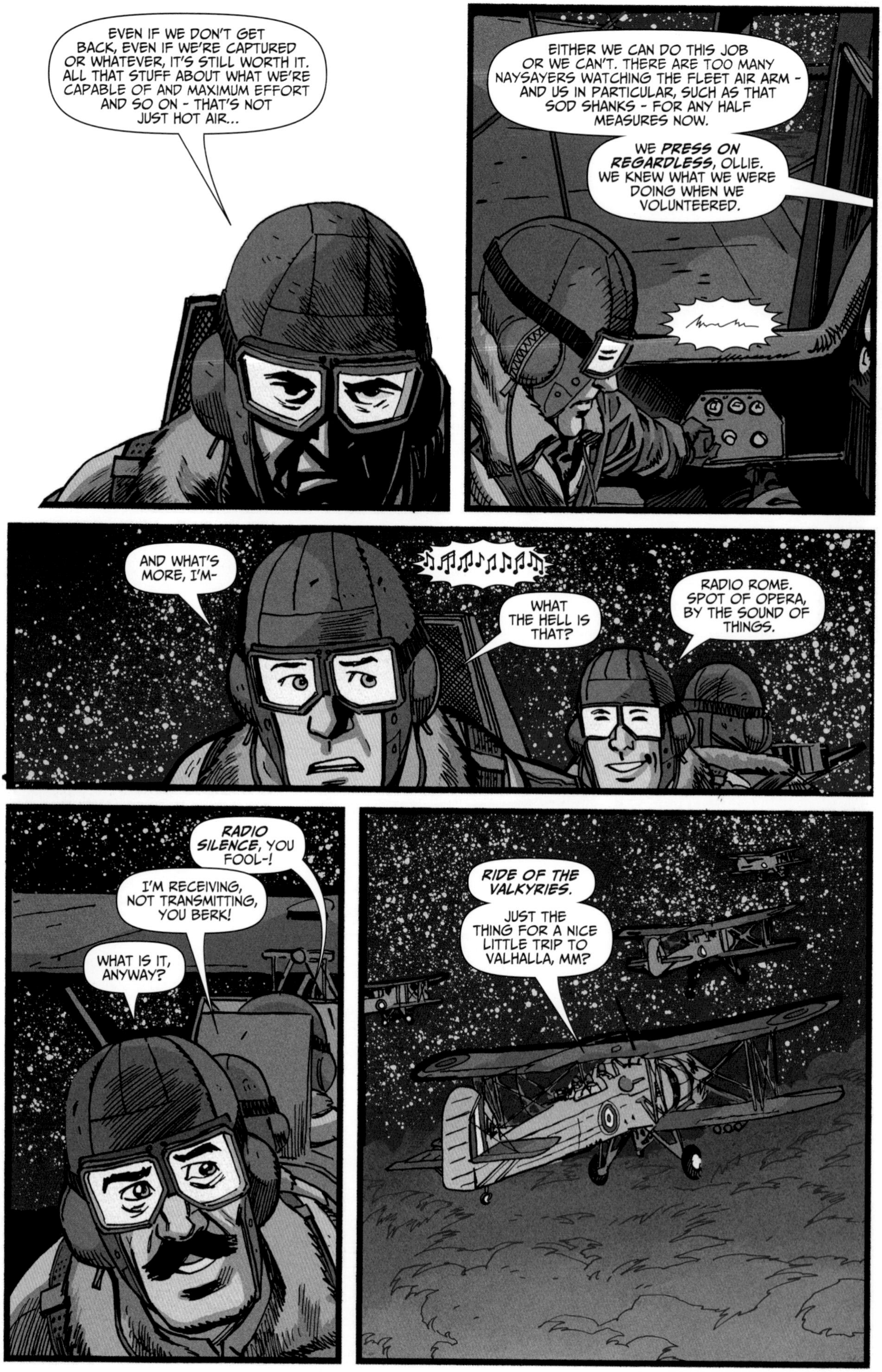
EVEN IF WE DON'T GET BACK, EVEN IF WE'RE CAPTURED OR WHATEVER, IT'S STILL WORTH IT. ALL THAT STUFF ABOUT WHAT WE'RE CAPABLE OF AND MAXIMUM EFFORT AND SO ON - THAT'S NOT JUST HOT AIR...
EITHER WE CAN DO THIS JOB OR WE CAN'T. THERE ARE TOO MANY NAYSAYERS WATCHING THE FLEET AIR ARM - AND US IN PARTICULAR, SUCH AS THAT SOD SHANKS - FOR ANY HALF MEASURES NOW.
WE PRESS ON REGARDLESS, OLLIE. WE KNEW WHAT WE WERE DOING WHEN WE VOLUNTEERED.
AND WHAT'S MORE, I'M-
WHAT THE HELL IS THAT?
RADIO ROME. SPOT OF OPERA, BY THE SOUND OF THINGS.
RADIO SILENCE, YOU FOOL-!
I'M RECEIVING, NOT TRANSMITTING, YOU BERK!
WHAT IS IT, ANYWAY?
RIDE OF THE VALKYRIES.
JUST THE THING FOR A NICE LITTLE TRIP TO VALHALLA, MM?

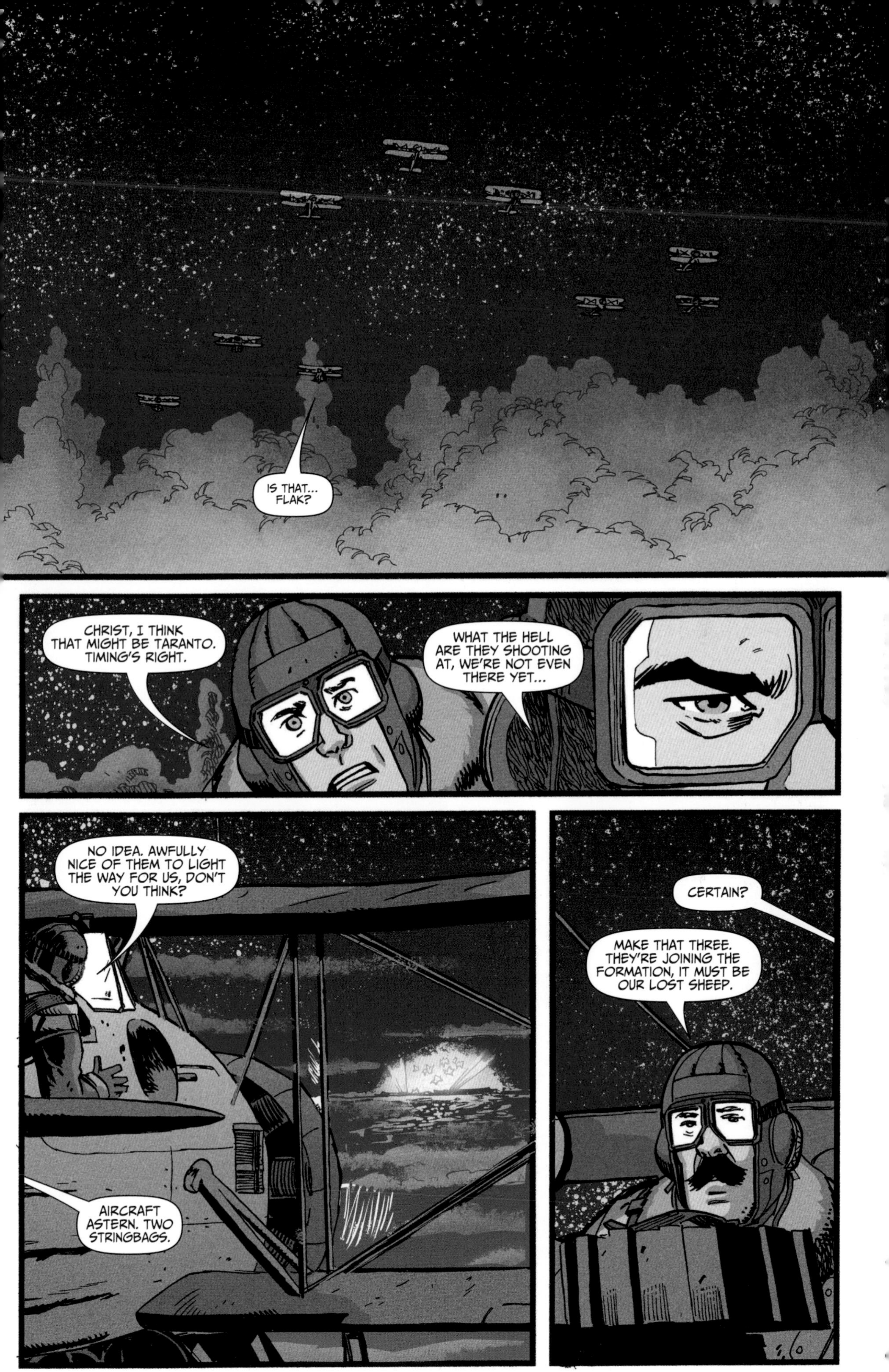
IS THAT... FLAK?
CHRIST, I THINK THAT MIGHT BE TARANTO. TIMING'S RIGHT.
WHAT THE HELL ARE THEY SHOOTING AT, WE'RE NOT EVEN THERE YET...
NO IDEA. AWFULLY NICE OF THEM TO LIGHT THE WAY FOR US, DON'T YOU THINK?
AIRCRAFT ASTERN. TWO STRINGBAGS.
CERTAIN?
MAKE THAT THREE. THEY'RE JOINING THE FORMATION, IT MUST BE OUR LOST SHEEP.

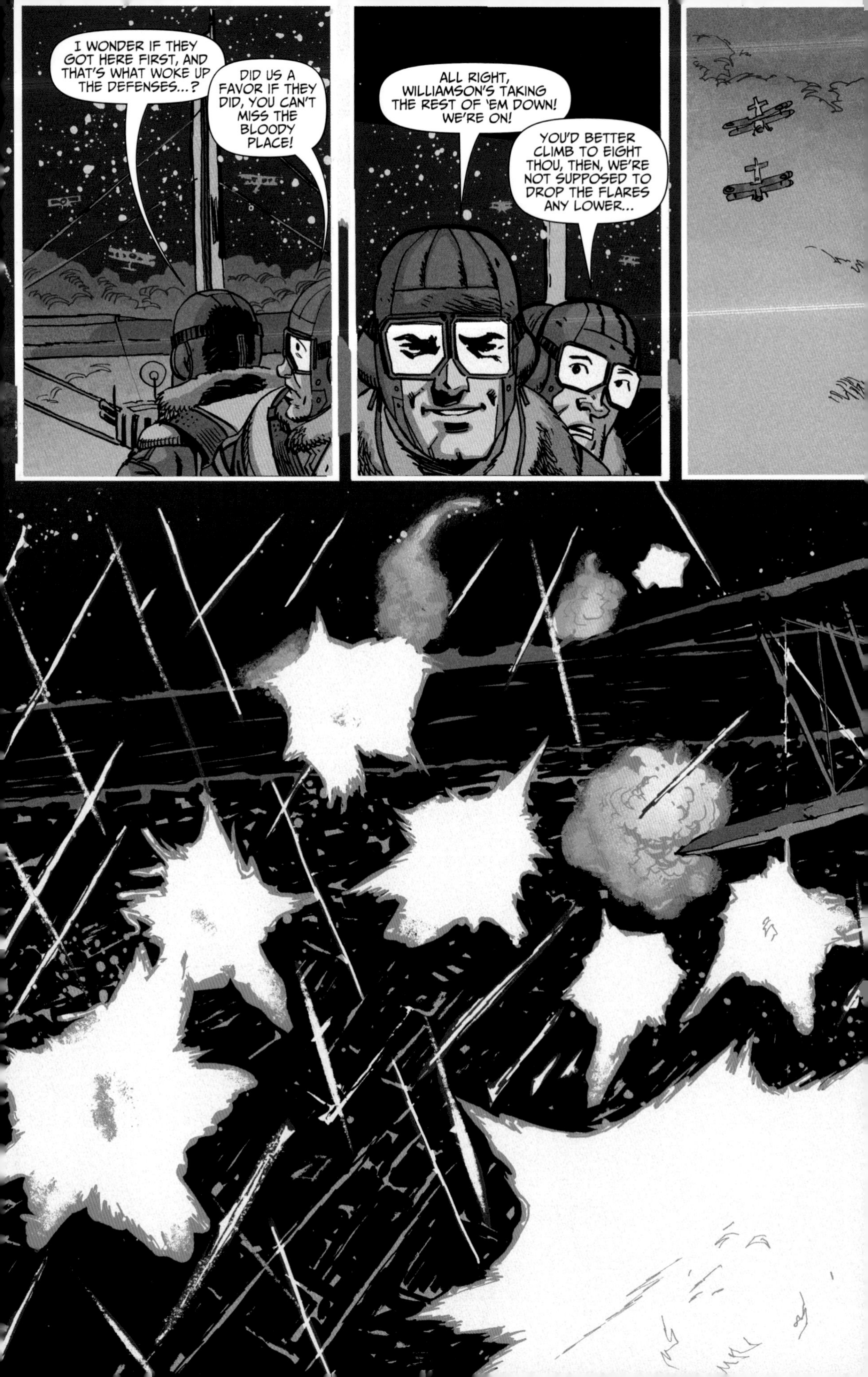
I WONDER IF THEY GOT HERE FIRST, AND THAT'S WHAT WOKE UP THE DEFENSES...?
DID US A FAVOR IF THEY DID, YOU CAN'T MISS THE BLOODY PLACE!
ALL RIGHT, WILLIAMSON'S TAKING THE REST OF 'EM DOWN! WE'RE ON!
YOU'D BETTER CLIMB TO EIGHT THOU, THEN, WE'RE NOT SUPPOSED TO DROP THE FLARES ANY LOWER...

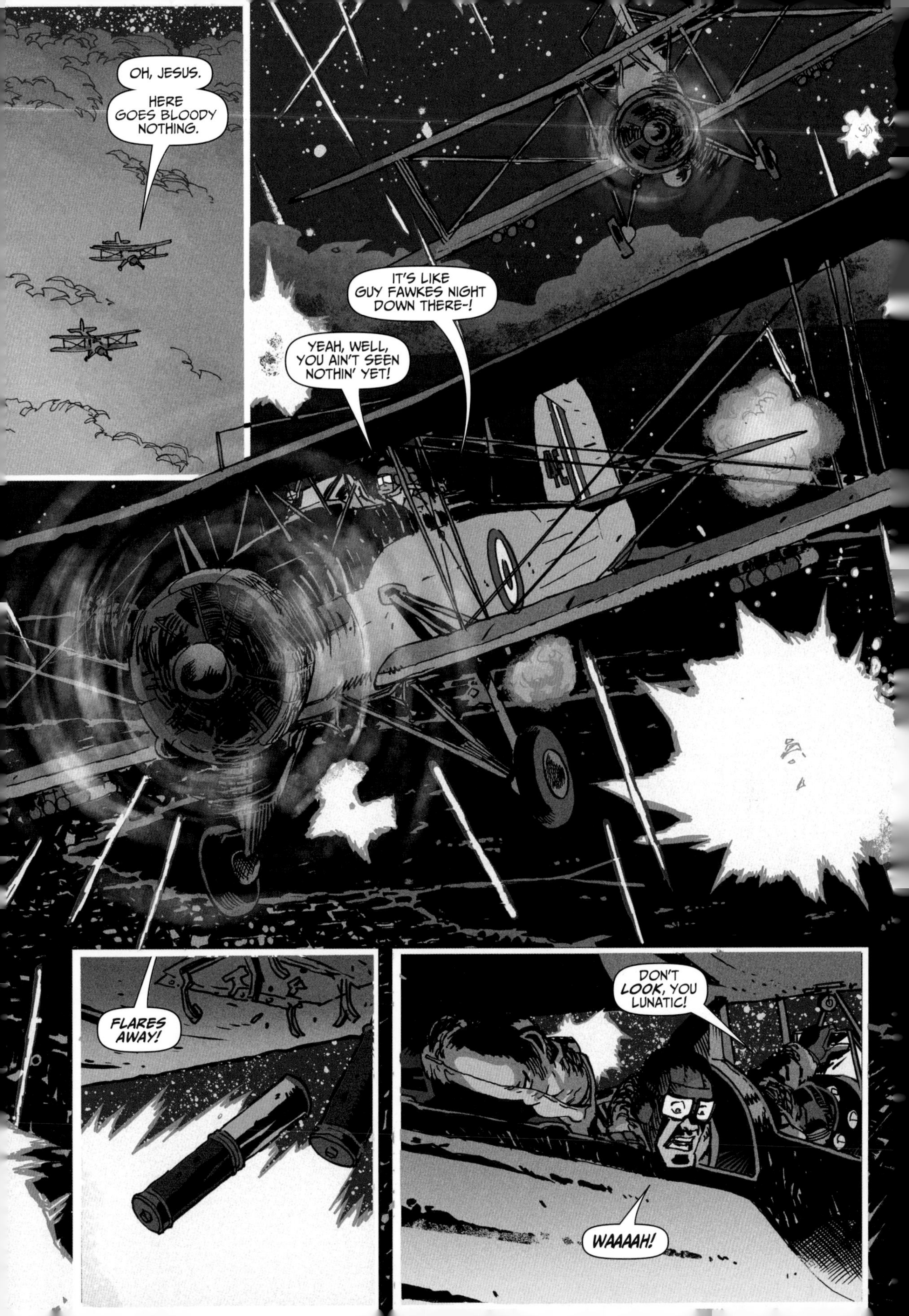
OH, JESUS.
HERE GOES BLOODY NOTHING.
IT'S LIKE GUY FAWKES NIGHT DOWN THERE-!
YEAH, WELL, YOU AIN'T SEEN NOTHIN' YET!
FLARES AWAY!
DON'T LOOK, YOU LUNATIC!
WAAAAH!

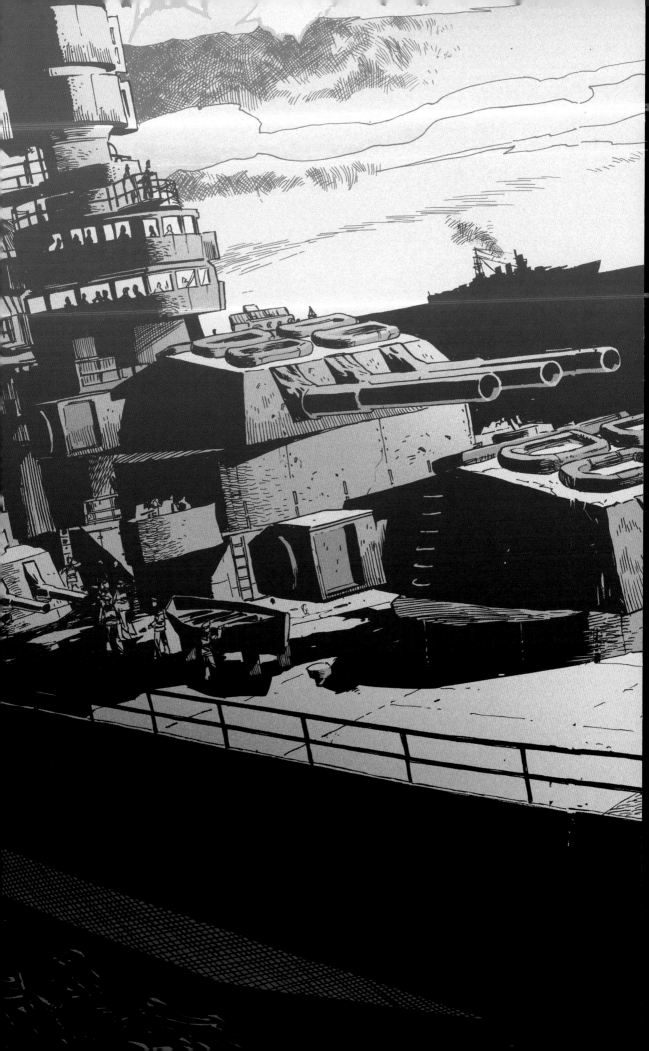

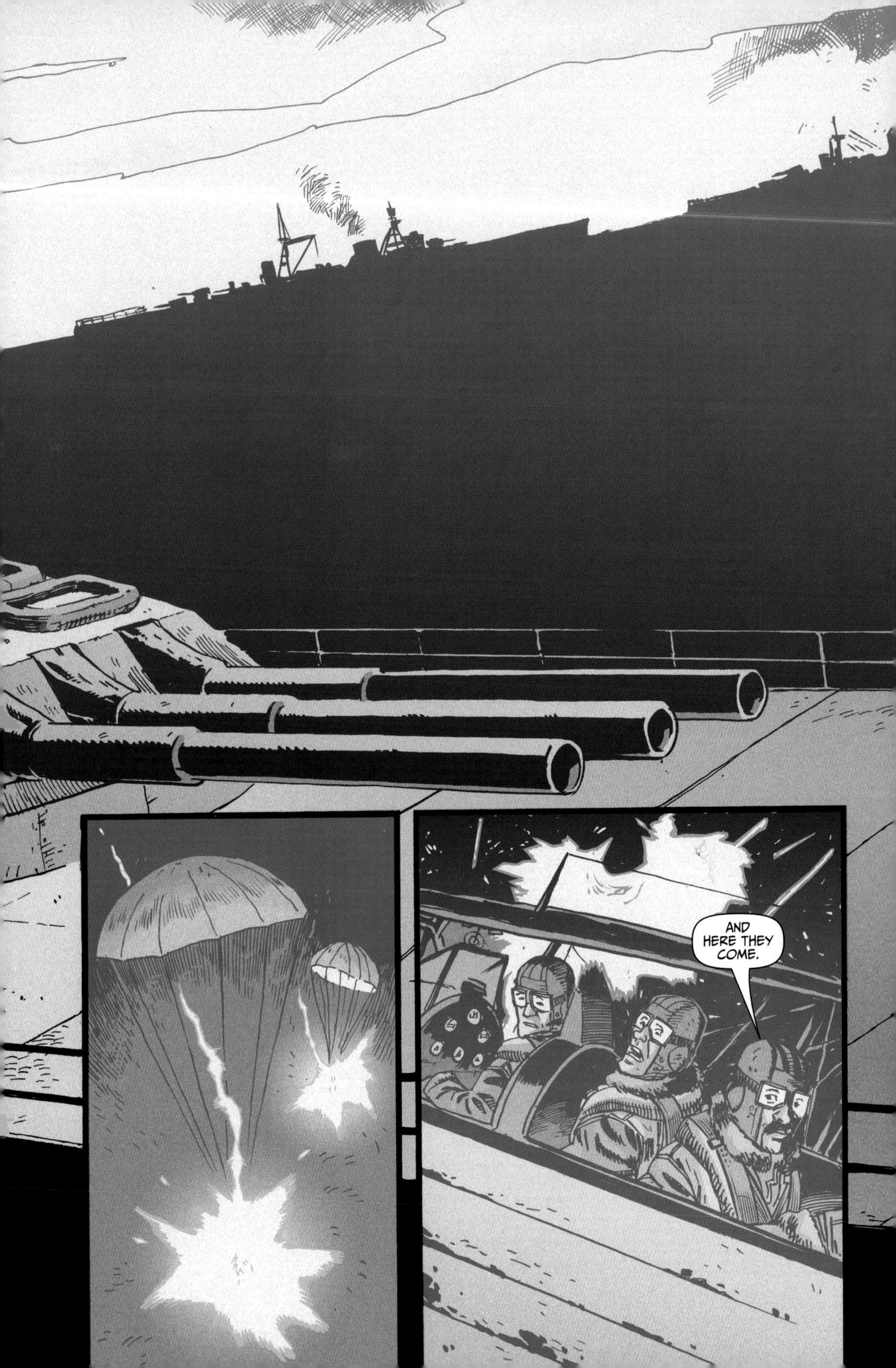
AND HERE THEY COME.

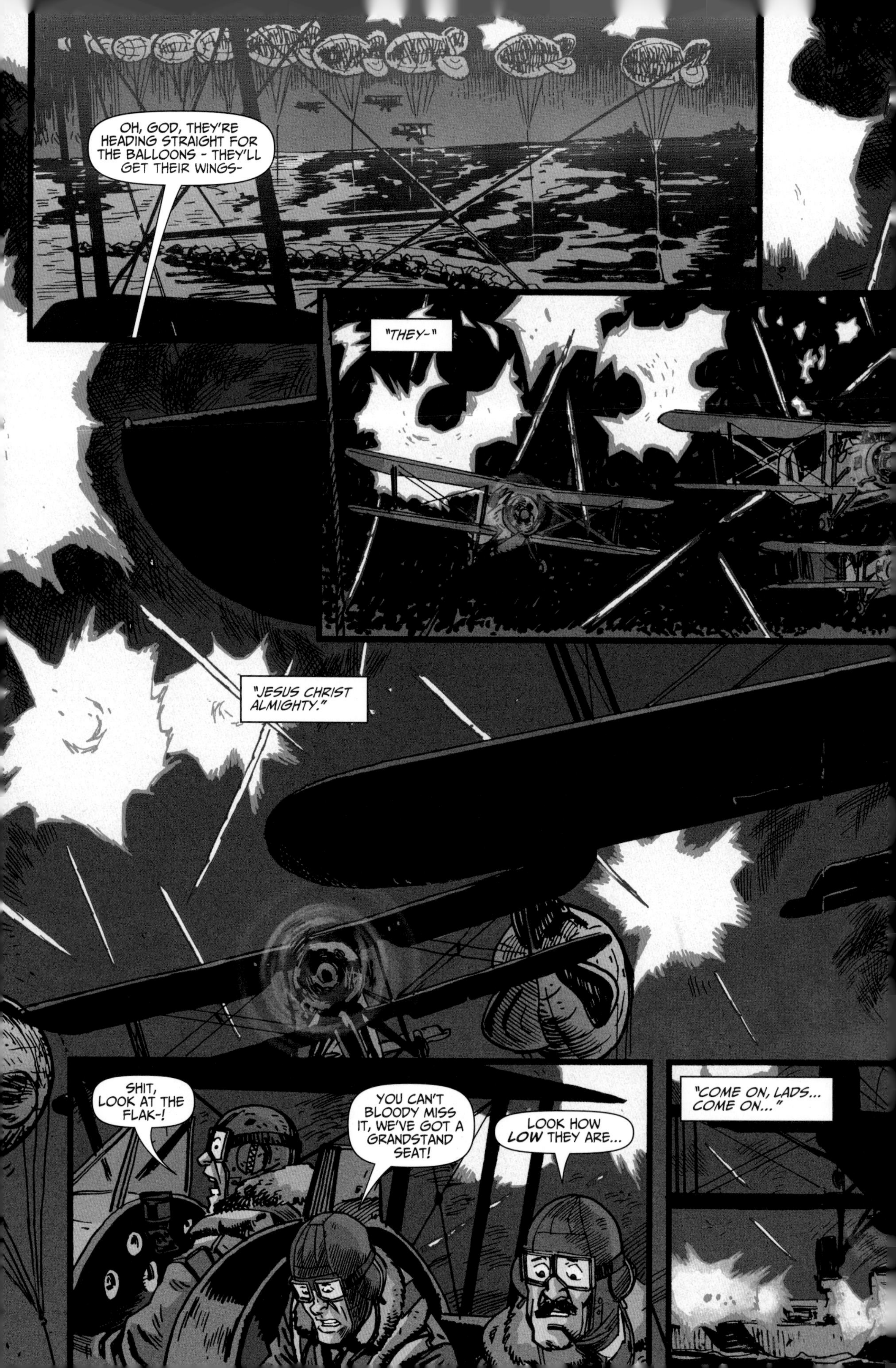
OH, GOD, THEY'RE HEADING STRAIGHT FOR THE BALLOONS - THEY'LL GET THEIR WINGS-
"THEY-"
"JESUS CHRIST ALMIGHTY."
SHIT, LOOK AT THE FLAK-!
YOU CAN'T BLOODY MISS IT, WE'VE GOT A GRANDSTAND SEAT!
LOOK HOW LOW THEY ARE...
"COME ON, LADS... COME ON..."

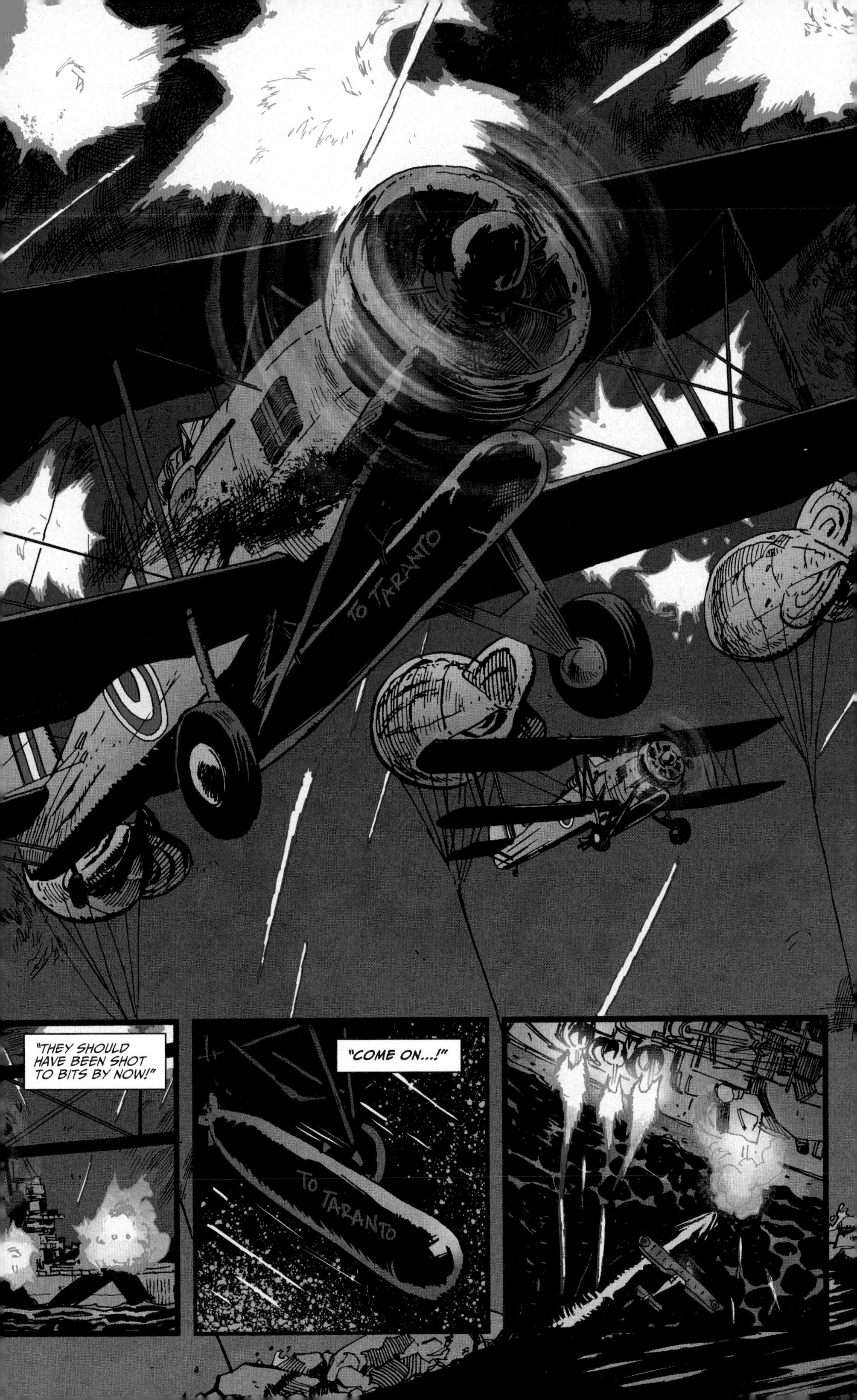
TO TARANTO
"THEY SHOULD HAVE BEEN SHOT TO BITS BY NOW!"
"COME ON...!"
TO TARANTO

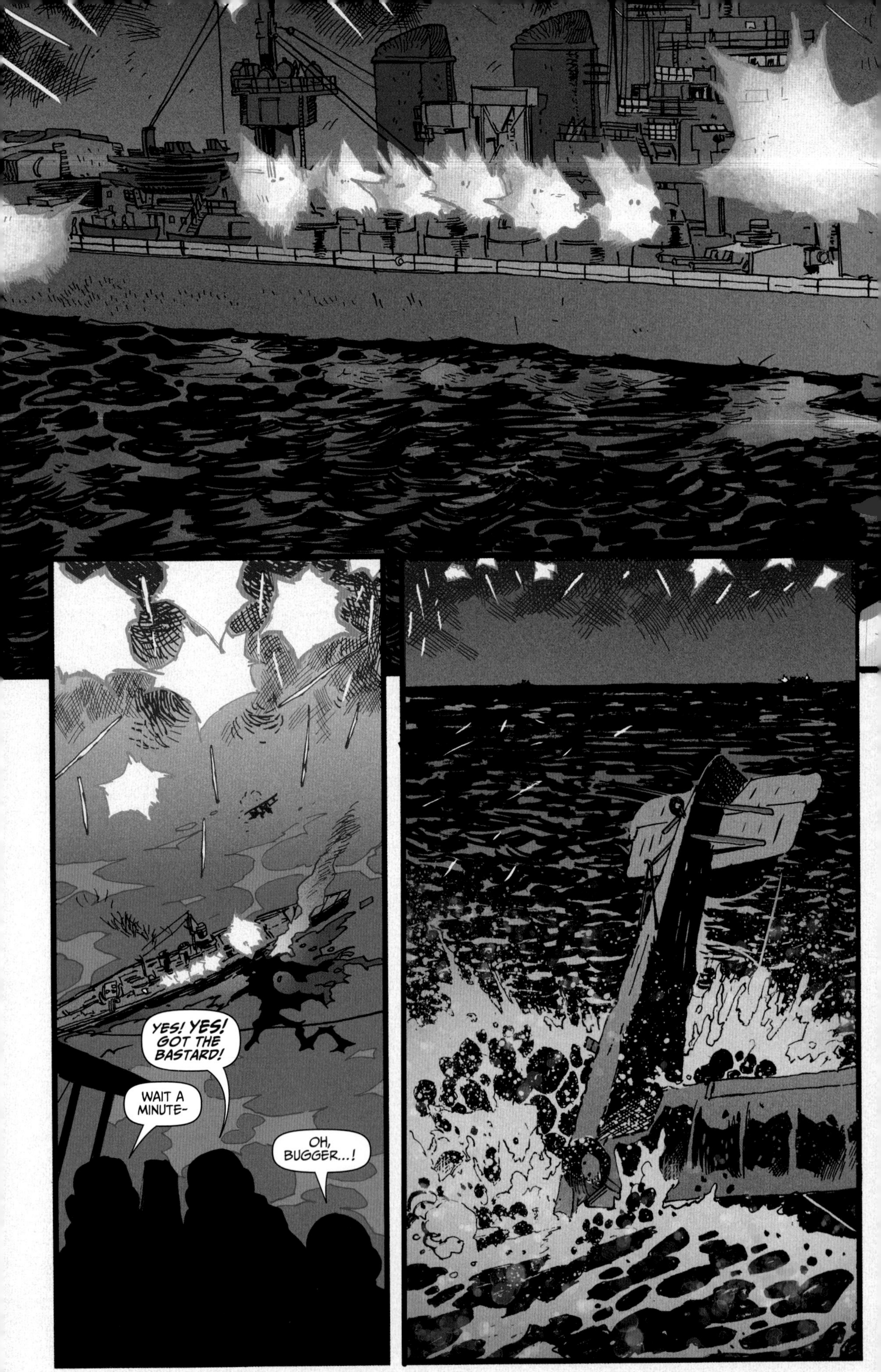
YES! YES! GOT THE BASTARD!
WAIT A MINUTE-
OH, BUGGER...!

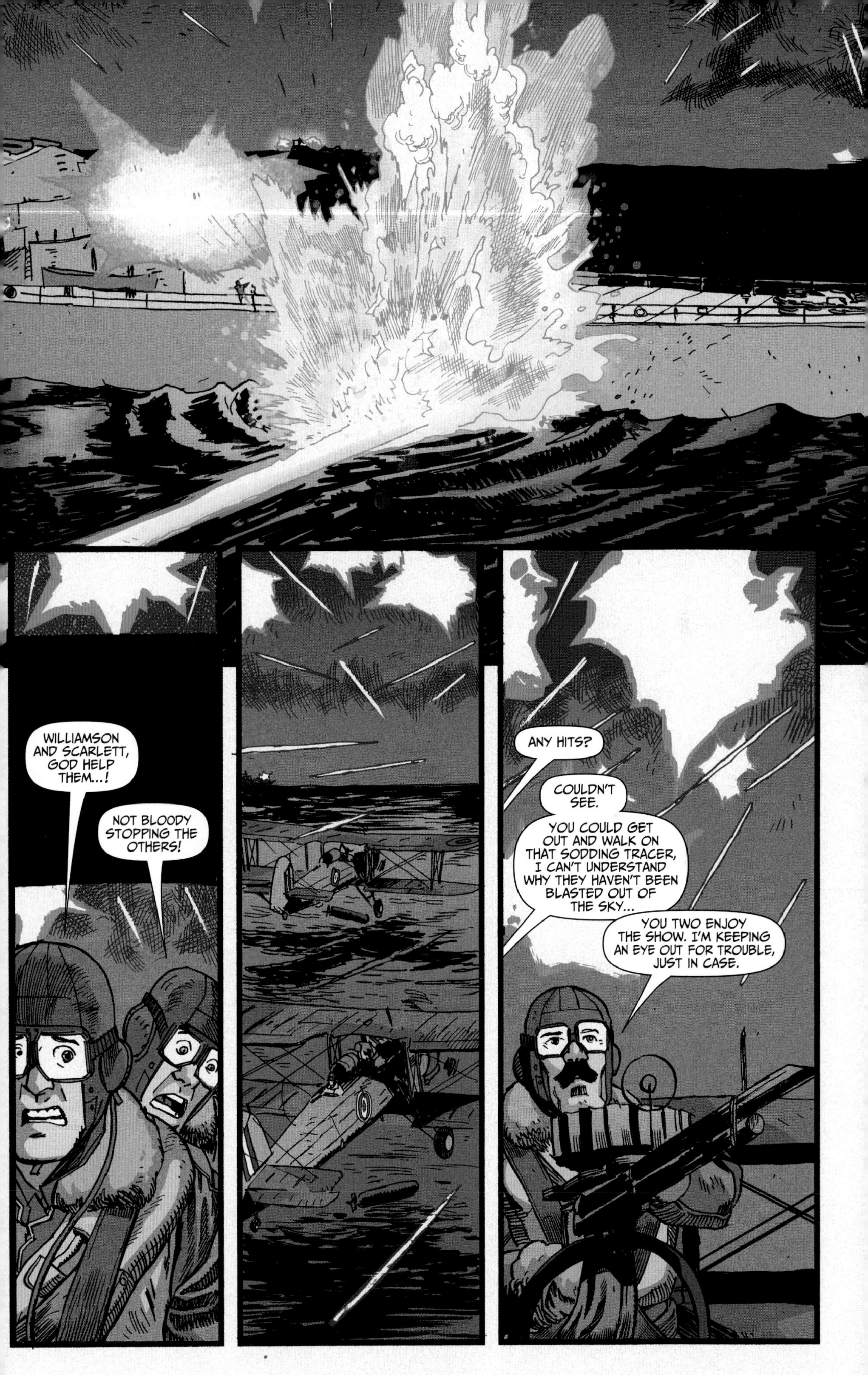
WILLIAMSON AND SCARLETT, GOD HELP THEM...!
NOT BLOODY STOPPING THE OTHERS!
ANY HITS?
COULDN'T SEE.
YOU COULD GET OUT AND WALK ON THAT SODDING TRACER, I CAN'T UNDERSTAND WHY THEY HAVEN'T BEEN BLASTED OUT OF THE SKY...
YOU TWO ENJOY THE SHOW. I'M KEEPING AN EYE OUT FOR TROUBLE, JUST IN CASE.

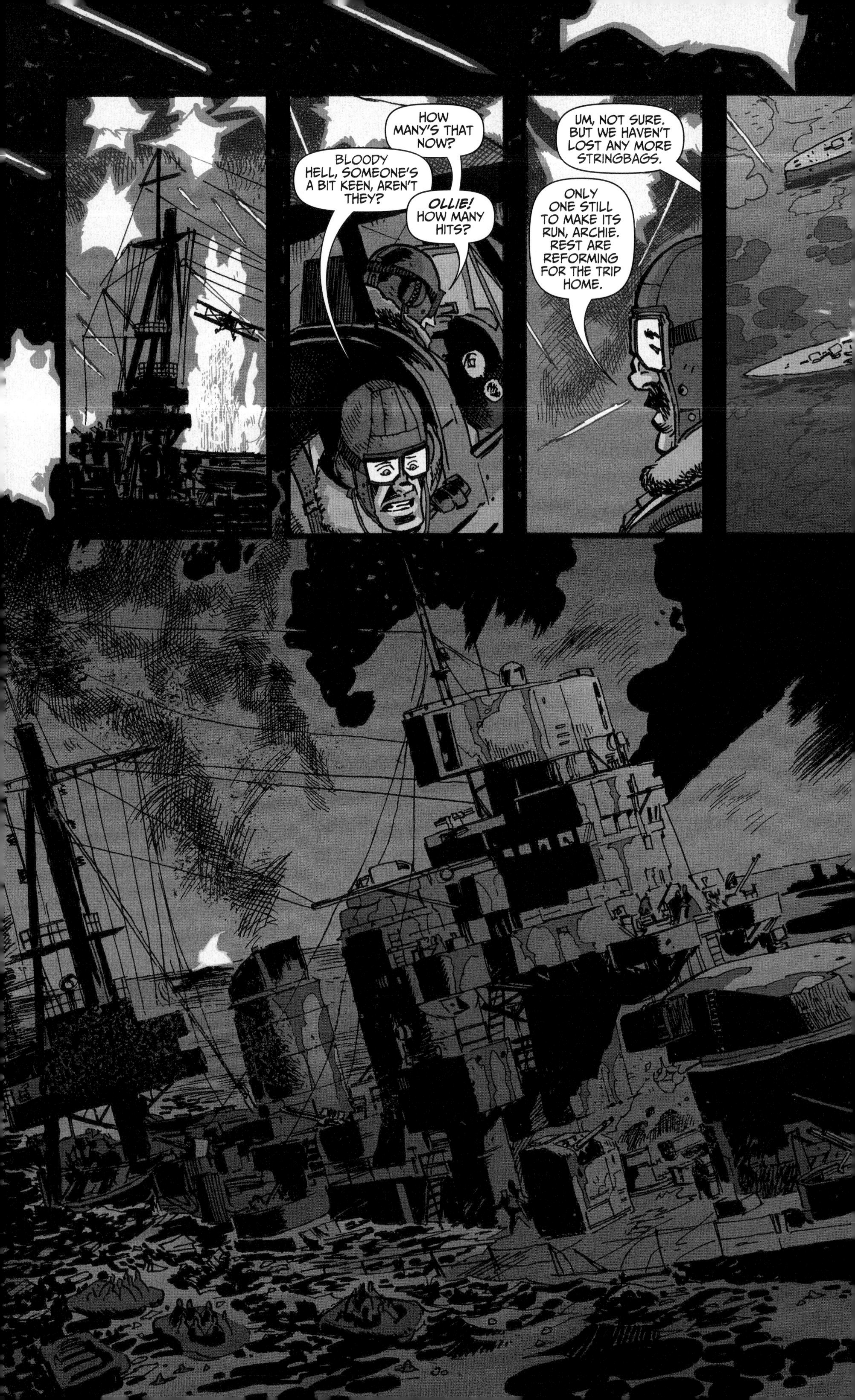

BLOODY HELL, SOMEONE'S A BIT KEEN, AREN'T THEY?
HOW MANY'S THAT NOW?
OLLIE! HOW MANY HITS?
UM, NOT SURE. BUT WE HAVEN'T LOST ANY MORE STRINGBAGS.
ONLY ONE STILL TO MAKE ITS RUN, ARCHIE. REST ARE REFORMING FOR THE TRIP HOME.

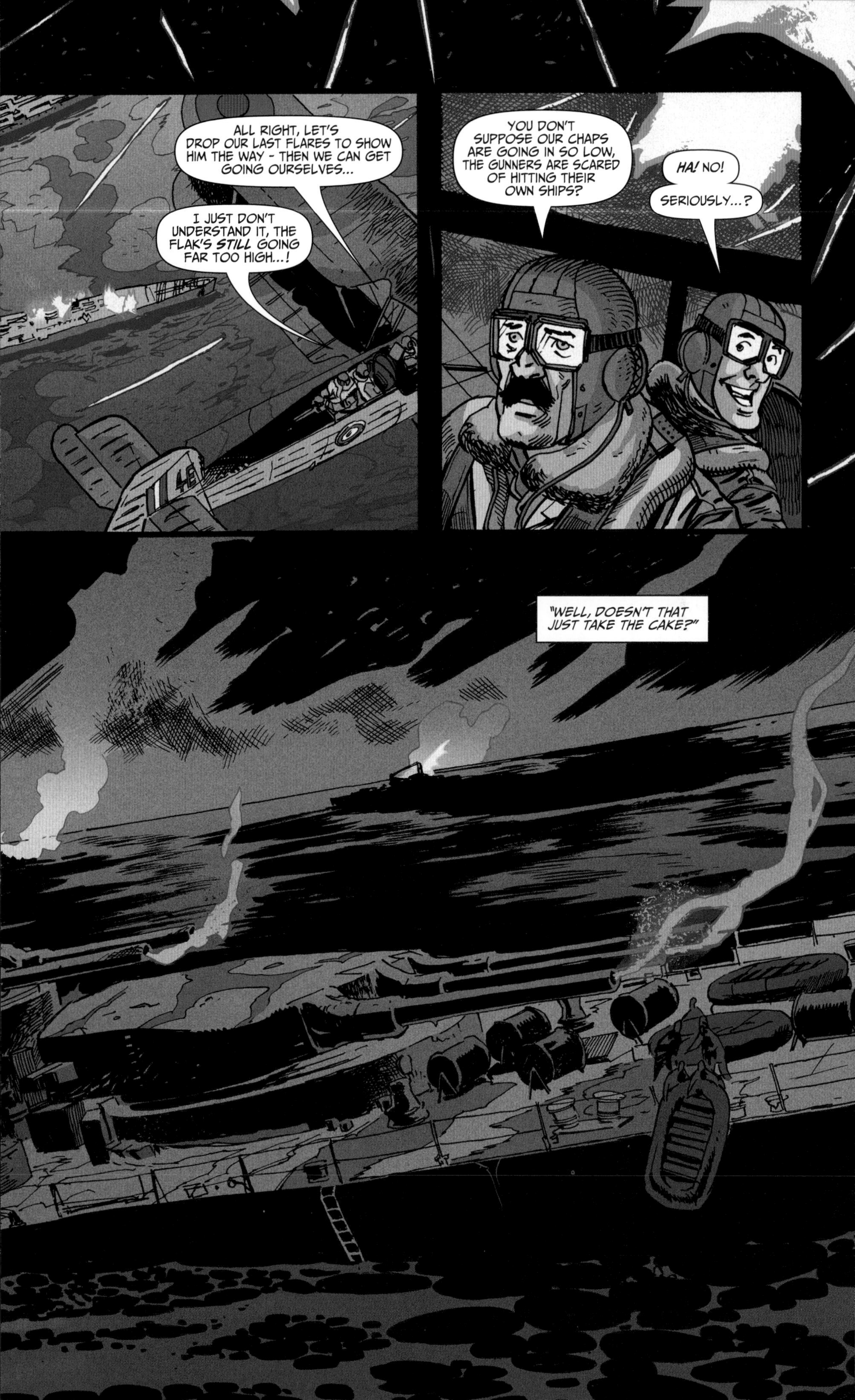
ALL RIGHT, LET'S DROP OUR LAST FLARES TO SHOW HIM THE WAY - THEN WE CAN GET GOING OURSELVES...
I JUST DON'T UNDERSTAND IT, THE FLAK'S STILL GOING FAR TOO HIGH...!
YOU DON'T SUPPOSE OUR CHAPS ARE GOING IN SO LOW, THE GUNNERS ARE SCARED OF HITTING THEIR OWN SHIPS?
HA! NO!
SERIOUSLY...?
"WELL, DOESN'T THAT JUST TAKE THE CAKE?"

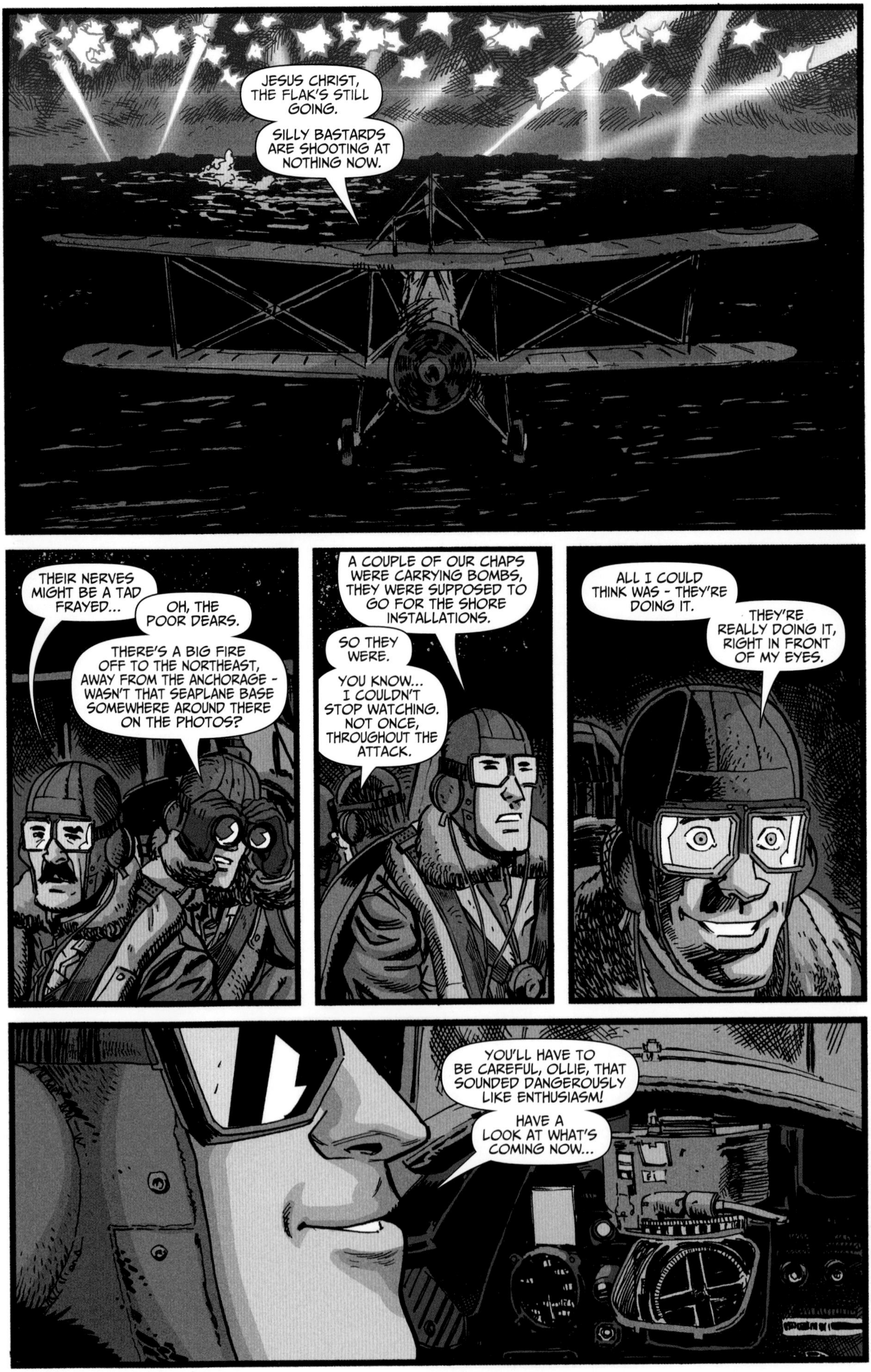
JESUS CHRIST, THE FLAK'S STILL GOING.
SILLY BASTARDS ARE SHOOTING AT NOTHING NOW.
THEIR NERVES MIGHT BE A TAD FRAYED...
OH, THE POOR DEARS.
THERE'S A BIG FIRE OFF TO THE NORTHEAST, AWAY FROM THE ANCHORAGE - WASN'T THAT SEAPLANE BASE SOMEWHERE AROUND THERE ON THE PHOTOS?
A COUPLE OF OUR CHAPS WERE CARRYING BOMBS, THEY WERE SUPPOSED TO GO FOR THE SHORE INSTALLATIONS.
SO THEY WERE.
YOU KNOW... I COULDN'T STOP WATCHING. NOT ONCE, THROUGHOUT THE ATTACK.
ALL I COULD THINK WAS - THEY'RE DOING IT.
THEY'RE REALLY DOING IT, RIGHT IN FRONT OF MY EYES.
YOU'LL HAVE TO BE CAREFUL, OLLIE, THAT SOUNDED DANGEROUSLY LIKE ENTHUSIASM!
HAVE A LOOK AT WHAT'S COMING NOW...

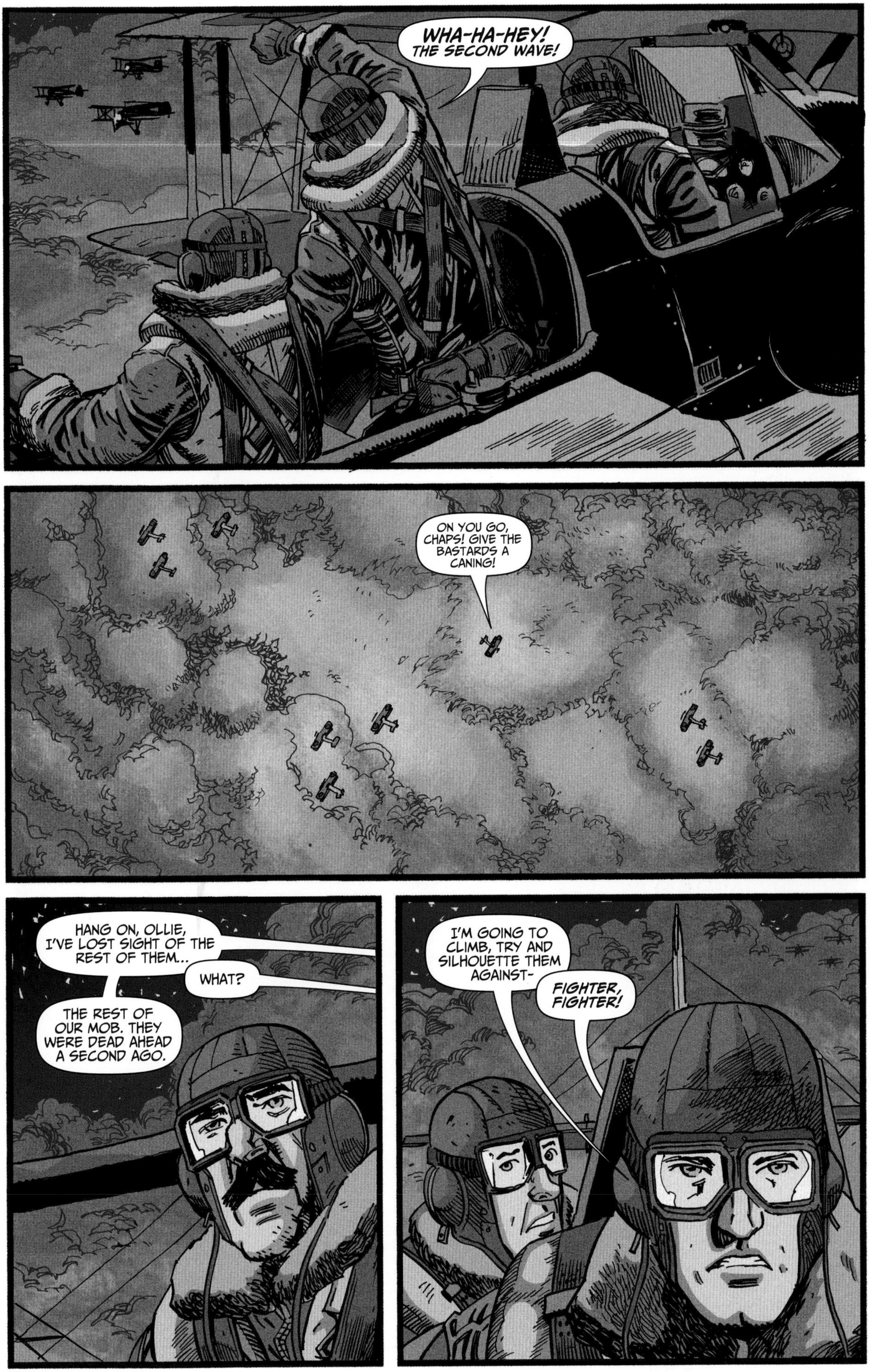
WHA-HA-HEY! THE SECOND WAVE!
ON YOU GO, CHAPS! GIVE THE BASTARDS A CANING!
HANG ON, OLLIE, I'VE LOST SIGHT OF THE REST OF THEM...
WHAT?
THE REST OF OUR MOB. THEY WERE DEAD AHEAD A SECOND AGO.
I'M GOING TO CLIMB, TRY AND SILHOUETTE THEM AGAINST-
FIGHTER, FIGHTER!

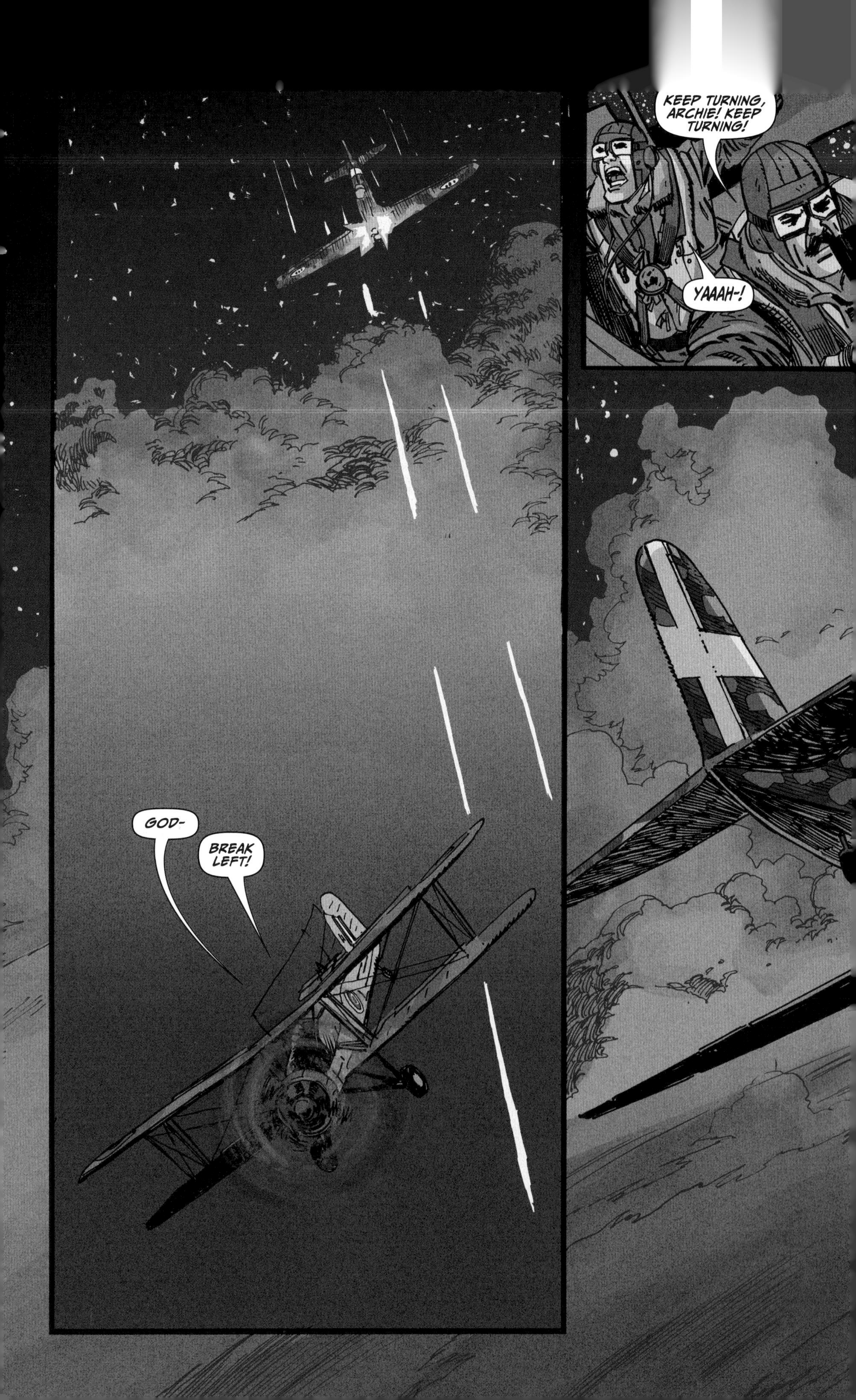
GOD-
BREAK LEFT!
KEEP TURNING, ARCHIE! KEEP TURNING!
YAAAH-!

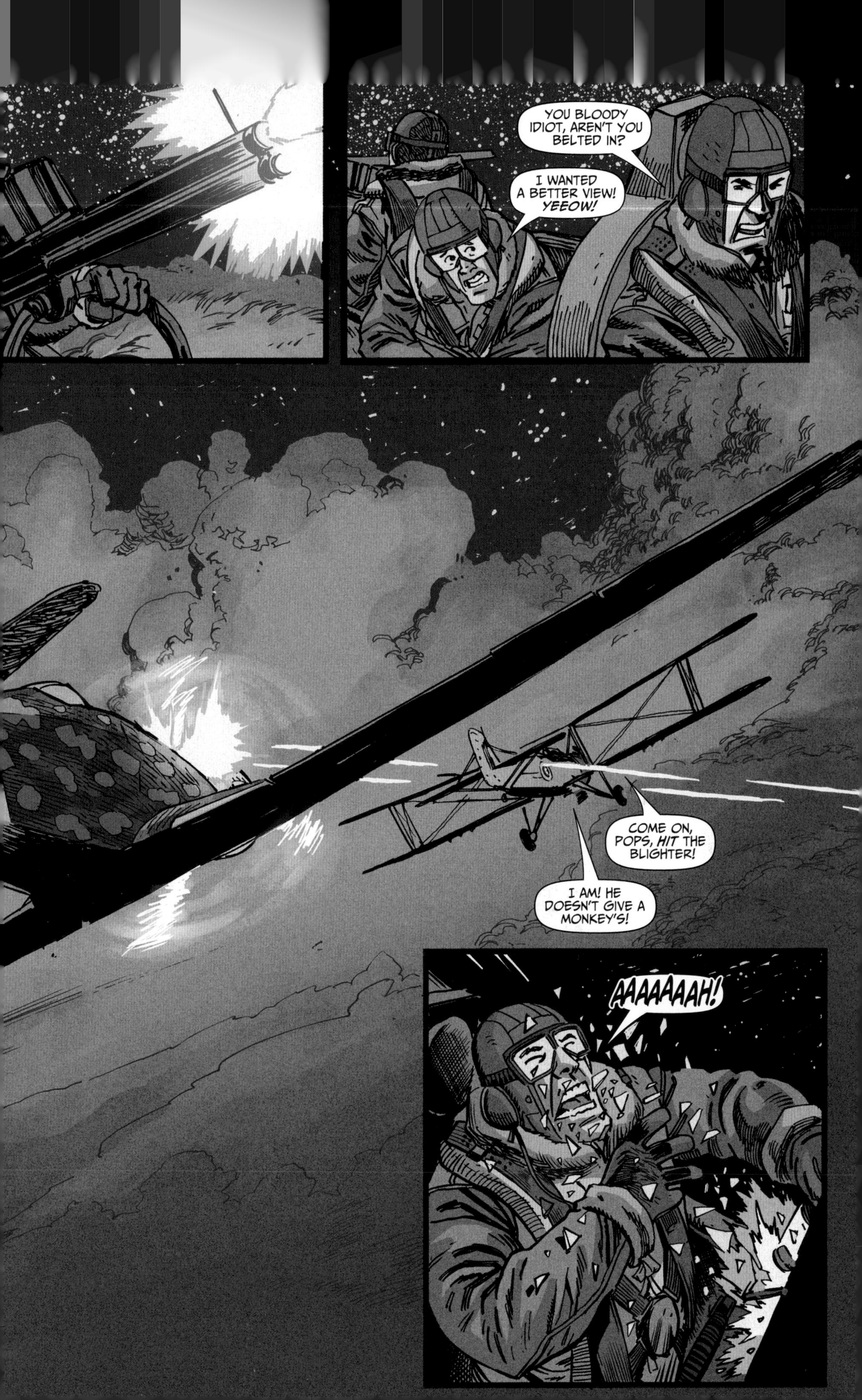
YOU BLOODY IDIOT, AREN'T YOU BELTED IN?
I WANTED A BETTER VIEW! YEEOW!
COME ON, POPS, HIT THE BLIGHTER!
I AM! HE DOESN'T GIVE A MONKEY'S!
AAAAAAAH!

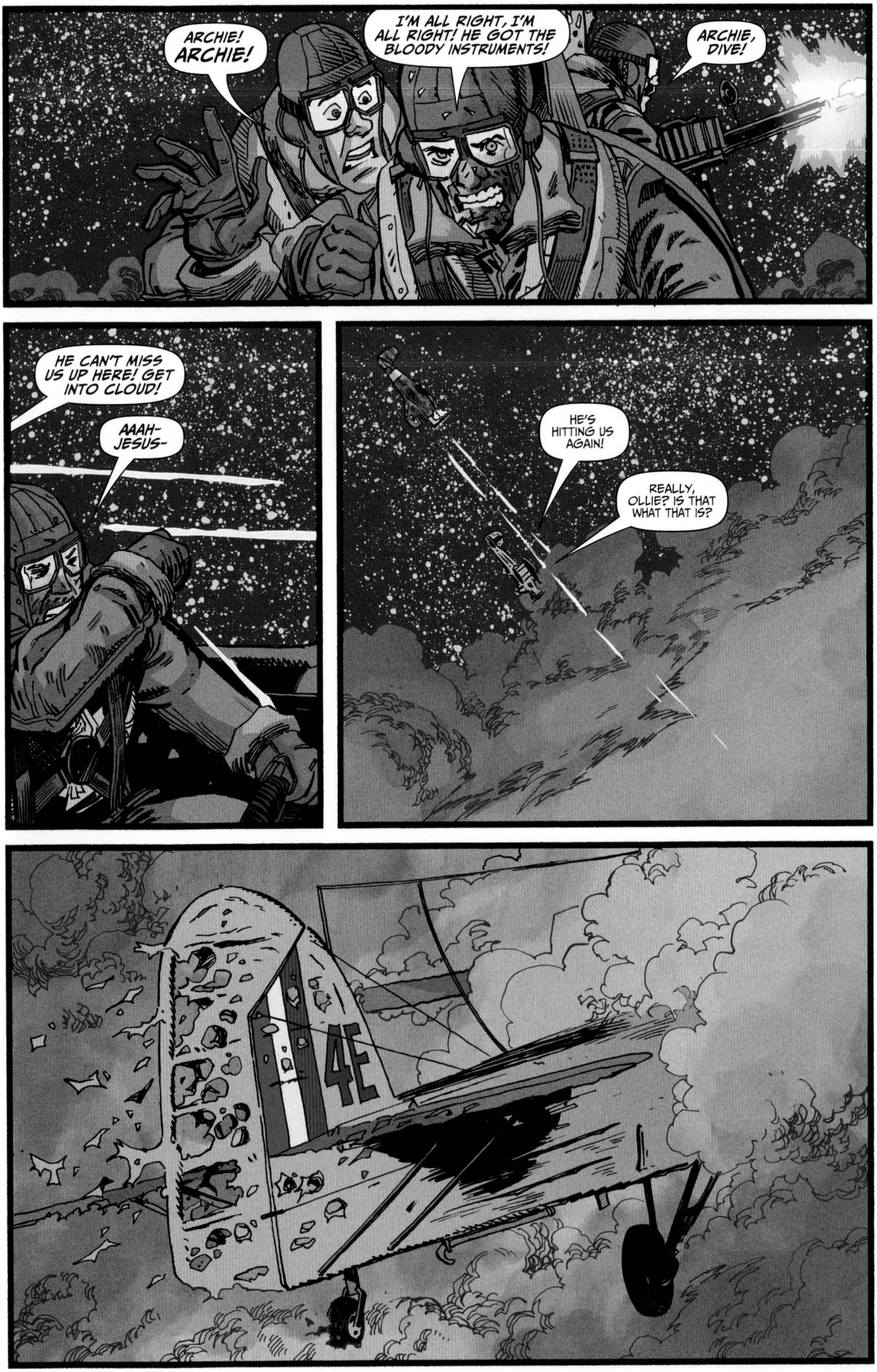
ARCHIE! ARCHIE!
I'M ALL RIGHT, I'M ALL RIGHT! HE GOT THE BLOODY INSTRUMENTS!
ARCHIE, DIVE!
HE CAN'T MISS US UP HERE! GET INTO CLOUD!
AAAH- JESUS-
HE'S HITTING US AGAIN!
REALLY, OLLIE? IS THAT WHAT THAT IS?
4E

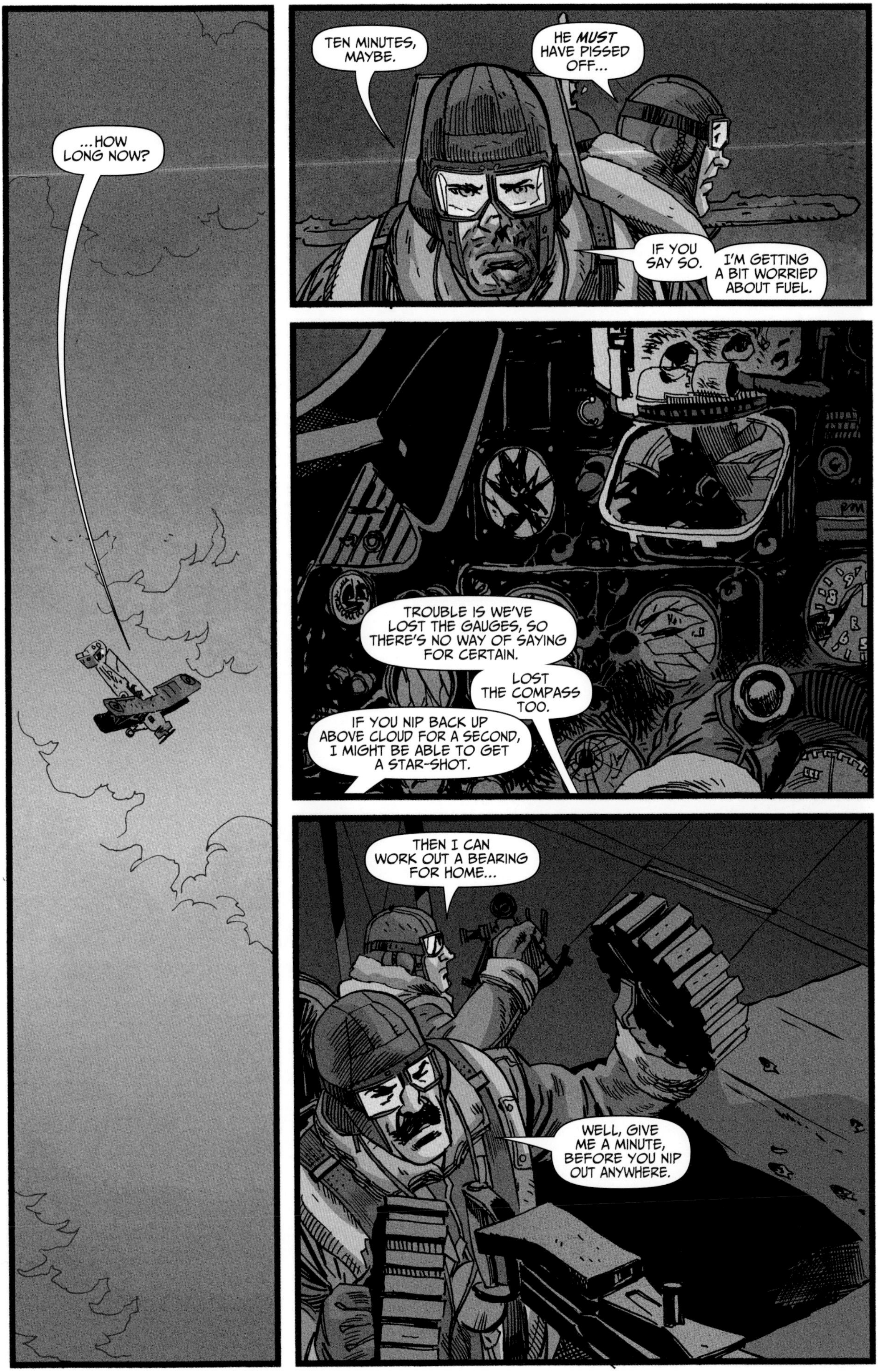
...HOW LONG NOW?
TEN MINUTES, MAYBE.
HE MUST HAVE PISSED OFF...
IF YOU SAY SO.
I'M GETTING A BIT WORRIED ABOUT FUEL.
TROUBLE IS WE'VE LOST THE GAUGES, SO THERE'S NO WAY OF SAYING FOR CERTAIN.
LOST THE COMPASS TOO.
IF YOU NIP BACK UP ABOVE CLOUD FOR A SECOND, I MIGHT BE ABLE TO GET A STAR-SHOT.
THEN I CAN WORK OUT A BEARING FOR HOME...
WELL, GIVE ME A MINUTE, BEFORE YOU NIP OUT ANYWHERE.

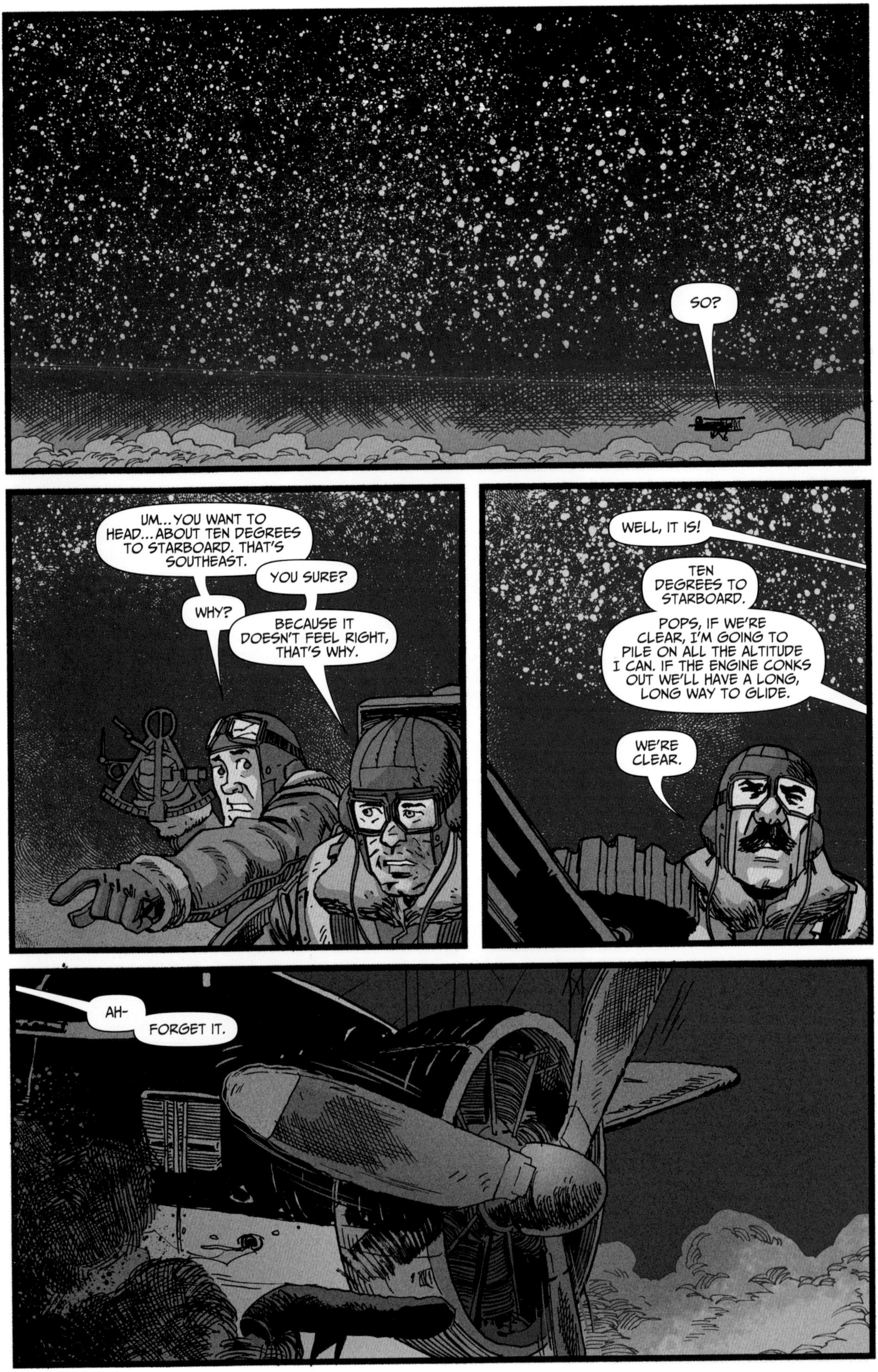
SO?
UM...YOU WANT TO HEAD...ABOUT TEN DEGREES TO STARBOARD. THAT'S SOUTHEAST.
YOU SURE?
WHY?
BECAUSE IT DOESN'T FEEL RIGHT, THAT'S WHY.
WELL, IT IS!
TEN DEGREES TO STARBOARD.
POPS, IF WE'RE CLEAR, I'M GOING TO PILE ON ALL THE ALTITUDE I CAN. IF THE ENGINE CONKS OUT WE'LL HAVE A LONG, LONG WAY TO GLIDE.
WE'RE CLEAR.
AH-
FORGET IT.

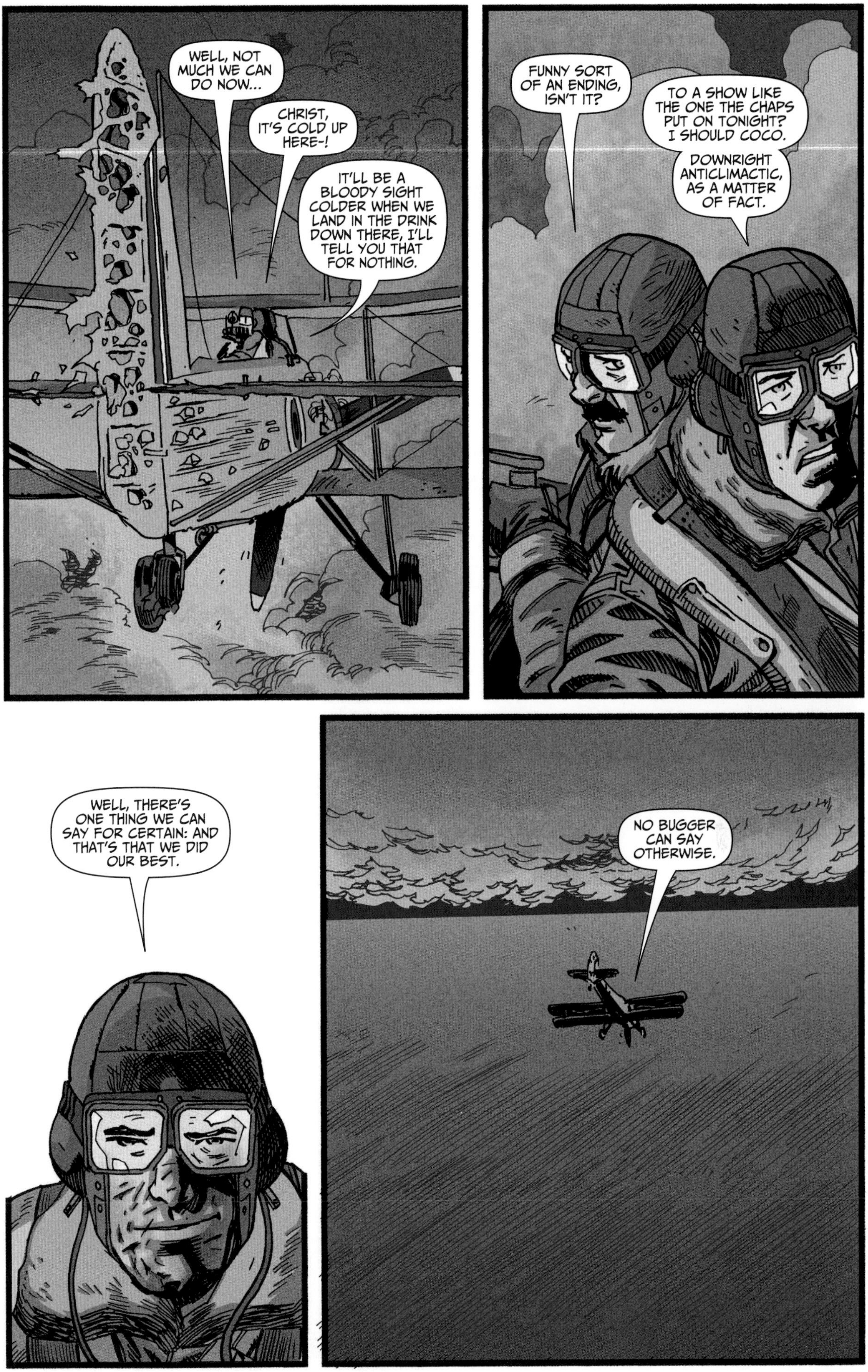
WELL, NOT MUCH WE CAN DO NOW...
CHRIST, IT'S COLD UP HERE-!
IT'LL BE A BLOODY SIGHT COLDER WHEN WE LAND IN THE DRINK DOWN THERE, I'LL TELL YOU THAT FOR NOTHING.
FUNNY SORT OF AN ENDING, ISN'T IT?
TO A SHOW LIKE THE ONE THE CHAPS PUT ON TONIGHT? I SHOULD COCO.
DOWNRIGHT ANTICLIMACTIC, AS A MATTER OF FACT.
WELL, THERE'S ONE THING WE CAN SAY FOR CERTAIN: AND THAT'S THAT WE DID OUR BEST.
NO BUGGER CAN SAY OTHERWISE.

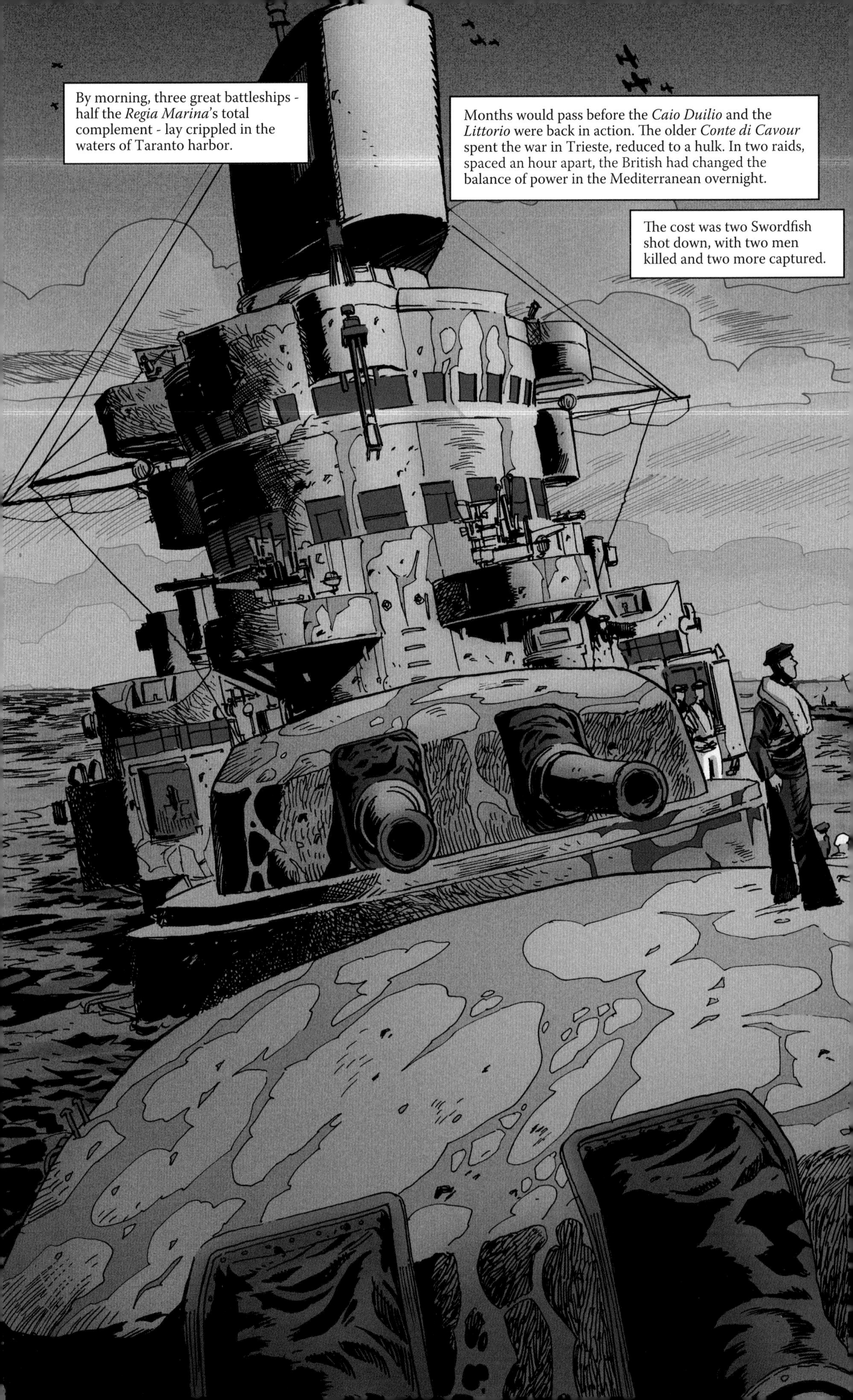
By morning, three great battleships - half the *Regia Marina*'s total complement - lay crippled in the waters of Taranto harbor.
Months would pass before the *Caio Duilio* and the *Littorio* were back in action. The older *Conte di Cavour* spent the war in Trieste, reduced to a hulk. In two raids, spaced an hour apart, the British had changed the balance of power in the Mediterranean overnight.
The cost was two Swordfish shot down, with two men killed and two more captured.

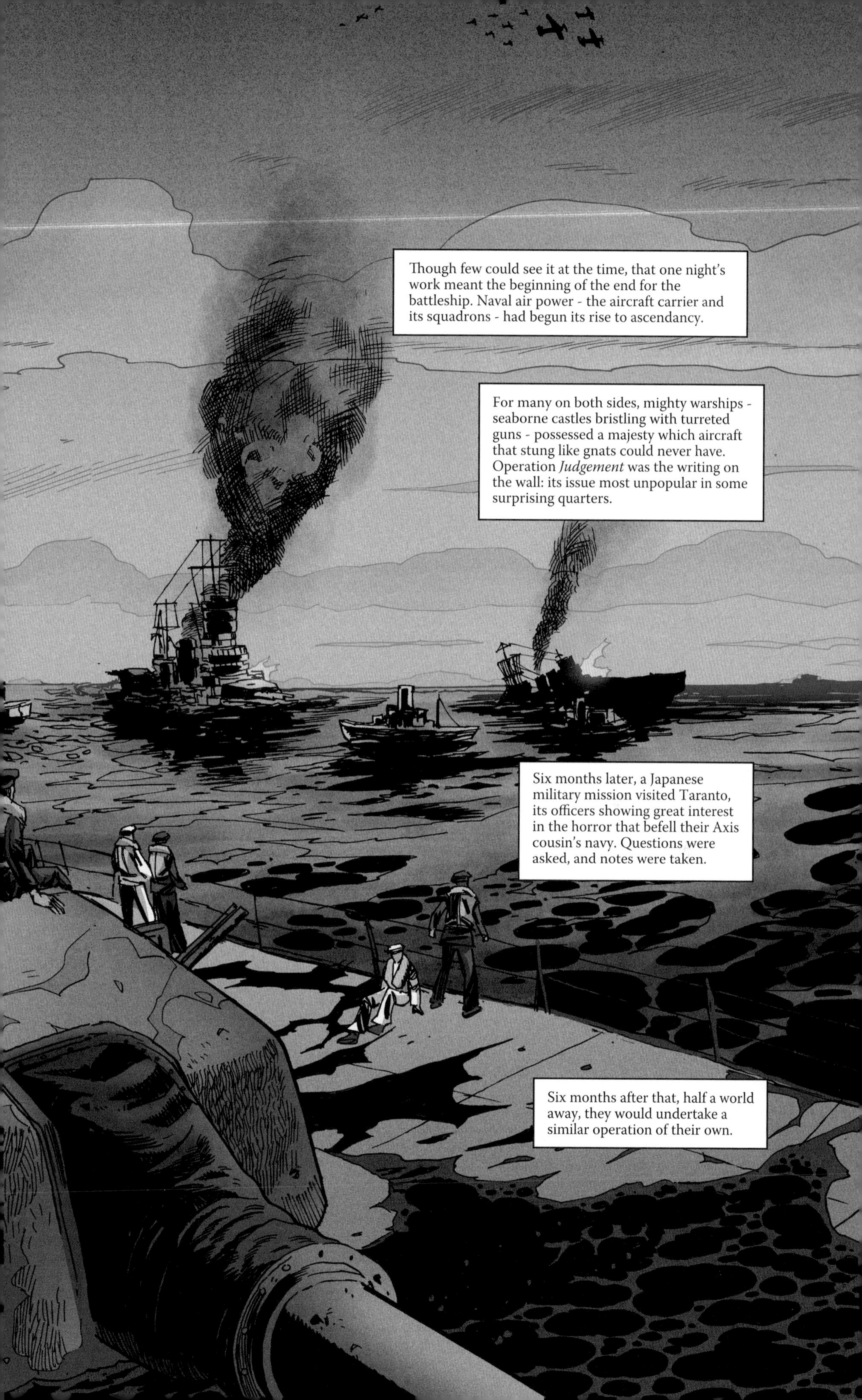
Though few could see it at the time, that one night's work meant the beginning of the end for the battleship. Naval air power - the aircraft carrier and its squadrons - had begun its rise to ascendancy.
For many on both sides, mighty warships - seaborne castles bristling with turreted guns - possessed a majesty which aircraft that stung like gnats could never have. Operation *Judgement* was the writing on the wall: its issue most unpopular in some surprising quarters.
Six months later, a Japanese military mission visited Taranto, its officers showing great interest in the horror that befell their Axis cousin's navy. Questions were asked, and notes were taken.
Six months after that, half a world away, they would undertake a similar operation of their own.

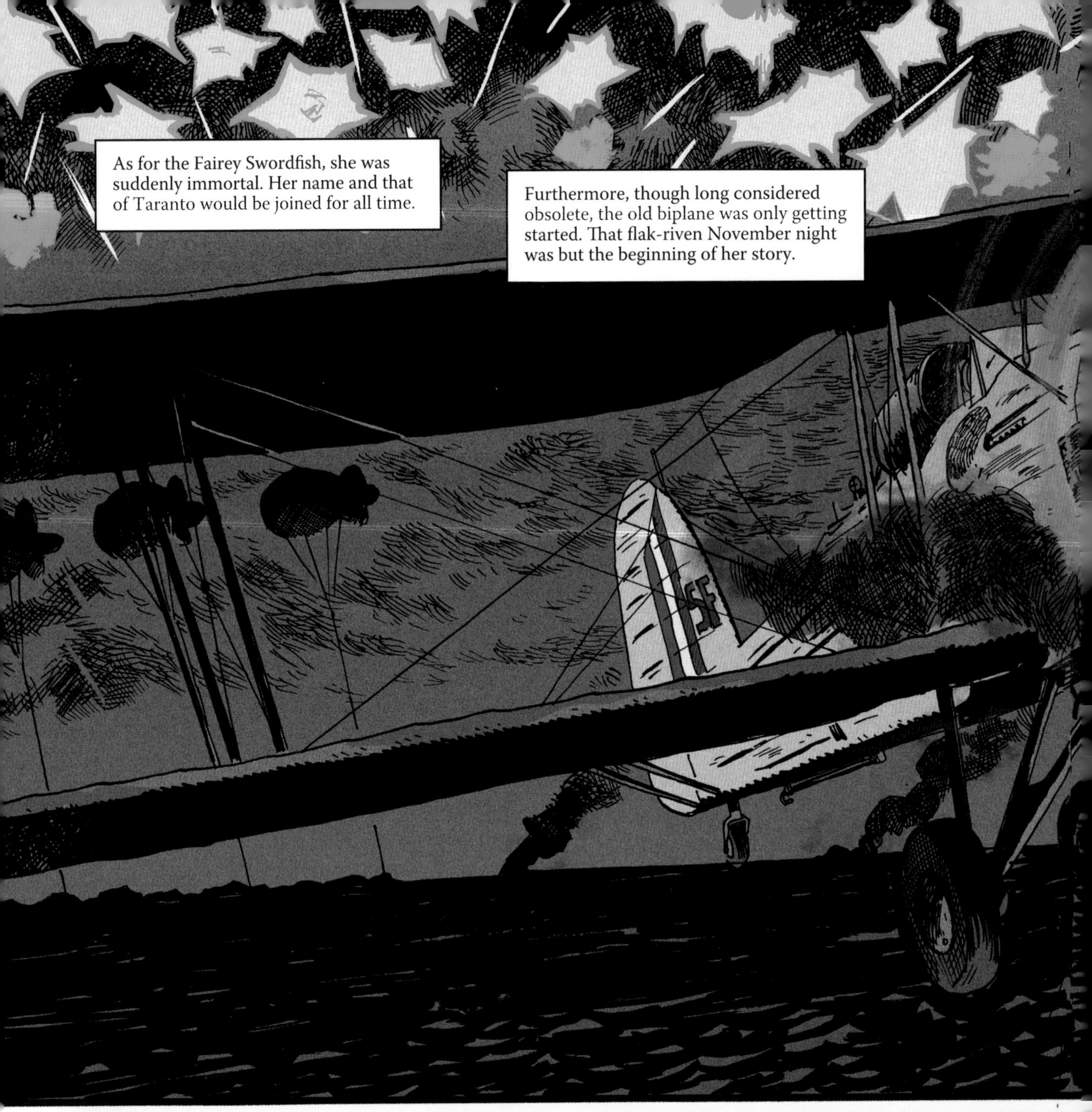
As for the Fairey Swordfish, she was suddenly immortal. Her name and that of Taranto would be joined for all time.
Furthermore, though long considered obsolete, the old biplane was only getting started. That flak-riven November night was but the beginning of her story.
SF

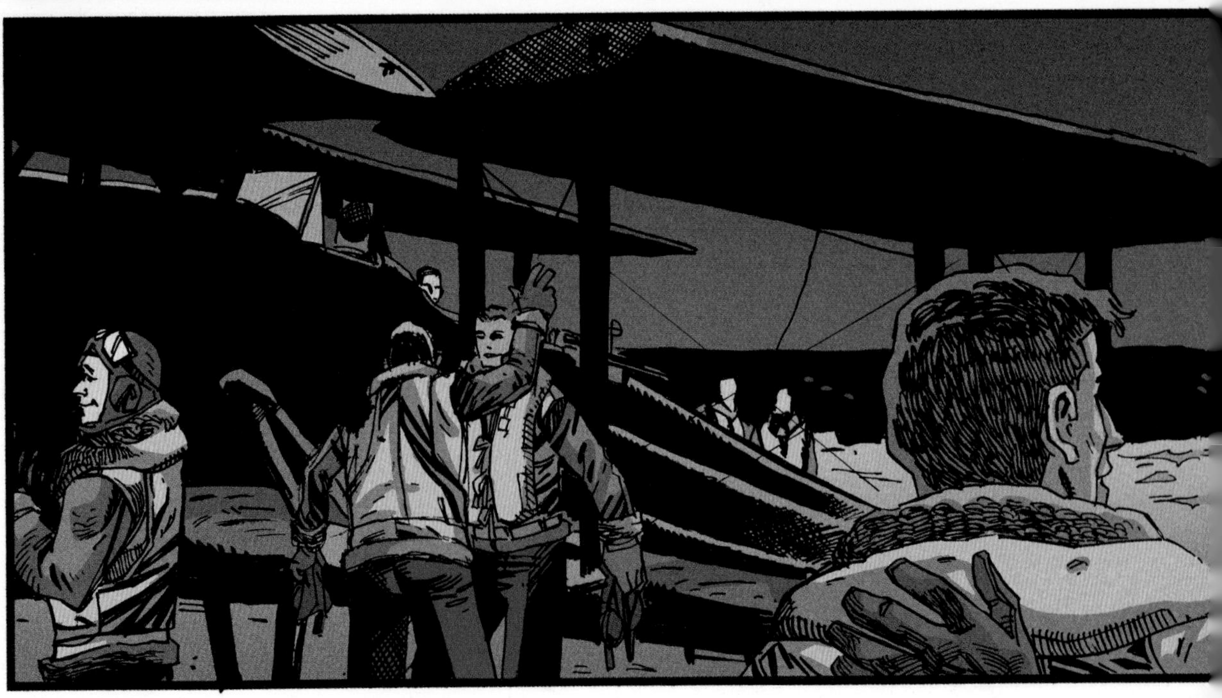

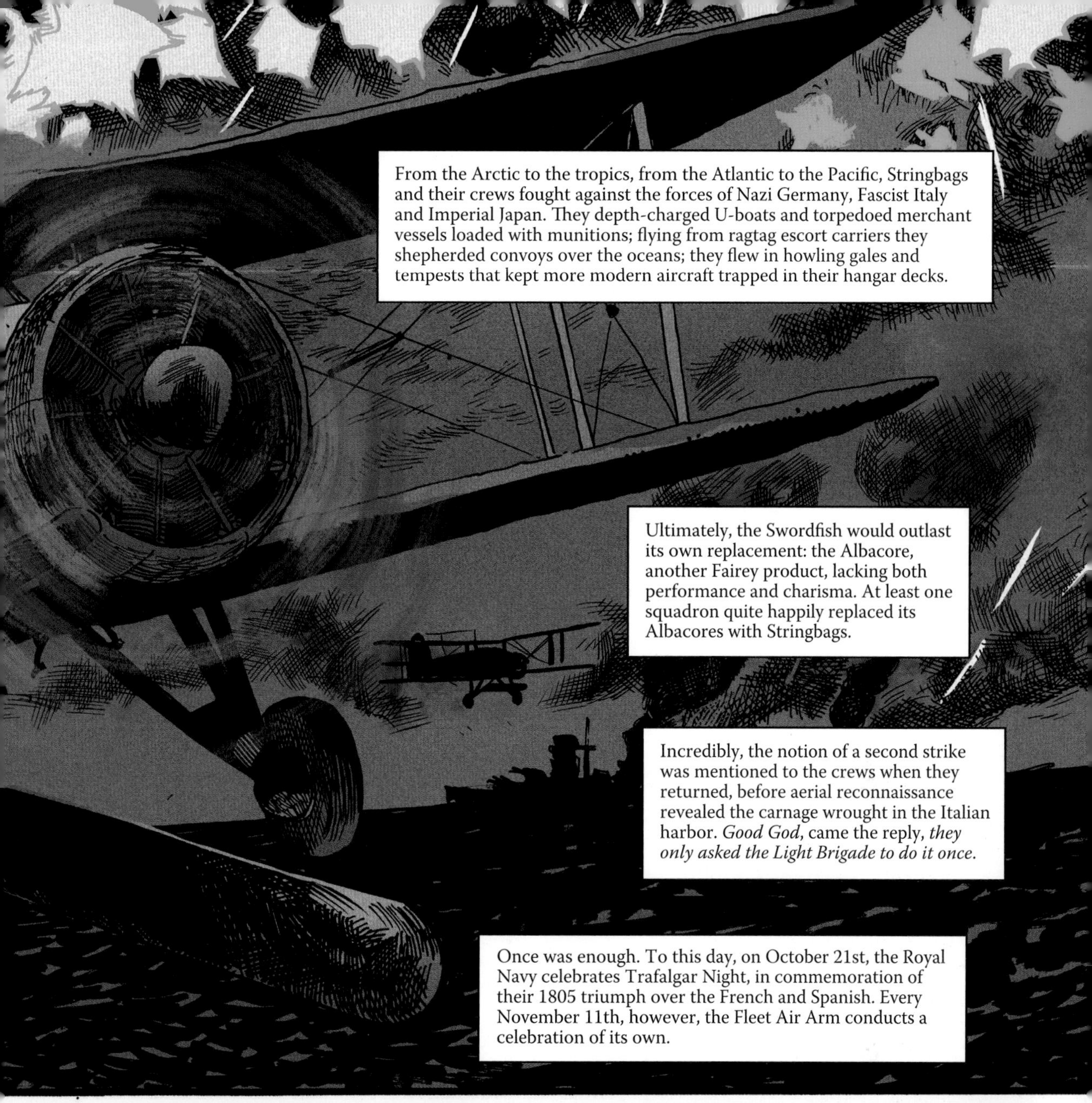
From the Arctic to the tropics, from the Atlantic to the Pacific, Stringbags and their crews fought against the forces of Nazi Germany, Fascist Italy and Imperial Japan. They depth-charged U-boats and torpedoed merchant vessels loaded with munitions; flying from ragtag escort carriers they shepherded convoys over the oceans; they flew in howling gales and tempests that kept more modern aircraft trapped in their hangar decks.
Ultimately, the Swordfish would outlast its own replacement: the Albacore, another Fairey product, lacking both performance and charisma. At least one squadron quite happily replaced its Albacores with Stringbags.
Incredibly, the notion of a second strike was mentioned to the crews when they returned, before aerial reconnaissance revealed the carnage wrought in the Italian harbor. *Good God*, came the reply, *they only asked the Light Brigade to do it once.*
Once was enough. To this day, on October 21st, the Royal Navy celebrates Trafalgar Night, in commemoration of their 1805 triumph over the French and Spanish. Every November 11th, however, the Fleet Air Arm conducts a celebration of its own.

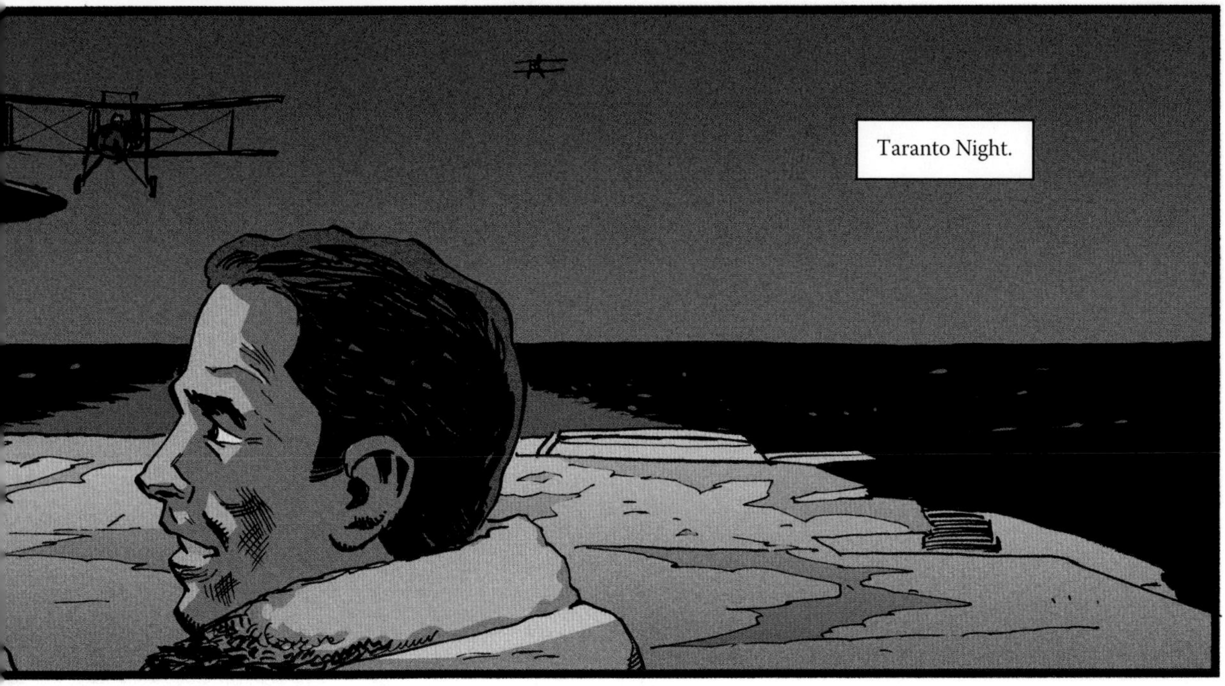
Taranto Night.

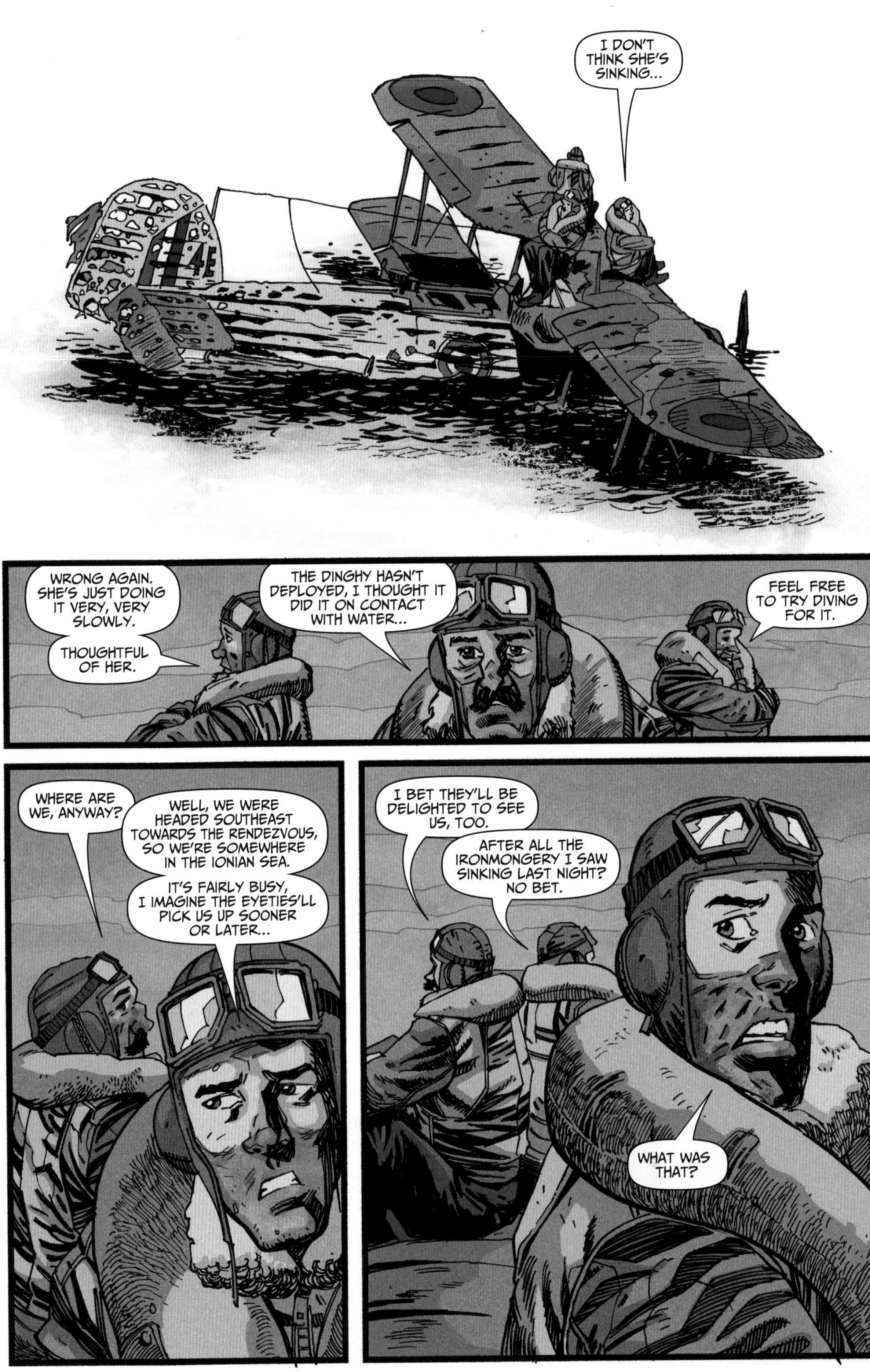
I DON'T THINK SHE'S SINKING...
WRONG AGAIN. SHE'S JUST DOING IT VERY, VERY SLOWLY.
THOUGHTFUL OF HER.
THE DINGHY HASN'T DEPLOYED, I THOUGHT IT DID IT ON CONTACT WITH WATER...
FEEL FREE TO TRY DIVING FOR IT.
WHERE ARE WE, ANYWAY?
WELL, WE WERE HEADED SOUTHEAST TOWARDS THE RENDEZVOUS, SO WE'RE SOMEWHERE IN THE IONIAN SEA.
IT'S FAIRLY BUSY, I IMAGINE THE EYETIES'LL PICK US UP SOONER OR LATER...
I BET THEY'LL BE DELIGHTED TO SEE US, TOO.
AFTER ALL THE IRONMONGERY I SAW SINKING LAST NIGHT? NO BET.
WHAT WAS THAT?

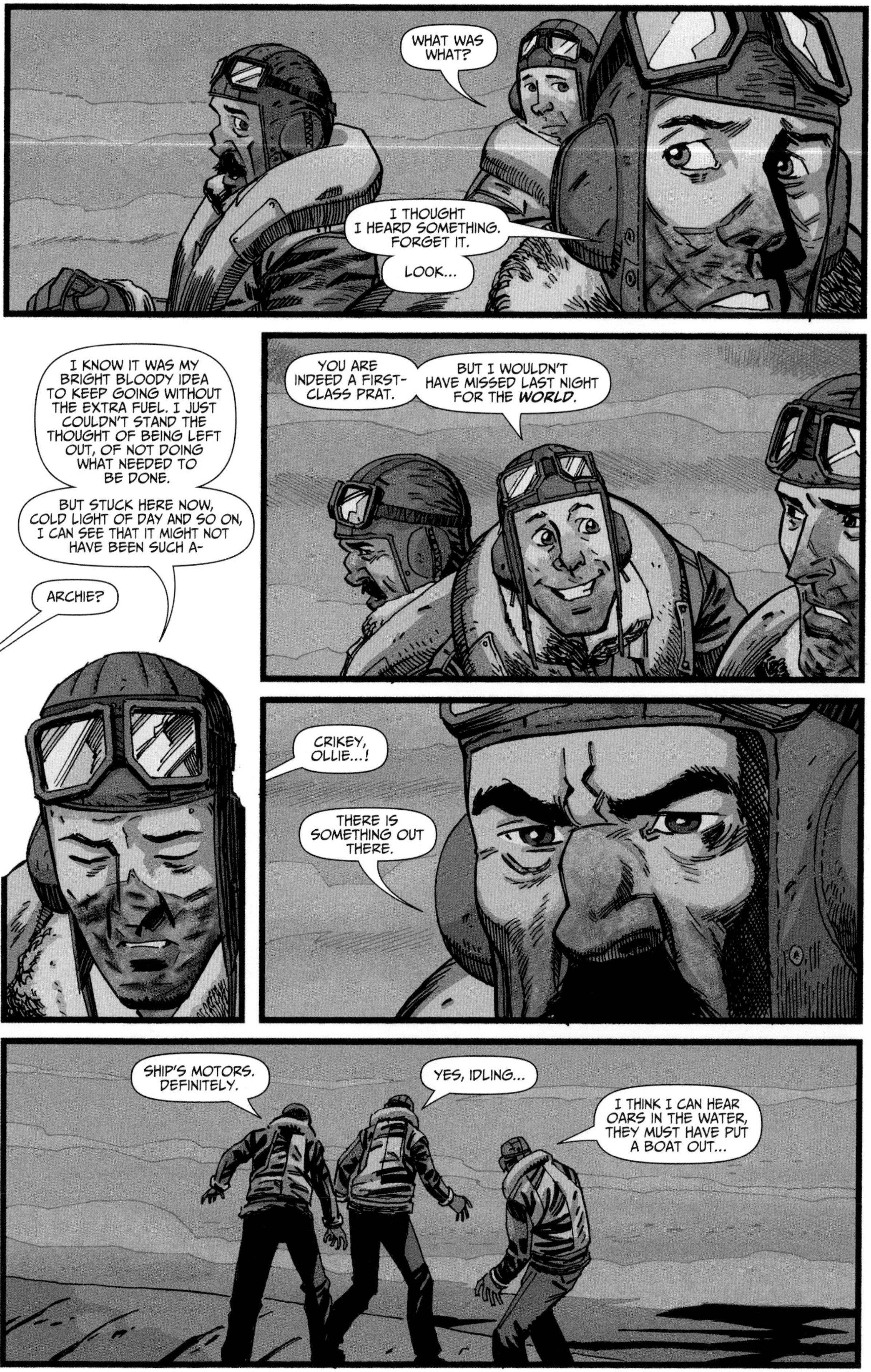
WHAT WAS WHAT?
I THOUGHT I HEARD SOMETHING. FORGET IT.
LOOK...
I KNOW IT WAS MY BRIGHT BLOODY IDEA TO KEEP GOING WITHOUT THE EXTRA FUEL. I JUST COULDN'T STAND THE THOUGHT OF BEING LEFT OUT, OF NOT DOING WHAT NEEDED TO BE DONE.
BUT STUCK HERE NOW, COLD LIGHT OF DAY AND SO ON, I CAN SEE THAT IT MIGHT NOT HAVE BEEN SUCH A-
YOU ARE INDEED A FIRST-CLASS PRAT.
BUT I WOULDN'T HAVE MISSED LAST NIGHT FOR THE **WORLD**.
ARCHIE?
CRIKEY, OLLIE...!
THERE IS SOMETHING OUT THERE.
SHIP'S MOTORS. DEFINITELY.
YES, IDLING...
I THINK I CAN HEAR OARS IN THE WATER, THEY MUST HAVE PUT A BOAT OUT...

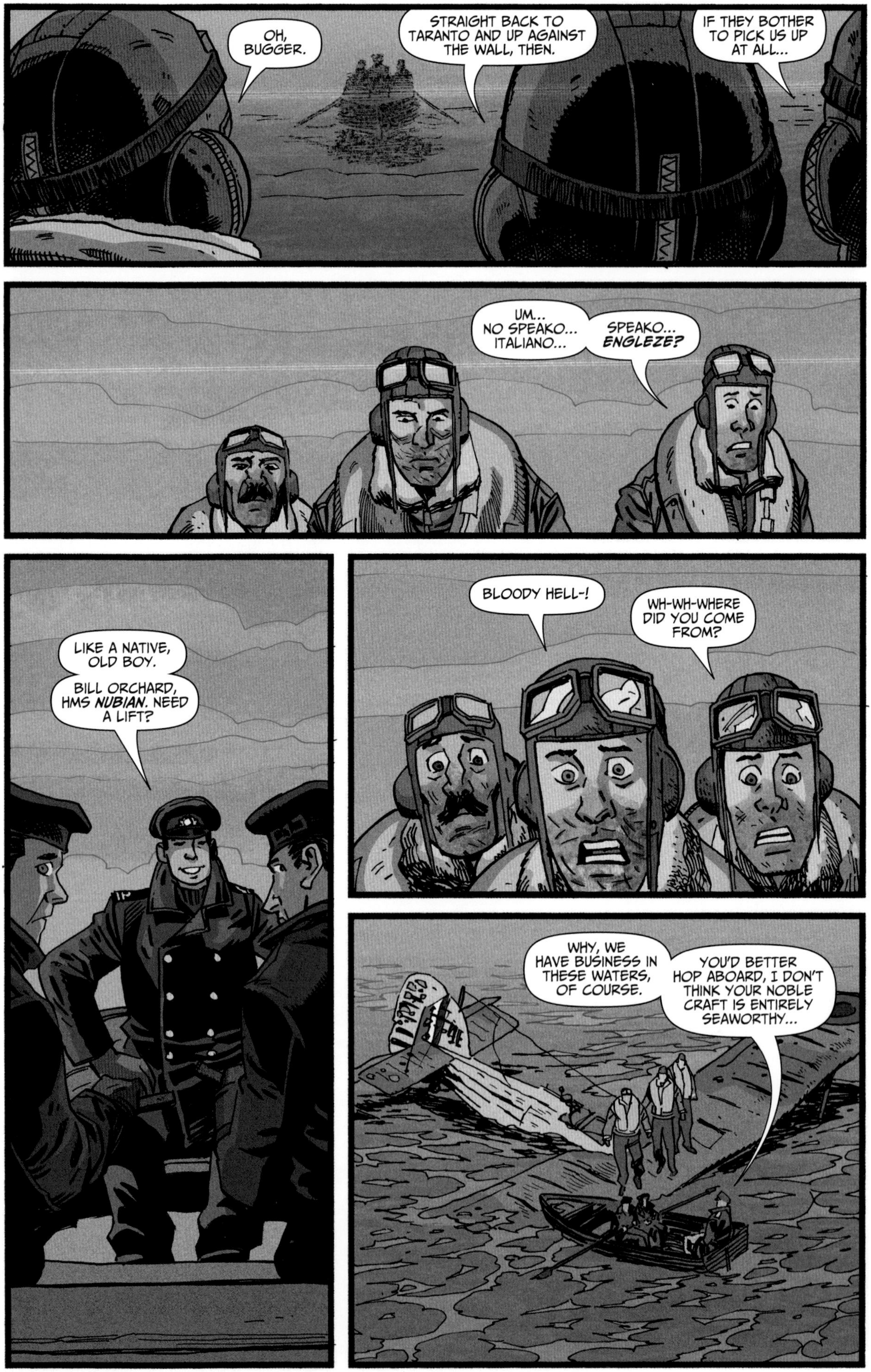
OH, BUGGER.
STRAIGHT BACK TO TARANTO AND UP AGAINST THE WALL, THEN.
IF THEY BOTHER TO PICK US UP AT ALL...
UM... NO SPEAKO... ITALIANO...
SPEAKO... ENGLEZE?
LIKE A NATIVE, OLD BOY.
BILL ORCHARD, HMS NUBIAN. NEED A LIFT?
BLOODY HELL-!
WH-WH-WHERE DID YOU COME FROM?
WHY, WE HAVE BUSINESS IN THESE WATERS, OF COURSE.
YOU'D BETTER HOP ABOARD, I DON'T THINK YOUR NOBLE CRAFT IS ENTIRELY SEAWORTHY...

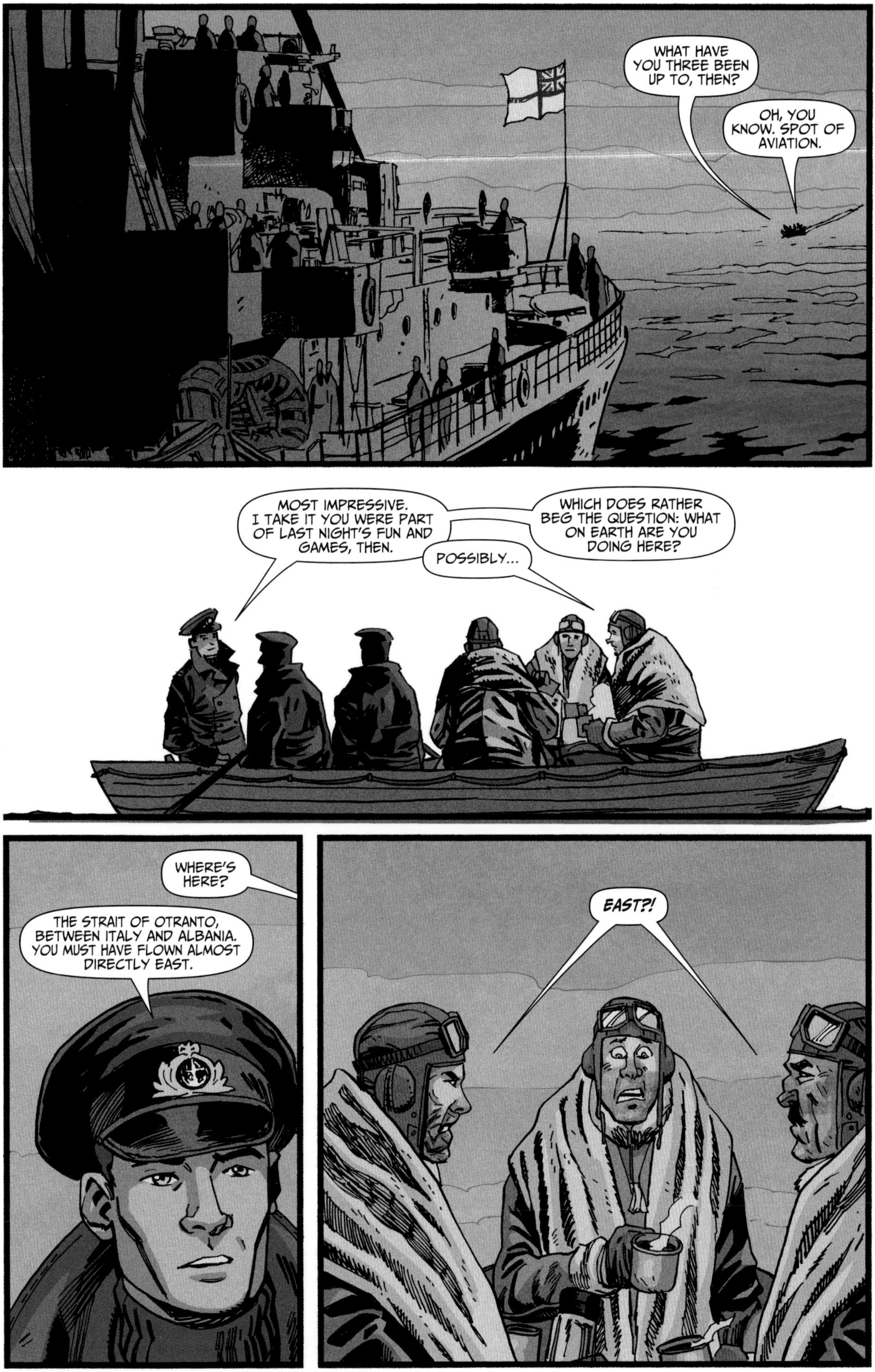
WHAT HAVE YOU THREE BEEN UP TO, THEN?
OH, YOU KNOW. SPOT OF AVIATION.
MOST IMPRESSIVE. I TAKE IT YOU WERE PART OF LAST NIGHT'S FUN AND GAMES, THEN.
POSSIBLY...
WHICH DOES RATHER BEG THE QUESTION: WHAT ON EARTH ARE YOU DOING HERE?
WHERE'S HERE?
THE STRAIT OF OTRANTO, BETWEEN ITALY AND ALBANIA. YOU MUST HAVE FLOWN ALMOST DIRECTLY EAST.
EAST?!

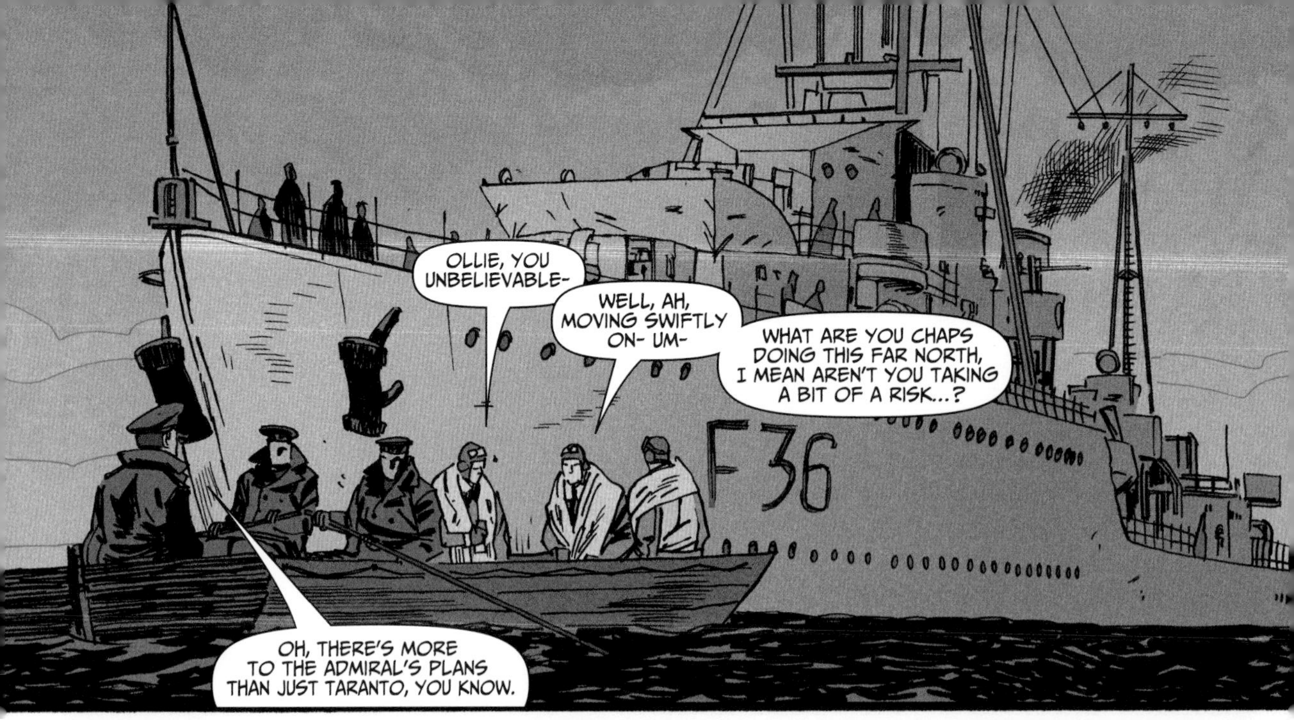
OLLIE, YOU UNBELIEVABLE-
WELL, AH, MOVING SWIFTLY ON- UM-
WHAT ARE YOU CHAPS DOING THIS FAR NORTH, I MEAN AREN'T YOU TAKING A BIT OF A RISK...?
F36
OH, THERE'S MORE TO THE ADMIRAL'S PLANS THAN JUST TARANTO, YOU KNOW.

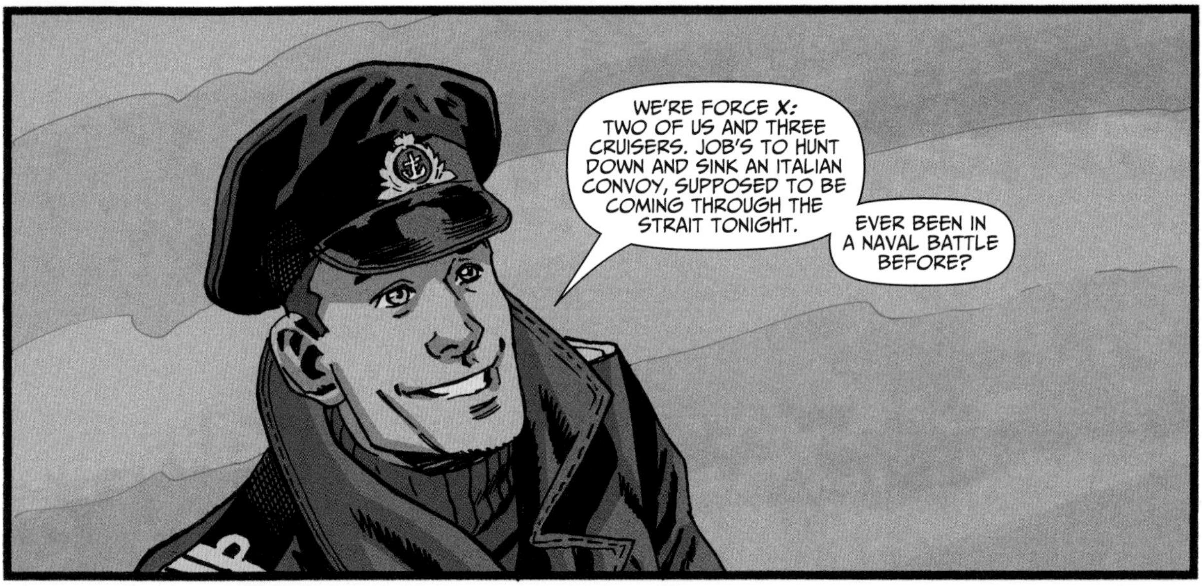
WE'RE FORCE X: TWO OF US AND THREE CRUISERS. JOB'S TO HUNT DOWN AND SINK AN ITALIAN CONVOY, SUPPOSED TO BE COMING THROUGH THE STRAIT TONIGHT.
EVER BEEN IN A NAVAL BATTLE BEFORE?

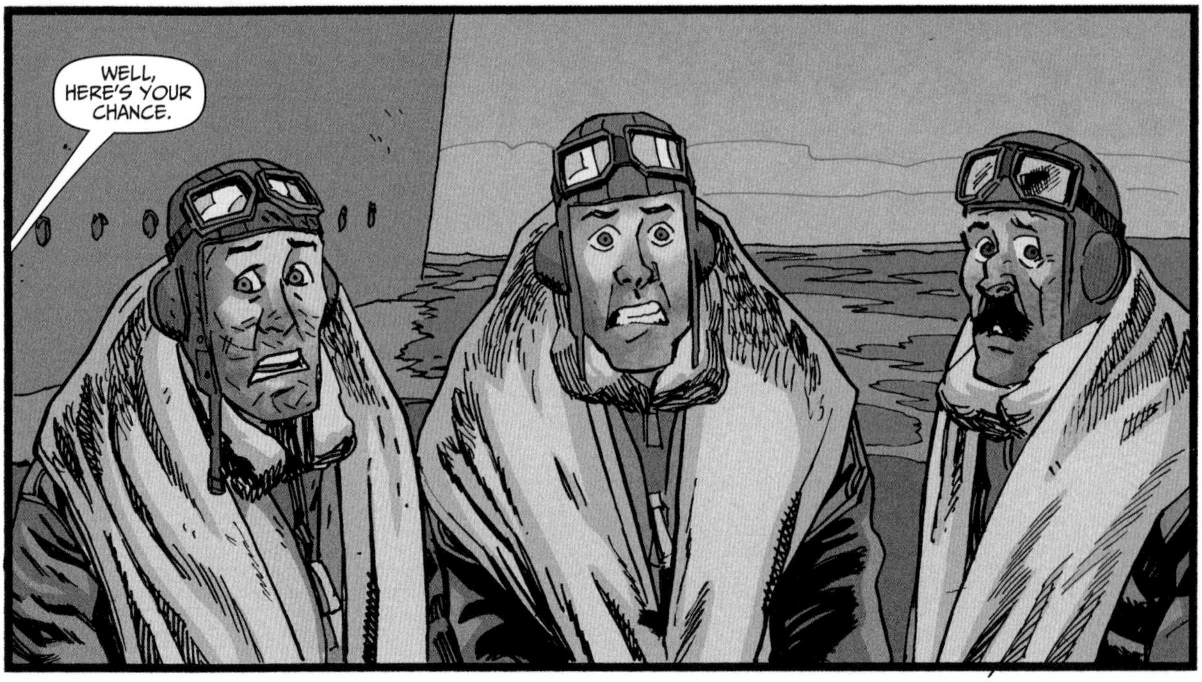
WELL, HERE'S YOUR CHANCE.

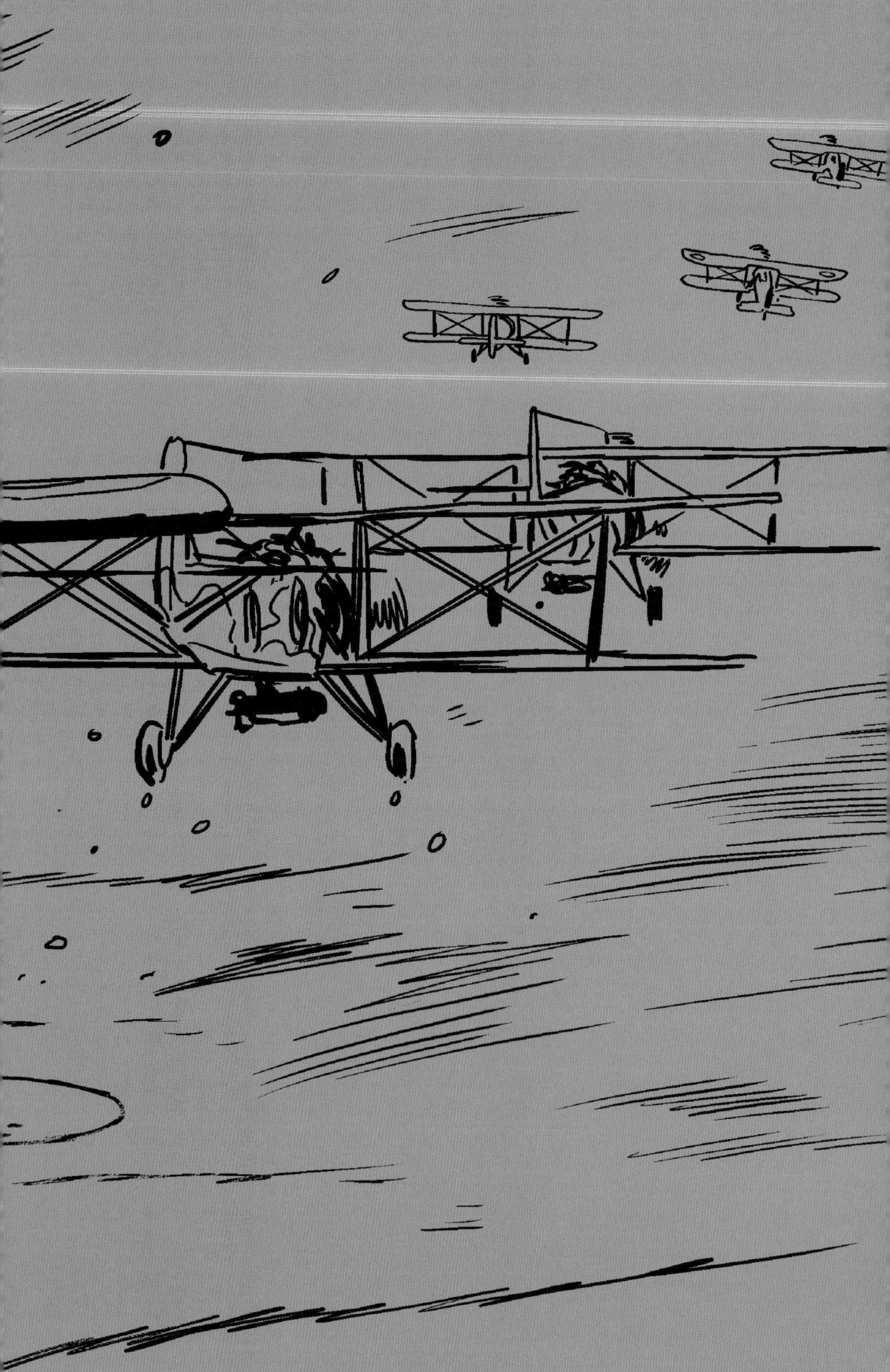

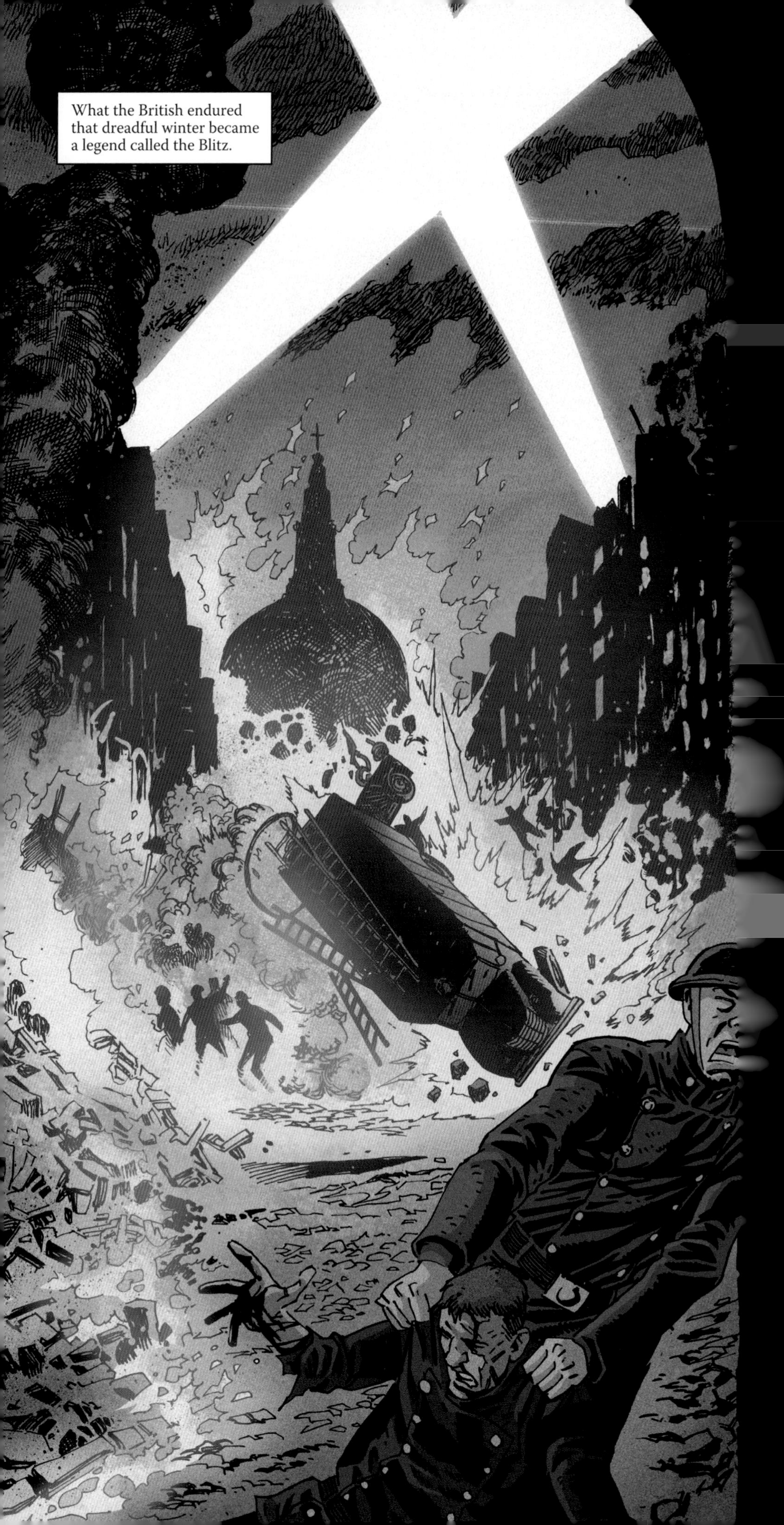
What the British endured that dreadful winter became a legend called the Blitz.

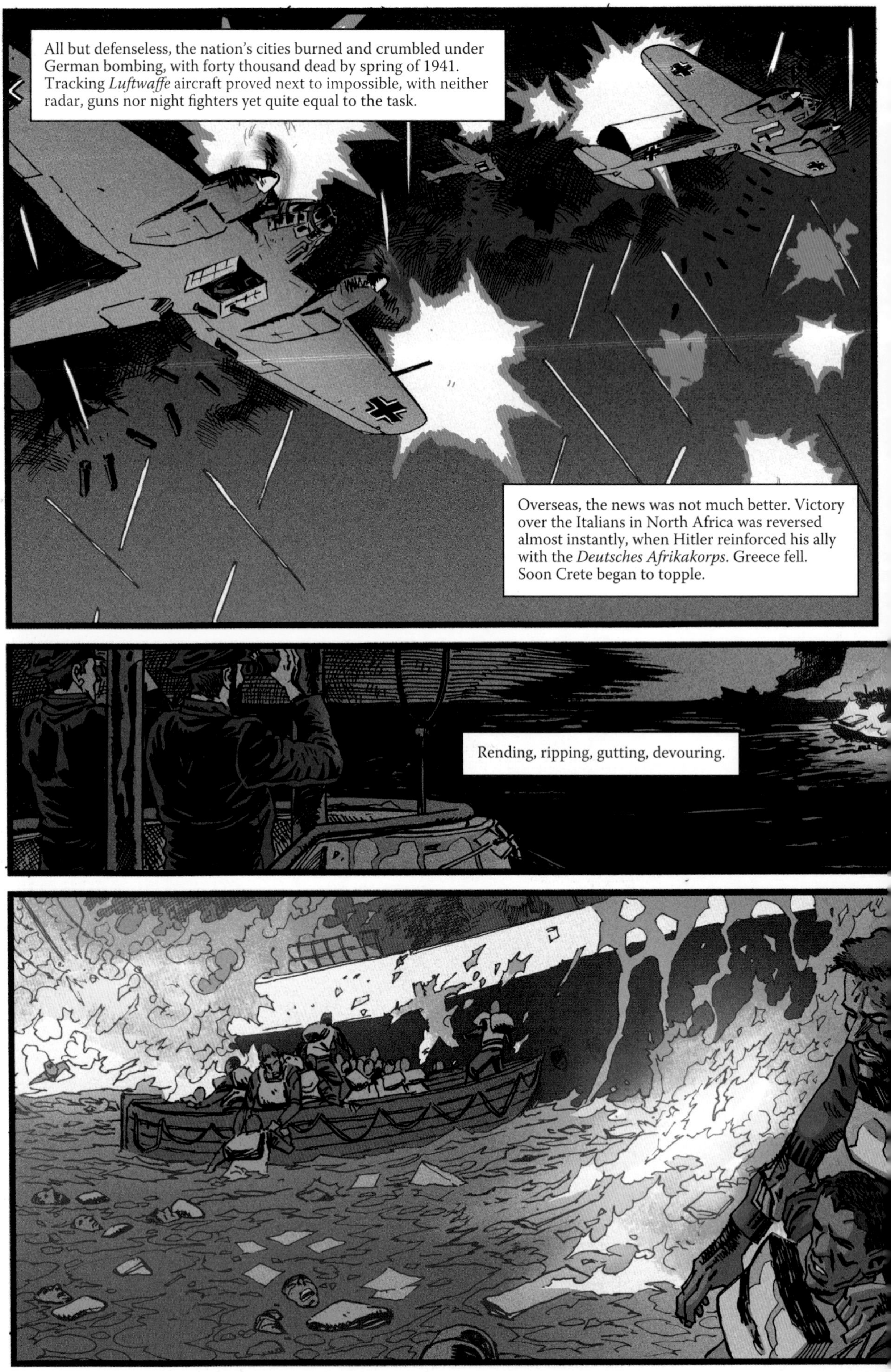
All but defenseless, the nation's cities burned and crumbled under German bombing, with forty thousand dead by spring of 1941. Tracking *Luftwaffe* aircraft proved next to impossible, with neither radar, guns nor night fighters yet quite equal to the task.
Overseas, the news was not much better. Victory over the Italians in North Africa was reversed almost instantly, when Hitler reinforced his ally with the *Deutsches Afrikakorps.* Greece fell. Soon Crete began to topple.
Rending, ripping, gutting, devouring.

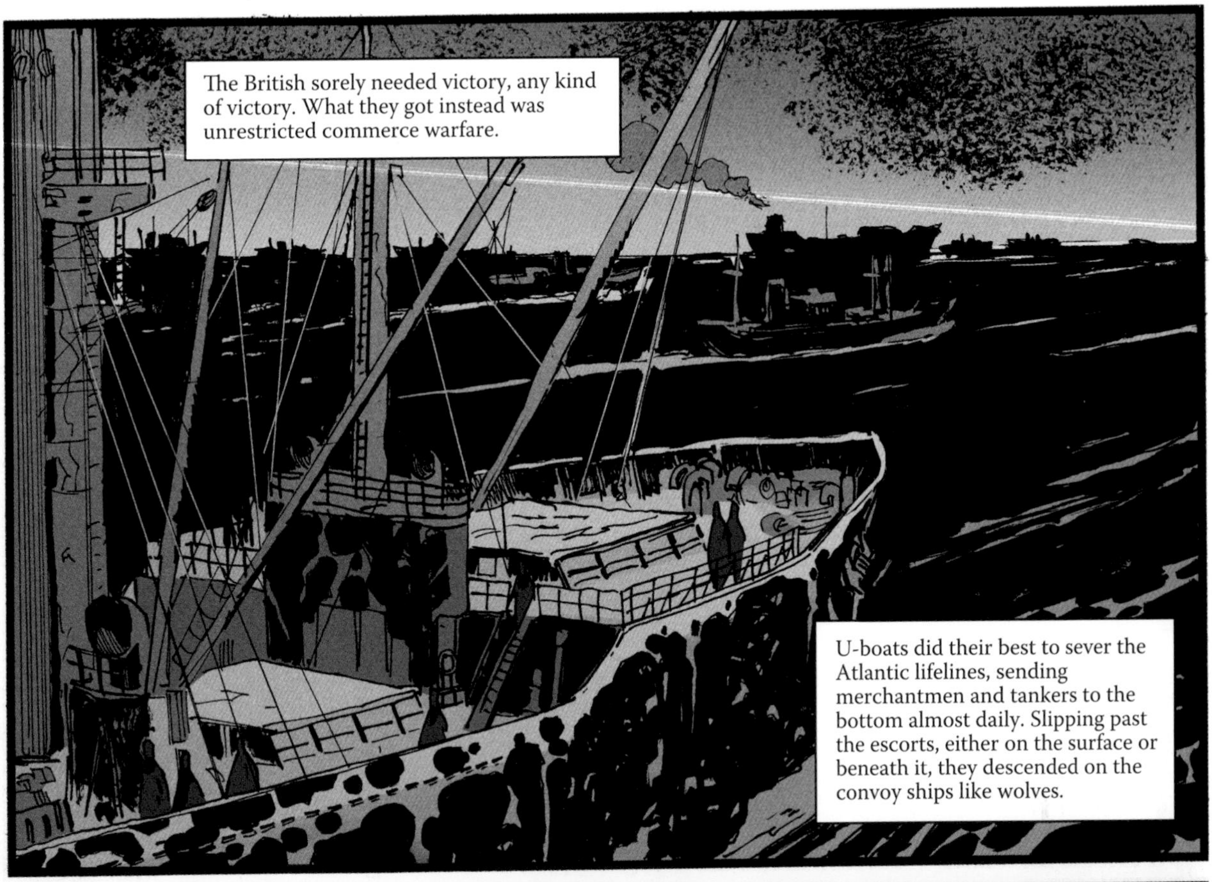
The British sorely needed victory, any kind of victory. What they got instead was unrestricted commerce warfare.
U-boats did their best to sever the Atlantic lifelines, sending merchantmen and tankers to the bottom almost daily. Slipping past the escorts, either on the surface or beneath it, they descended on the convoy ships like wolves.

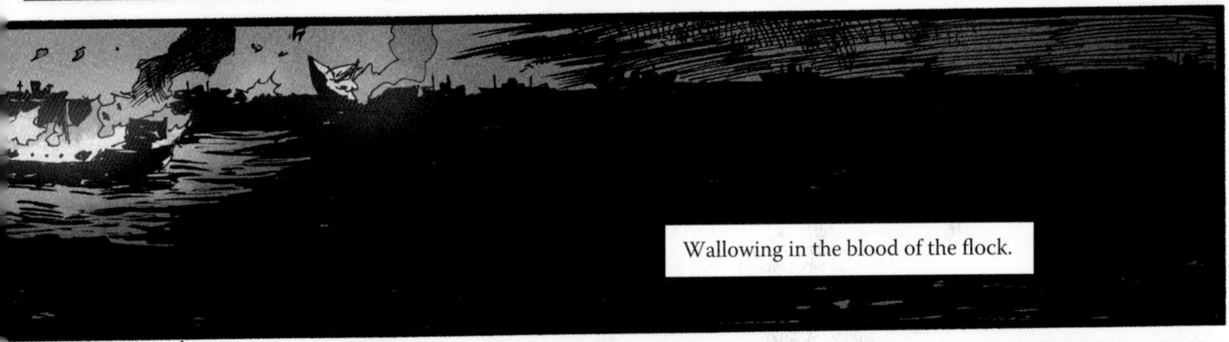
Wallowing in the blood of the flock.

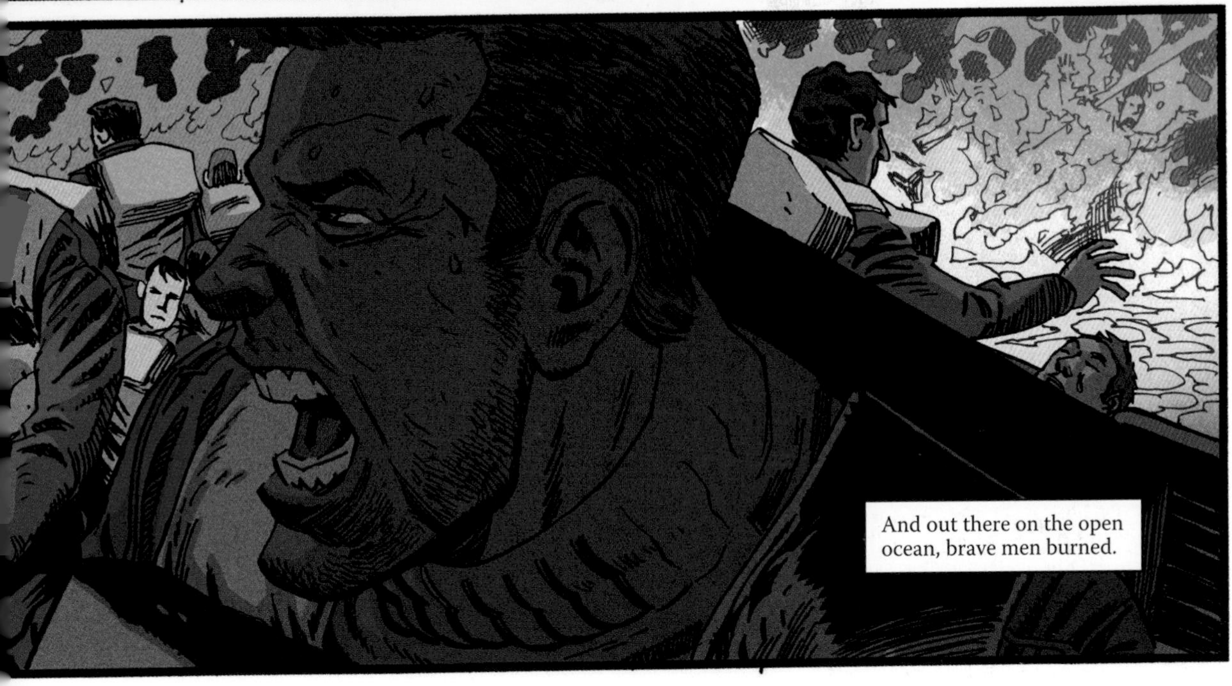
And out there on the open ocean, brave men burned.

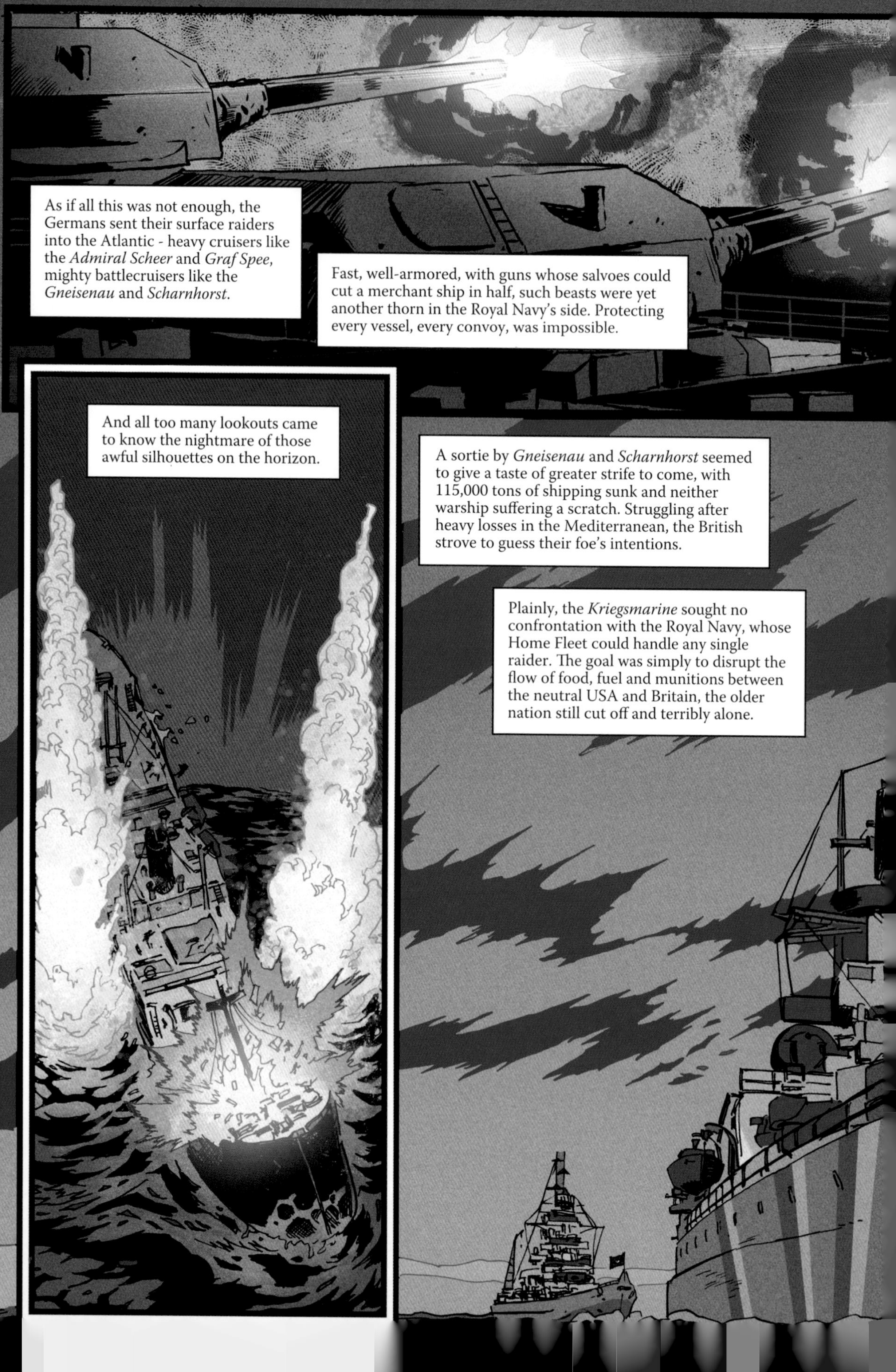
As if all this was not enough, the Germans sent their surface raiders into the Atlantic - heavy cruisers like the *Admiral Scheer* and *Graf Spee*, mighty battlecruisers like the *Gneisenau* and *Scharnhorst*.
Fast, well-armored, with guns whose salvoes could cut a merchant ship in half, such beasts were yet another thorn in the Royal Navy's side. Protecting every vessel, every convoy, was impossible.
And all too many lookouts came to know the nightmare of those awful silhouettes on the horizon.
A sortie by *Gneisenau* and *Scharnhorst* seemed to give a taste of greater strife to come, with 115,000 tons of shipping sunk and neither warship suffering a scratch. Struggling after heavy losses in the Mediterranean, the British strove to guess their foe's intentions.
Plainly, the *Kriegsmarine* sought no confrontation with the Royal Navy, whose Home Fleet could handle any single raider. The goal was simply to disrupt the flow of food, fuel and munitions between the neutral USA and Britain, the older nation still cut off and terribly alone.

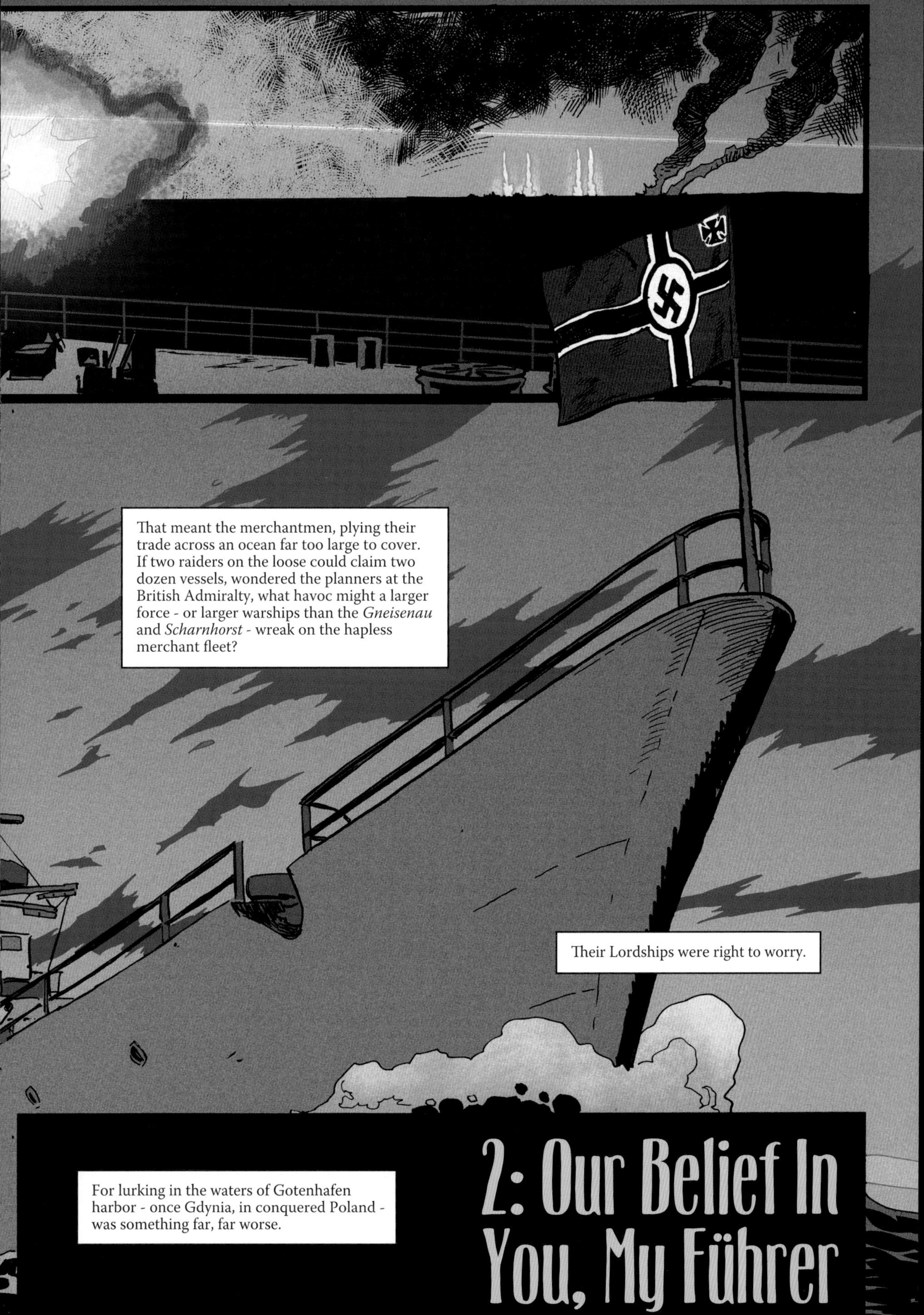
That meant the merchantmen, plying their trade across an ocean far too large to cover. If two raiders on the loose could claim two dozen vessels, wondered the planners at the British Admiralty, what havoc might a larger force - or larger warships than the *Gneisenau* and *Scharnhorst* - wreak on the hapless merchant fleet?
Their Lordships were right to worry.
For lurking in the waters of Gotenhafen harbor - once Gdynia, in conquered Poland - was something far, far worse.
2: Our Belief In You, My Führer

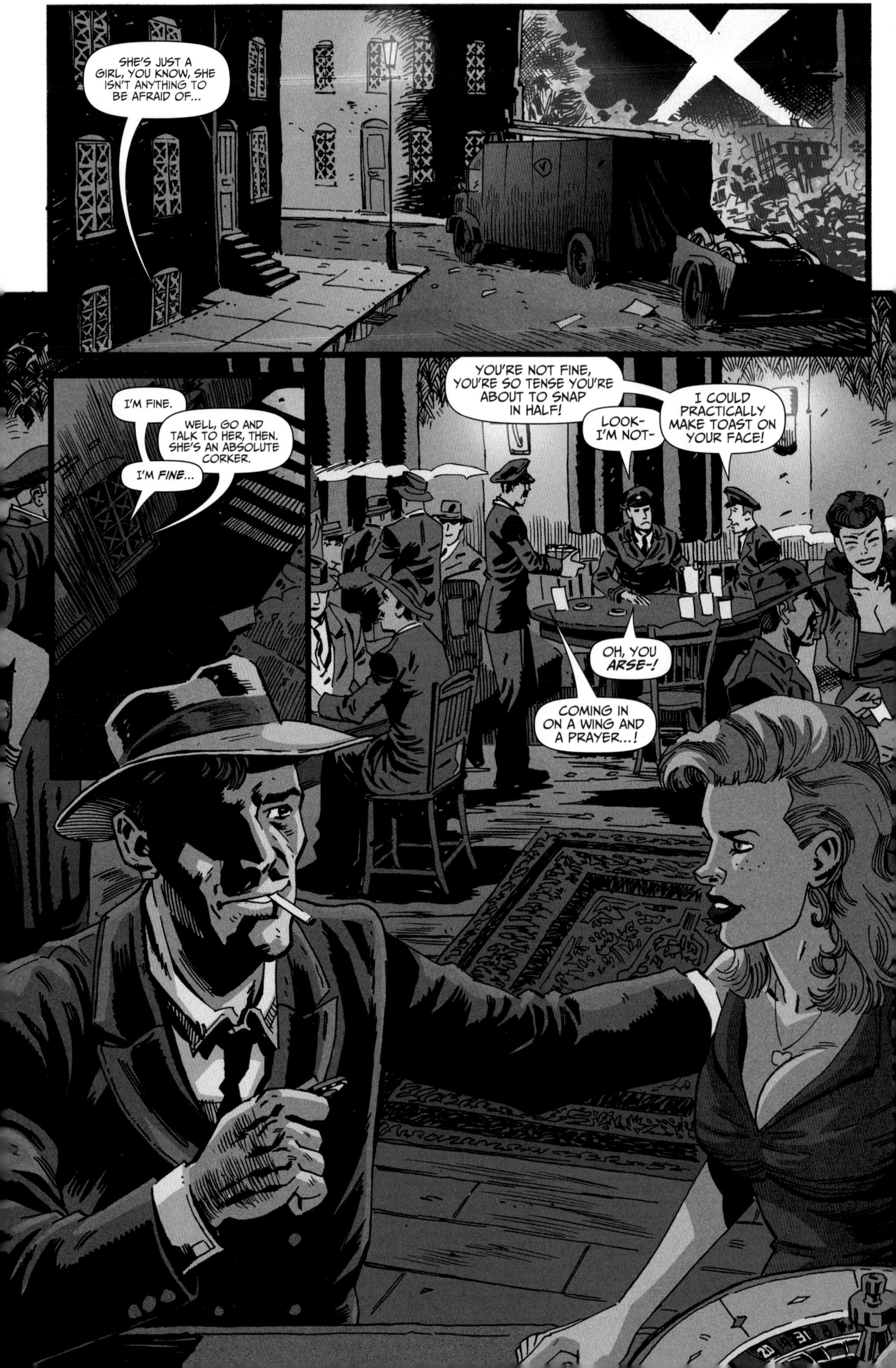
SHE'S JUST A GIRL, YOU KNOW, SHE ISN'T ANYTHING TO BE AFRAID OF...
I'M FINE.
WELL, GO AND TALK TO HER, THEN. SHE'S AN ABSOLUTE CORKER.
I'M *FINE*...
YOU'RE NOT FINE, YOU'RE SO TENSE YOU'RE ABOUT TO SNAP IN HALF!
LOOK- I'M NOT-
I COULD PRACTICALLY MAKE TOAST ON YOUR FACE!
OH, YOU *ARSE*-!
COMING IN ON A WING AND A PRAYER...!

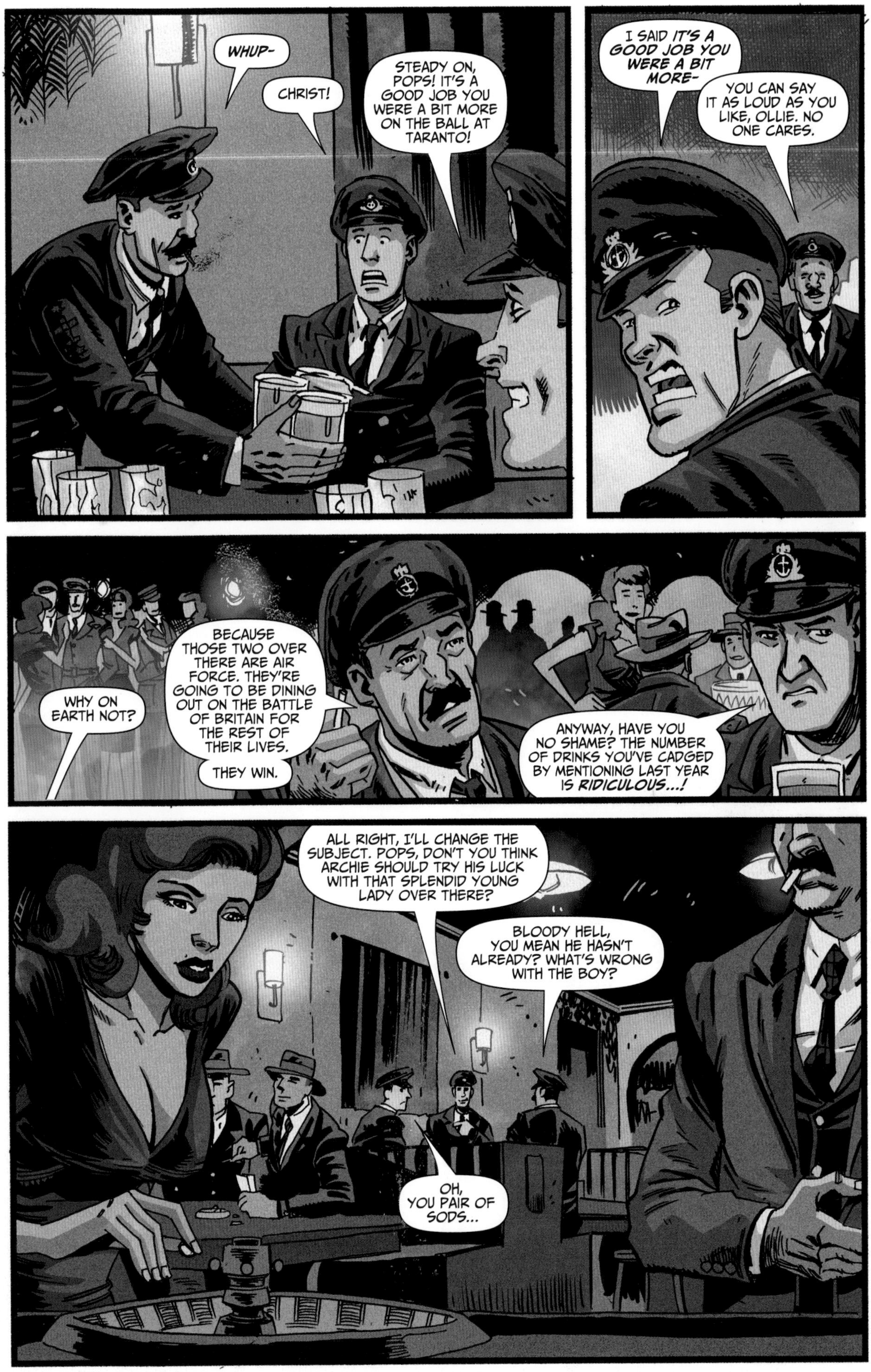
WHUP-
CHRIST!
STEADY ON, POPS! IT'S A GOOD JOB YOU WERE A BIT MORE ON THE BALL AT TARANTO!
I SAID IT'S A GOOD JOB YOU WERE A BIT MORE-
YOU CAN SAY IT AS LOUD AS YOU LIKE, OLLIE. NO ONE CARES.
WHY ON EARTH NOT?
BECAUSE THOSE TWO OVER THERE ARE AIR FORCE. THEY'RE GOING TO BE DINING OUT ON THE BATTLE OF BRITAIN FOR THE REST OF THEIR LIVES.
THEY WIN.
ANYWAY, HAVE YOU NO SHAME? THE NUMBER OF DRINKS YOU'VE CADGED BY MENTIONING LAST YEAR IS RIDICULOUS...!
ALL RIGHT, I'LL CHANGE THE SUBJECT. POPS, DON'T YOU THINK ARCHIE SHOULD TRY HIS LUCK WITH THAT SPLENDID YOUNG LADY OVER THERE?
BLOODY HELL, YOU MEAN HE HASN'T ALREADY? WHAT'S WRONG WITH THE BOY?
OH, YOU PAIR OF SODS...

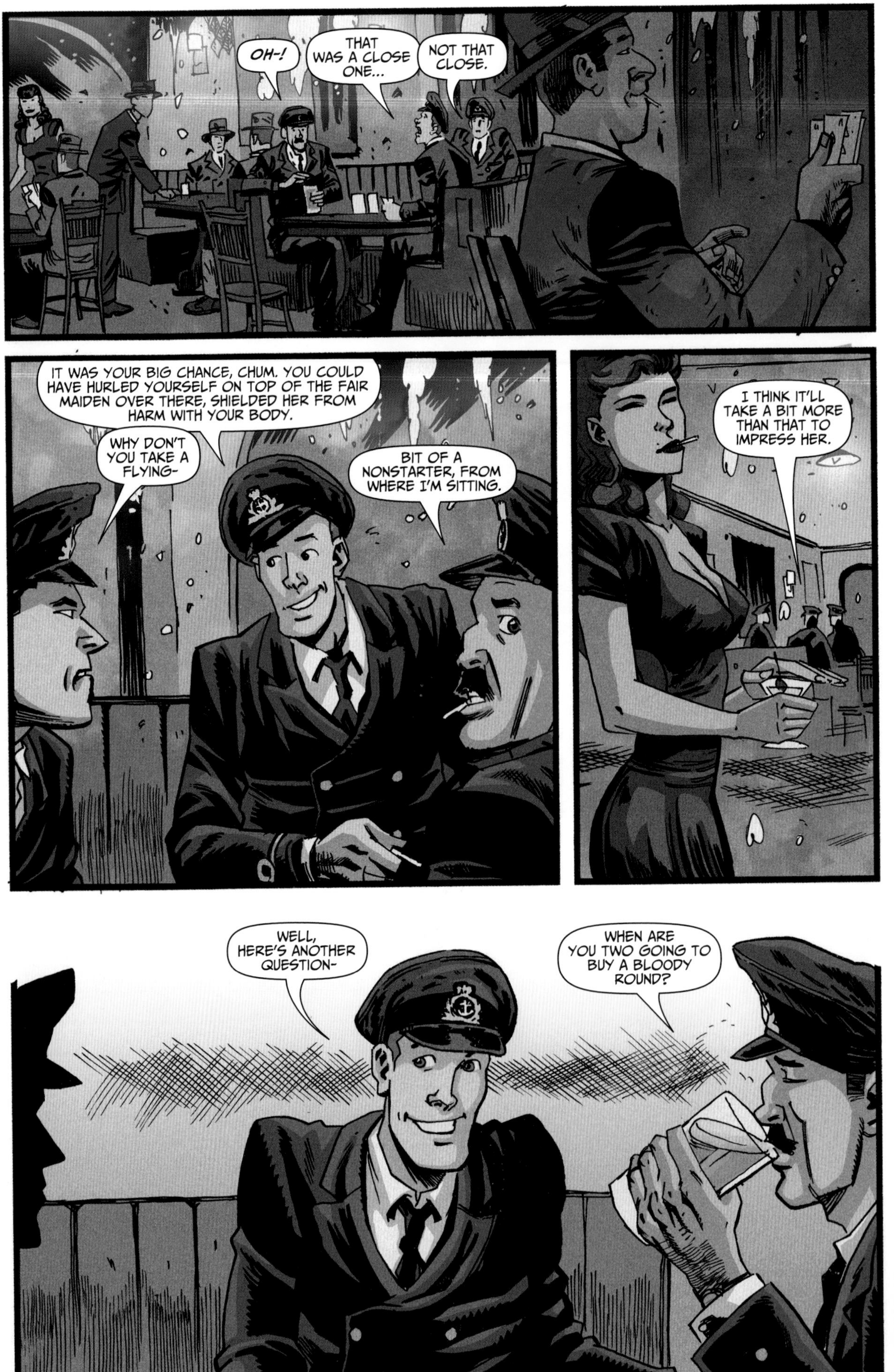
OH-!
THAT WAS A CLOSE ONE...
NOT THAT CLOSE.
IT WAS YOUR BIG CHANCE, CHUM. YOU COULD HAVE HURLED YOURSELF ON TOP OF THE FAIR MAIDEN OVER THERE, SHIELDED HER FROM HARM WITH YOUR BODY.
WHY DON'T YOU TAKE A FLYING-
BIT OF A NONSTARTER, FROM WHERE I'M SITTING.
I THINK IT'LL TAKE A BIT MORE THAN THAT TO IMPRESS HER.
WELL, HERE'S ANOTHER QUESTION-
WHEN ARE YOU TWO GOING TO BUY A BLOODY ROUND?

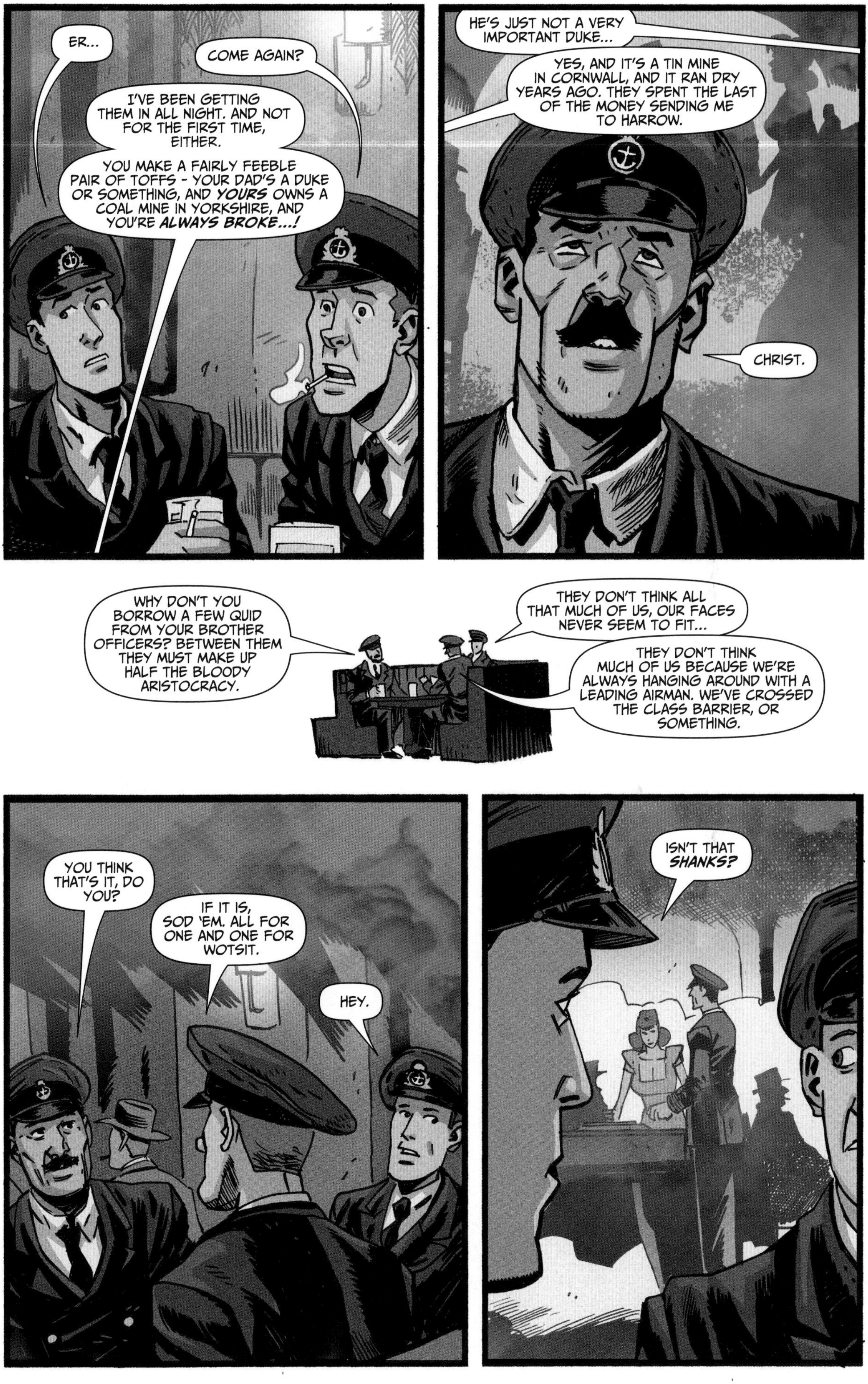
ER...
COME AGAIN?
I'VE BEEN GETTING THEM IN ALL NIGHT. AND NOT FOR THE FIRST TIME, EITHER.
YOU MAKE A FAIRLY FEEBLE PAIR OF TOFFS - YOUR DAD'S A DUKE OR SOMETHING, AND YOURS OWNS A COAL MINE IN YORKSHIRE, AND YOU'RE ALWAYS BROKE...!
HE'S JUST NOT A VERY IMPORTANT DUKE...
YES, AND IT'S A TIN MINE IN CORNWALL, AND IT RAN DRY YEARS AGO. THEY SPENT THE LAST OF THE MONEY SENDING ME TO HARROW.
CHRIST.
WHY DON'T YOU BORROW A FEW QUID FROM YOUR BROTHER OFFICERS? BETWEEN THEM THEY MUST MAKE UP HALF THE BLOODY ARISTOCRACY.
THEY DON'T THINK ALL THAT MUCH OF US, OUR FACES NEVER SEEM TO FIT...
THEY DON'T THINK MUCH OF US BECAUSE WE'RE ALWAYS HANGING AROUND WITH A LEADING AIRMAN. WE'VE CROSSED THE CLASS BARRIER, OR SOMETHING.
YOU THINK THAT'S IT, DO YOU?
IF IT IS, SOD 'EM. ALL FOR ONE AND ONE FOR WOTSIT.
HEY.
ISN'T THAT SHANKS?

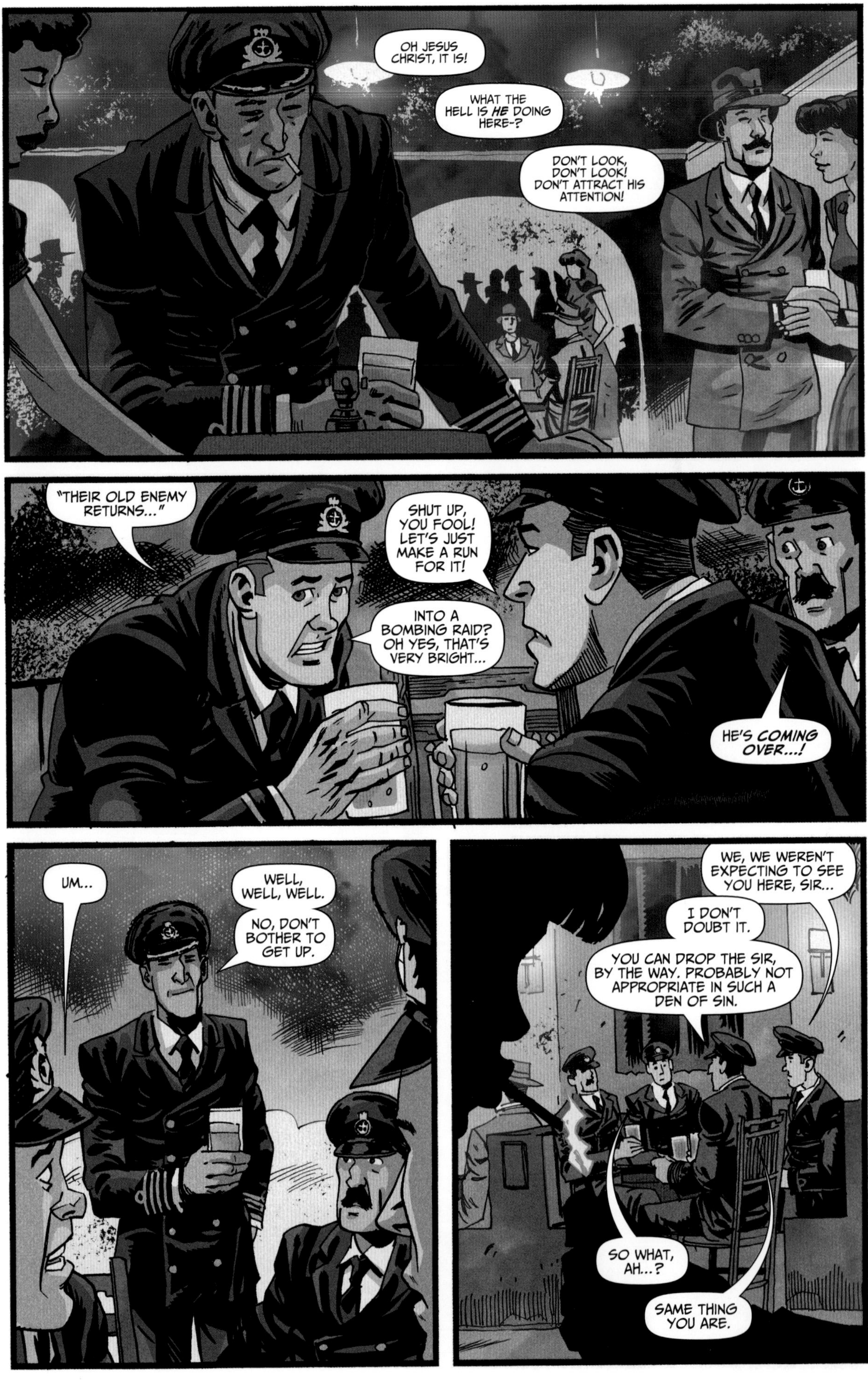
OH JESUS CHRIST, IT IS!
WHAT THE HELL IS *HE* DOING HERE-?
DON'T LOOK, DON'T LOOK! DON'T ATTRACT HIS ATTENTION!
"THEIR OLD ENEMY RETURNS..."
SHUT UP, YOU FOOL! LET'S JUST MAKE A RUN FOR IT!
INTO A BOMBING RAID? OH YES, THAT'S VERY BRIGHT...
HE'S *COMING OVER...!*
UM..
WELL, WELL, WELL.
NO, DON'T BOTHER TO GET UP.
WE, WE WEREN'T EXPECTING TO SEE YOU HERE, SIR...
I DON'T DOUBT IT.
YOU CAN DROP THE SIR, BY THE WAY. PROBABLY NOT APPROPRIATE IN SUCH A DEN OF SIN.
SO WHAT, AH...?
SAME THING YOU ARE.

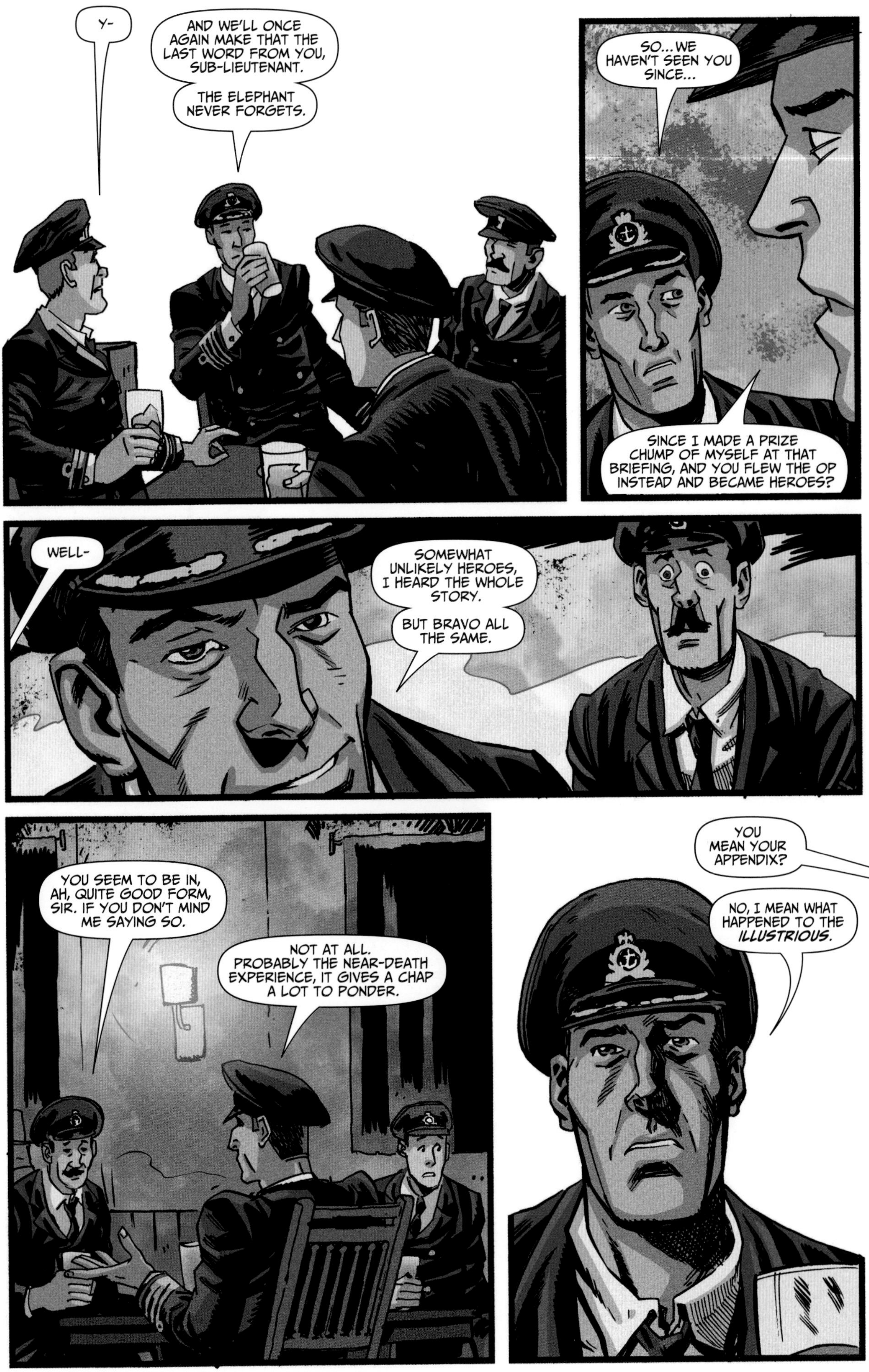
Y-
AND WE'LL ONCE AGAIN MAKE THAT THE LAST WORD FROM YOU, SUB-LIEUTENANT.
THE ELEPHANT NEVER FORGETS.
SO...WE HAVEN'T SEEN YOU SINCE...
SINCE I MADE A PRIZE CHUMP OF MYSELF AT THAT BRIEFING, AND YOU FLEW THE OP INSTEAD AND BECAME HEROES?
WELL-
SOMEWHAT UNLIKELY HEROES, I HEARD THE WHOLE STORY.
BUT BRAVO ALL THE SAME.
YOU SEEM TO BE IN, AH, QUITE GOOD FORM, SIR. IF YOU DON'T MIND ME SAYING SO.
NOT AT ALL. PROBABLY THE NEAR-DEATH EXPERIENCE, IT GIVES A CHAP A LOT TO PONDER.
YOU MEAN YOUR APPENDIX?
NO, I MEAN WHAT HAPPENED TO THE *ILLUSTRIOUS*.

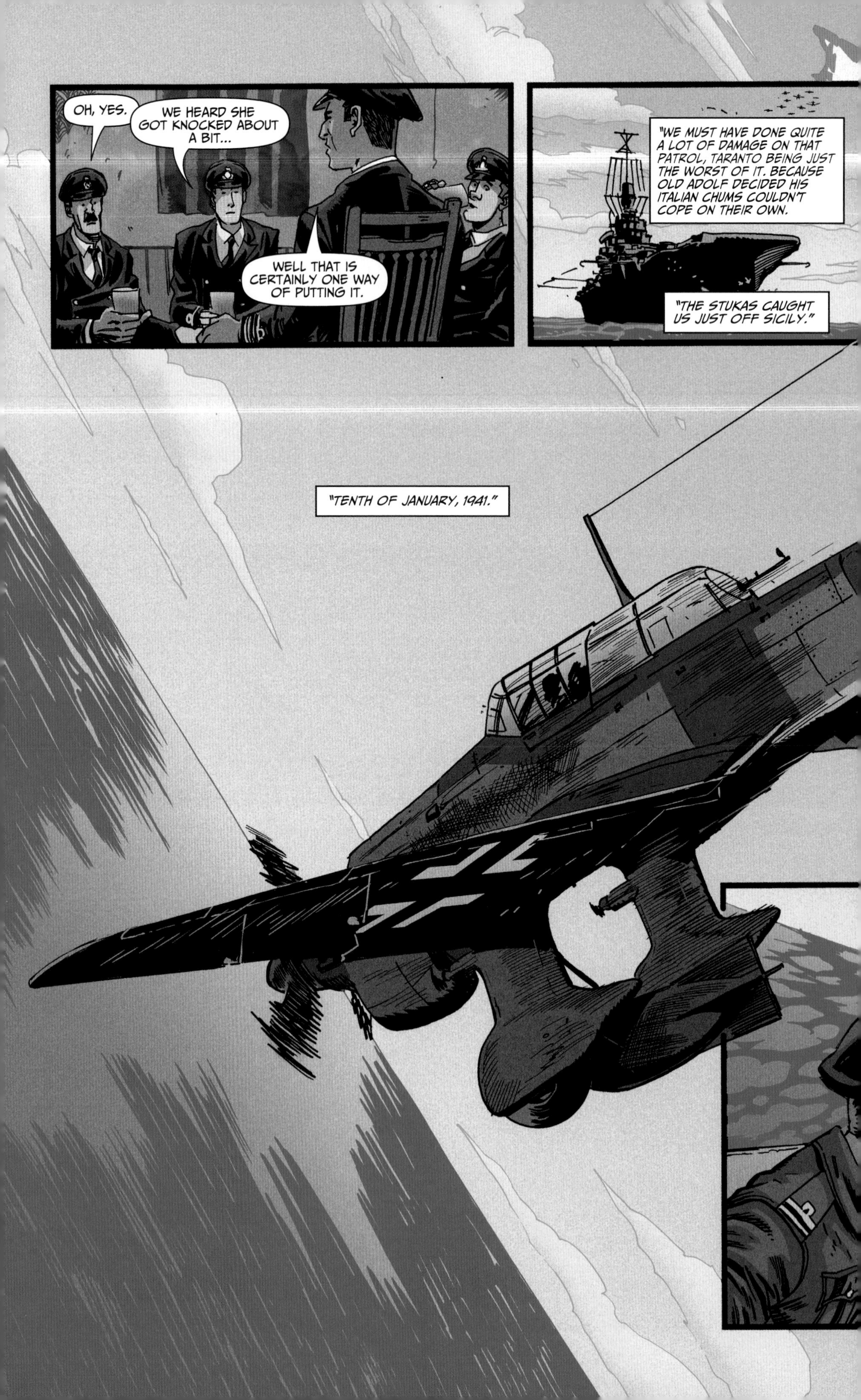
OH, YES.
WE HEARD SHE GOT KNOCKED ABOUT A BIT...
WELL THAT IS CERTAINLY ONE WAY OF PUTTING IT.
"WE MUST HAVE DONE QUITE A LOT OF DAMAGE ON THAT PATROL, TARANTO BEING JUST THE WORST OF IT. BECAUSE OLD ADOLF DECIDED HIS ITALIAN CHUMS COULDN'T COPE ON THEIR OWN.
"THE STUKAS CAUGHT US JUST OFF SICILY."
"TENTH OF JANUARY, 1941."

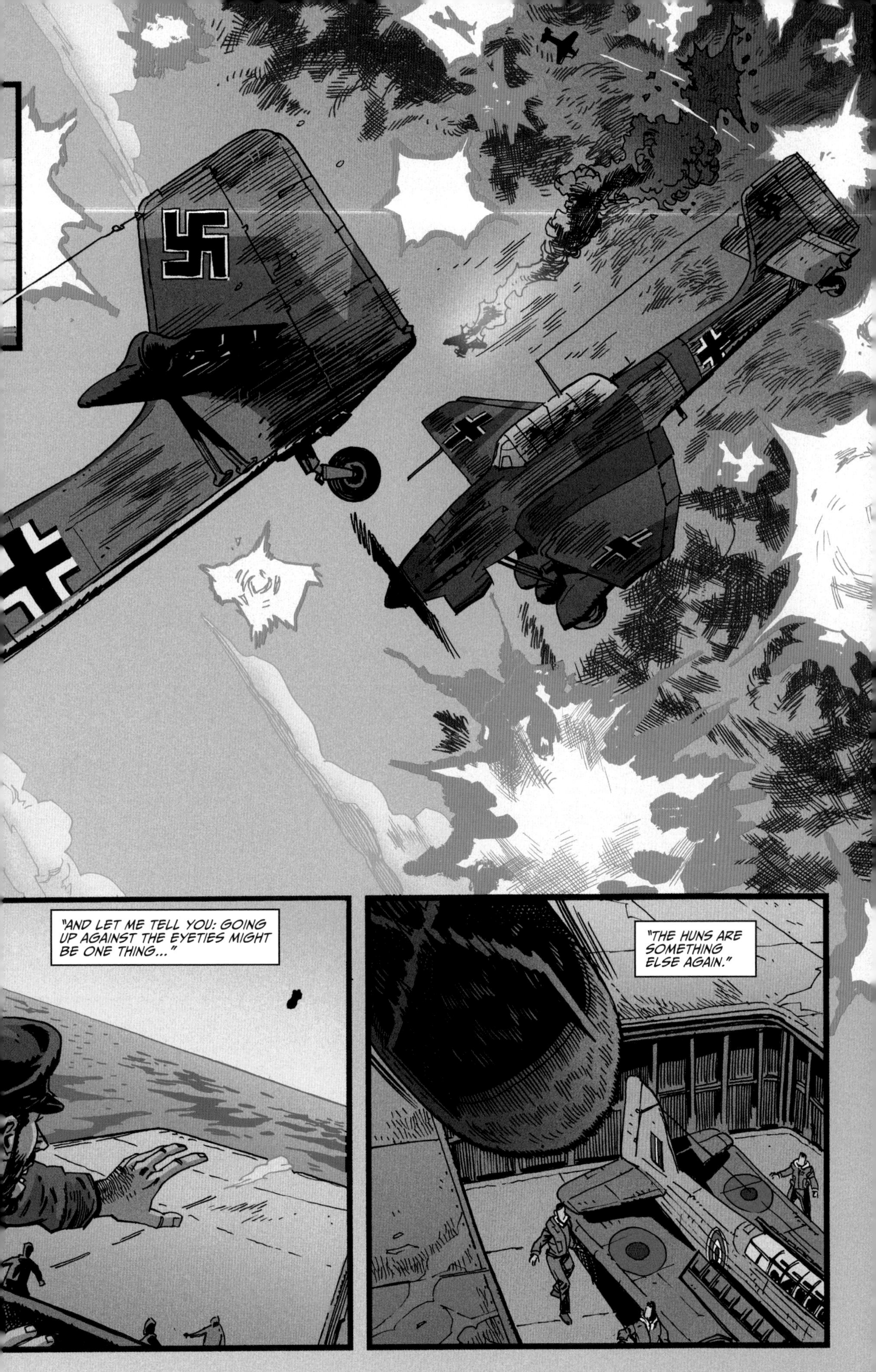
"AND LET ME TELL YOU: GOING UP AGAINST THE EYETIES MIGHT BE ONE THING..."
"THE HUNS ARE SOMETHING ELSE AGAIN."

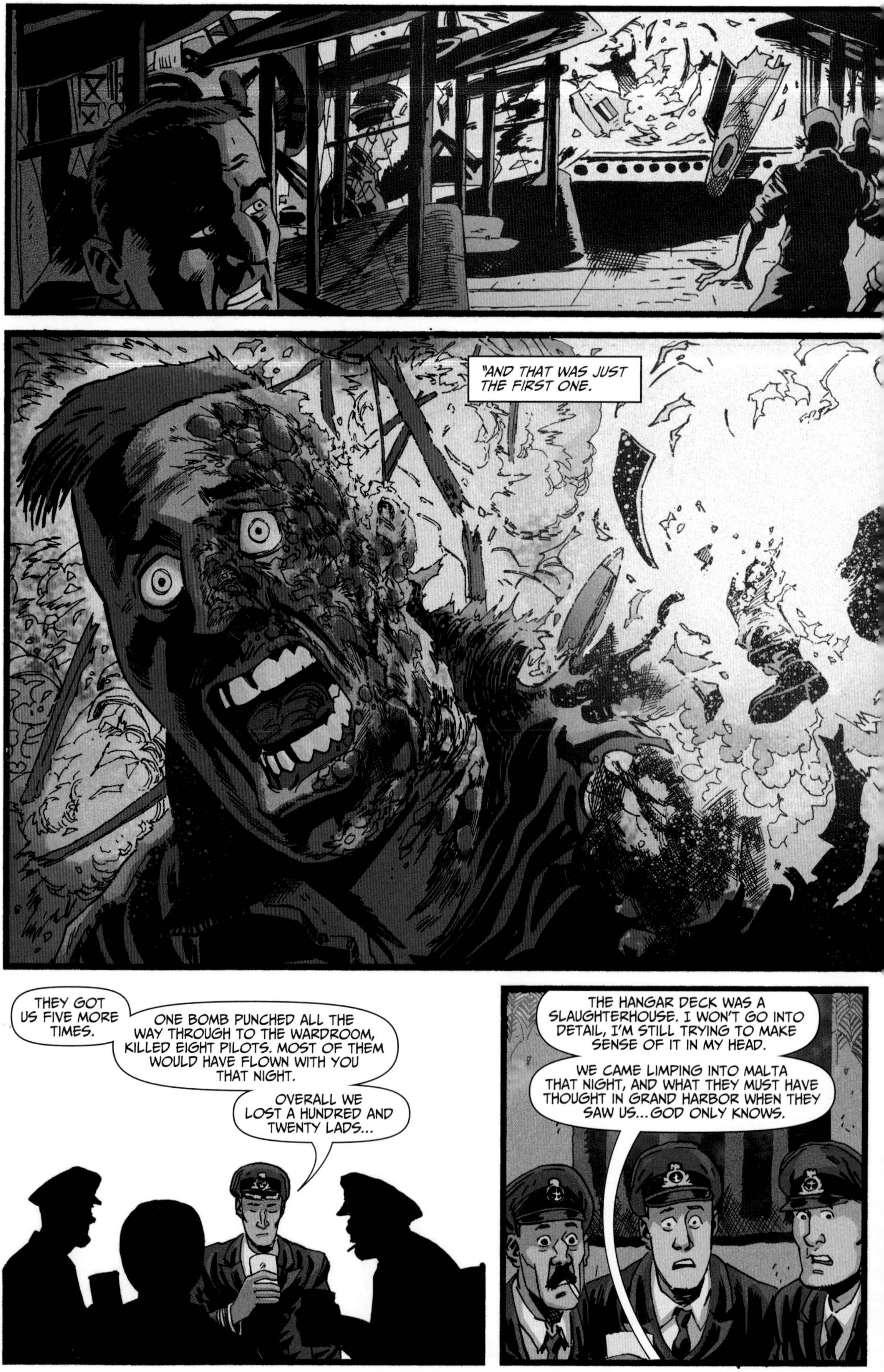
"AND THAT WAS JUST THE FIRST ONE.
THEY GOT US FIVE MORE TIMES.
ONE BOMB PUNCHED ALL THE WAY THROUGH TO THE WARDROOM, KILLED EIGHT PILOTS. MOST OF THEM WOULD HAVE FLOWN WITH YOU THAT NIGHT.
OVERALL WE LOST A HUNDRED AND TWENTY LADS...
THE HANGAR DECK WAS A SLAUGHTERHOUSE. I WON'T GO INTO DETAIL, I'M STILL TRYING TO MAKE SENSE OF IT IN MY HEAD.
WE CAME LIMPING INTO MALTA THAT NIGHT, AND WHAT THEY MUST HAVE THOUGHT IN GRAND HARBOR WHEN THEY SAW US...GOD ONLY KNOWS.

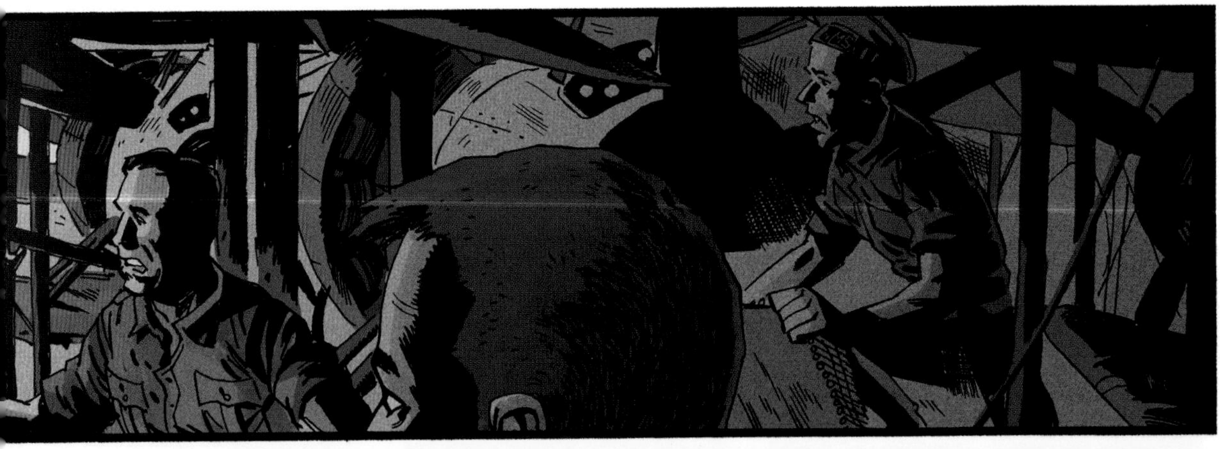

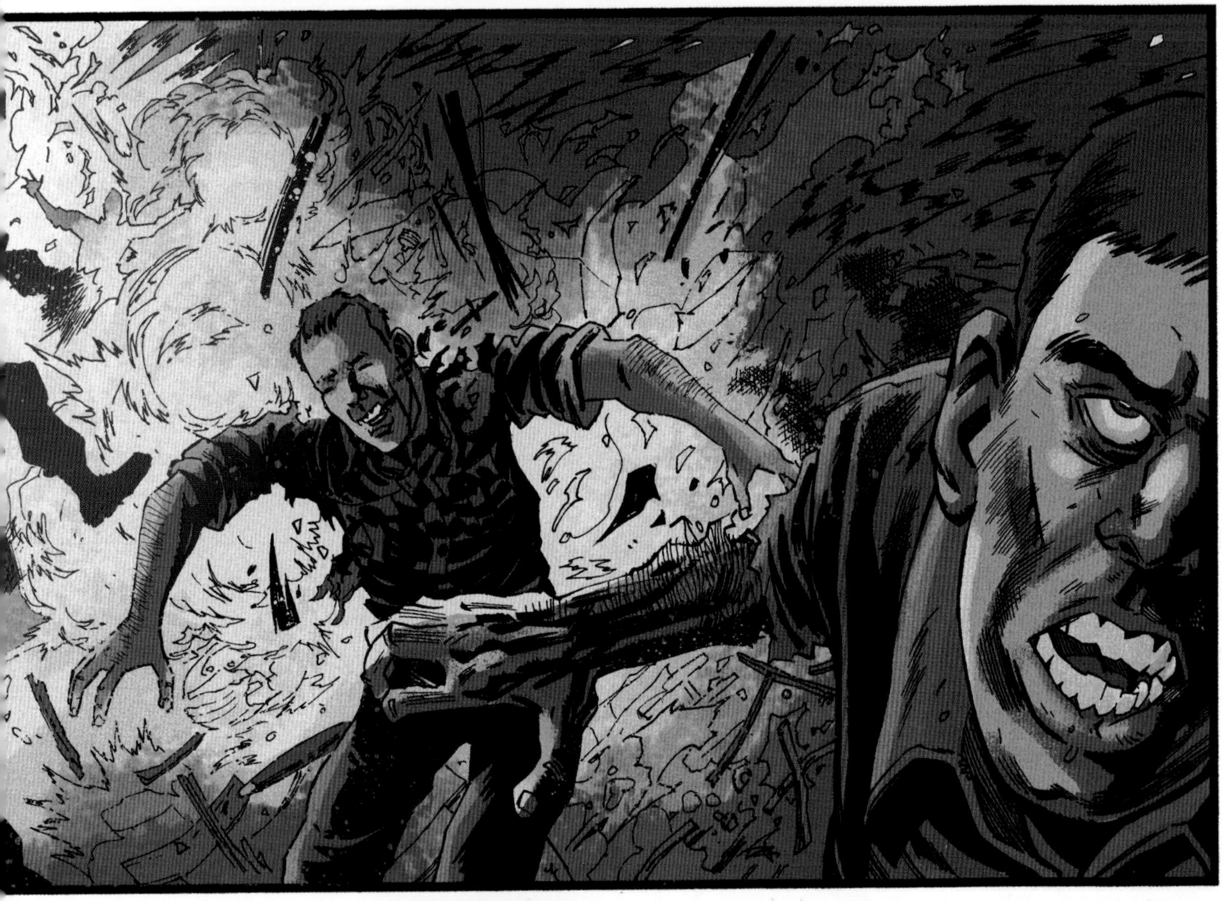

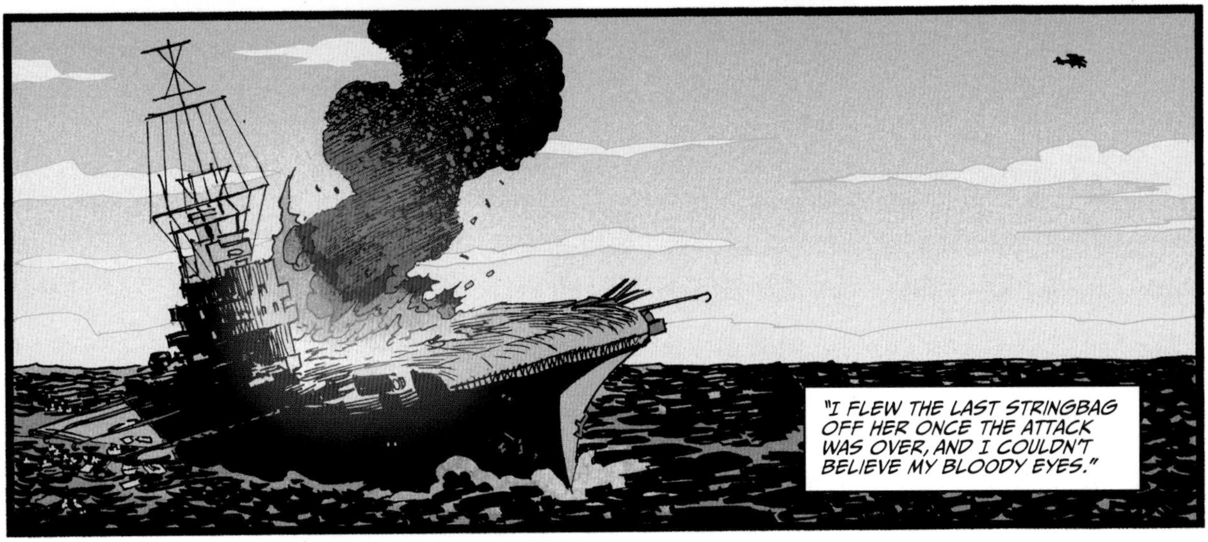
"I FLEW THE LAST STRINGBAG OFF HER ONCE THE ATTACK WAS OVER, AND I COULDN'T BELIEVE MY BLOODY EYES."

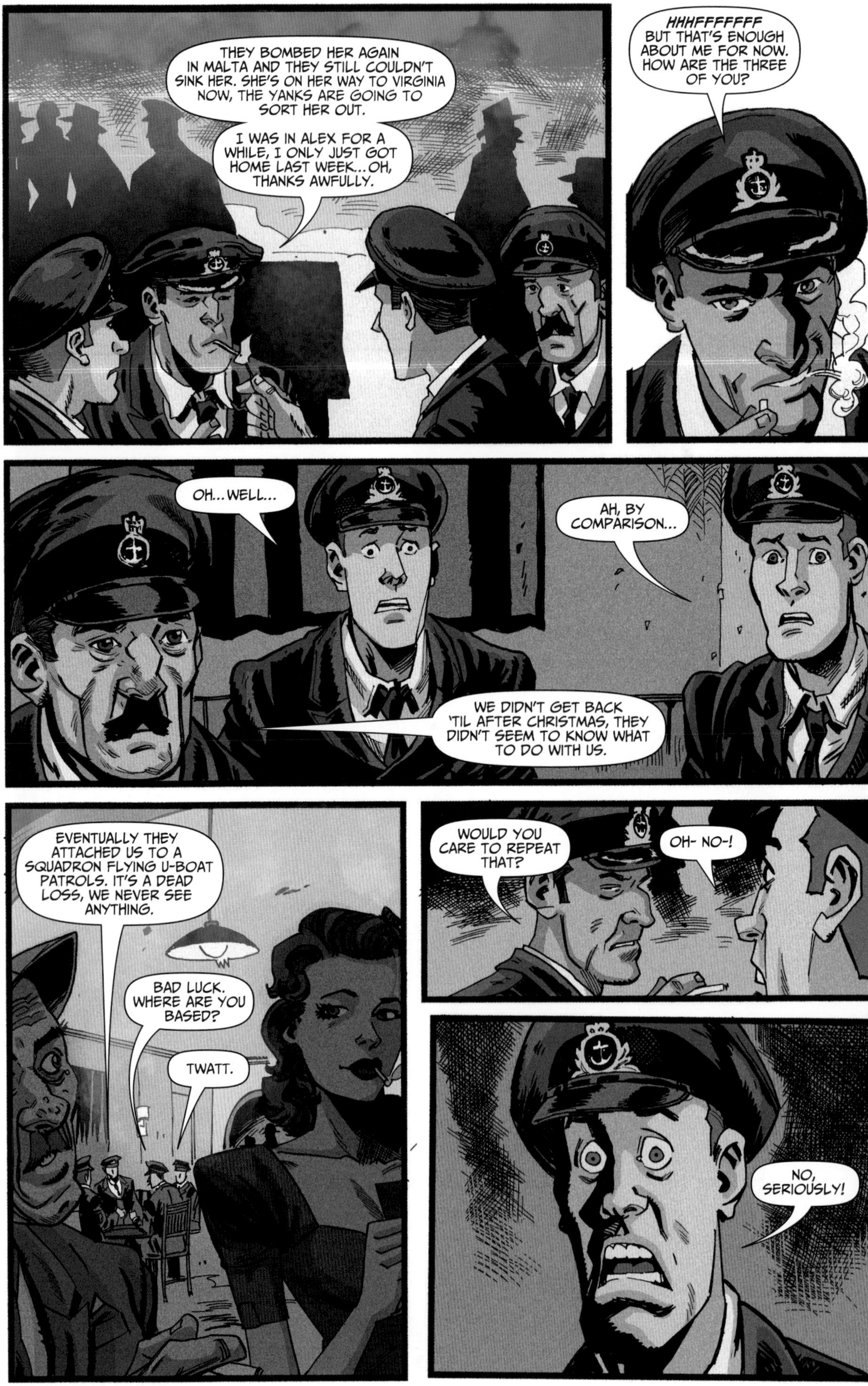
THEY BOMBED HER AGAIN IN MALTA AND THEY STILL COULDN'T SINK HER. SHE'S ON HER WAY TO VIRGINIA NOW, THE YANKS ARE GOING TO SORT HER OUT.
I WAS IN ALEX FOR A WHILE, I ONLY JUST GOT HOME LAST WEEK...OH, THANKS AWFULLY.
HHHFFFFFFF
BUT THAT'S ENOUGH ABOUT ME FOR NOW. HOW ARE THE THREE OF YOU?
OH...WELL...
AH, BY COMPARISON...
WE DIDN'T GET BACK 'TIL AFTER CHRISTMAS, THEY DIDN'T SEEM TO KNOW WHAT TO DO WITH US.
EVENTUALLY THEY ATTACHED US TO A SQUADRON FLYING U-BOAT PATROLS. IT'S A DEAD LOSS, WE NEVER SEE ANYTHING.
BAD LUCK. WHERE ARE YOU BASED?
TWATT.
WOULD YOU CARE TO REPEAT THAT?
OH- NO-!
NO, SERIOUSLY!

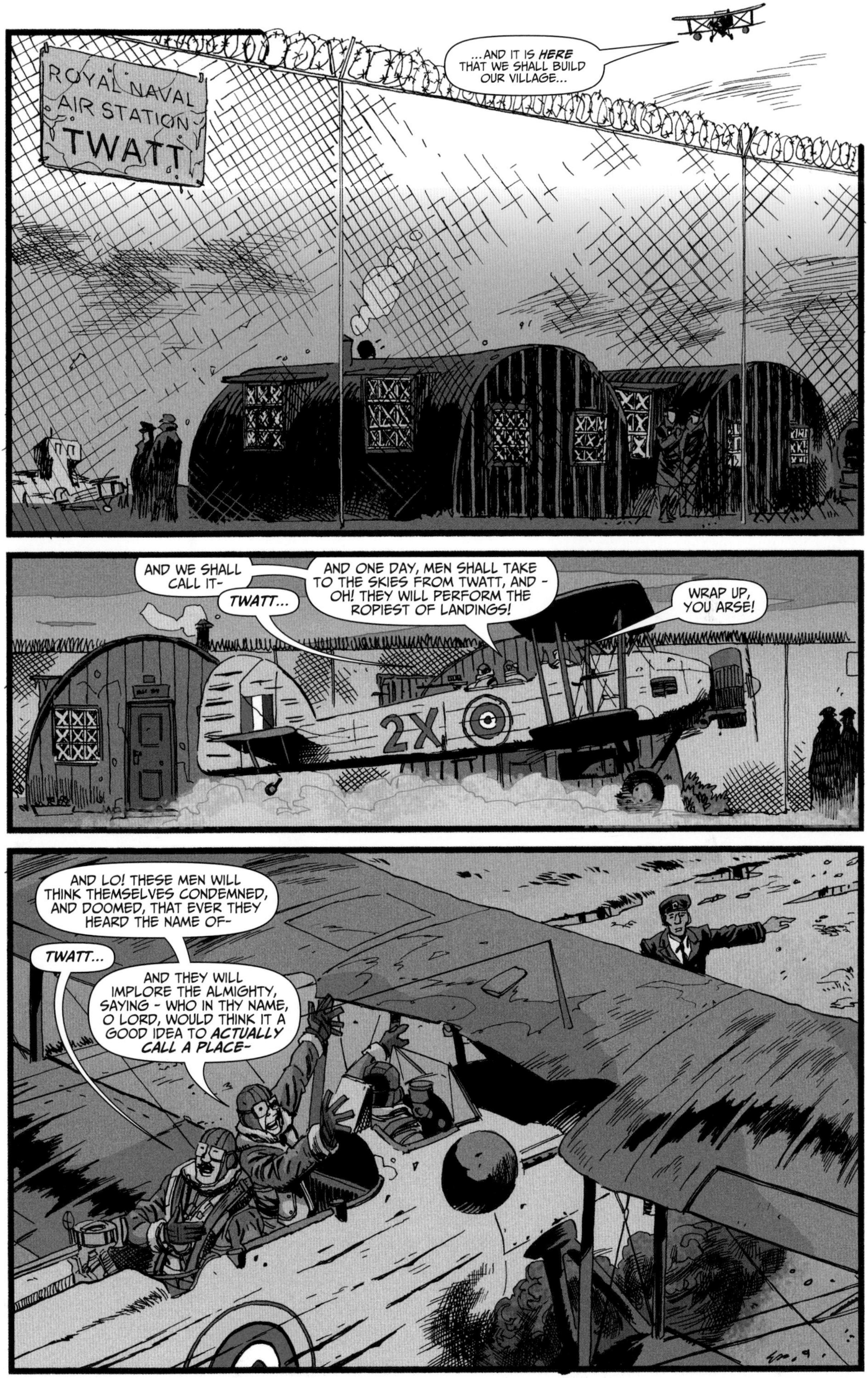
ROYAL NAVAL AIR STATION TWATT
...AND IT IS HERE THAT WE SHALL BUILD OUR VILLAGE...
AND WE SHALL CALL IT-
TWATT...
AND ONE DAY, MEN SHALL TAKE TO THE SKIES FROM TWATT, AND - OH! THEY WILL PERFORM THE ROPIEST OF LANDINGS!
WRAP UP, YOU ARSE!
2X
AND LO! THESE MEN WILL THINK THEMSELVES CONDEMNED, AND DOOMED, THAT EVER THEY HEARD THE NAME OF-
TWATT...
AND THEY WILL IMPLORE THE ALMIGHTY, SAYING - WHO IN THY NAME, O LORD, WOULD THINK IT A GOOD IDEA TO ACTUALLY CALL A PLACE-

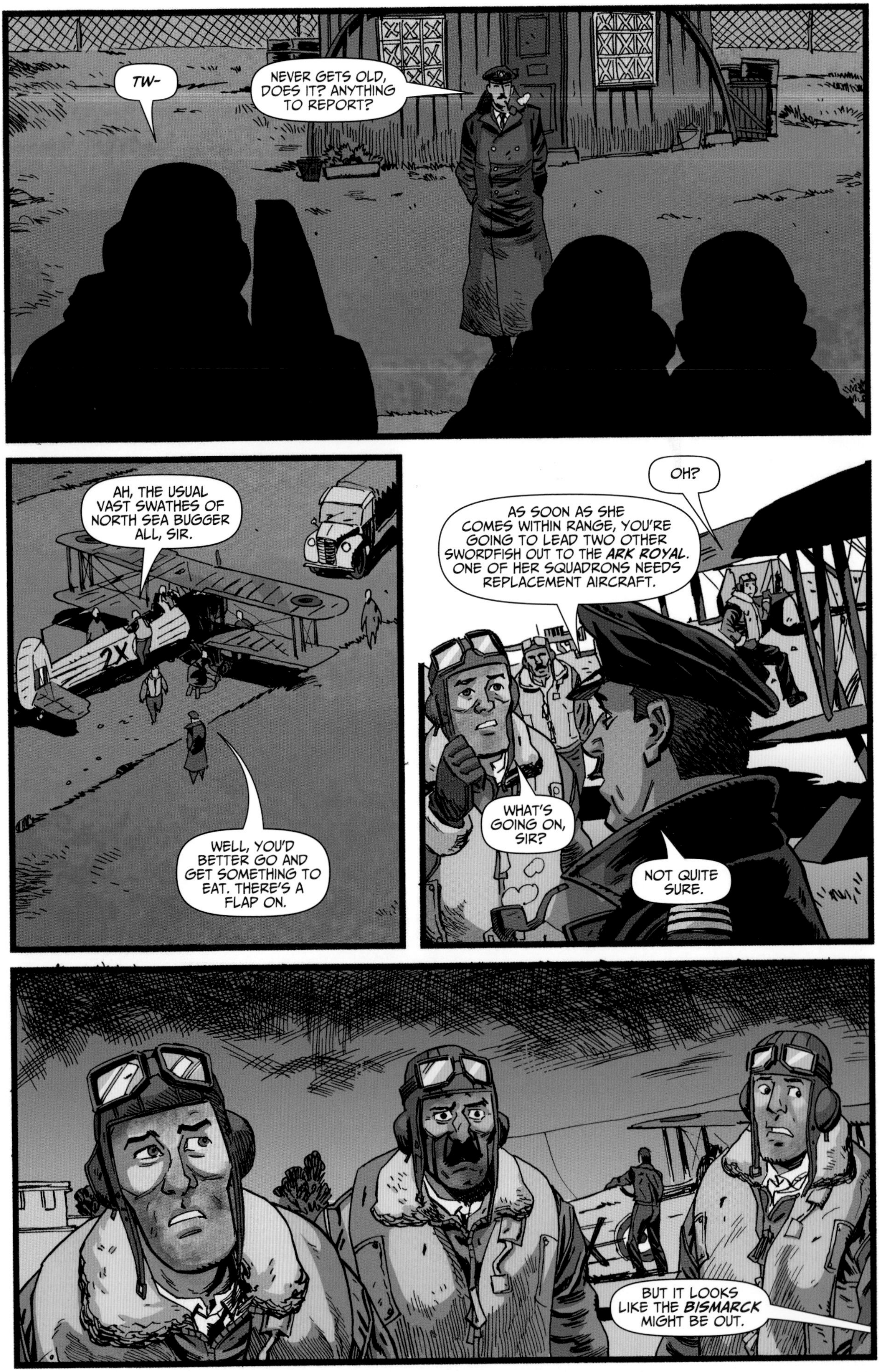
TW-
NEVER GETS OLD, DOES IT? ANYTHING TO REPORT?
AH, THE USUAL VAST SWATHES OF NORTH SEA BUGGER ALL, SIR.
WELL, YOU'D BETTER GO AND GET SOMETHING TO EAT. THERE'S A FLAP ON.
OH?
AS SOON AS SHE COMES WITHIN RANGE, YOU'RE GOING TO LEAD TWO OTHER SWORDFISH OUT TO THE ARK ROYAL. ONE OF HER SQUADRONS NEEDS REPLACEMENT AIRCRAFT.
WHAT'S GOING ON, SIR?
NOT QUITE SURE.
BUT IT LOOKS LIKE THE BISMARCK MIGHT BE OUT.

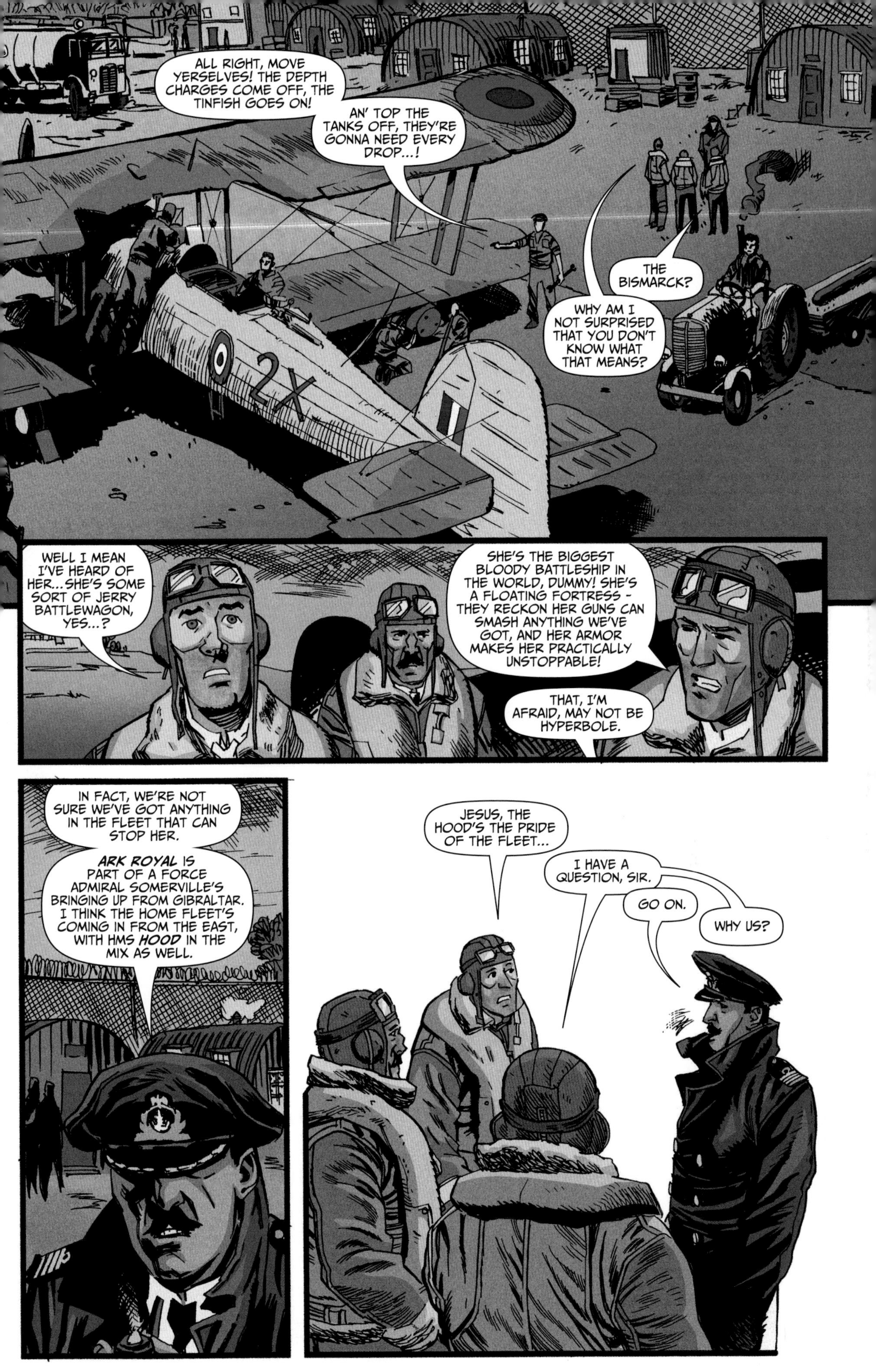
ALL RIGHT, MOVE YERSELVES! THE DEPTH CHARGES COME OFF, THE TINFISH GOES ON!
AN' TOP THE TANKS OFF, THEY'RE GONNA NEED EVERY DROP...!
THE BISMARCK?
WHY AM I NOT SURPRISED THAT YOU DON'T KNOW WHAT THAT MEANS?
WELL I MEAN I'VE HEARD OF HER...SHE'S SOME SORT OF JERRY BATTLEWAGON, YES...?
SHE'S THE BIGGEST BLOODY BATTLESHIP IN THE WORLD, DUMMY! SHE'S A FLOATING FORTRESS - THEY RECKON HER GUNS CAN SMASH ANYTHING WE'VE GOT, AND HER ARMOR MAKES HER PRACTICALLY UNSTOPPABLE!
THAT, I'M AFRAID, MAY NOT BE HYPERBOLE.
IN FACT, WE'RE NOT SURE WE'VE GOT ANYTHING IN THE FLEET THAT CAN STOP HER.
ARK ROYAL IS PART OF A FORCE ADMIRAL SOMERVILLE'S BRINGING UP FROM GIBRALTAR. I THINK THE HOME FLEET'S COMING IN FROM THE EAST, WITH HMS *HOOD* IN THE MIX AS WELL.
JESUS, THE HOOD'S THE PRIDE OF THE FLEET...
I HAVE A QUESTION, SIR.
GO ON.
WHY US?

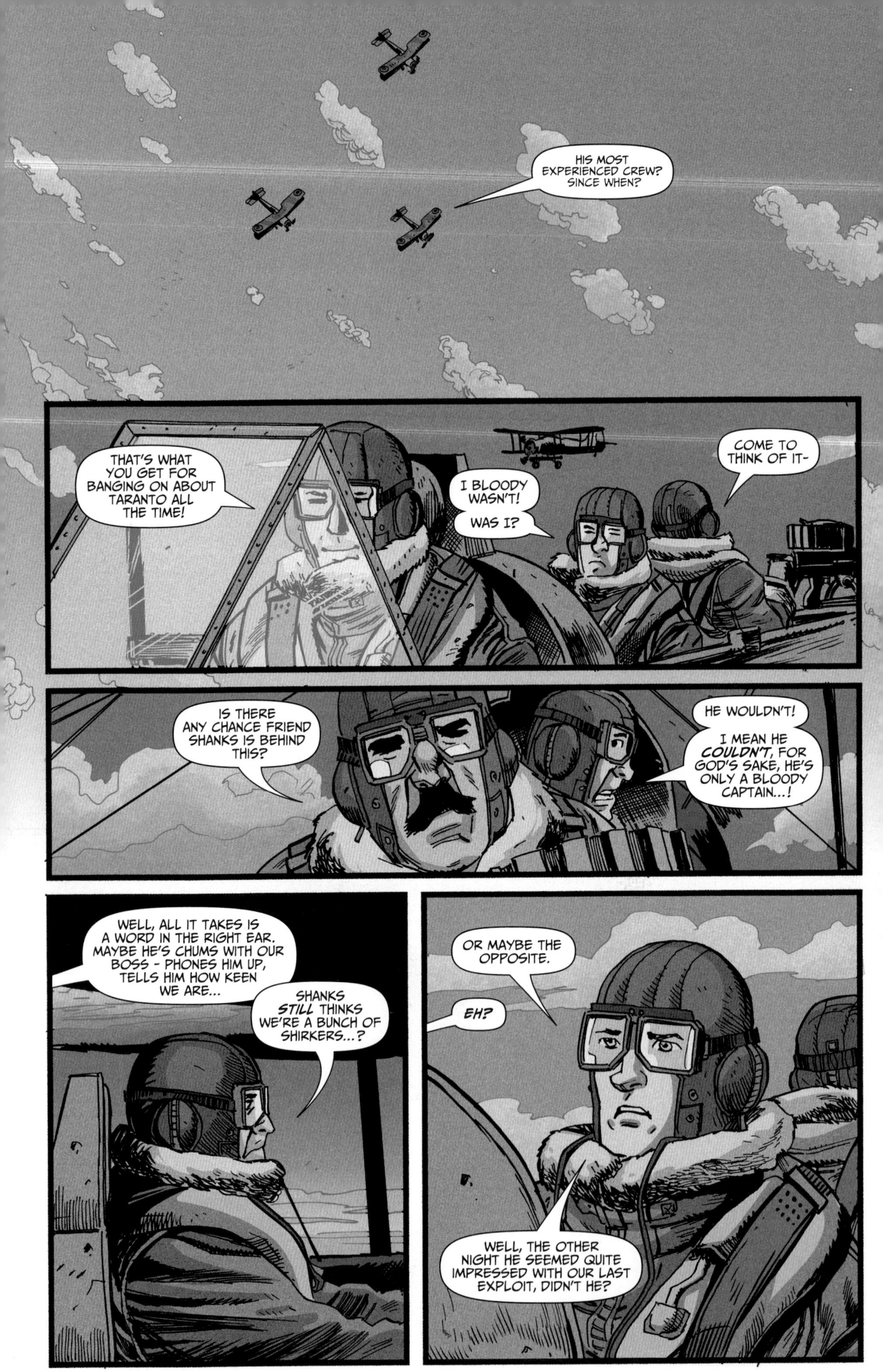
HIS MOST EXPERIENCED CREW? SINCE WHEN?
THAT'S WHAT YOU GET FOR BANGING ON ABOUT TARANTO ALL THE TIME!
I BLOODY WASN'T!
WAS I?
COME TO THINK OF IT-
IS THERE ANY CHANCE FRIEND SHANKS IS BEHIND THIS?
HE WOULDN'T!
I MEAN HE COULDN'T, FOR GOD'S SAKE, HE'S ONLY A BLOODY CAPTAIN...!
WELL, ALL IT TAKES IS A WORD IN THE RIGHT EAR. MAYBE HE'S CHUMS WITH OUR BOSS - PHONES HIM UP, TELLS HIM HOW KEEN WE ARE...
SHANKS STILL THINKS WE'RE A BUNCH OF SHIRKERS...?
OR MAYBE THE OPPOSITE.
EH?
WELL, THE OTHER NIGHT HE SEEMED QUITE IMPRESSED WITH OUR LAST EXPLOIT, DIDN'T HE?

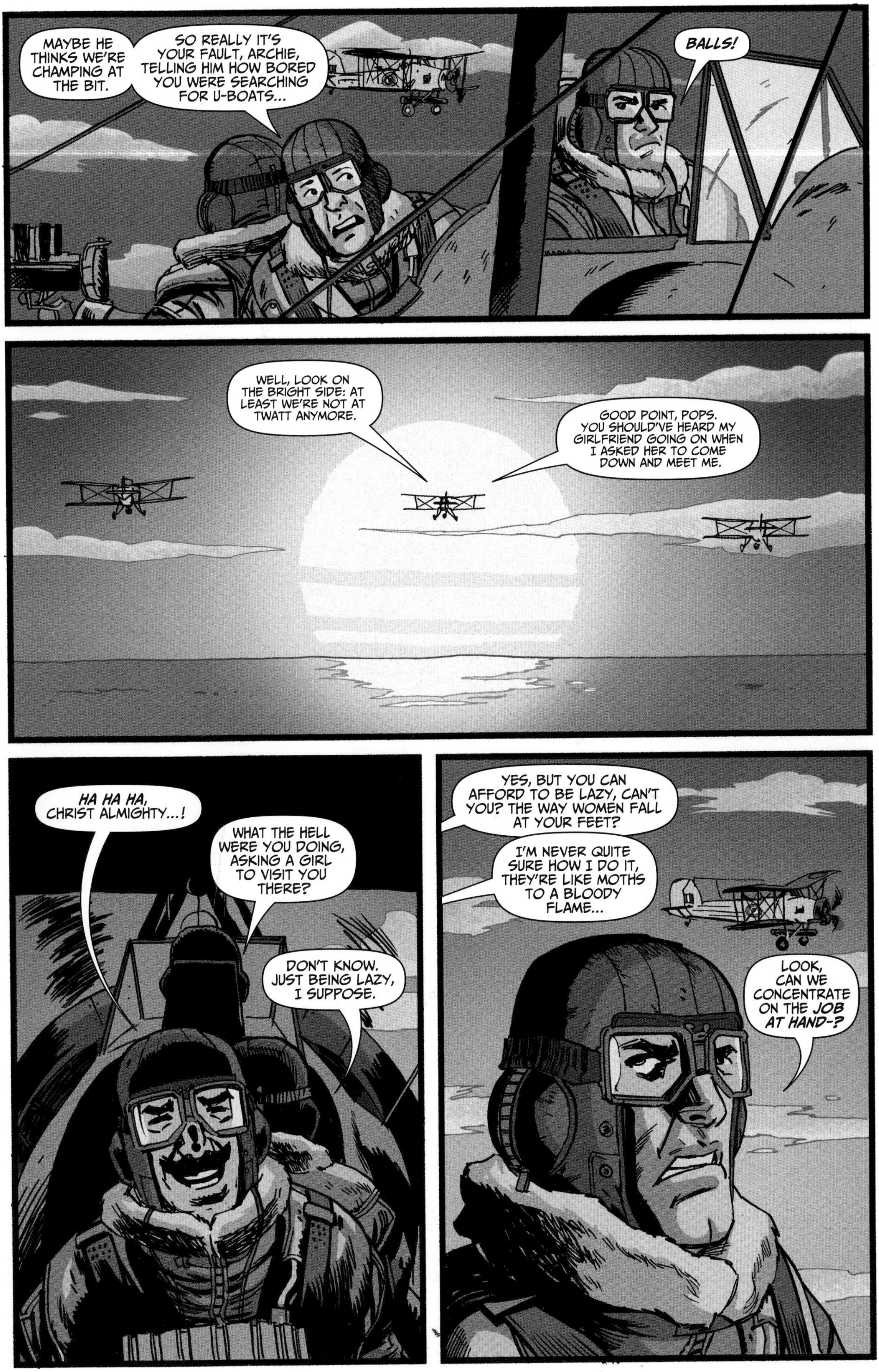
MAYBE HE THINKS WE'RE CHAMPING AT THE BIT.
SO REALLY IT'S YOUR FAULT, ARCHIE, TELLING HIM HOW BORED YOU WERE SEARCHING FOR U-BOATS...
BALLS!
WELL, LOOK ON THE BRIGHT SIDE: AT LEAST WE'RE NOT AT TWATT ANYMORE.
GOOD POINT, POPS. YOU SHOULD'VE HEARD MY GIRLFRIEND GOING ON WHEN I ASKED HER TO COME DOWN AND MEET ME.
HA HA HA, CHRIST ALMIGHTY...!
WHAT THE HELL WERE YOU DOING, ASKING A GIRL TO VISIT YOU THERE?
DON'T KNOW. JUST BEING LAZY, I SUPPOSE.
YES, BUT YOU CAN AFFORD TO BE LAZY, CAN'T YOU? THE WAY WOMEN FALL AT YOUR FEET?
I'M NEVER QUITE SURE HOW I DO IT, THEY'RE LIKE MOTHS TO A BLOODY FLAME...
LOOK, CAN WE CONCENTRATE ON THE JOB AT HAND-?

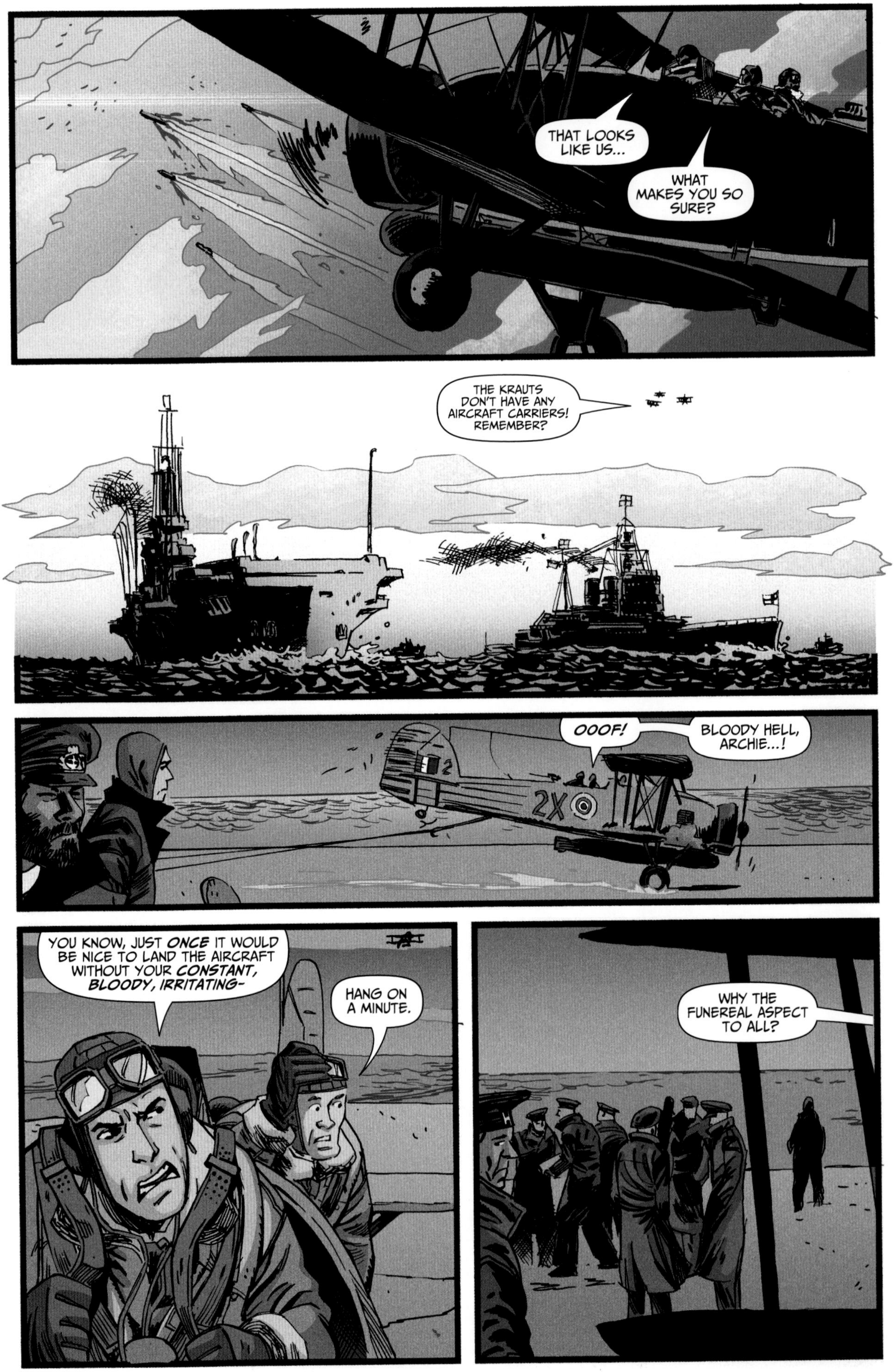
THAT LOOKS LIKE US...
WHAT MAKES YOU SO SURE?
THE KRAUTS DON'T HAVE ANY AIRCRAFT CARRIERS! REMEMBER?
OOOF!
BLOODY HELL, ARCHIE...!
YOU KNOW, JUST ONCE IT WOULD BE NICE TO LAND THE AIRCRAFT WITHOUT YOUR CONSTANT, BLOODY, IRRITATING-
HANG ON A MINUTE.
WHY THE FUNEREAL ASPECT TO ALL?

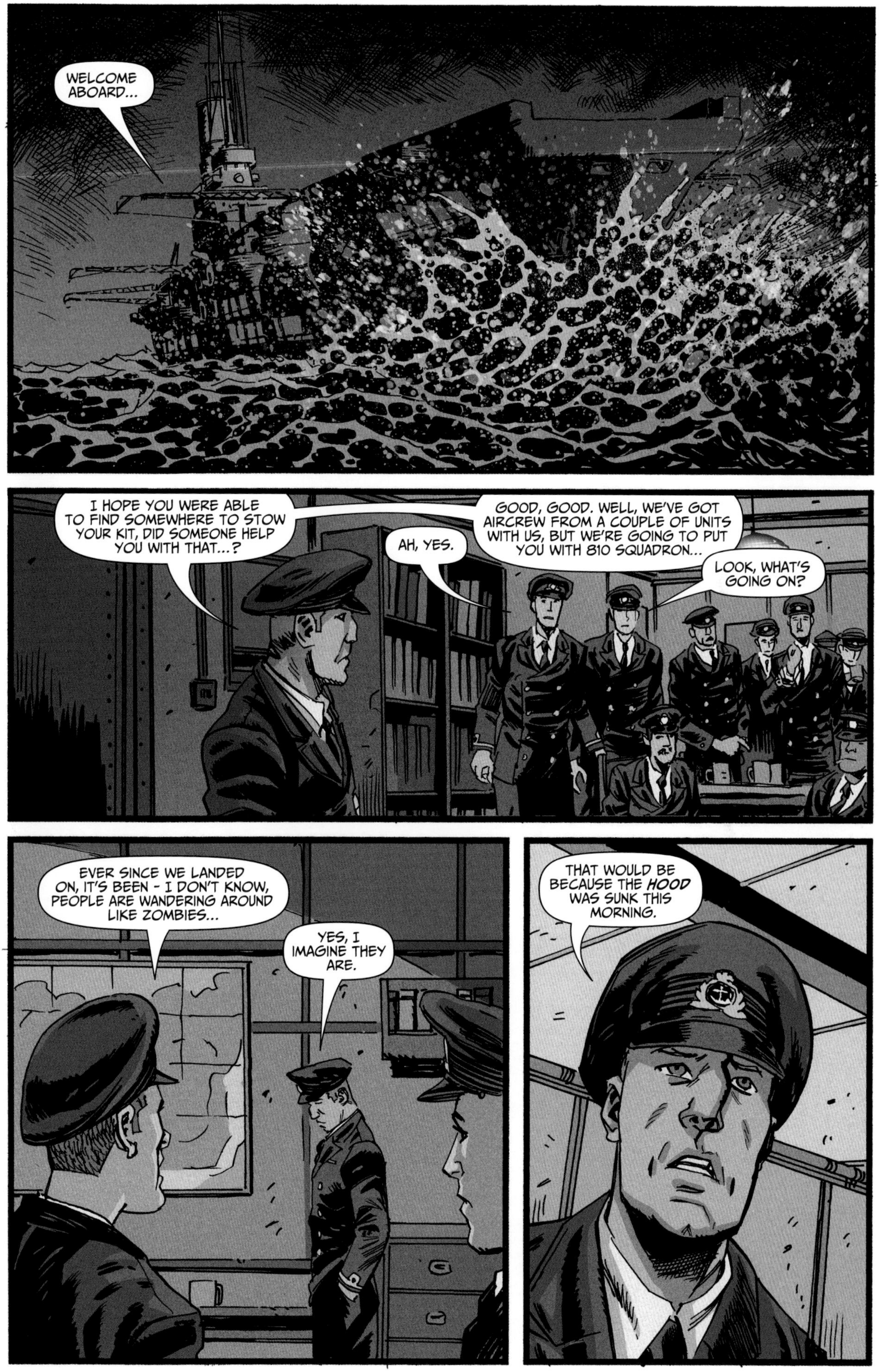
WELCOME ABOARD...
I HOPE YOU WERE ABLE TO FIND SOMEWHERE TO STOW YOUR KIT, DID SOMEONE HELP YOU WITH THAT...?
AH, YES.
GOOD, GOOD. WELL, WE'VE GOT AIRCREW FROM A COUPLE OF UNITS WITH US, BUT WE'RE GOING TO PUT YOU WITH 810 SQUADRON...
LOOK, WHAT'S GOING ON?
EVER SINCE WE LANDED ON, IT'S BEEN - I DON'T KNOW, PEOPLE ARE WANDERING AROUND LIKE ZOMBIES...
YES, I IMAGINE THEY ARE.
THAT WOULD BE BECAUSE THE *HOOD* WAS SUNK THIS MORNING.

WHAT?

I CAN UNDERSTAND YOUR SURPRISE.

THE LONG AND THE SHORT OF IT IS THAT THE *HOOD* AND THE *PRINCE OF WALES* CAUGHT UP WITH THE *BISMARCK* AROUND DAWN. OUR SHIPS WERE OUT IN FRONT OF THE HOME FLEET, THE HUNS WERE COMING SOUTHWEST OUT OF THE DENMARK STRAIT.

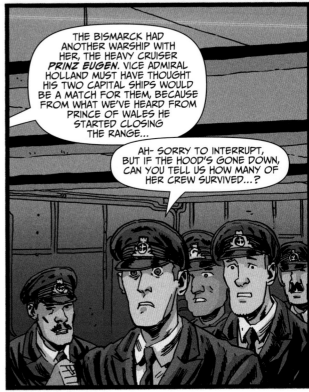

THE *BISMARCK* HAD ANOTHER WARSHIP WITH HER, THE HEAVY CRUISER *PRINZ EUGEN.* VICE ADMIRAL HOLLAND MUST HAVE THOUGHT HIS TWO CAPITAL SHIPS WOULD BE A MATCH FOR THEM, BECAUSE FROM WHAT WE'VE HEARD FROM *PRINCE OF WALES* HE STARTED CLOSING THE RANGE...

AH- SORRY TO INTERRUPT, BUT IF THE *HOOD'S* GONE DOWN, CAN YOU TELL US HOW MANY OF HER CREW SURVIVED...?

WE BELIEVE... THREE.

OUT OF *FOURTEEN HUNDRED?*

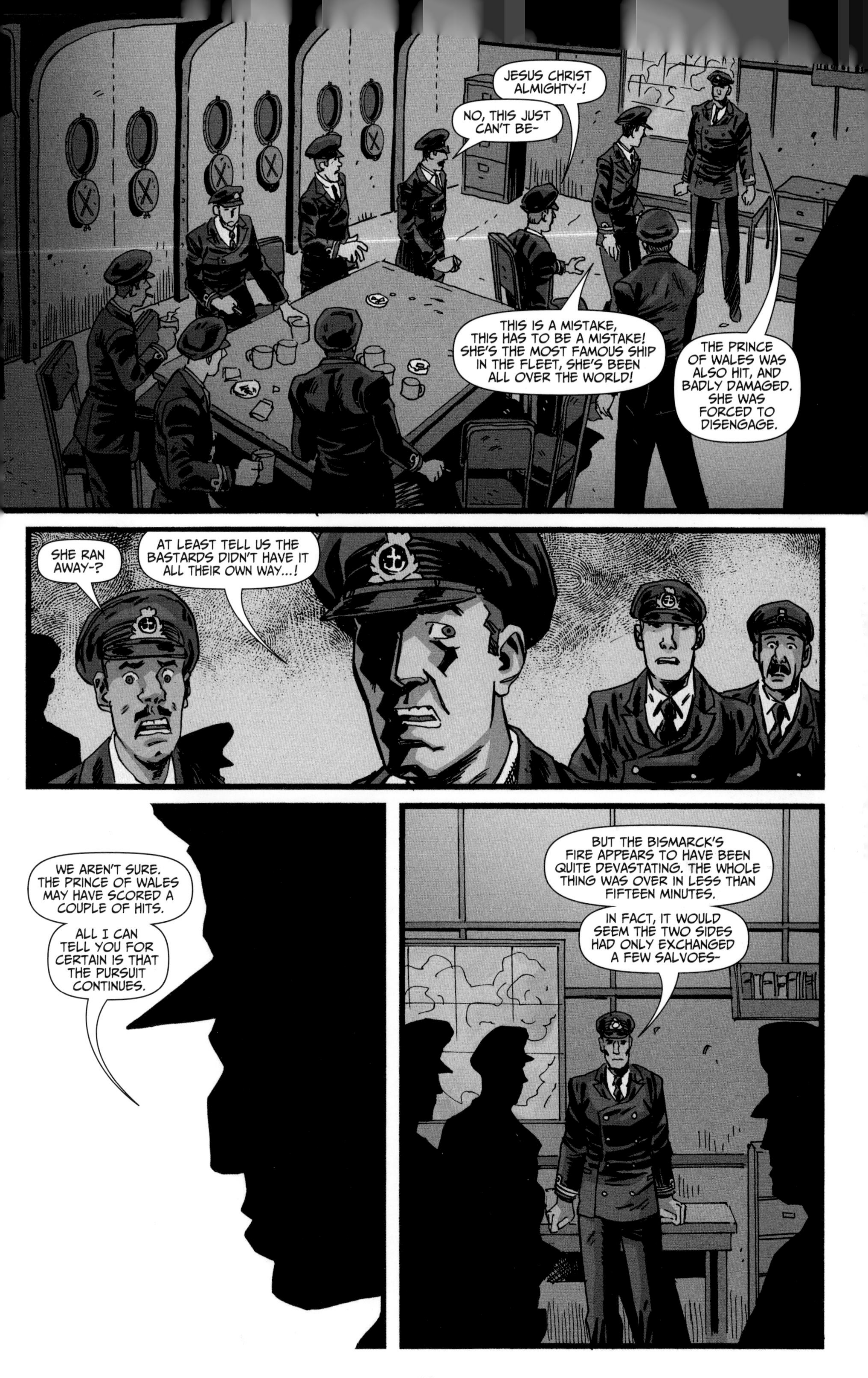
JESUS CHRIST ALMIGHTY-!
NO, THIS JUST CAN'T BE-
THIS IS A MISTAKE, THIS HAS TO BE A MISTAKE! SHE'S THE MOST FAMOUS SHIP IN THE FLEET, SHE'S BEEN ALL OVER THE WORLD!
THE PRINCE OF WALES WAS ALSO HIT, AND BADLY DAMAGED. SHE WAS FORCED TO DISENGAGE.
SHE RAN AWAY-?
AT LEAST TELL US THE BASTARDS DIDN'T HAVE IT ALL THEIR OWN WAY...!
WE AREN'T SURE. THE PRINCE OF WALES MAY HAVE SCORED A COUPLE OF HITS.
ALL I CAN TELL YOU FOR CERTAIN IS THAT THE PURSUIT CONTINUES.
BUT THE BISMARCK'S FIRE APPEARS TO HAVE BEEN QUITE DEVASTATING. THE WHOLE THING WAS OVER IN LESS THAN FIFTEEN MINUTES.
IN FACT, IT WOULD SEEM THE TWO SIDES HAD ONLY EXCHANGED A FEW SALVOES-

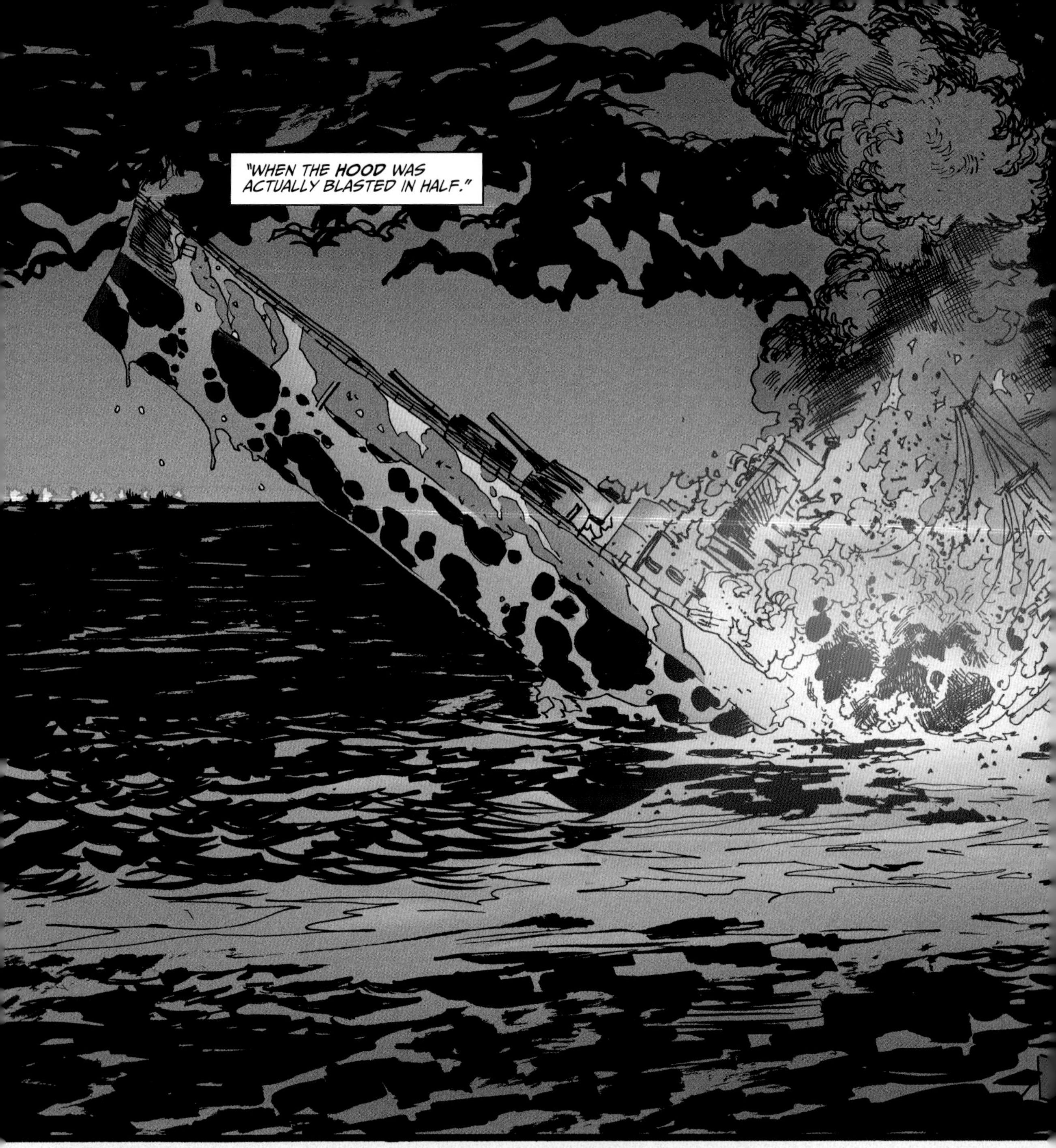
"WHEN THE **HOOD** WAS ACTUALLY BLASTED IN HALF."

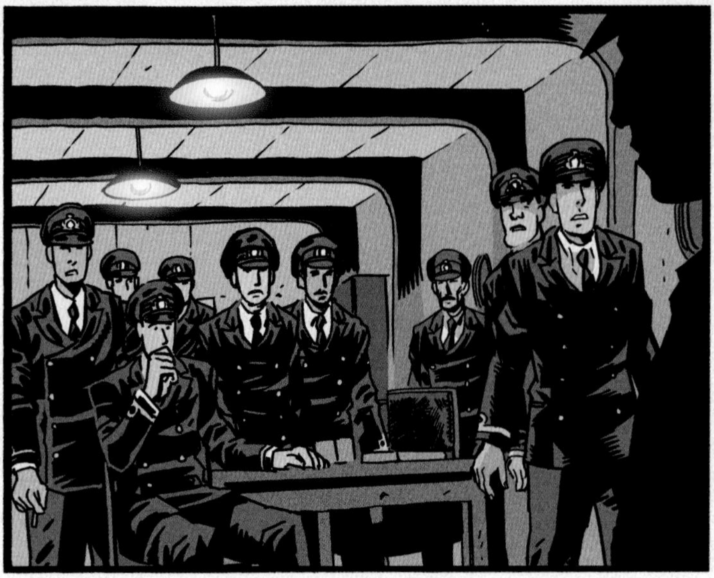

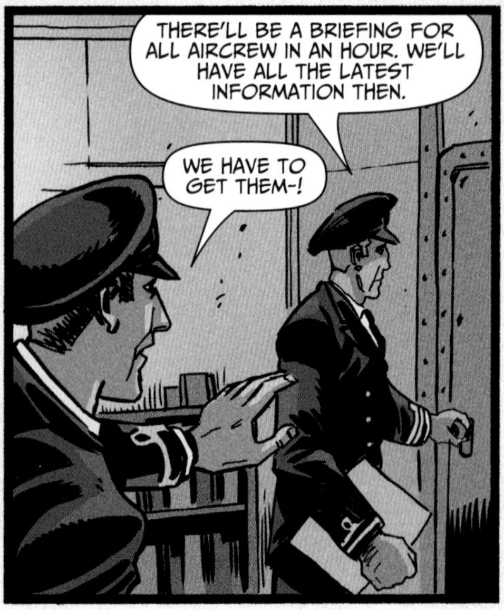
THERE'LL BE A BRIEFING FOR ALL AIRCREW IN AN HOUR. WE'LL HAVE ALL THE LATEST INFORMATION THEN.
WE HAVE TO GET THEM-!

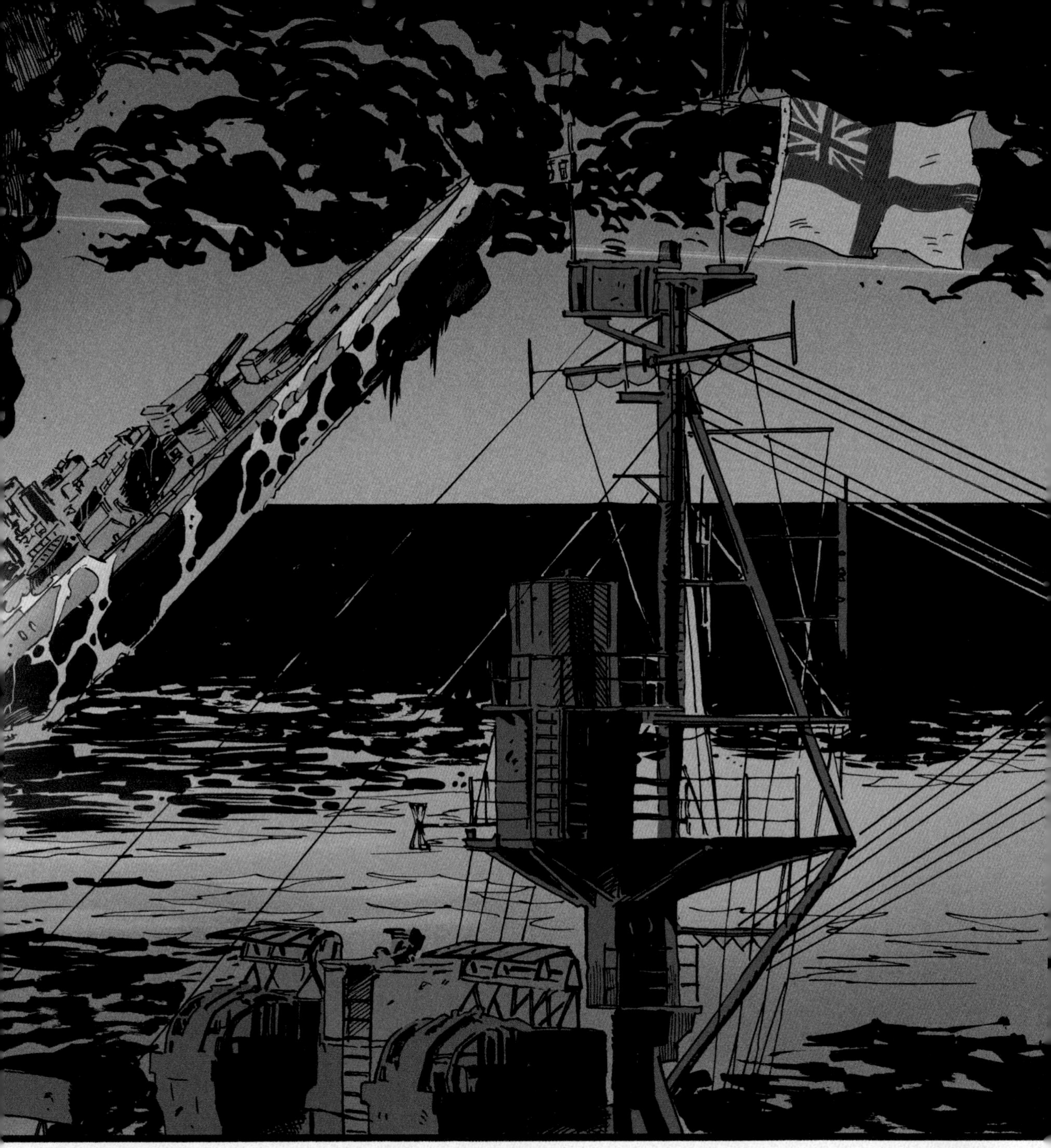

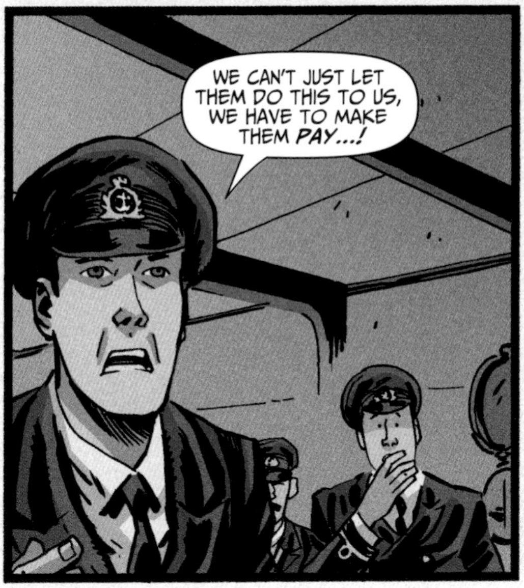
WE CAN'T JUST LET THEM DO THIS TO US, WE HAVE TO MAKE THEM *PAY...!*

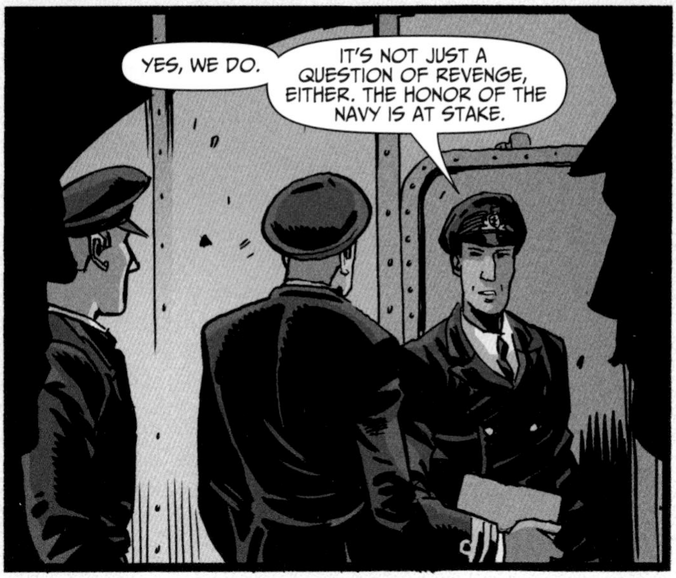
YES, WE DO.
IT'S NOT JUST A QUESTION OF REVENGE, EITHER. THE HONOR OF THE NAVY IS AT STAKE.

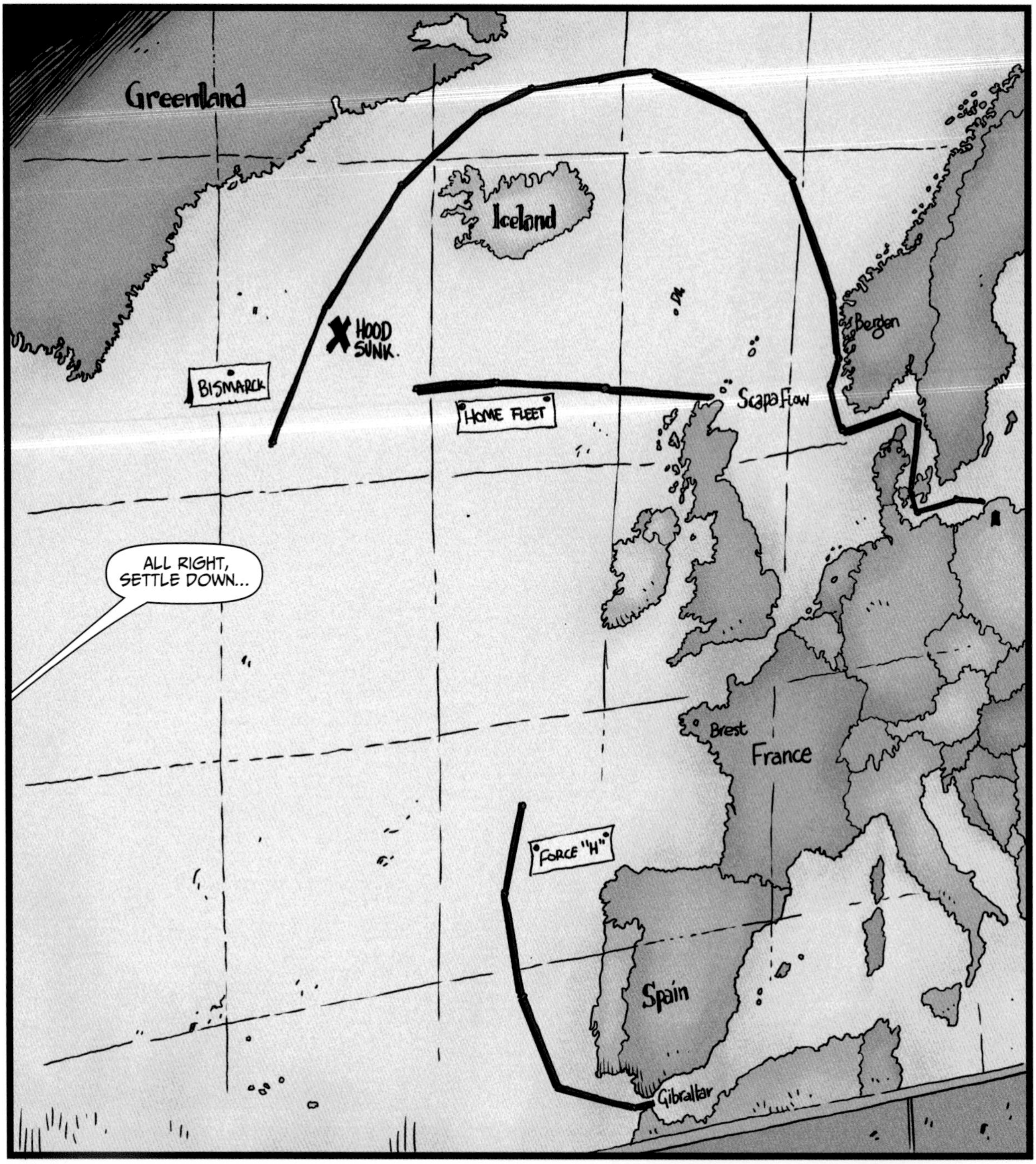
Greenland
Iceland
HOOD SUNK.
BISMARCK
HOME FLEET
Scapa Flow
Bergen
ALL RIGHT, SETTLE DOWN...
Brest
France
FORCE "H"
Spain
Gibraltar

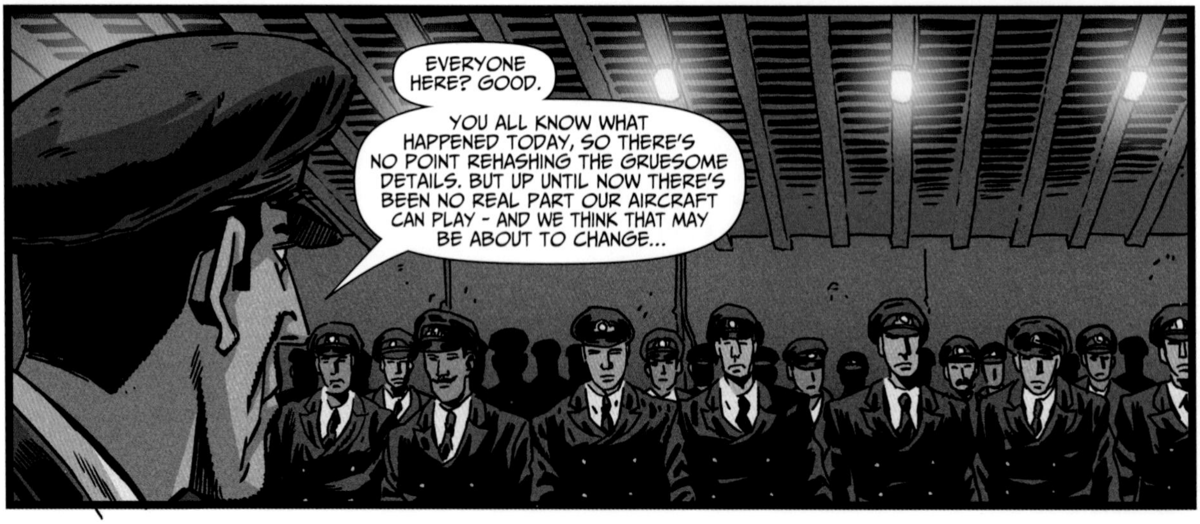
EVERYONE HERE? GOOD.
YOU ALL KNOW WHAT HAPPENED TODAY, SO THERE'S NO POINT REHASHING THE GRUESOME DETAILS. BUT UP UNTIL NOW THERE'S BEEN NO REAL PART OUR AIRCRAFT CAN PLAY - AND WE THINK THAT MAY BE ABOUT TO CHANGE...

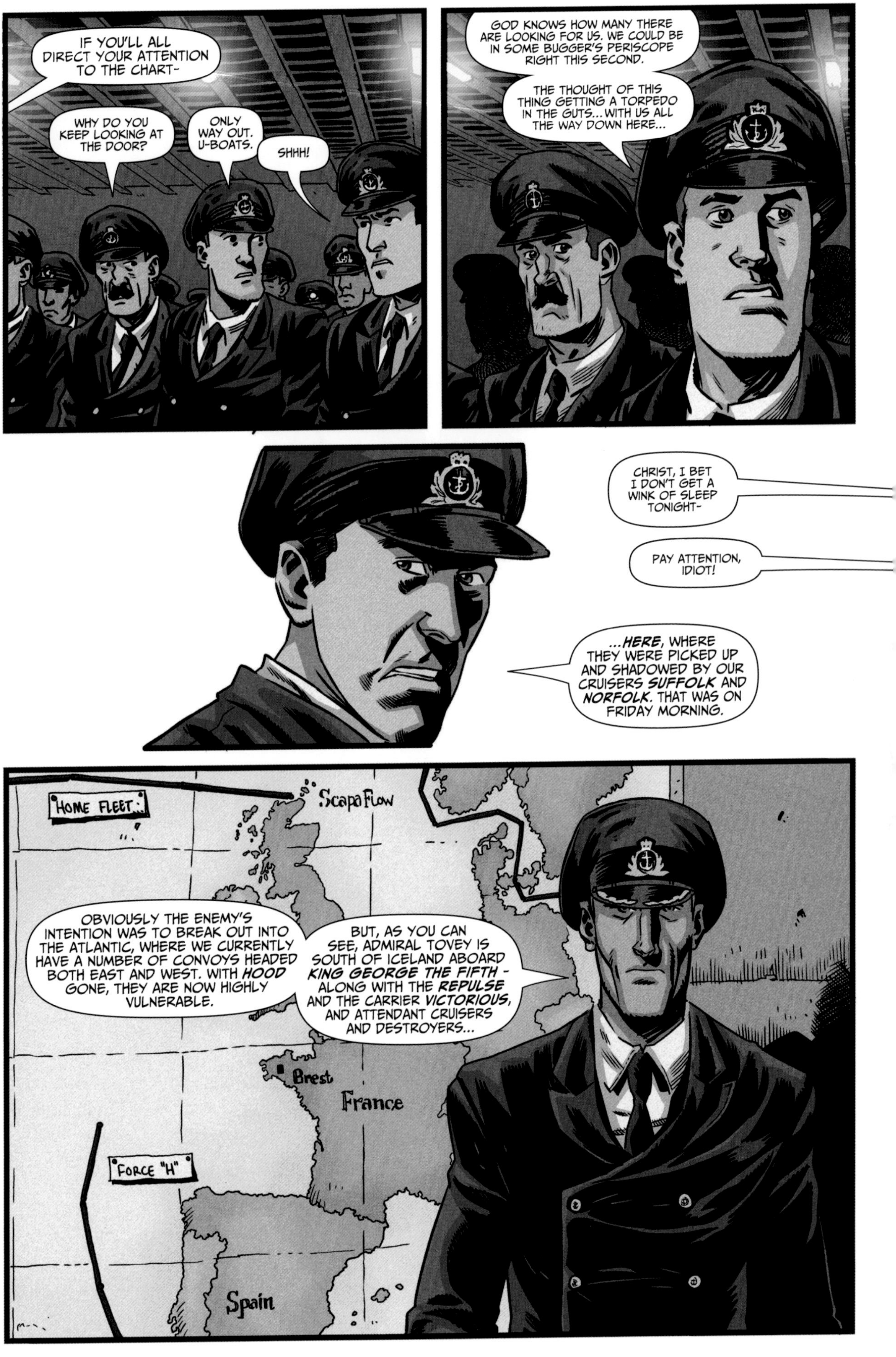
IF YOU'LL ALL DIRECT YOUR ATTENTION TO THE CHART-
WHY DO YOU KEEP LOOKING AT THE DOOR?
ONLY WAY OUT. U-BOATS.
SHHH!
GOD KNOWS HOW MANY THERE ARE LOOKING FOR US. WE COULD BE IN SOME BUGGER'S PERISCOPE RIGHT THIS SECOND.
THE THOUGHT OF THIS THING GETTING A TORPEDO IN THE GUTS...WITH US ALL THE WAY DOWN HERE...
CHRIST, I BET I DON'T GET A WINK OF SLEEP TONIGHT-
PAY ATTENTION, IDIOT!
...*HERE*, WHERE THEY WERE PICKED UP AND SHADOWED BY OUR CRUISERS *SUFFOLK* AND *NORFOLK*. THAT WAS ON FRIDAY MORNING.
HOME FLEET
Scapa Flow
Brest
France
FORCE "H"
Spain
OBVIOUSLY THE ENEMY'S INTENTION WAS TO BREAK OUT INTO THE ATLANTIC, WHERE WE CURRENTLY HAVE A NUMBER OF CONVOYS HEADED BOTH EAST AND WEST. WITH *HOOD* GONE, THEY ARE NOW HIGHLY VULNERABLE.
BUT, AS YOU CAN SEE, ADMIRAL TOVEY IS SOUTH OF ICELAND ABOARD *KING GEORGE THE FIFTH* - ALONG WITH THE *REPULSE* AND THE CARRIER *VICTORIOUS*, AND ATTENDANT CRUISERS AND DESTROYERS...

WE KNOW THE BISMARCK CANNOT BE ALONE, AND I'M NOT JUST TALKING ABOUT THE *PRINZ EUGEN* AND WHATEVER U-BOATS ARE IN THE VICINITY. SHE MUST HAVE TANKERS AND SUPPLY VESSELS WAITING TO RENDEZVOUS WITH HER, TO SUSTAIN HER FOR A PROLONGED CAMPAIGN, AND THE HUNT IS OF COURSE ON FOR THOSE ASSETS AS WE SPEAK.

BUT THAT IS NOT OUR JOB. OUR ONE AND ONLY CONCERN IS THE BEAST HERSELF.

IT IS ADMIRAL TOVEY'S INTENTION TO INTERCEPT HER - IDEALLY CATCHING HER BETWEEN HIS FORCE AND OUR OWN - AND TO SINK HER WITHOUT DELAY.

EASIER SAID THAN BLOODY DONE...!

AS SOON AS SHE COMES WITHIN RANGE - OF EITHER *VICTORIOUS* OR OURSELVES - THE SWORDFISH WILL BE LAUNCHED AGAINST HER. THE MORE DAMAGE WE CAN DO THE BETTER, BUT AT THE VERY LEAST WE MUST STRIVE TO SLOW HER DOWN FOR THE REST OF THE FLEET.

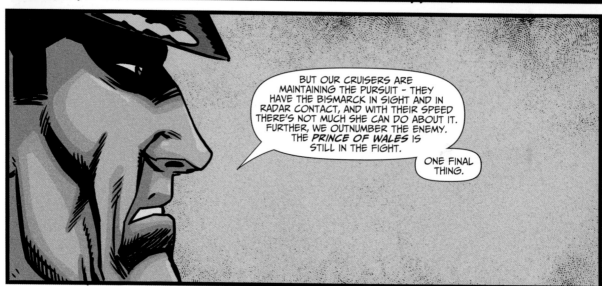

BUT OUR CRUISERS ARE MAINTAINING THE PURSUIT - THEY HAVE THE BISMARCK IN SIGHT AND IN RADAR CONTACT, AND WITH THEIR SPEED THERE'S NOT MUCH SHE CAN DO ABOUT IT. FURTHER, WE OUTNUMBER THE ENEMY. THE *PRINCE OF WALES* IS STILL IN THE FIGHT.

ONE FINAL THING.

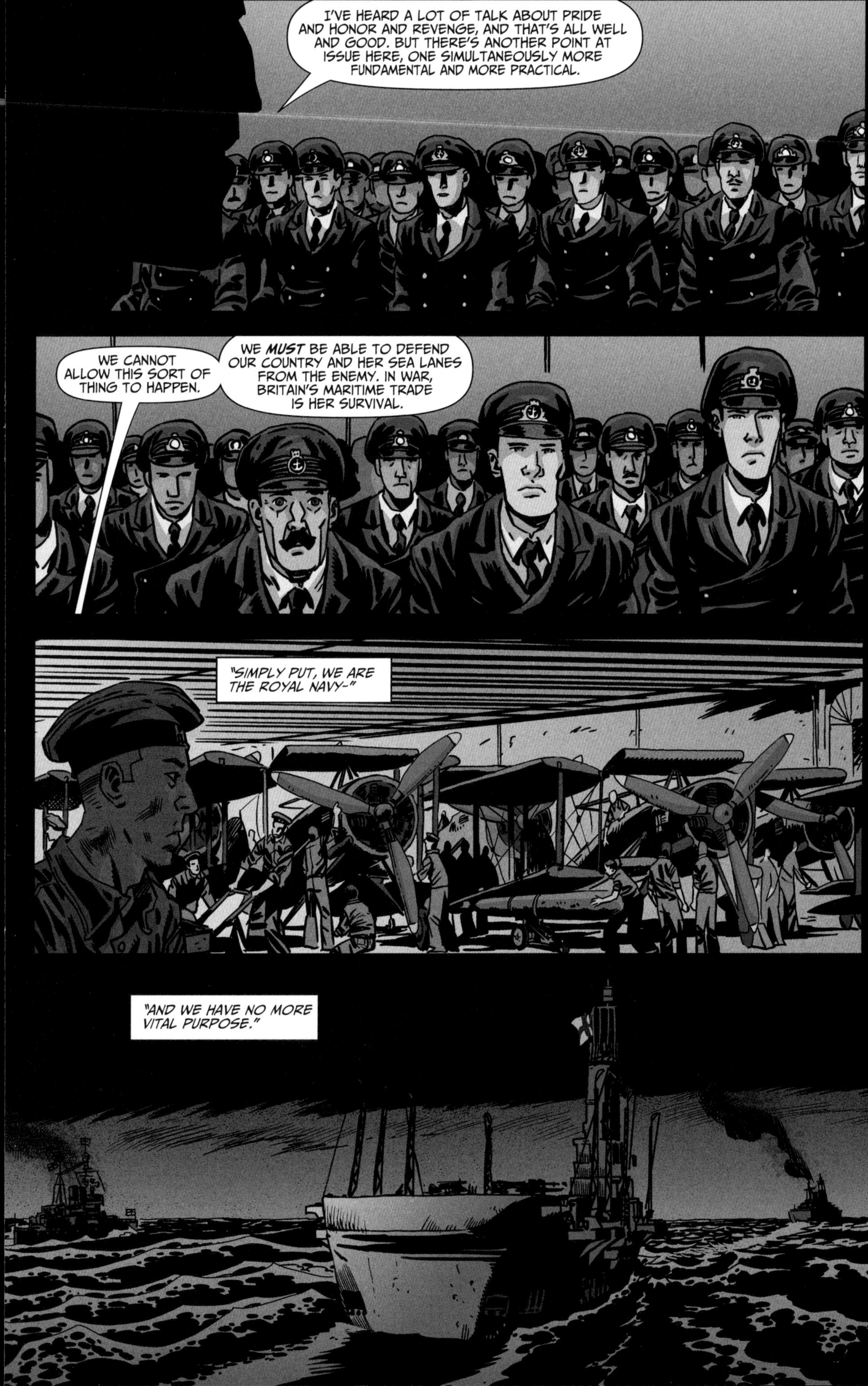
I'VE HEARD A LOT OF TALK ABOUT PRIDE AND HONOR AND REVENGE, AND THAT'S ALL WELL AND GOOD. BUT THERE'S ANOTHER POINT AT ISSUE HERE, ONE SIMULTANEOUSLY MORE FUNDAMENTAL AND MORE PRACTICAL.
WE CANNOT ALLOW THIS SORT OF THING TO HAPPEN.
WE MUST BE ABLE TO DEFEND OUR COUNTRY AND HER SEA LANES FROM THE ENEMY. IN WAR, BRITAIN'S MARITIME TRADE IS HER SURVIVAL.
"SIMPLY PUT, WE ARE THE ROYAL NAVY-"
"AND WE HAVE NO MORE VITAL PURPOSE."

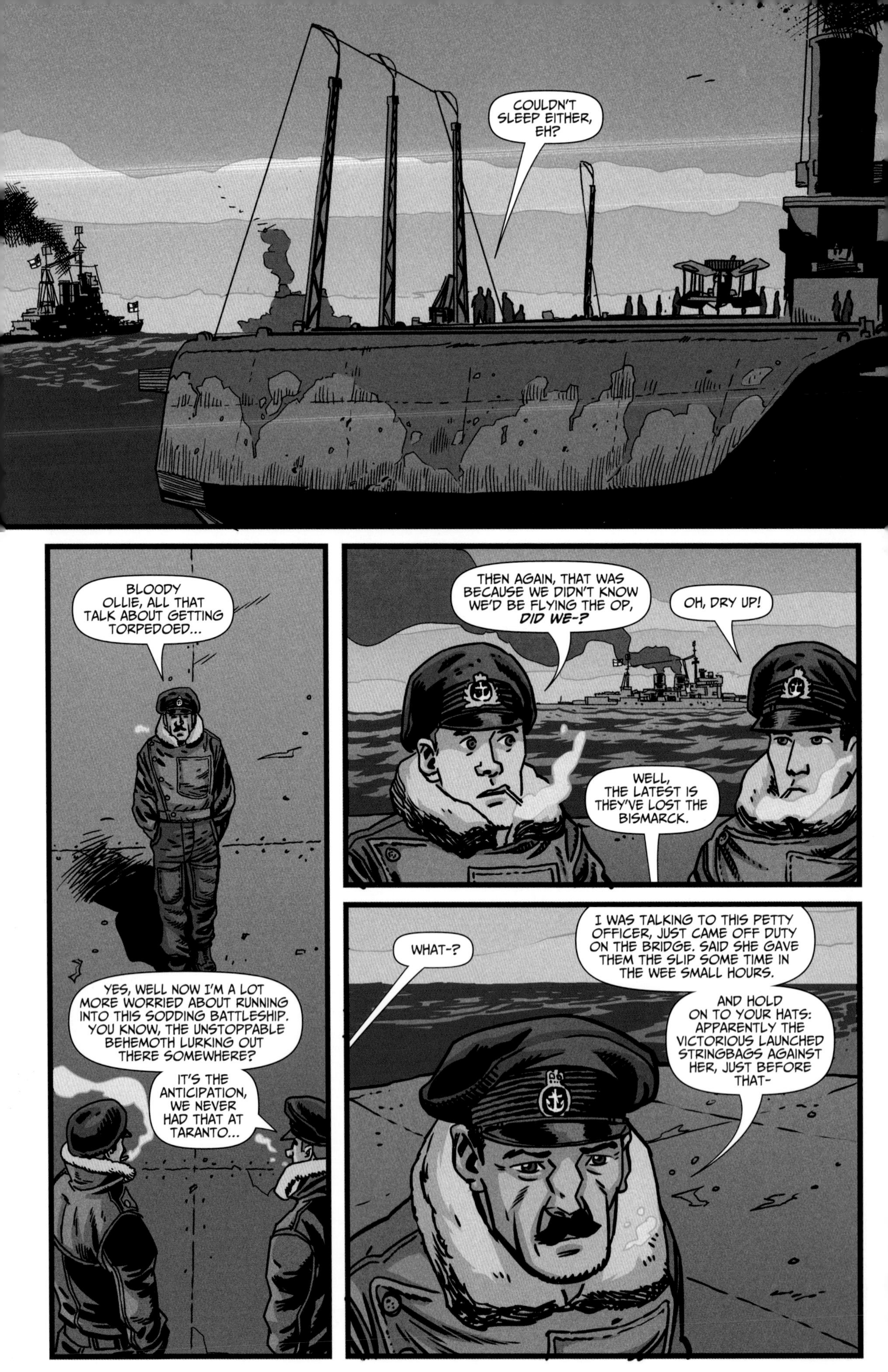
COULDN'T SLEEP EITHER, EH?
BLOODY OLLIE, ALL THAT TALK ABOUT GETTING TORPEDOED...
YES, WELL NOW I'M A LOT MORE WORRIED ABOUT RUNNING INTO THIS SODDING BATTLESHIP. YOU KNOW, THE UNSTOPPABLE BEHEMOTH LURKING OUT THERE SOMEWHERE?
IT'S THE ANTICIPATION, WE NEVER HAD THAT AT TARANTO...
THEN AGAIN, THAT WAS BECAUSE WE DIDN'T KNOW WE'D BE FLYING THE OP, *DID WE-?*
OH, DRY UP!
WELL, THE LATEST IS THEY'VE LOST THE BISMARCK.
WHAT-?
I WAS TALKING TO THIS PETTY OFFICER, JUST CAME OFF DUTY ON THE BRIDGE. SAID SHE GAVE THEM THE SLIP SOME TIME IN THE WEE SMALL HOURS.
AND HOLD ON TO YOUR HATS: APPARENTLY THE VICTORIOUS LAUNCHED STRINGBAGS AGAINST HER, JUST BEFORE THAT-

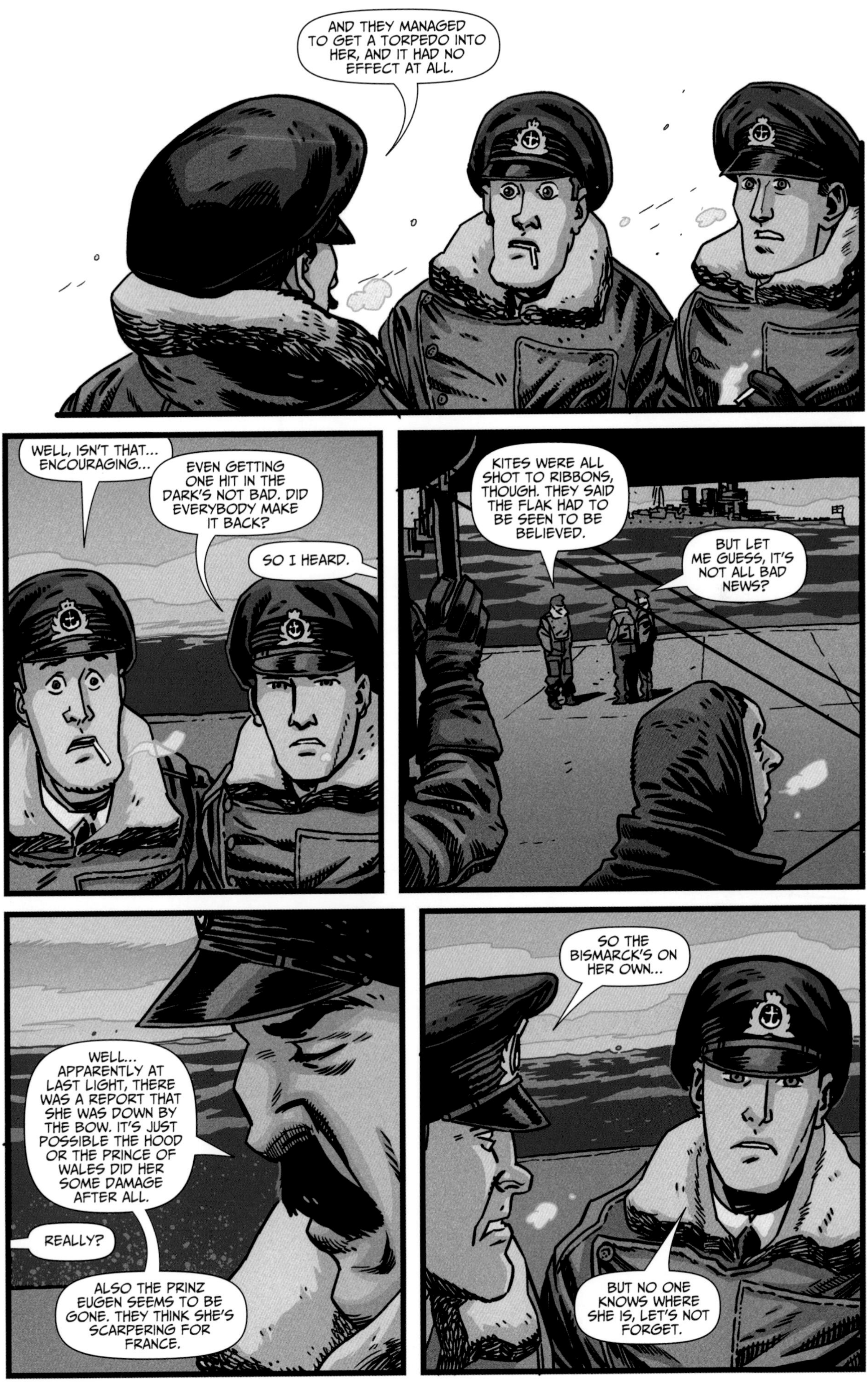
AND THEY MANAGED TO GET A TORPEDO INTO HER, AND IT HAD NO EFFECT AT ALL.
WELL, ISN'T THAT... ENCOURAGING...
EVEN GETTING ONE HIT IN THE DARK'S NOT BAD. DID EVERYBODY MAKE IT BACK?
SO I HEARD.
KITES WERE ALL SHOT TO RIBBONS, THOUGH. THEY SAID THE FLAK HAD TO BE SEEN TO BE BELIEVED.
BUT LET ME GUESS, IT'S NOT ALL BAD NEWS?
WELL... APPARENTLY AT LAST LIGHT, THERE WAS A REPORT THAT SHE WAS DOWN BY THE BOW. IT'S JUST POSSIBLE THE HOOD OR THE PRINCE OF WALES DID HER SOME DAMAGE AFTER ALL.
REALLY?
ALSO THE PRINZ EUGEN SEEMS TO BE GONE. THEY THINK SHE'S SCARPERING FOR FRANCE.
SO THE BISMARCK'S ON HER OWN...
BUT NO ONE KNOWS WHERE SHE IS, LET'S NOT FORGET.

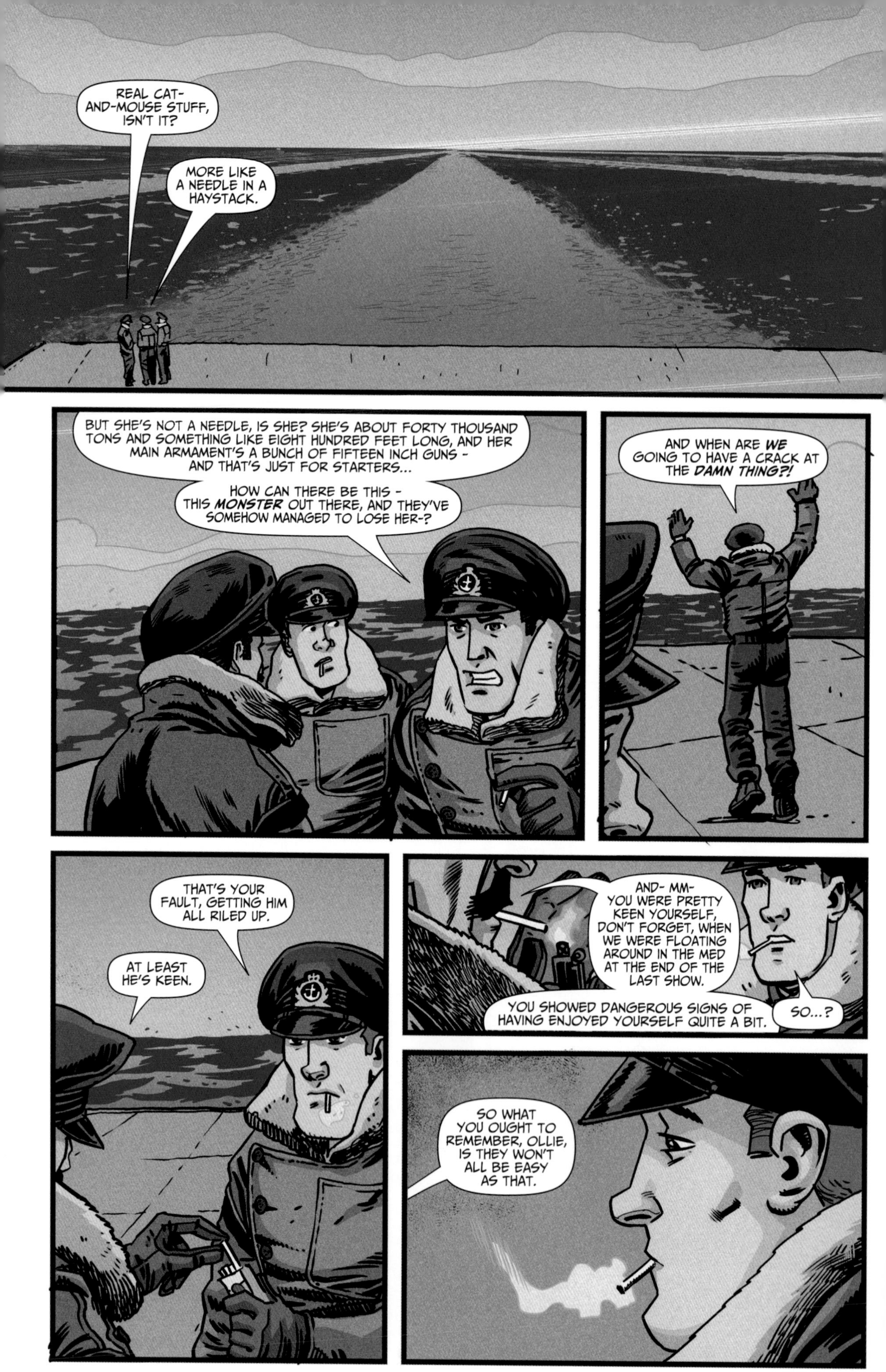
REAL CAT-AND-MOUSE STUFF, ISN'T IT?
MORE LIKE A NEEDLE IN A HAYSTACK.
BUT SHE'S NOT A NEEDLE, IS SHE? SHE'S ABOUT FORTY THOUSAND TONS AND SOMETHING LIKE EIGHT HUNDRED FEET LONG, AND HER MAIN ARMAMENT'S A BUNCH OF FIFTEEN INCH GUNS - AND THAT'S JUST FOR STARTERS...
HOW CAN THERE BE THIS - THIS MONSTER OUT THERE, AND THEY'VE SOMEHOW MANAGED TO LOSE HER-?
AND WHEN ARE WE GOING TO HAVE A CRACK AT THE DAMN THING?!
THAT'S YOUR FAULT, GETTING HIM ALL RILED UP.
AT LEAST HE'S KEEN.
AND- MM- YOU WERE PRETTY KEEN YOURSELF, DON'T FORGET, WHEN WE WERE FLOATING AROUND IN THE MED AT THE END OF THE LAST SHOW.
YOU SHOWED DANGEROUS SIGNS OF HAVING ENJOYED YOURSELF QUITE A BIT.
SO...?
SO WHAT YOU OUGHT TO REMEMBER, OLLIE, IS THEY WON'T ALL BE EASY AS THAT.

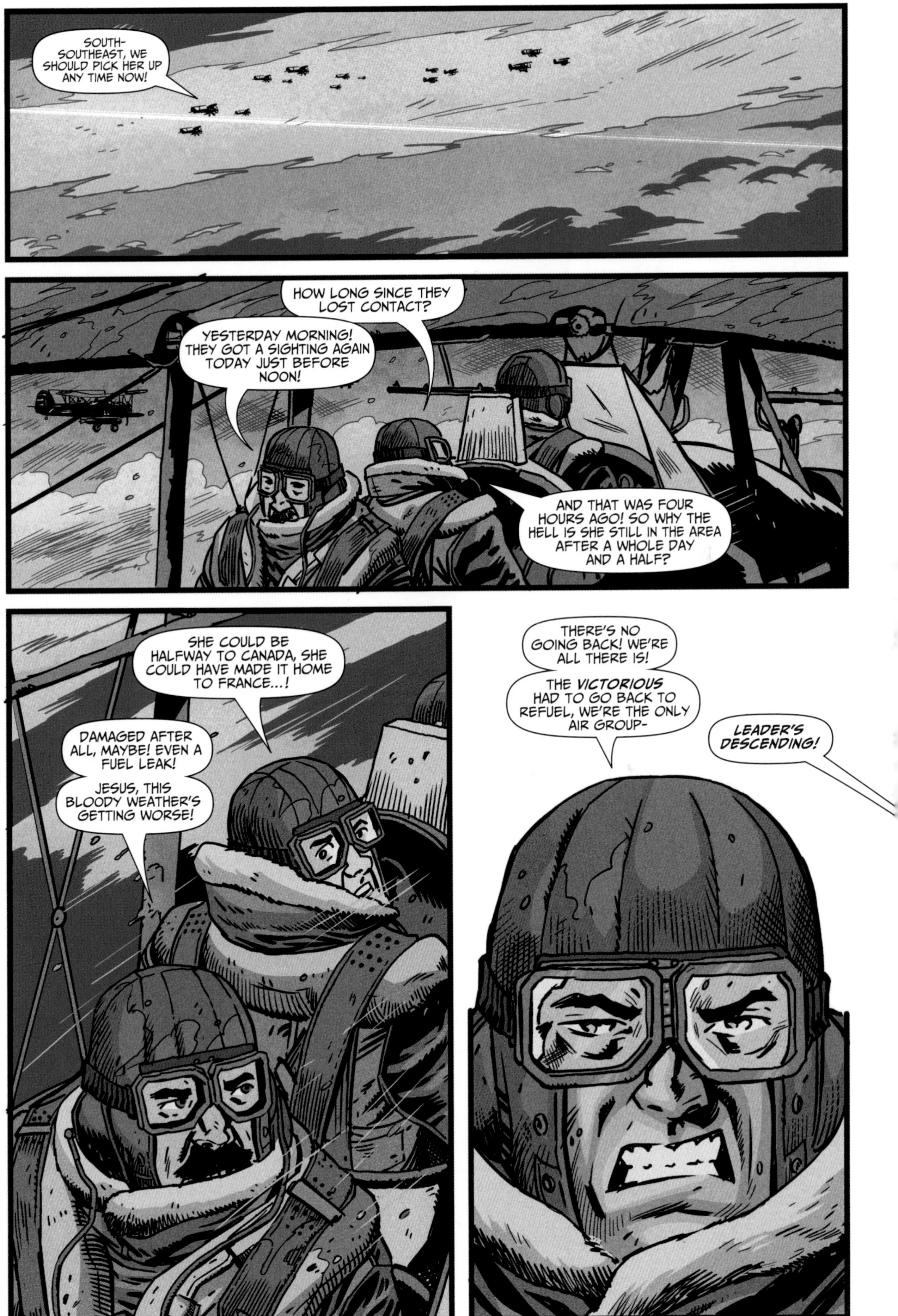
SOUTH-SOUTHEAST, WE SHOULD PICK HER UP ANY TIME NOW!
HOW LONG SINCE THEY LOST CONTACT?
YESTERDAY MORNING! THEY GOT A SIGHTING AGAIN TODAY JUST BEFORE NOON!
AND THAT WAS FOUR HOURS AGO! SO WHY THE HELL IS SHE STILL IN THE AREA AFTER A WHOLE DAY AND A HALF?
SHE COULD BE HALFWAY TO CANADA, SHE COULD HAVE MADE IT HOME TO FRANCE...!
DAMAGED AFTER ALL, MAYBE! EVEN A FUEL LEAK!
JESUS, THIS BLOODY WEATHER'S GETTING WORSE!
THERE'S NO GOING BACK! WE'RE ALL THERE IS!
THE *VICTORIOUS* HAD TO GO BACK TO REFUEL, WE'RE THE ONLY AIR GROUP-
LEADER'S DESCENDING!

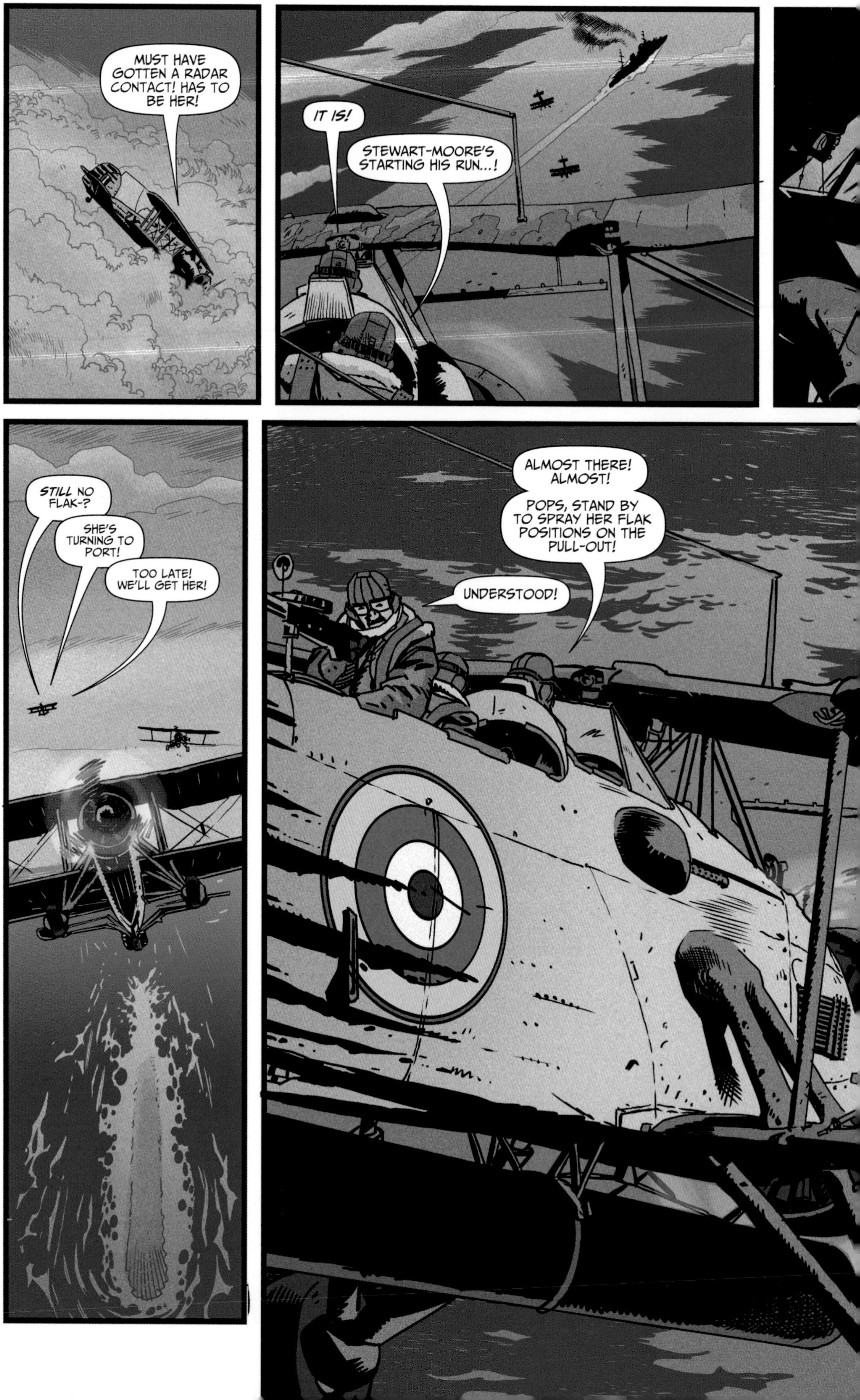
MUST HAVE GOTTEN A RADAR CONTACT! HAS TO BE HER!
IT IS!
STEWART-MOORE'S STARTING HIS RUN...!
STILL NO FLAK-?
SHE'S TURNING TO PORT!
TOO LATE! WE'LL GET HER!
ALMOST THERE! ALMOST!
POPS, STAND BY TO SPRAY HER FLAK POSITIONS ON THE PULL-OUT!
UNDERSTOOD!

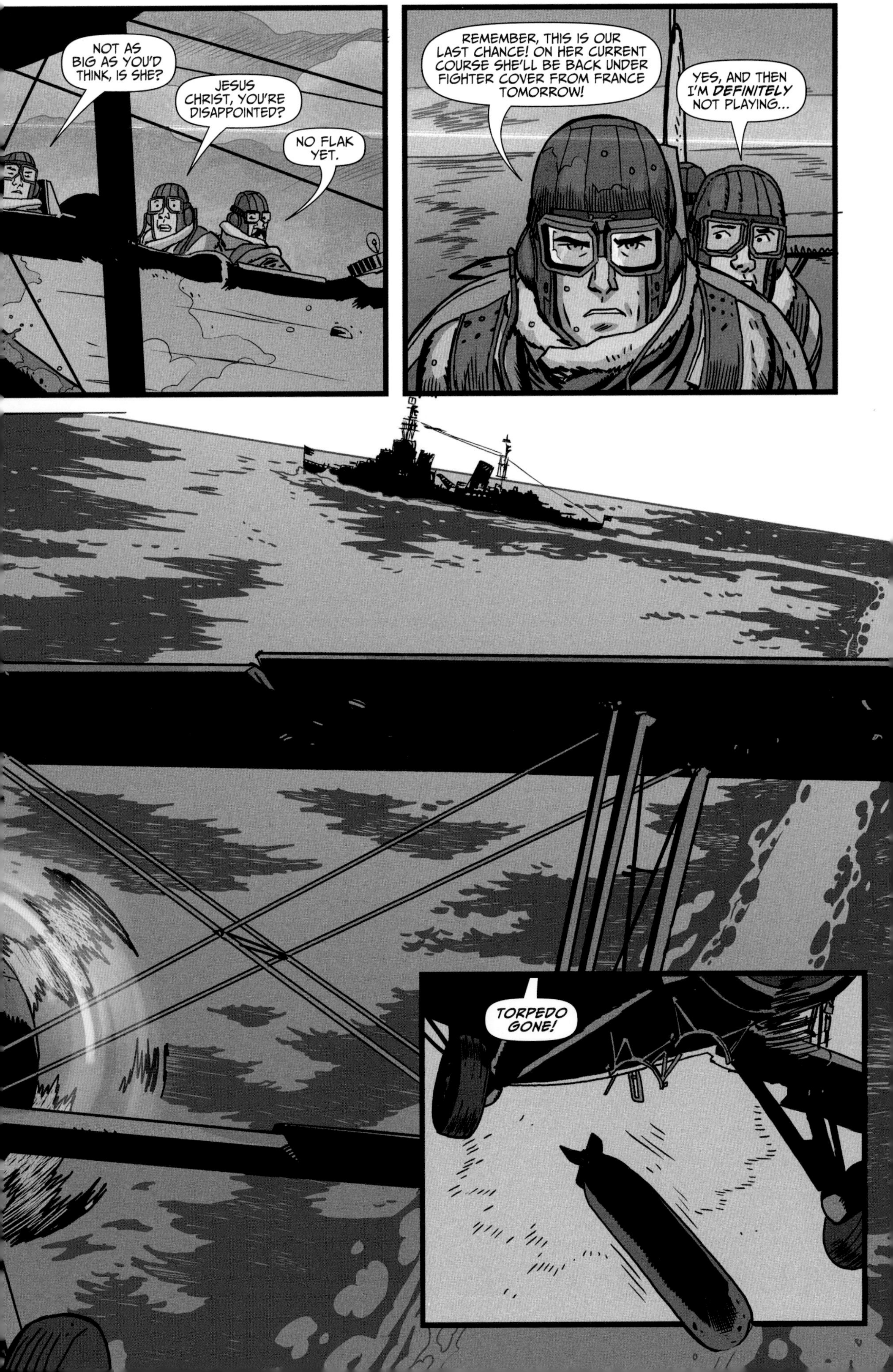
NOT AS BIG AS YOU'D THINK, IS SHE?
JESUS CHRIST, YOU'RE DISAPPOINTED?
NO FLAK YET.
REMEMBER, THIS IS OUR LAST CHANCE! ON HER CURRENT COURSE SHE'LL BE BACK UNDER FIGHTER COVER FROM FRANCE TOMORROW!
YES, AND THEN I'M *DEFINITELY* NOT PLAYING...
TORPEDO GONE!

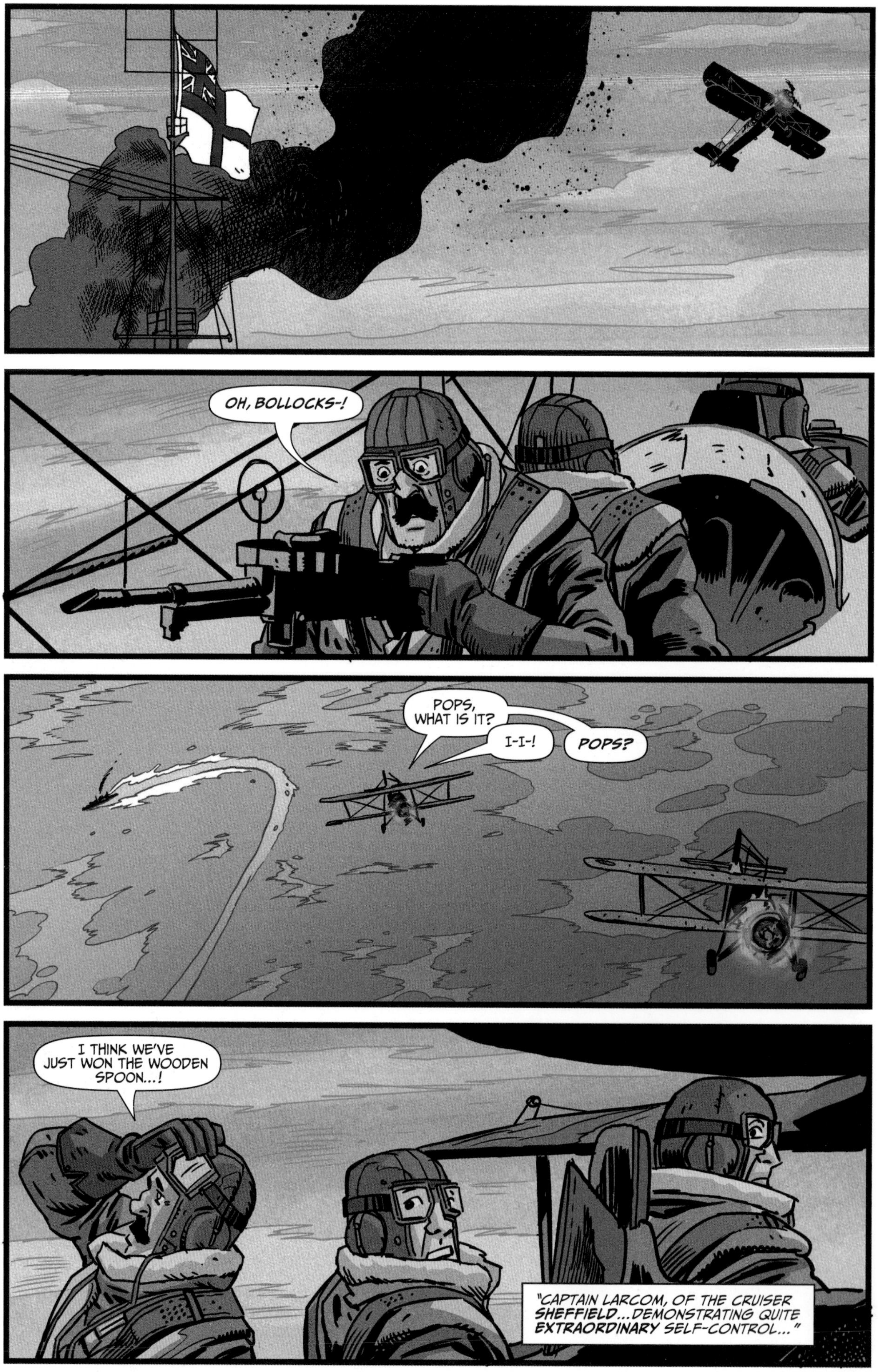
OH, BOLLOCKS-!
POPS, WHAT IS IT?
I-I-!
POPS?
I THINK WE'VE JUST WON THE WOODEN SPOON...!
"CAPTAIN LARCOM, OF THE CRUISER SHEFFIELD...DEMONSTRATING QUITE EXTRAORDINARY SELF-CONTROL..."

"SOMEHOW REFRAINED FROM HAVING HIS GUNNERS OPEN FIRE ON YOU. HIS AIRCRAFT RECOGNITION WAS CLEARLY BETTER THAN YOUR SHIP RECOGNITION."

ONLY THAT — AND HIS EXPERTISE IN HANDLING HIS SHIP — PREVENTED A WORLD-CLASS COCK-UP.

SIR, WE WERE TOLD THE BISMARCK WAS THE ONLY WARSHIP IN THE VICINITY...

AND THE SHEFFIELD WAS TWENTY MILES NORTH OF THE BISMARCK'S REPORTED POSITION.

I—

THIS DOES US NO GOOD.

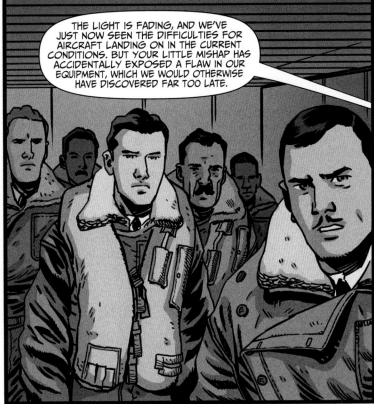

THE LIGHT IS FADING, AND WE'VE JUST NOW SEEN THE DIFFICULTIES FOR AIRCRAFT LANDING ON IN THE CURRENT CONDITIONS. BUT YOUR LITTLE MISHAP HAS ACCIDENTALLY EXPOSED A FLAW IN OUR EQUIPMENT, WHICH WE WOULD OTHERWISE HAVE DISCOVERED FAR TOO LATE.

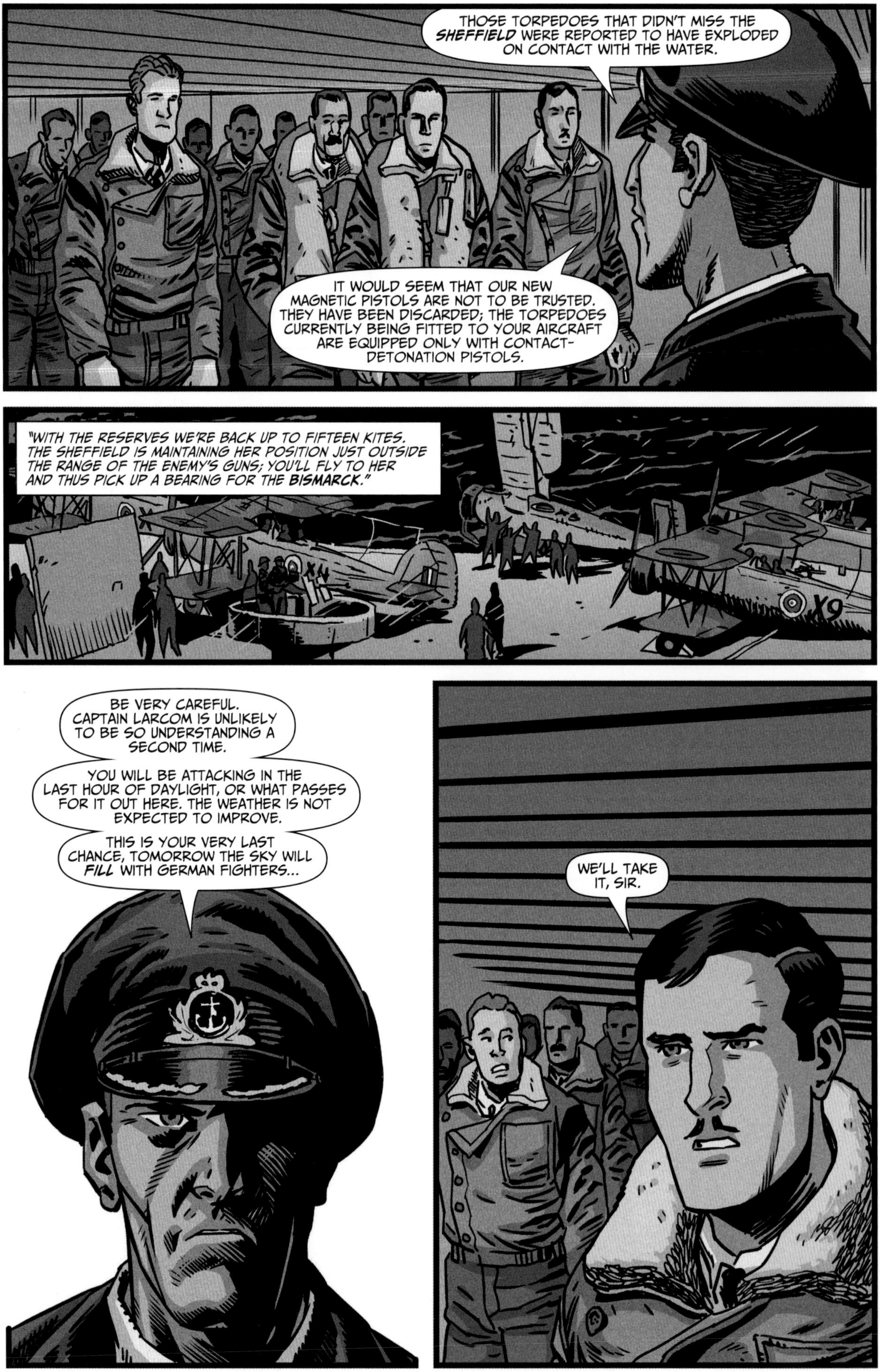
THOSE TORPEDOES THAT DIDN'T MISS THE *SHEFFIELD* WERE REPORTED TO HAVE EXPLODED ON CONTACT WITH THE WATER.
IT WOULD SEEM THAT OUR NEW MAGNETIC PISTOLS ARE NOT TO BE TRUSTED. THEY HAVE BEEN DISCARDED; THE TORPEDOES CURRENTLY BEING FITTED TO YOUR AIRCRAFT ARE EQUIPPED ONLY WITH CONTACT-DETONATION PISTOLS.
"WITH THE RESERVES WE'RE BACK UP TO FIFTEEN KITES. THE SHEFFIELD IS MAINTAINING HER POSITION JUST OUTSIDE THE RANGE OF THE ENEMY'S GUNS; YOU'LL FLY TO HER AND THUS PICK UP A BEARING FOR THE ***BISMARCK.****"*
BE VERY CAREFUL. CAPTAIN LARCOM IS UNLIKELY TO BE SO UNDERSTANDING A SECOND TIME.
YOU WILL BE ATTACKING IN THE LAST HOUR OF DAYLIGHT, OR WHAT PASSES FOR IT OUT HERE. THE WEATHER IS NOT EXPECTED TO IMPROVE.
THIS IS YOUR VERY LAST CHANCE, TOMORROW THE SKY WILL *FILL* WITH GERMAN FIGHTERS...
WE'LL TAKE IT, SIR.

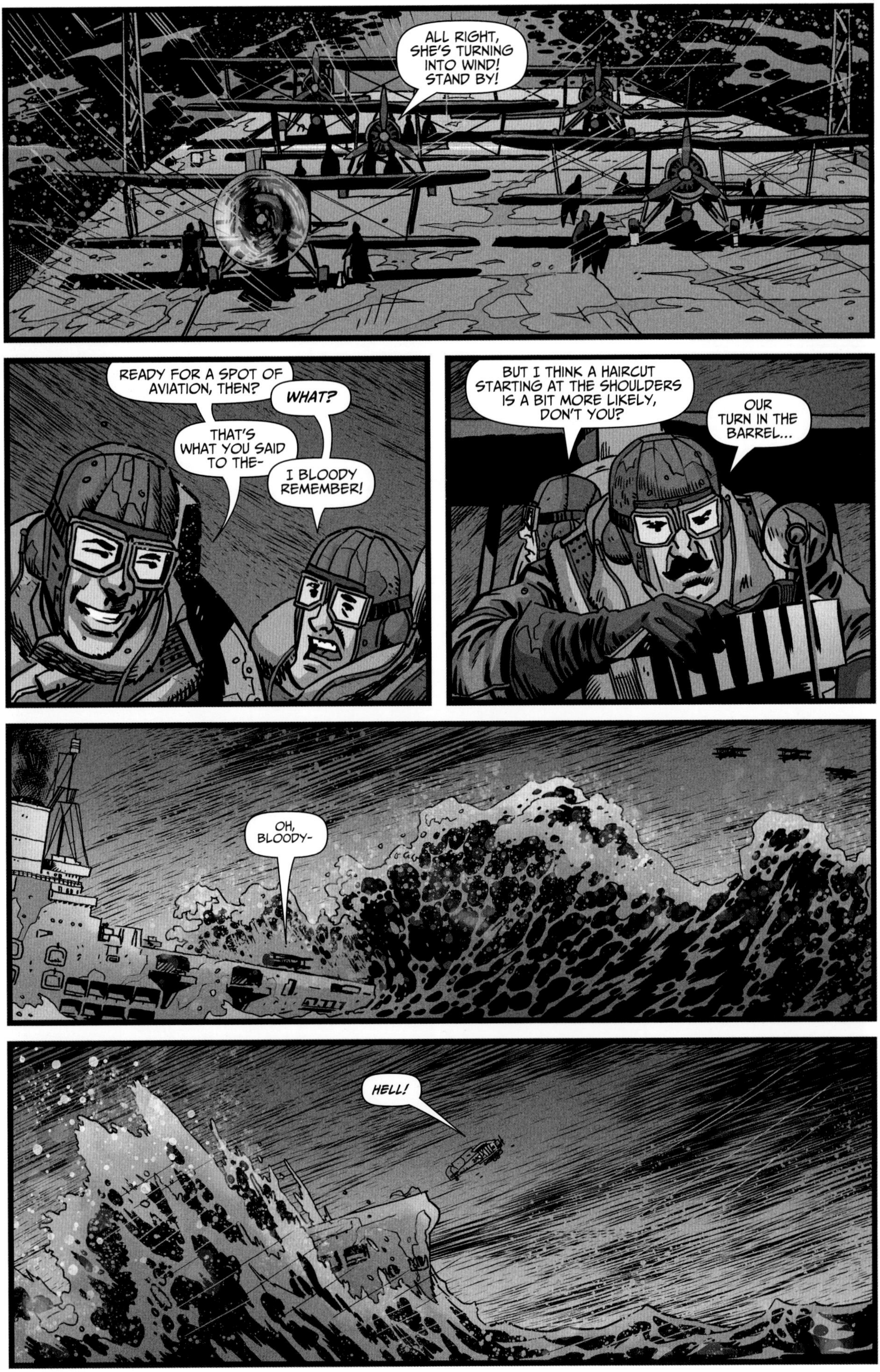
ALL RIGHT, SHE'S TURNING INTO WIND! STAND BY!
READY FOR A SPOT OF AVIATION, THEN?
WHAT?
THAT'S WHAT YOU SAID TO THE-
I BLOODY REMEMBER!
BUT I THINK A HAIRCUT STARTING AT THE SHOULDERS IS A BIT MORE LIKELY, DON'T YOU?
OUR TURN IN THE BARREL...
OH, BLOODY-
HELL!

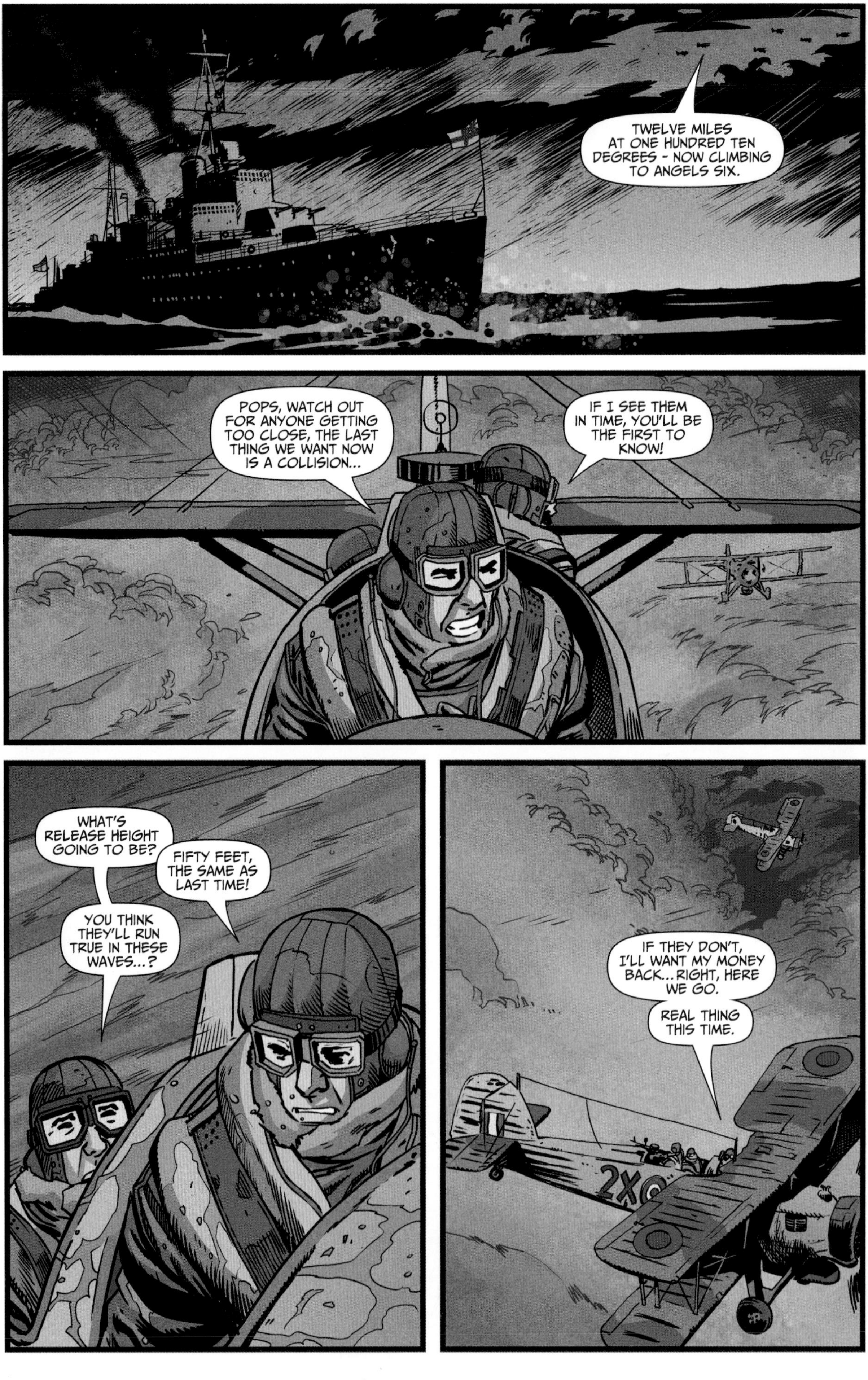
TWELVE MILES AT ONE HUNDRED TEN DEGREES - NOW CLIMBING TO ANGELS SIX.
POPS, WATCH OUT FOR ANYONE GETTING TOO CLOSE, THE LAST THING WE WANT NOW IS A COLLISION...
IF I SEE THEM IN TIME, YOU'LL BE THE FIRST TO KNOW!
WHAT'S RELEASE HEIGHT GOING TO BE?
FIFTY FEET, THE SAME AS LAST TIME!
YOU THINK THEY'LL RUN TRUE IN THESE WAVES...?
IF THEY DON'T, I'LL WANT MY MONEY BACK...RIGHT, HERE WE GO.
REAL THING THIS TIME.
2X

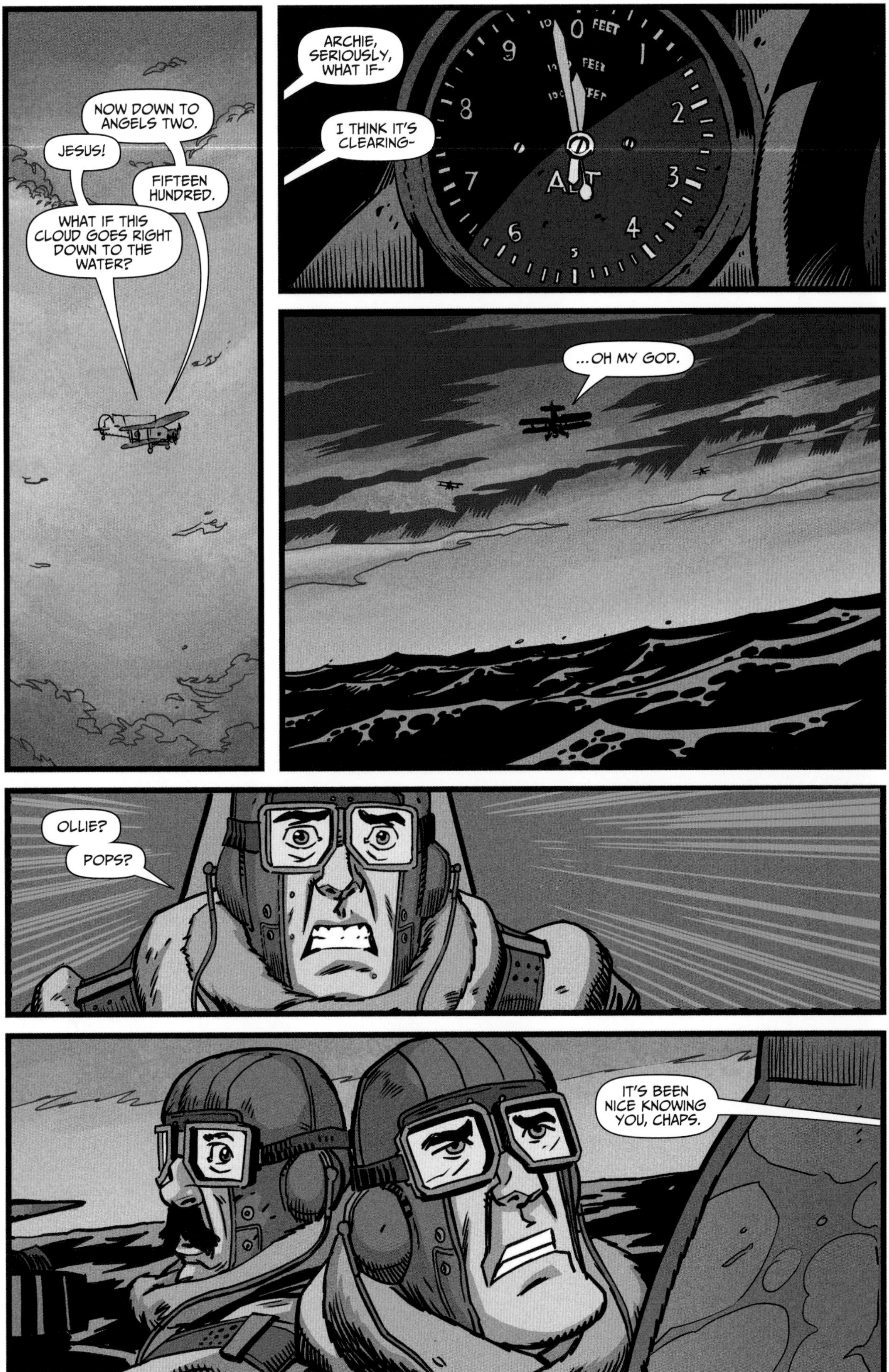
NOW DOWN TO ANGELS TWO.
JESUS!
FIFTEEN HUNDRED.
WHAT IF THIS CLOUD GOES RIGHT DOWN TO THE WATER?
ARCHIE, SERIOUSLY, WHAT IF-
I THINK IT'S CLEARING-
FEET
ALT
...OH MY GOD.
OLLIE?
POPS?
IT'S BEEN NICE KNOWING YOU, CHAPS.

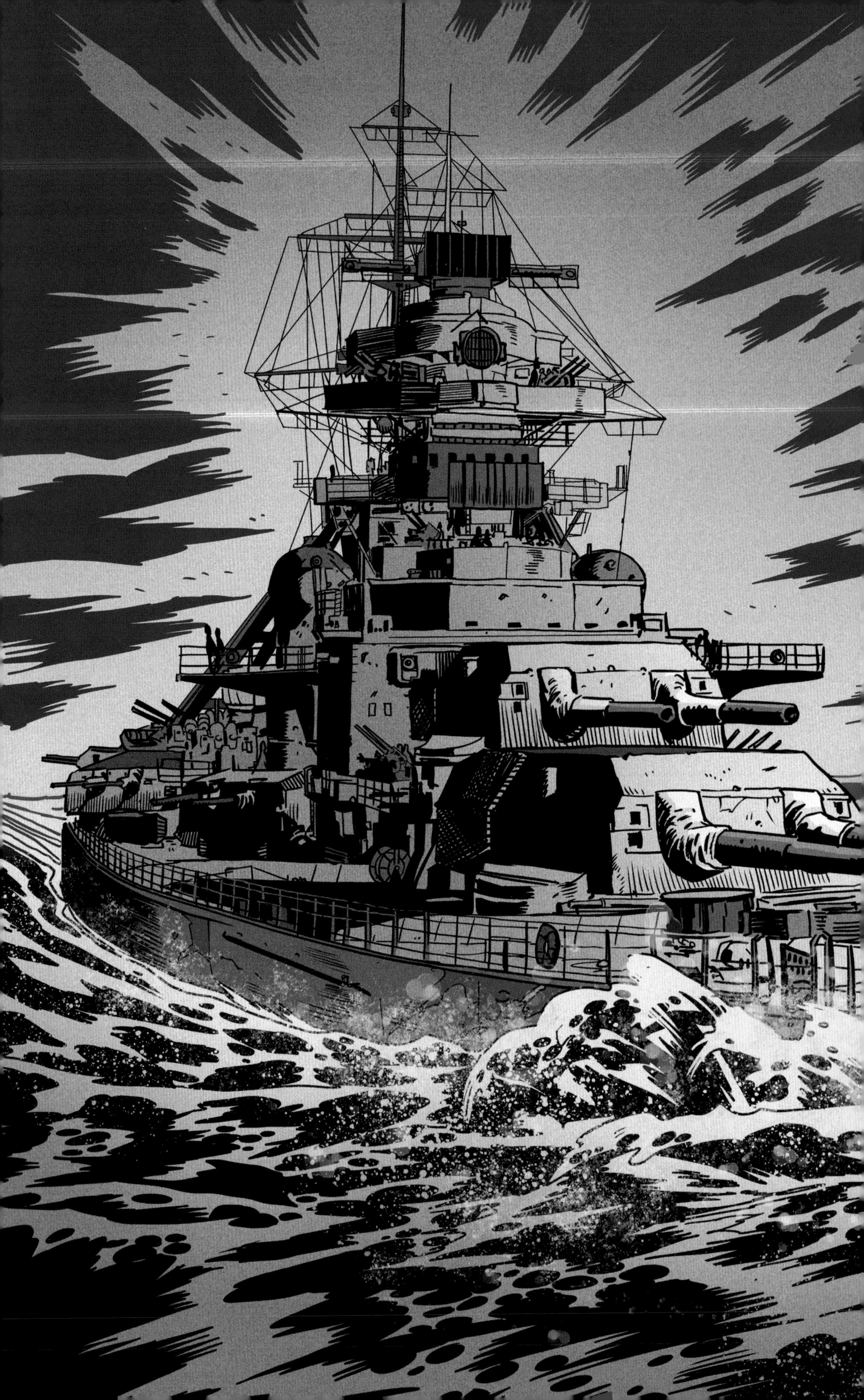

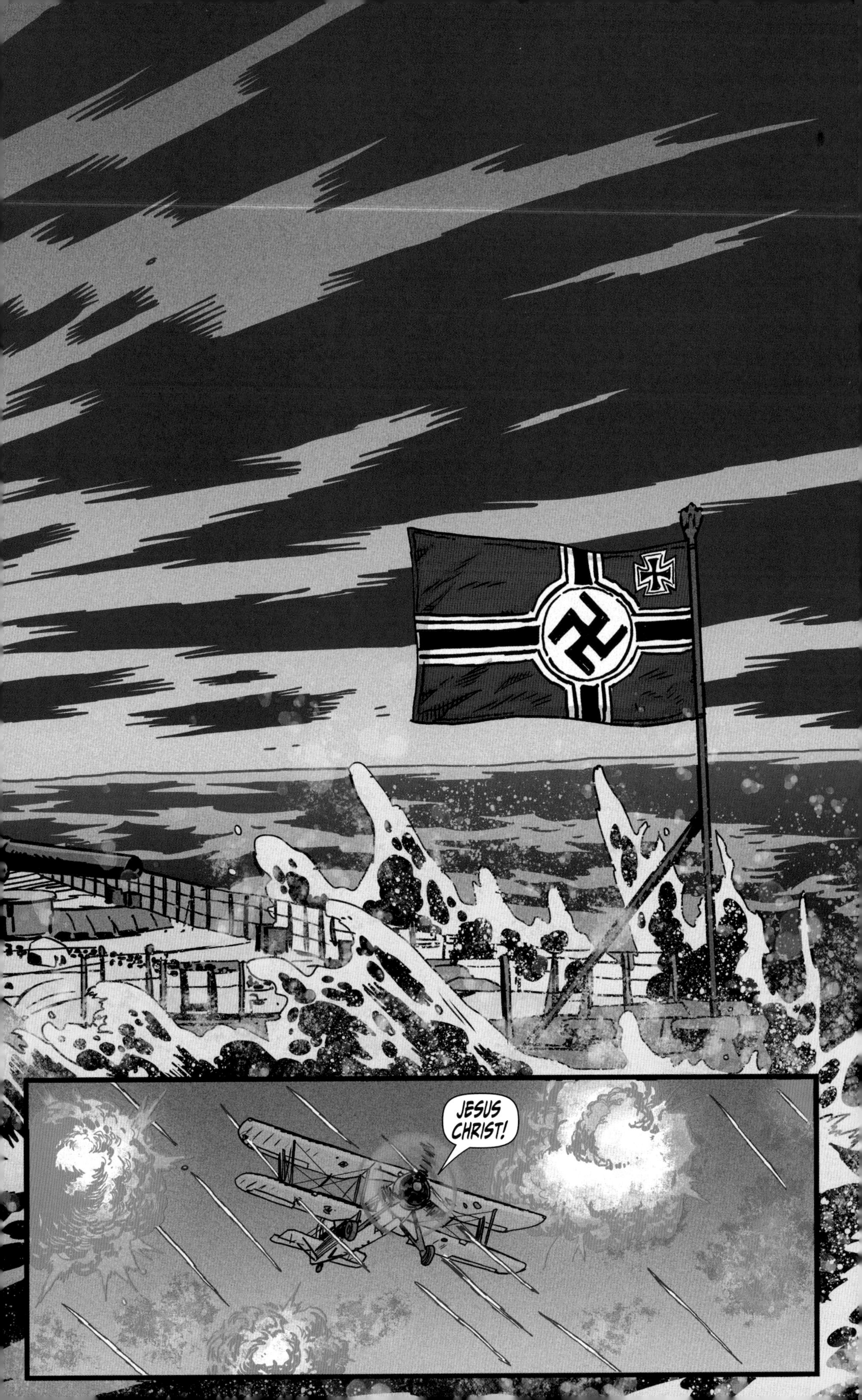
JESUS CHRIST!

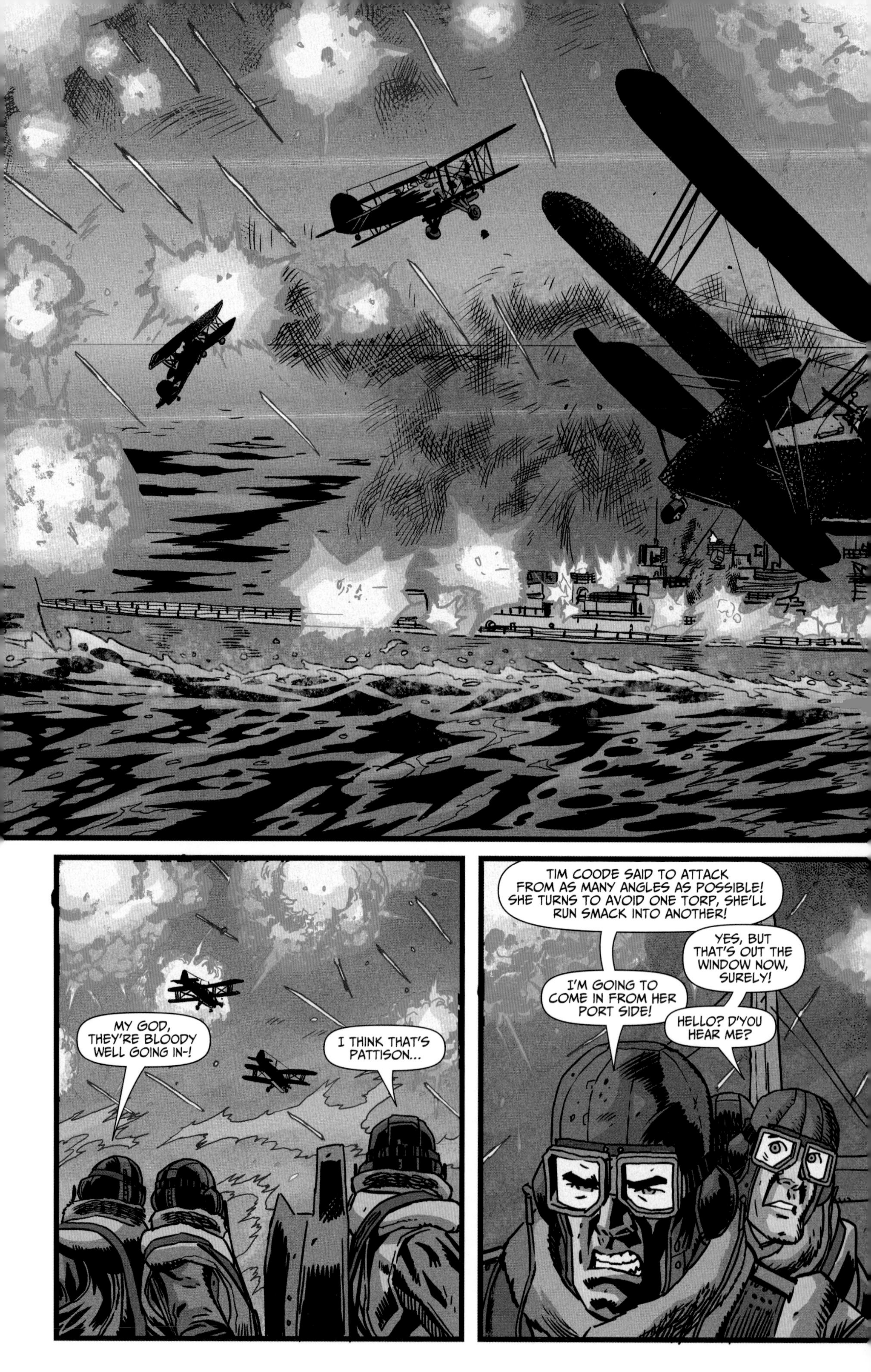
MY GOD, THEY'RE BLOODY WELL GOING IN-!
I THINK THAT'S PATTISON...
TIM COODE SAID TO ATTACK FROM AS MANY ANGLES AS POSSIBLE! SHE TURNS TO AVOID ONE TORP, SHE'LL RUN SMACK INTO ANOTHER!
YES, BUT THAT'S OUT THE WINDOW NOW, SURELY!
I'M GOING TO COME IN FROM HER PORT SIDE!
HELLO? D'YOU HEAR ME?

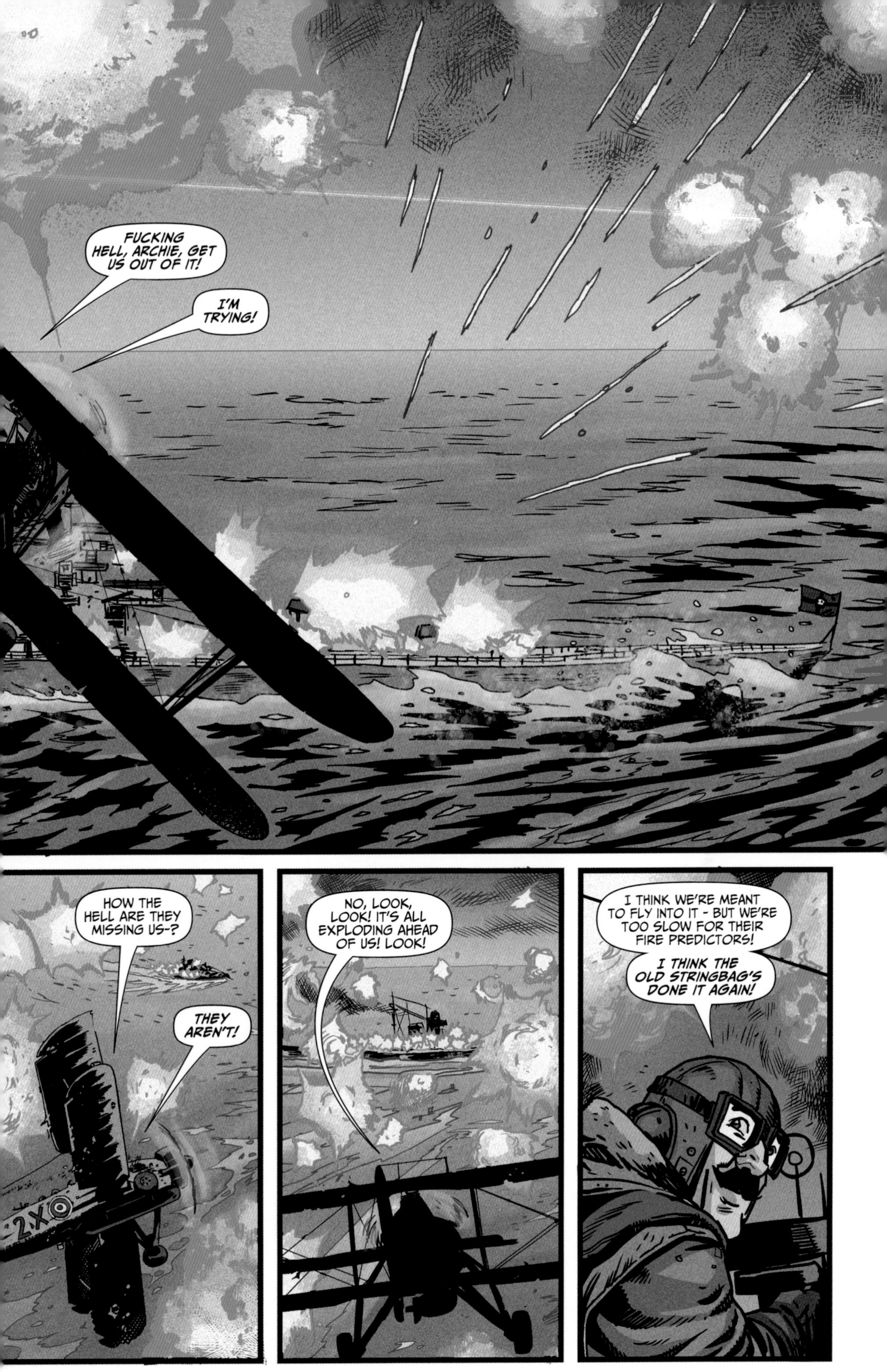
FUCKING HELL, ARCHIE, GET US OUT OF IT!
I'M TRYING!
HOW THE HELL ARE THEY MISSING US-?
THEY AREN'T!
NO, LOOK, LOOK! IT'S ALL EXPLODING AHEAD OF US! LOOK!
I THINK WE'RE MEANT TO FLY INTO IT - BUT WE'RE TOO SLOW FOR THEIR FIRE PREDICTORS!
I THINK THE OLD STRINGBAG'S DONE IT AGAIN!

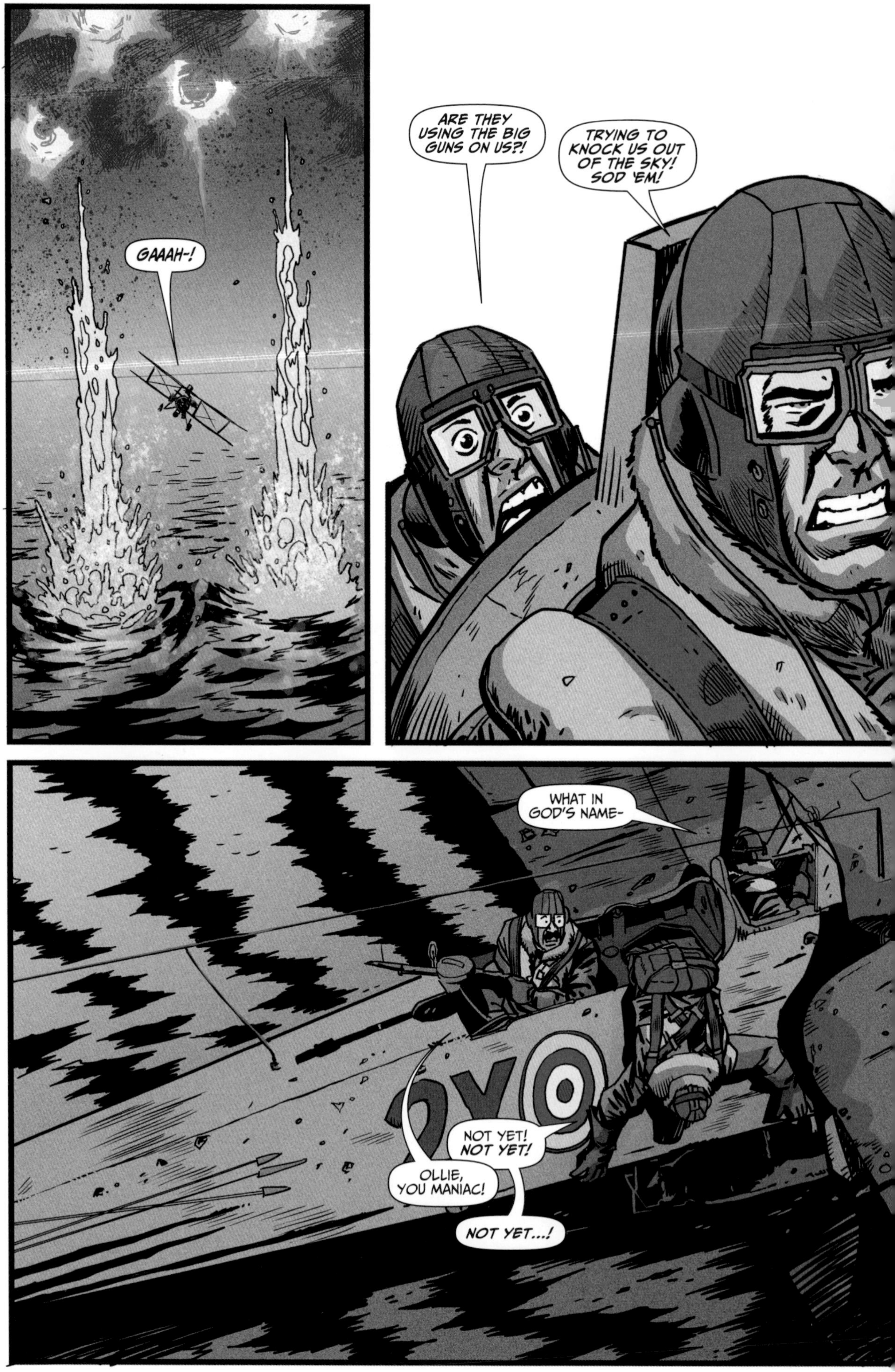
GAAAH-!
ARE THEY USING THE BIG GUNS ON US?!
TRYING TO KNOCK US OUT OF THE SKY! SOD 'EM!
WHAT IN GOD'S NAME-
NOT YET! NOT YET!
OLLIE, YOU MANIAC!
NOT YET...!

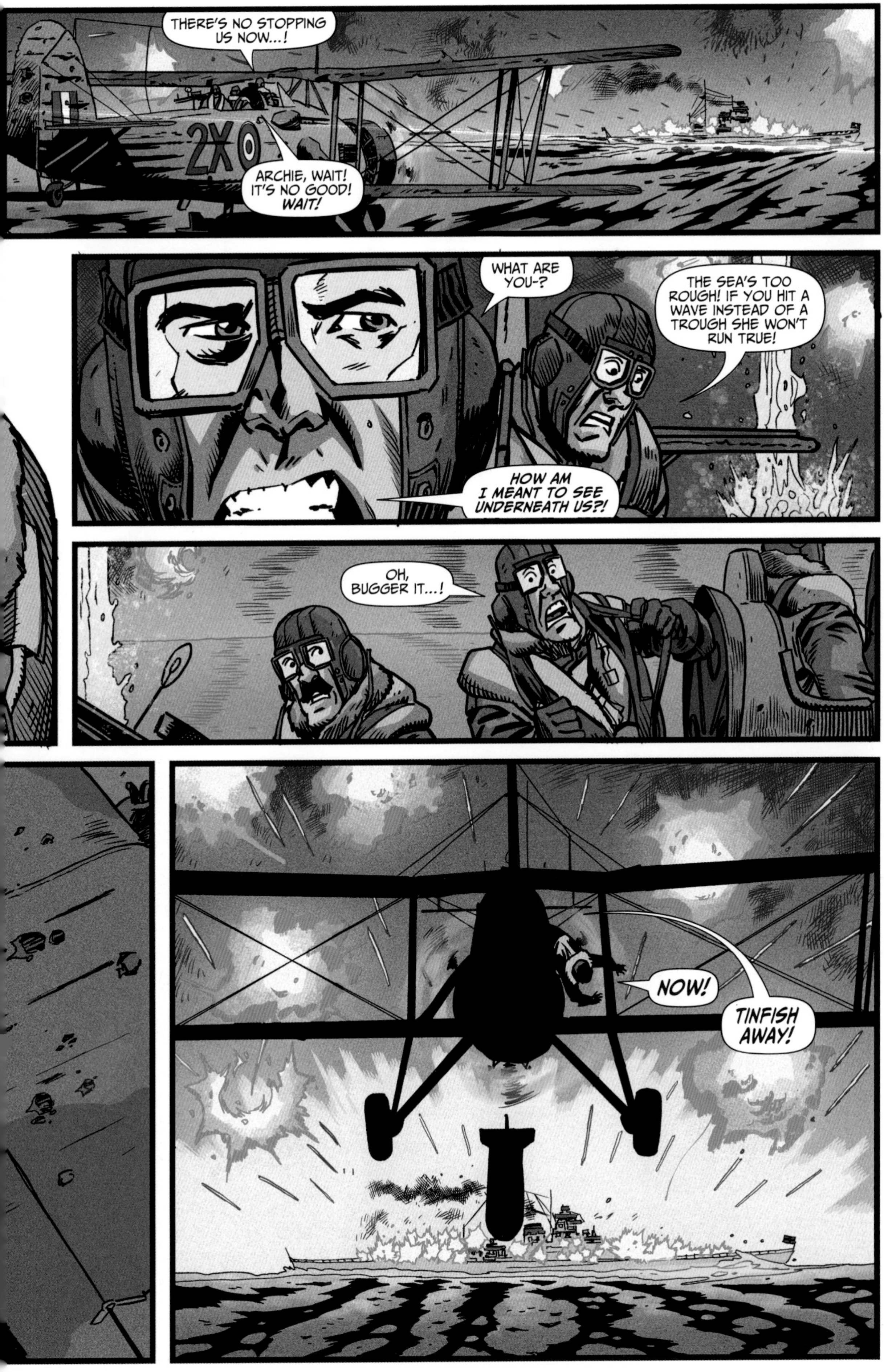
THERE'S NO STOPPING US NOW...!
ARCHIE, WAIT! IT'S NO GOOD! WAIT!
WHAT ARE YOU-?
THE SEA'S TOO ROUGH! IF YOU HIT A WAVE INSTEAD OF A TROUGH SHE WON'T RUN TRUE!
HOW AM I MEANT TO SEE UNDERNEATH US?!
OH, BUGGER IT...!
NOW!
TINFISH AWAY!

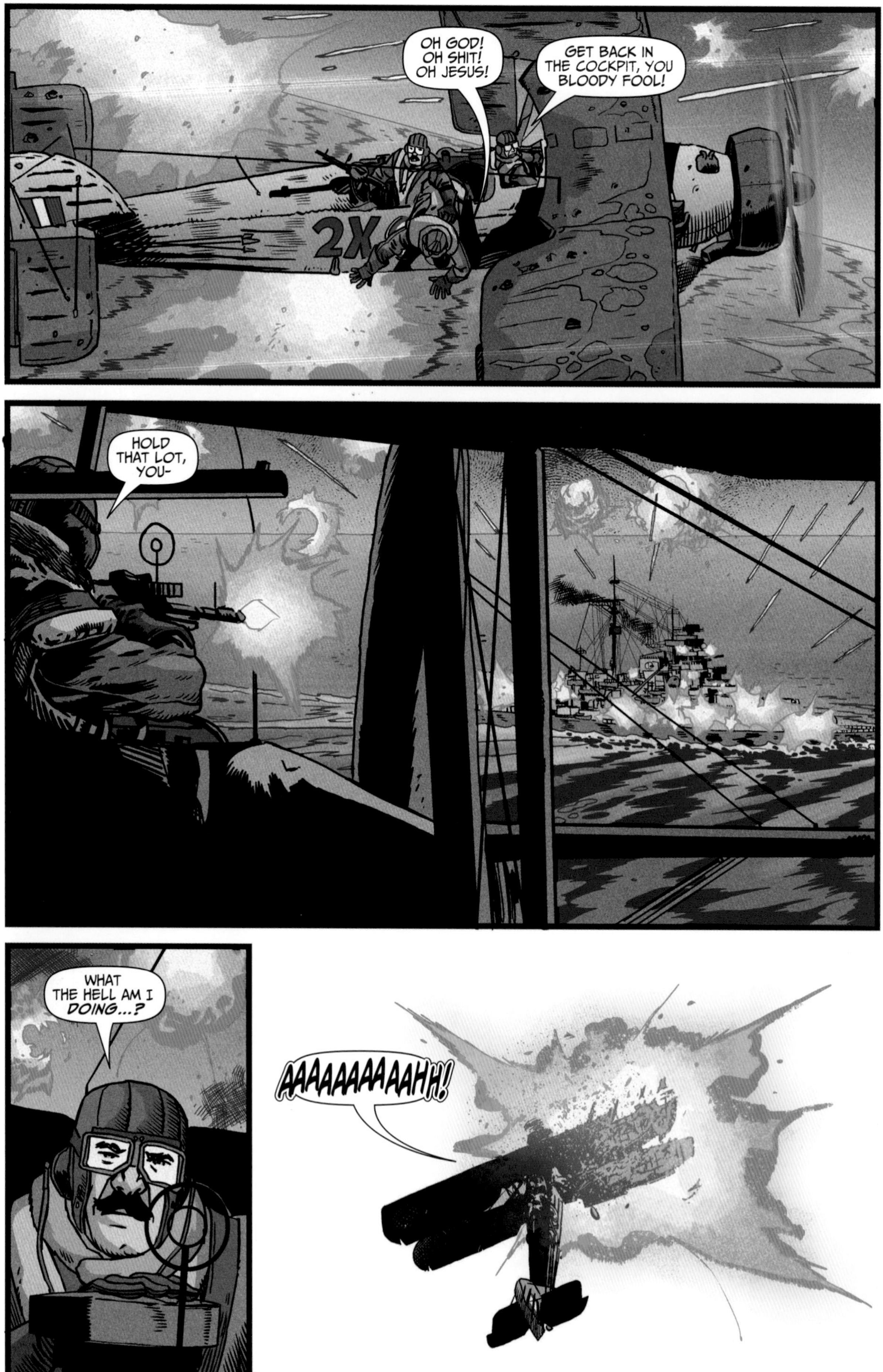
OH GOD! OH SHIT! OH JESUS!
GET BACK IN THE COCKPIT, YOU BLOODY FOOL!
2X
HOLD THAT LOT, YOU-
WHAT THE HELL AM I DOING...?
AAAAAAAAAAHH!

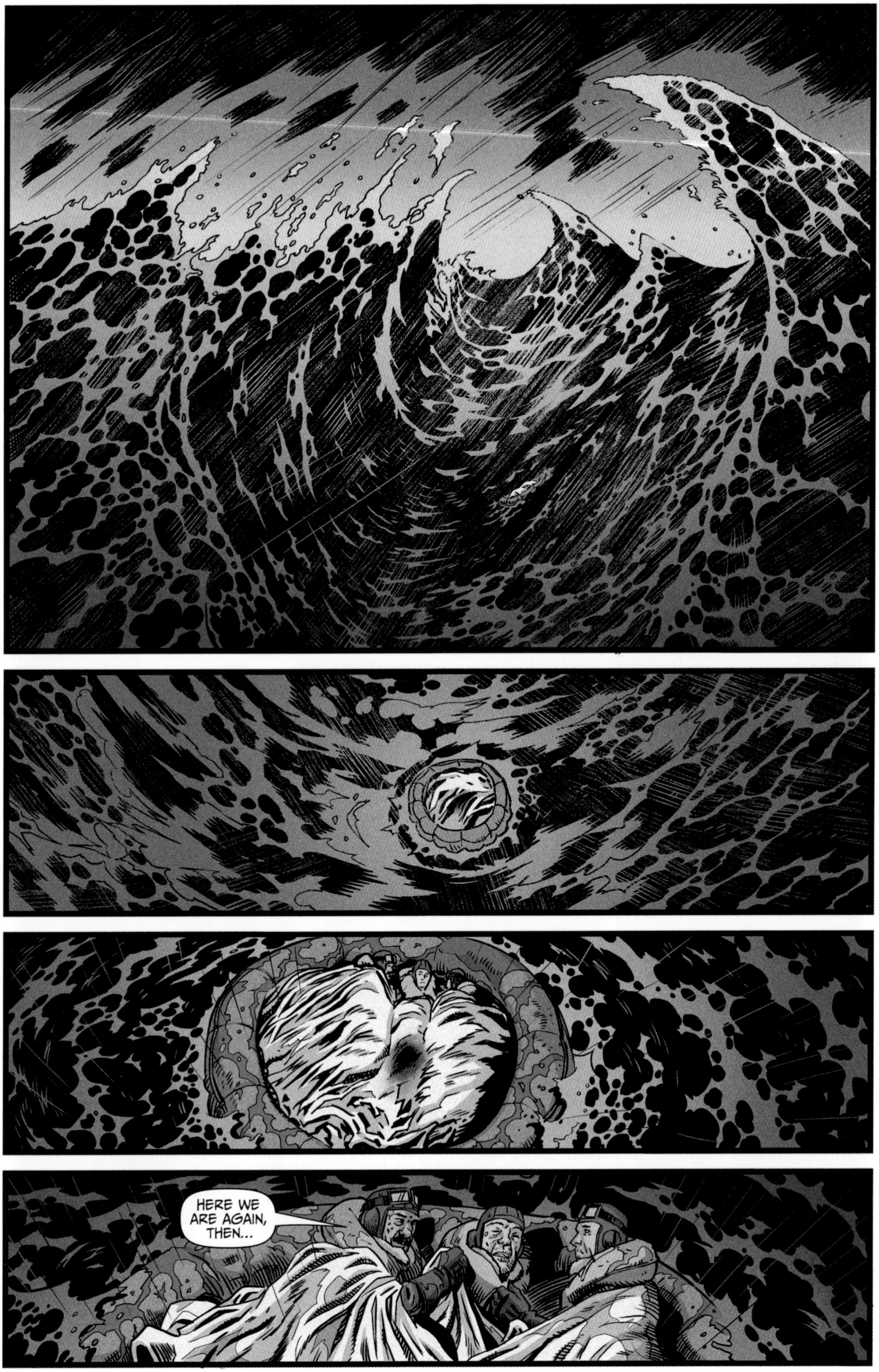
HERE WE ARE AGAIN, THEN...

YES, EXCEPT THE ATLANTIC'S NOT THE-BLOODY MED-

GOOD LANDING, MIND YOU.

I SEEM TO BE GETTING PLENTY OF PRACTICE.

HOW IS HE?

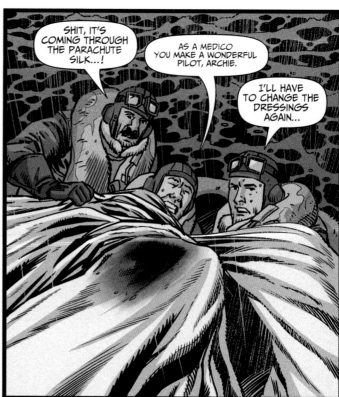

SHIT, IT'S COMING THROUGH THE PARACHUTE SILK...!

AS A MEDICO YOU MAKE A WONDERFUL PILOT, ARCHIE.

I'LL HAVE TO CHANGE THE DRESSINGS AGAIN...

DRESSINGS ARE ALL SOAKED ANYWAY. JUST LEAVE IT, IT HURTS TOO MUCH.

DID WE AT LEAST *HIT* THE BASTARD THING...?

I DON'T KNOW, I DIDN'T SEE.

ONE OF THE OTHERS MIGHT HAVE SCORED.

PROBABLY JUST BOUNCED OFF, LIKE THE ONES THE BOYS FROM VICTORIOUS DROPPED.

AND ON THE SUBJECT OF LOUSY ODDS...

THEY'RE BOUND TO BE OUT LOOKING FOR US. WE'VE STILL GOT A FEW MORE HOURS OF DAYLIGHT.

YOU THINK WE'LL LAST THAT LONG?

110

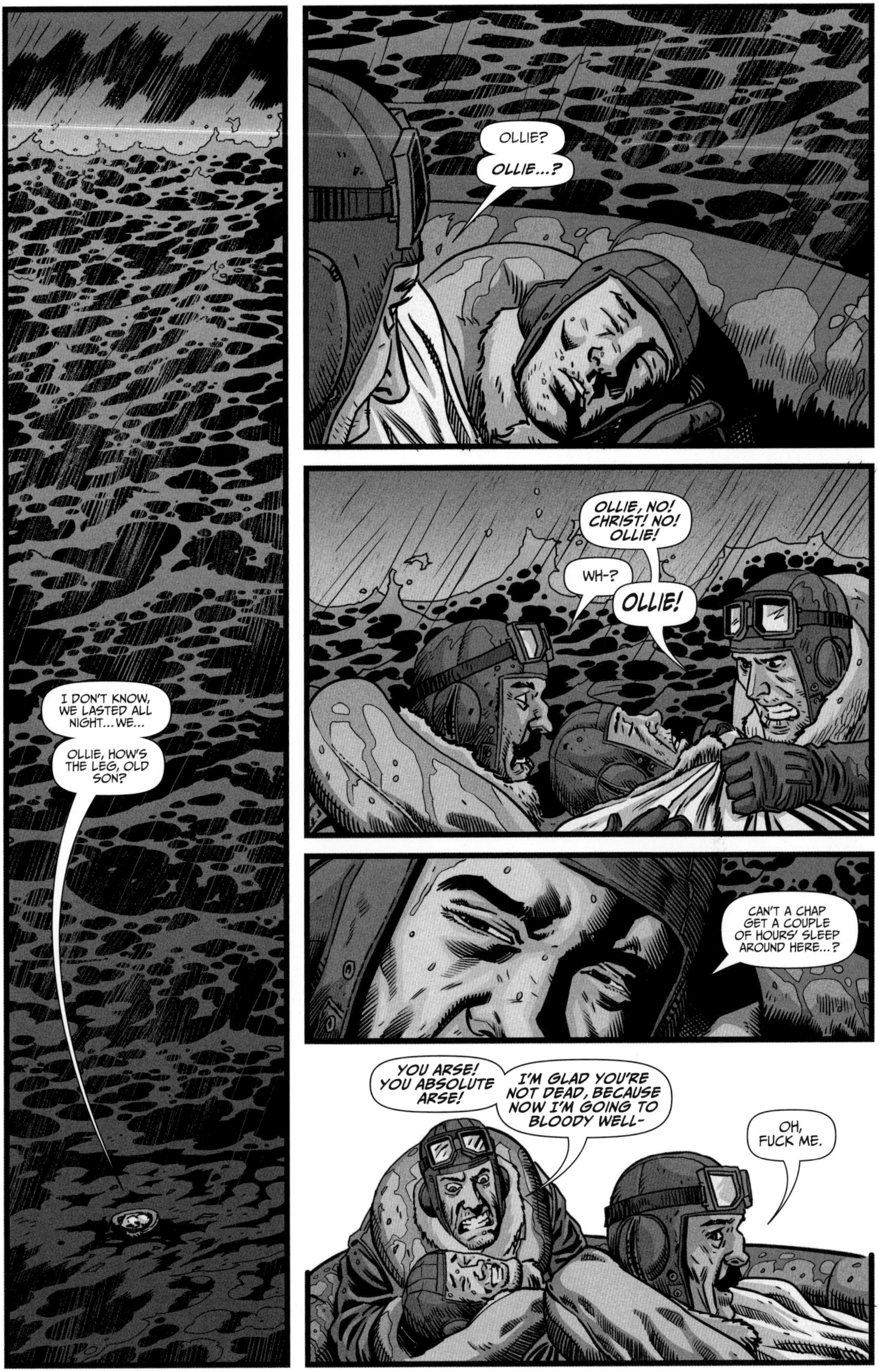
I DON'T KNOW, WE LASTED ALL NIGHT... WE...
OLLIE, HOW'S THE LEG, OLD SON?
OLLIE?
OLLIE...?
OLLIE, NO! CHRIST! NO! OLLIE!
WH-?
OLLIE!
CAN'T A CHAP GET A COUPLE OF HOURS' SLEEP AROUND HERE...?
YOU ARSE! YOU ABSOLUTE ARSE!
I'M GLAD YOU'RE NOT DEAD, BECAUSE NOW I'M GOING TO BLOODY WELL-
OH, FUCK ME.

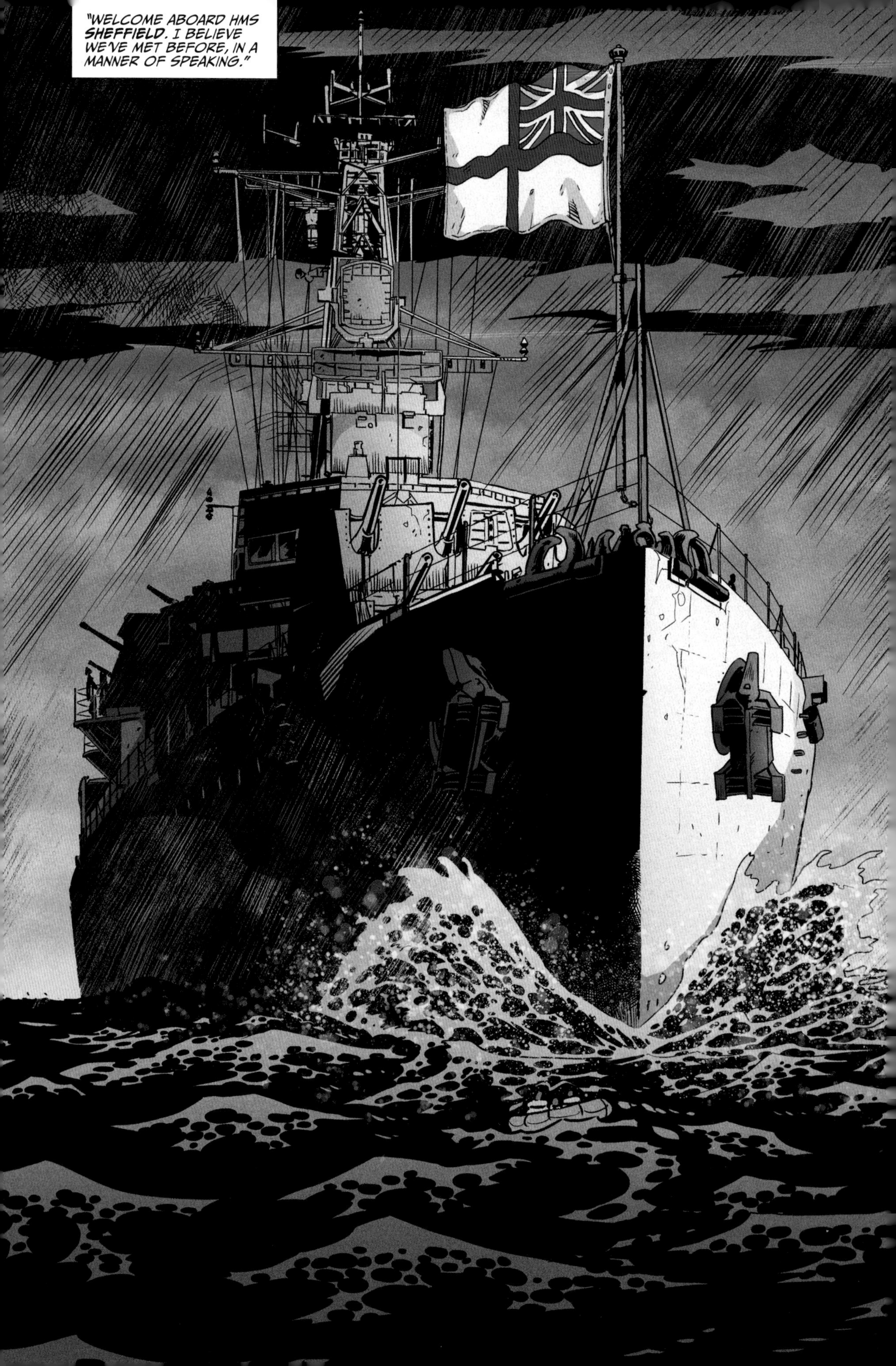
"WELCOME ABOARD HMS **SHEFFIELD**. I BELIEVE WE'VE MET BEFORE, IN A MANNER OF SPEAKING."

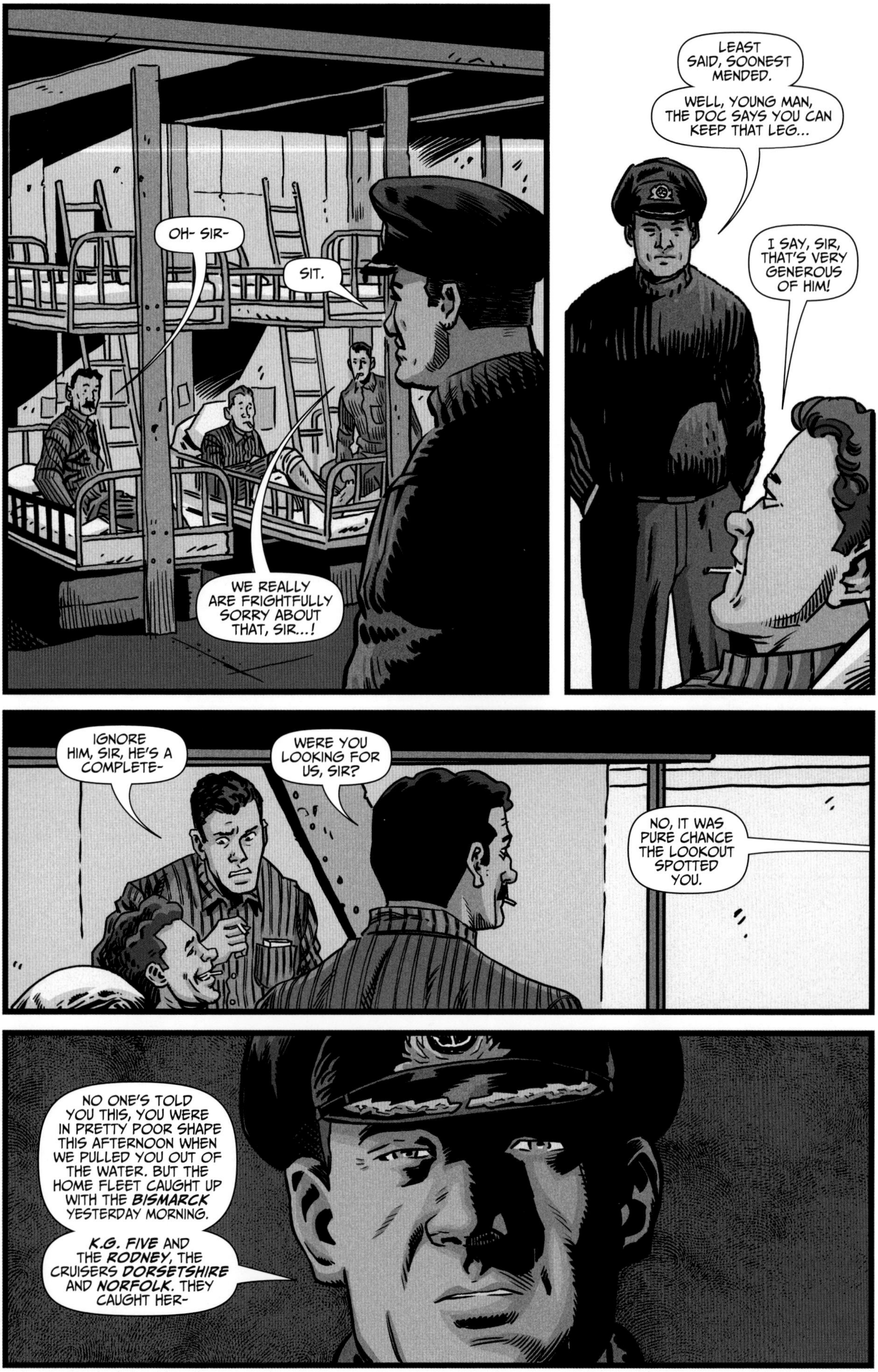
OH- SIR-
SIT.
WE REALLY ARE FRIGHTFULLY SORRY ABOUT THAT, SIR...!
LEAST SAID, SOONEST MENDED.
WELL, YOUNG MAN, THE DOC SAYS YOU CAN KEEP THAT LEG...
I SAY, SIR, THAT'S VERY GENEROUS OF HIM!
IGNORE HIM, SIR, HE'S A COMPLETE-
WERE YOU LOOKING FOR US, SIR?
NO, IT WAS PURE CHANCE THE LOOKOUT SPOTTED YOU.
NO ONE'S TOLD YOU THIS, YOU WERE IN PRETTY POOR SHAPE THIS AFTERNOON WHEN WE PULLED YOU OUT OF THE WATER. BUT THE HOME FLEET CAUGHT UP WITH THE *BISMARCK* YESTERDAY MORNING.
K.G. FIVE AND THE *RODNEY*, THE CRUISERS *DORSETSHIRE* AND *NORFOLK*. THEY CAUGHT HER-

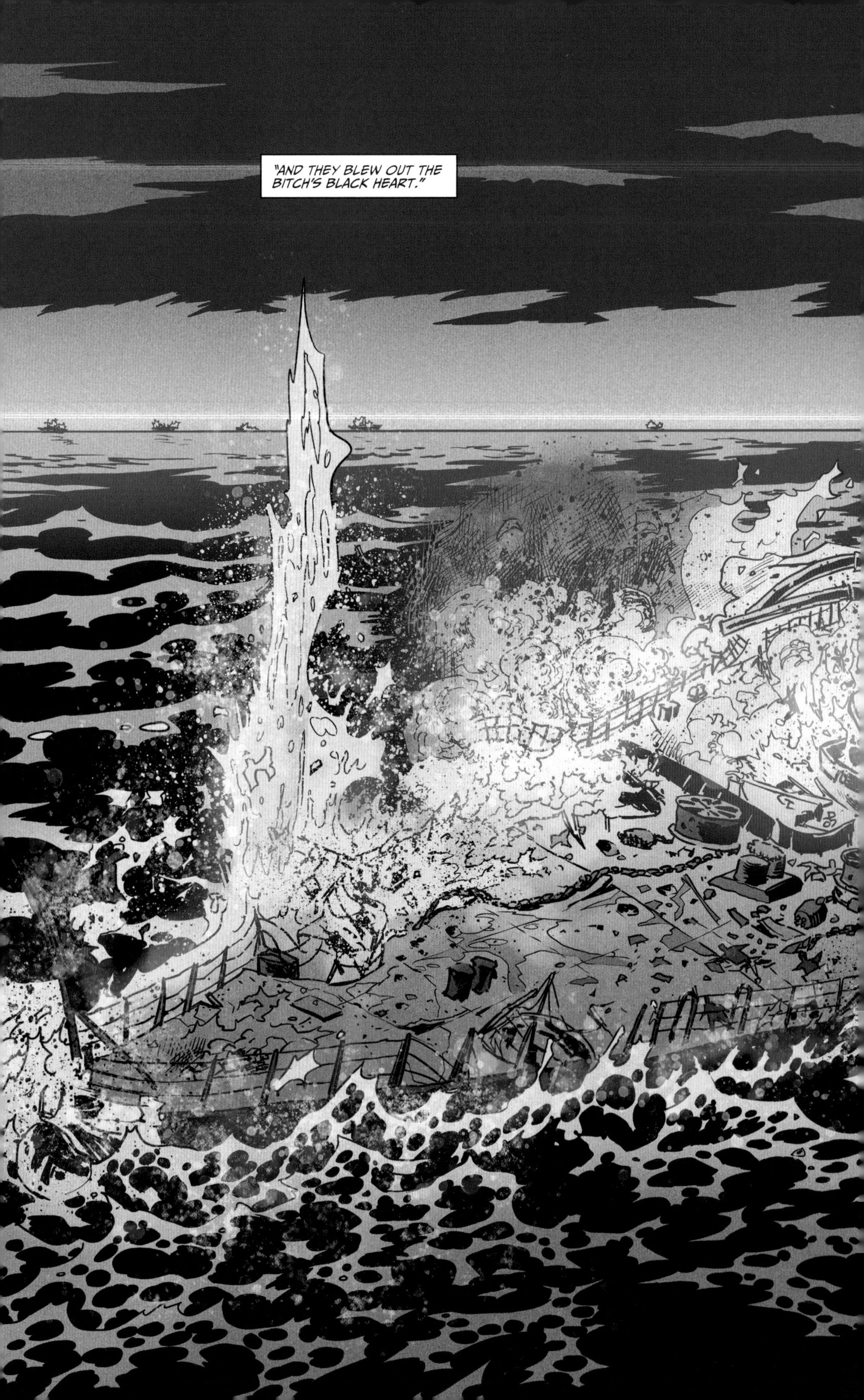
"AND THEY BLEW OUT THE BITCH'S BLACK HEART."

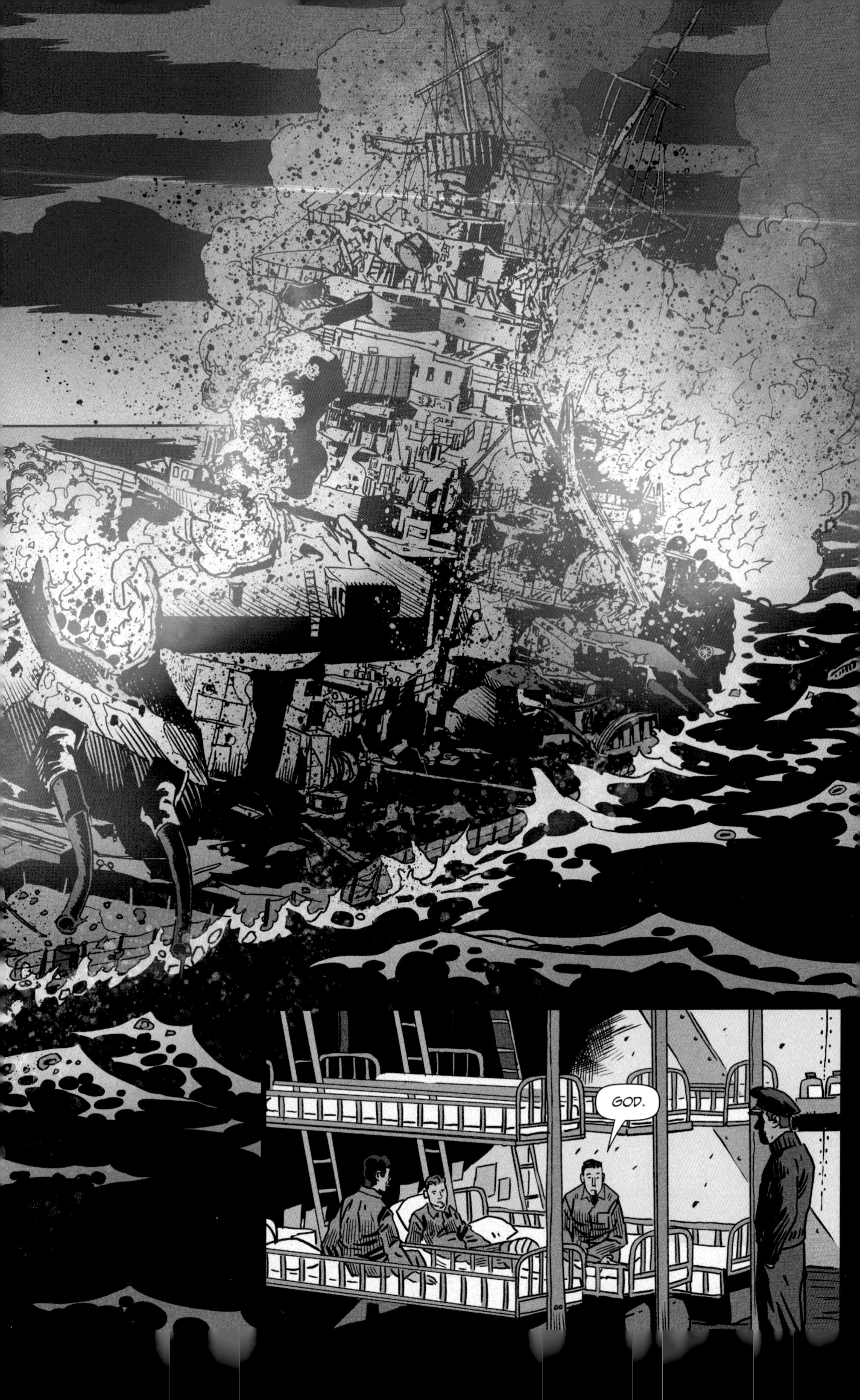
GOD.

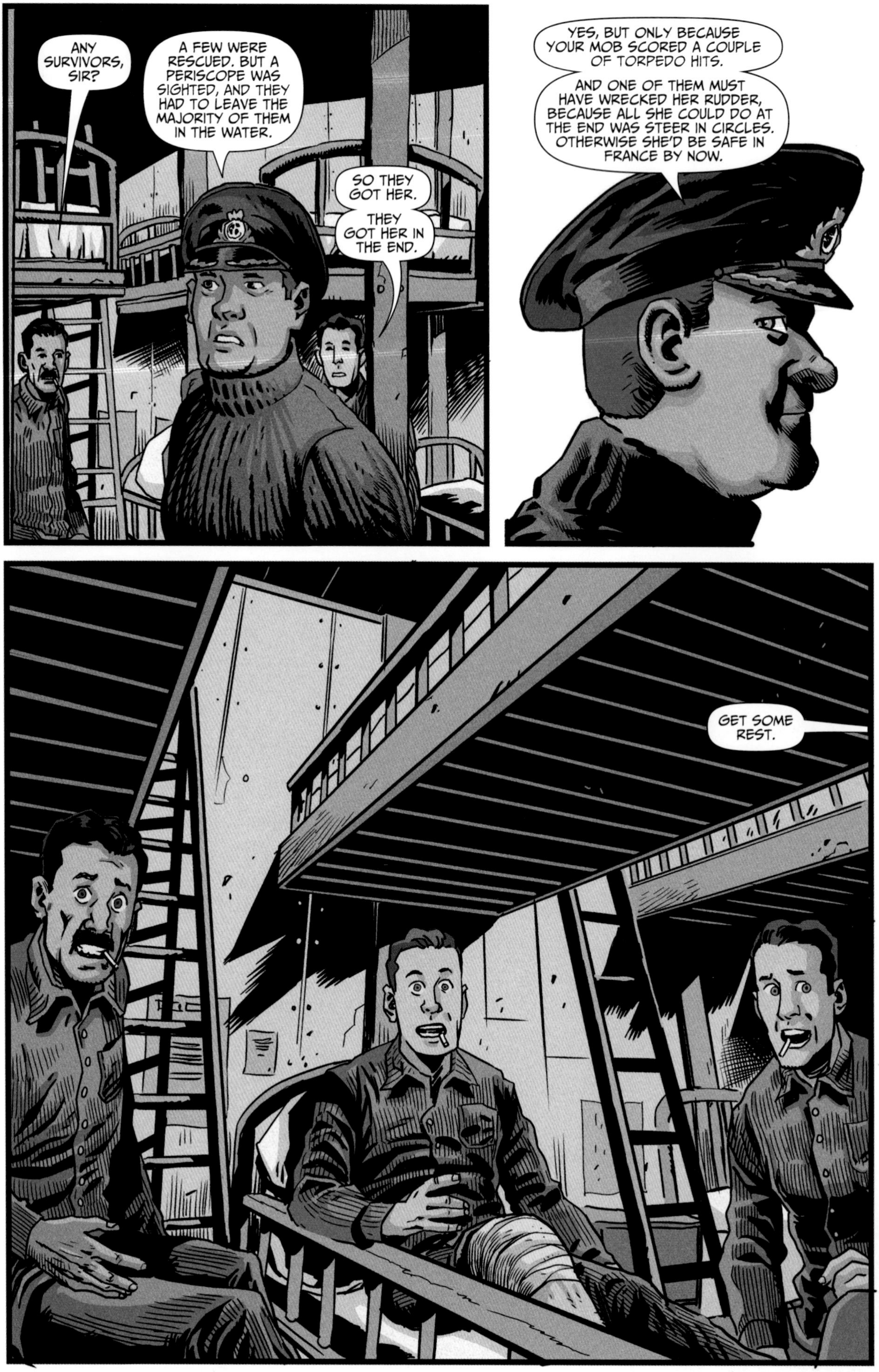
ANY SURVIVORS, SIR?
A FEW WERE RESCUED. BUT A PERISCOPE WAS SIGHTED, AND THEY HAD TO LEAVE THE MAJORITY OF THEM IN THE WATER.
SO THEY GOT HER.
THEY GOT HER IN THE END.
YES, BUT ONLY BECAUSE YOUR MOB SCORED A COUPLE OF TORPEDO HITS.
AND ONE OF THEM MUST HAVE WRECKED HER RUDDER, BECAUSE ALL SHE COULD DO AT THE END WAS STEER IN CIRCLES. OTHERWISE SHE'D BE SAFE IN FRANCE BY NOW.
GET SOME REST.

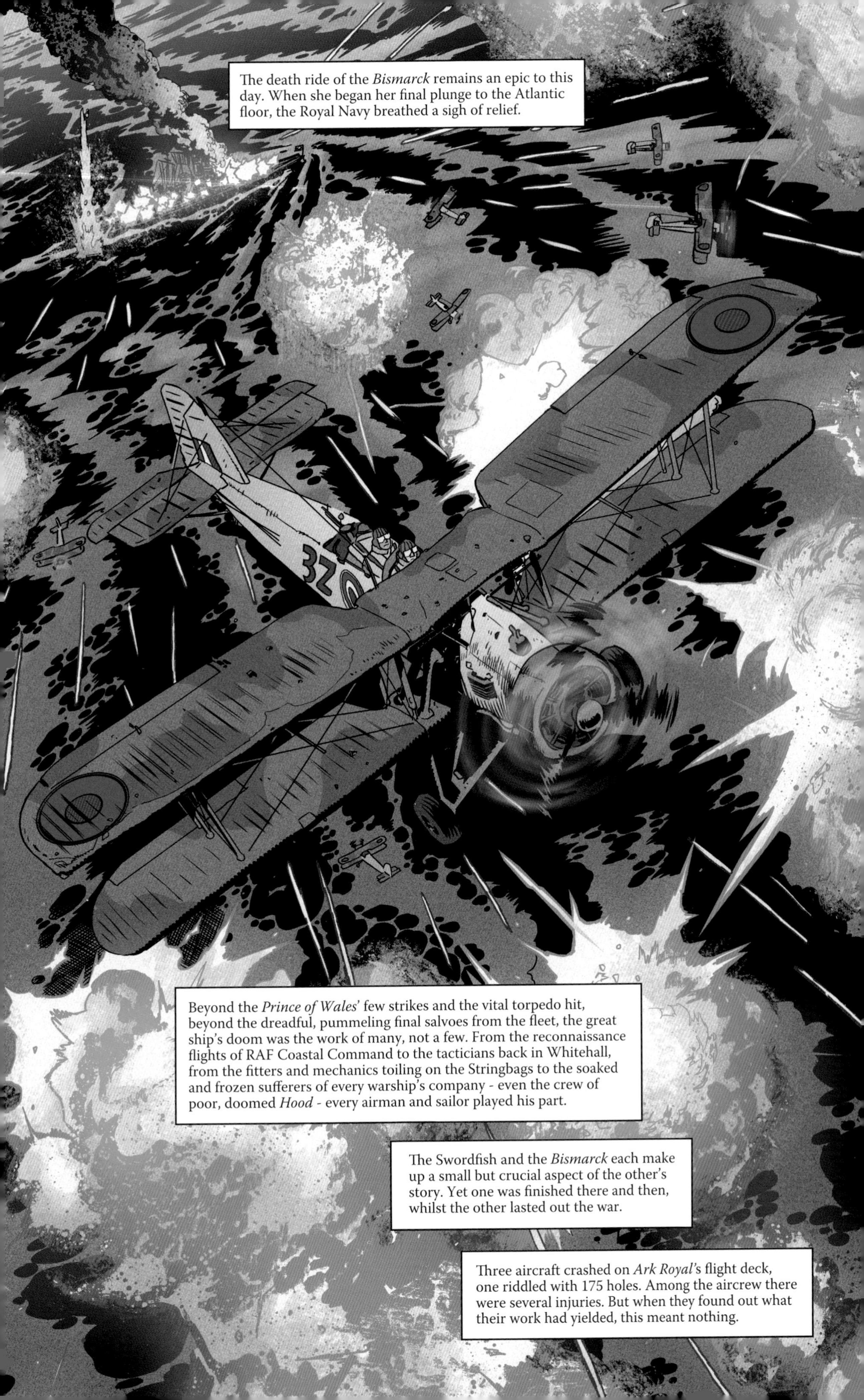
The death ride of the *Bismarck* remains an epic to this day. When she began her final plunge to the Atlantic floor, the Royal Navy breathed a sigh of relief.
3Z
Beyond the *Prince of Wales'* few strikes and the vital torpedo hit, beyond the dreadful, pummeling final salvoes from the fleet, the great ship's doom was the work of many, not a few. From the reconnaissance flights of RAF Coastal Command to the tacticians back in Whitehall, from the fitters and mechanics toiling on the Stringbags to the soaked and frozen sufferers of every warship's company - even the crew of poor, doomed *Hood* - every airman and sailor played his part.
The Swordfish and the *Bismarck* each make up a small but crucial aspect of the other's story. Yet one was finished there and then, whilst the other lasted out the war.
Three aircraft crashed on *Ark Royal*'s flight deck, one riddled with 175 holes. Among the aircrew there were several injuries. But when they found out what their work had yielded, this meant nothing.

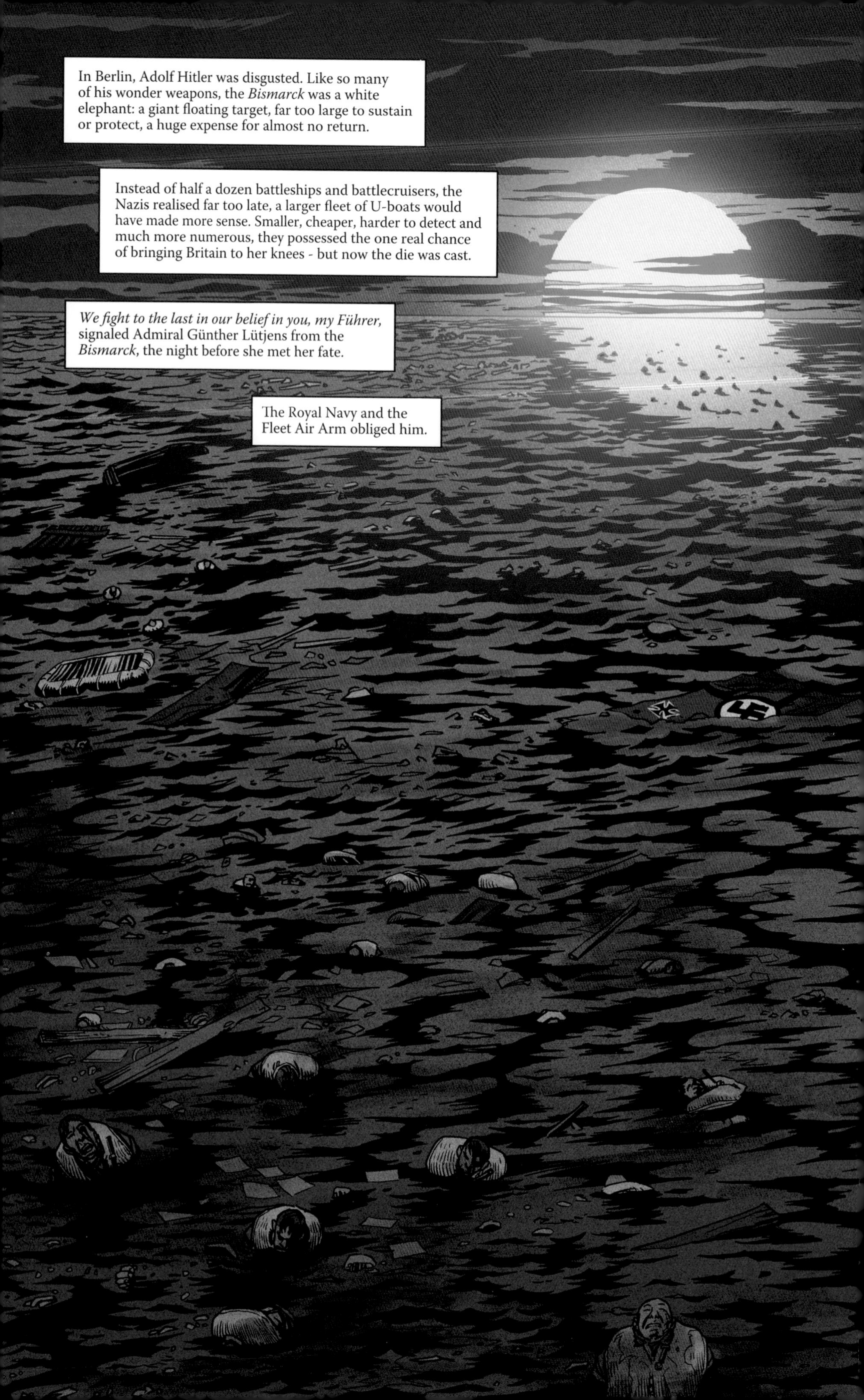
In Berlin, Adolf Hitler was disgusted. Like so many of his wonder weapons, the *Bismarck* was a white elephant: a giant floating target, far too large to sustain or protect, a huge expense for almost no return.
Instead of half a dozen battleships and battlecruisers, the Nazis realised far too late, a larger fleet of U-boats would have made more sense. Smaller, cheaper, harder to detect and much more numerous, they possessed the one real chance of bringing Britain to her knees - but now the die was cast.
We fight to the last in our belief in you, my Führer, signaled Admiral Günther Lütjens from the *Bismarck*, the night before she met her fate.
The Royal Navy and the Fleet Air Arm obliged him.

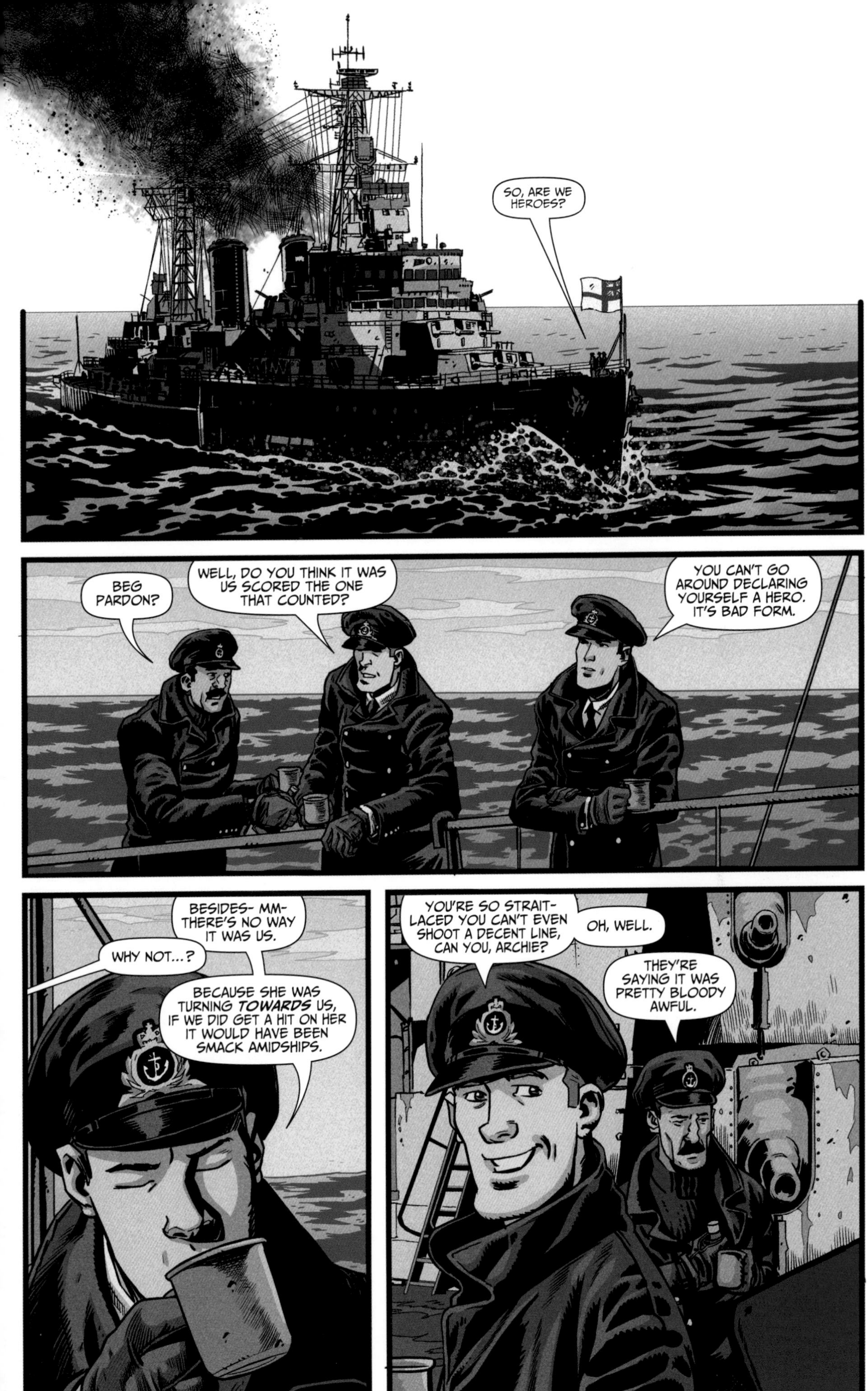
SO, ARE WE HEROES?
BEG PARDON?
WELL, DO YOU THINK IT WAS US SCORED THE ONE THAT COUNTED?
YOU CAN'T GO AROUND DECLARING YOURSELF A HERO. IT'S BAD FORM.
BESIDES- MM- THERE'S NO WAY IT WAS US.
WHY NOT...?
BECAUSE SHE WAS TURNING TOWARDS US, IF WE DID GET A HIT ON HER IT WOULD HAVE BEEN SMACK AMIDSHIPS.
YOU'RE SO STRAIT-LACED YOU CAN'T EVEN SHOOT A DECENT LINE, CAN YOU, ARCHIE?
OH, WELL.
THEY'RE SAYING IT WAS PRETTY BLOODY AWFUL.

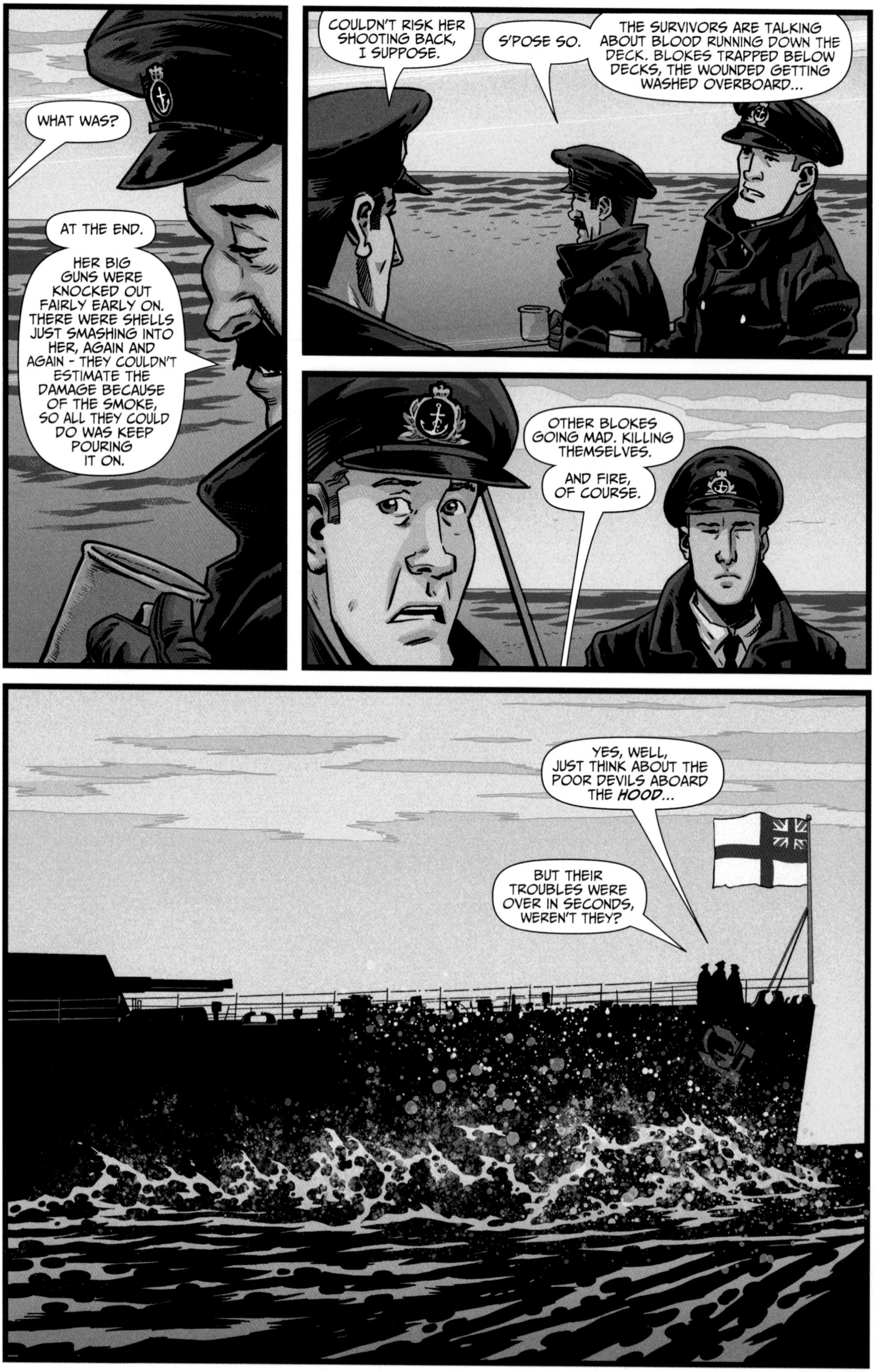
WHAT WAS?
AT THE END.
HER BIG GUNS WERE KNOCKED OUT FAIRLY EARLY ON. THERE WERE SHELLS JUST SMASHING INTO HER, AGAIN AND AGAIN - THEY COULDN'T ESTIMATE THE DAMAGE BECAUSE OF THE SMOKE, SO ALL THEY COULD DO WAS KEEP POURING IT ON.
COULDN'T RISK HER SHOOTING BACK, I SUPPOSE.
S'POSE SO.
THE SURVIVORS ARE TALKING ABOUT BLOOD RUNNING DOWN THE DECK. BLOKES TRAPPED BELOW DECKS, THE WOUNDED GETTING WASHED OVERBOARD...
OTHER BLOKES GOING MAD. KILLING THEMSELVES.
AND FIRE, OF COURSE.
YES, WELL, JUST THINK ABOUT THE POOR DEVILS ABOARD THE *HOOD*...
BUT THEIR TROUBLES WERE OVER IN SECONDS, WEREN'T THEY?

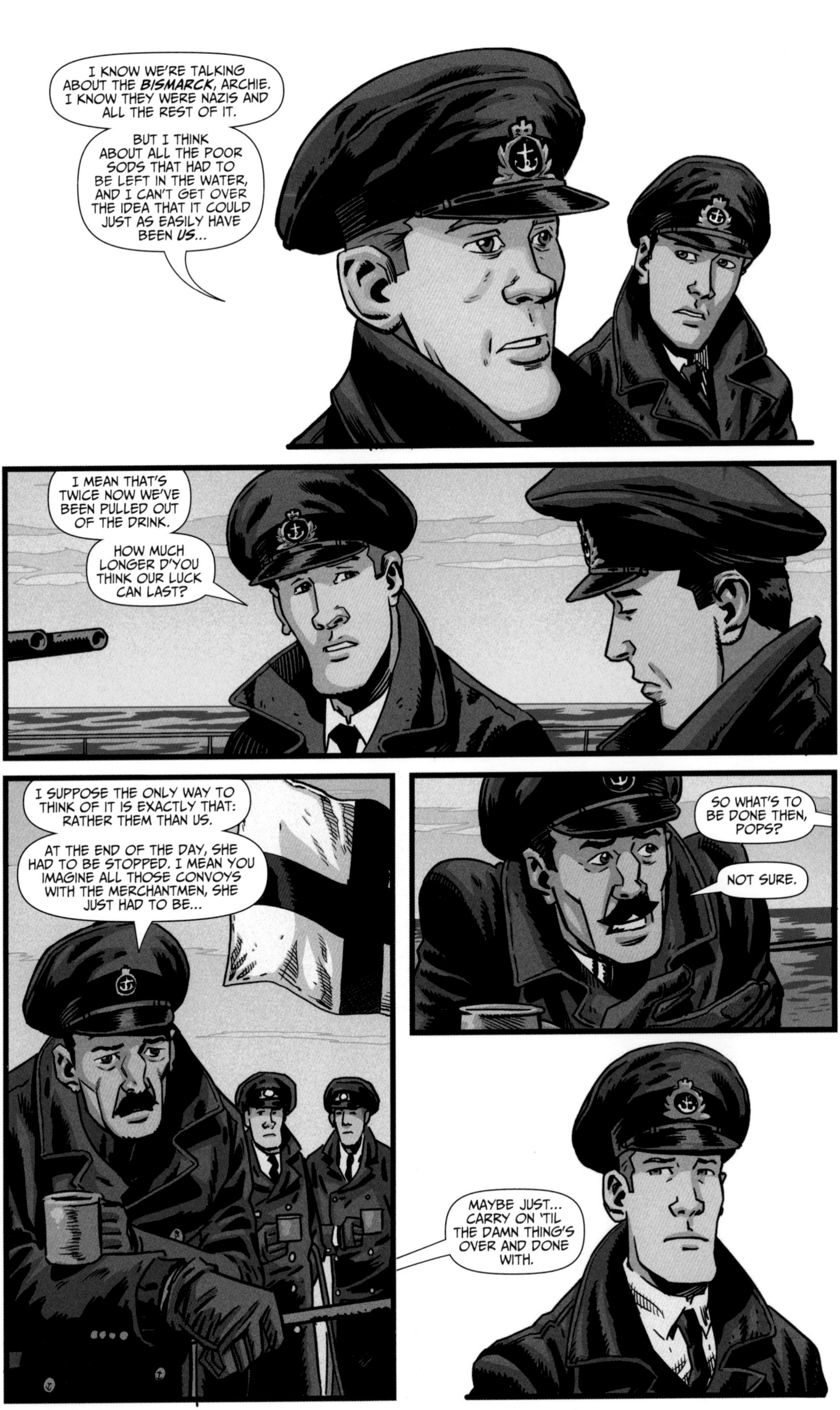
I KNOW WE'RE TALKING ABOUT THE BISMARCK, ARCHIE. I KNOW THEY WERE NAZIS AND ALL THE REST OF IT.
BUT I THINK ABOUT ALL THE POOR SODS THAT HAD TO BE LEFT IN THE WATER, AND I CAN'T GET OVER THE IDEA THAT IT COULD JUST AS EASILY HAVE BEEN US...
I MEAN THAT'S TWICE NOW WE'VE BEEN PULLED OUT OF THE DRINK.
HOW MUCH LONGER D'YOU THINK OUR LUCK CAN LAST?
I SUPPOSE THE ONLY WAY TO THINK OF IT IS EXACTLY THAT: RATHER THEM THAN US.
AT THE END OF THE DAY, SHE HAD TO BE STOPPED. I MEAN YOU IMAGINE ALL THOSE CONVOYS WITH THE MERCHANTMEN, SHE JUST HAD TO BE...
SO WHAT'S TO BE DONE THEN, POPS?
NOT SURE.
MAYBE JUST... CARRY ON 'TIL THE DAMN THING'S OVER AND DONE WITH.

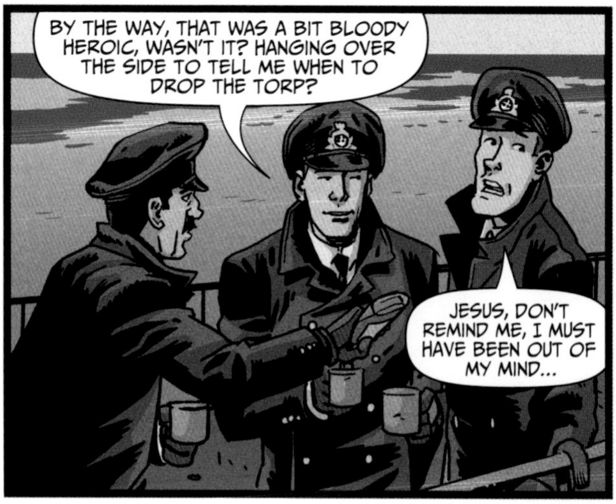
BY THE WAY, THAT WAS A BIT BLOODY HEROIC, WASN'T IT? HANGING OVER THE SIDE TO TELL ME WHEN TO DROP THE TORP?
JESUS, DON'T REMIND ME, I MUST HAVE BEEN OUT OF MY MIND...

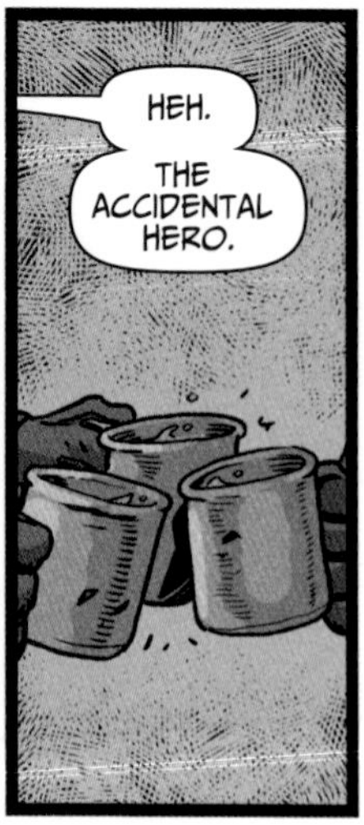
HEH.
THE ACCIDENTAL HERO.

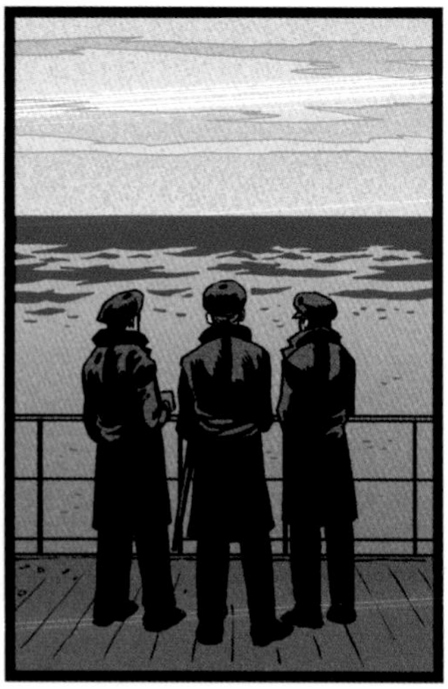

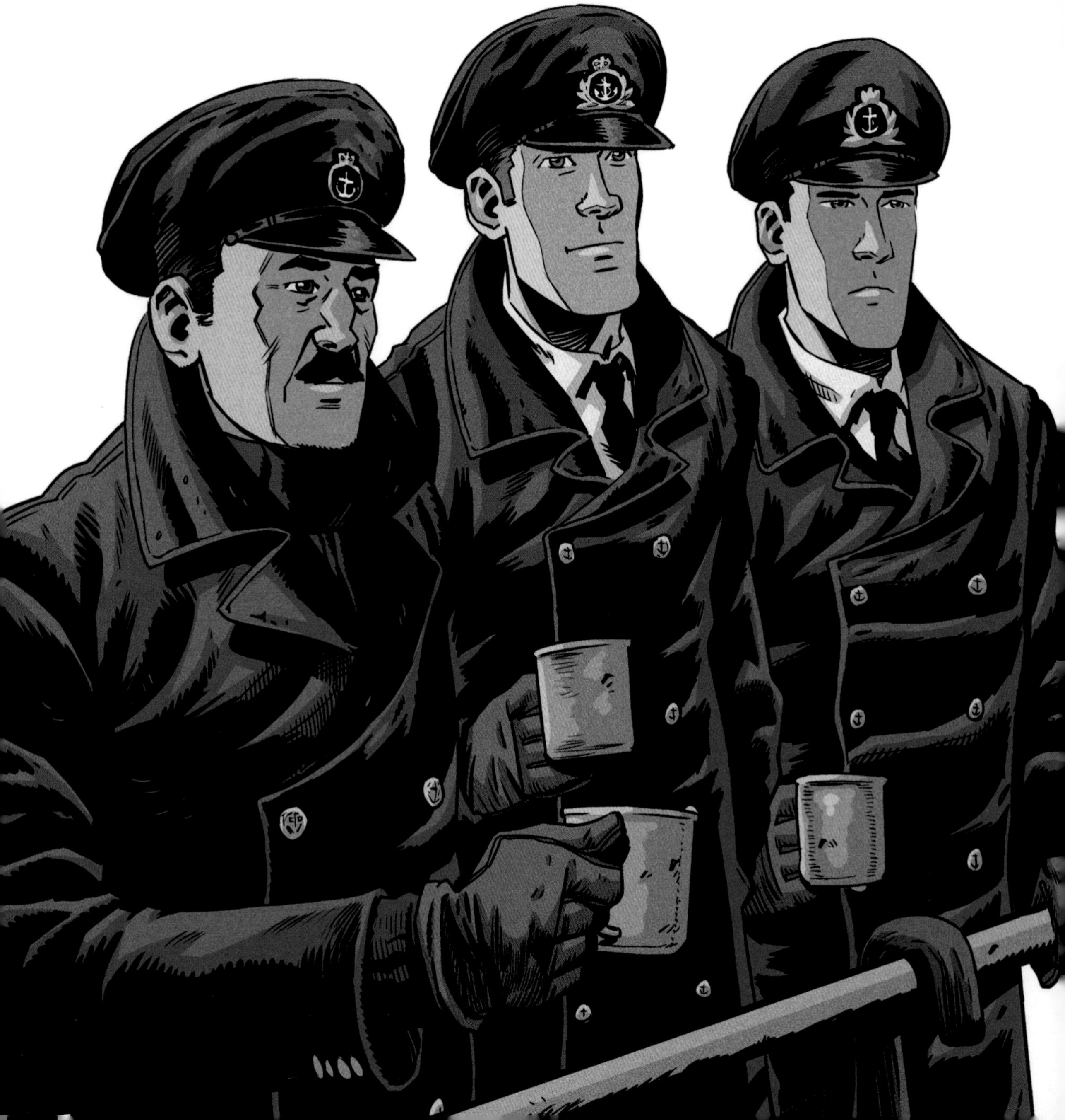

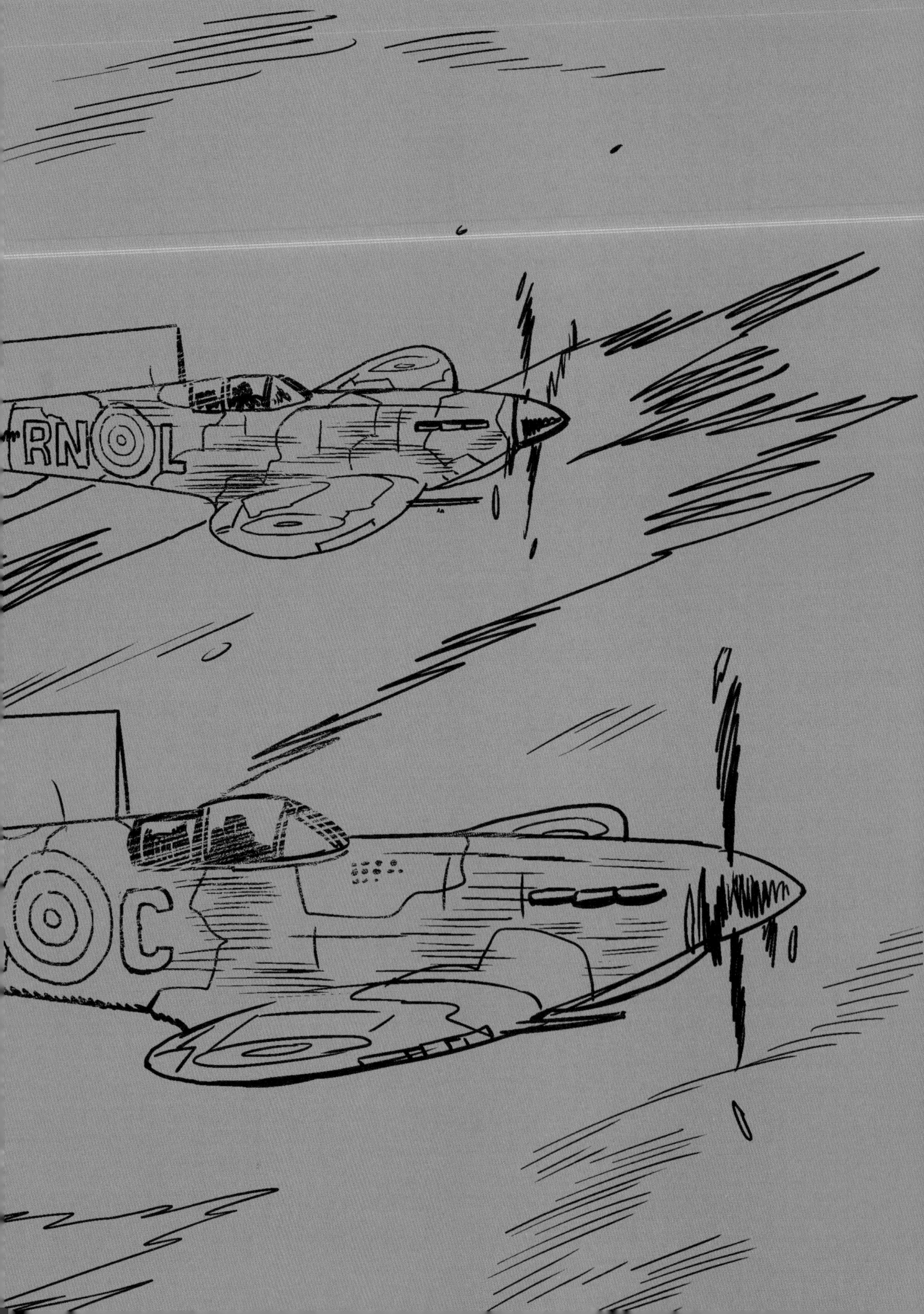
RN L
C

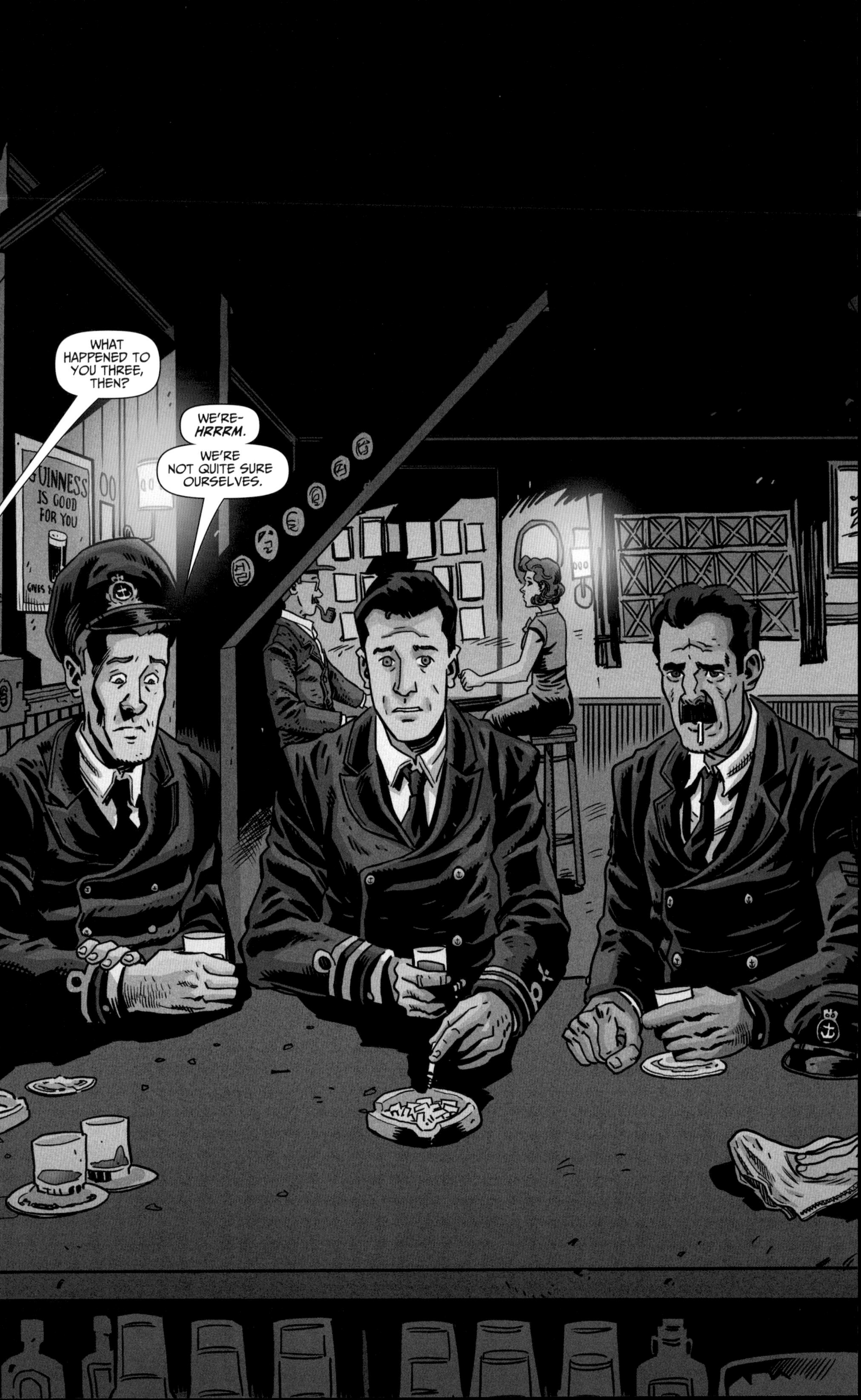
WHAT HAPPENED TO YOU THREE, THEN?
WE'RE- HRRRM.
WE'RE NOT QUITE SURE OURSELVES.
GUINNESS IS GOOD FOR YOU

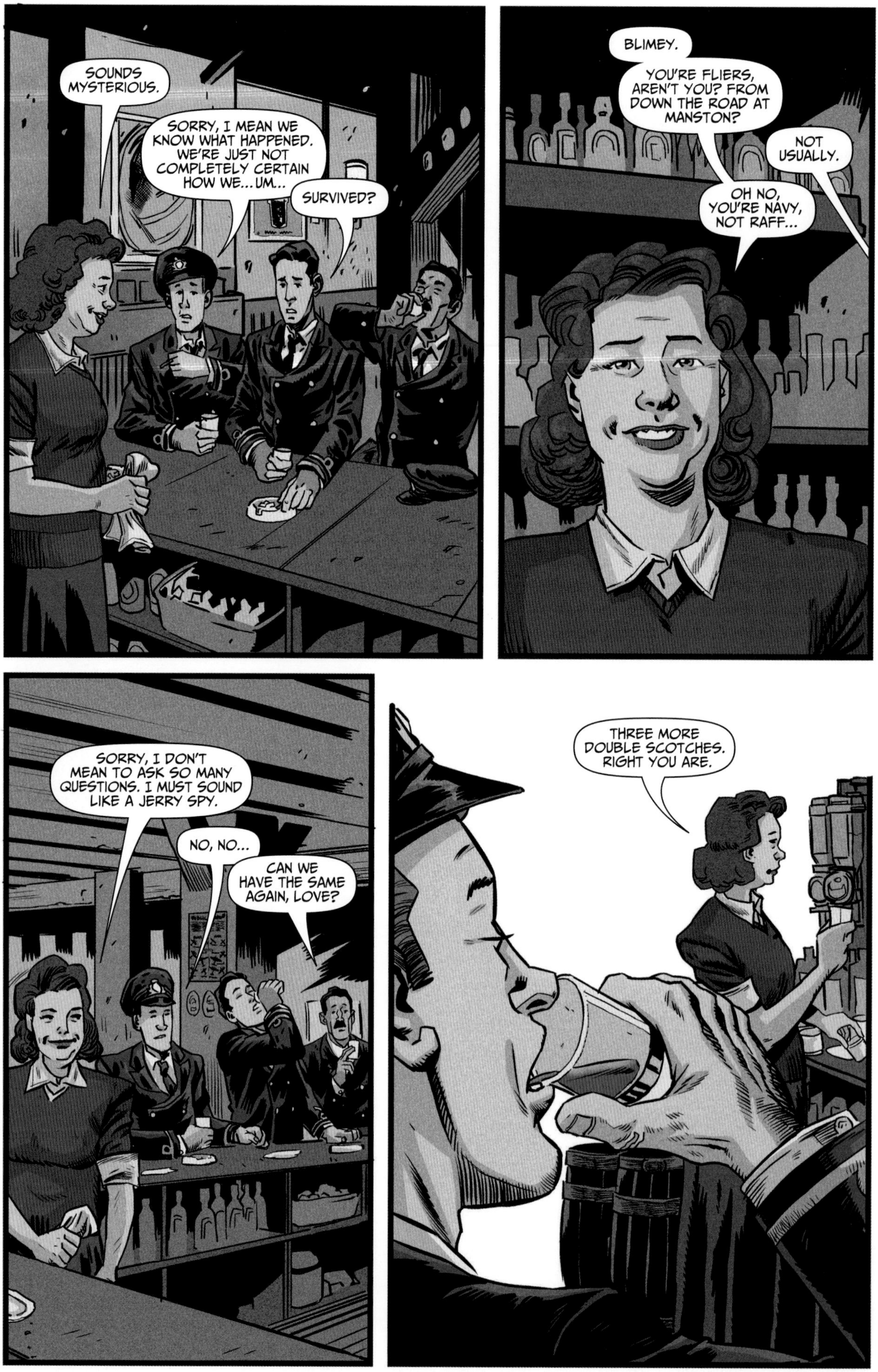
SOUNDS MYSTERIOUS.
SORRY, I MEAN WE KNOW WHAT HAPPENED. WE'RE JUST NOT COMPLETELY CERTAIN HOW WE...UM...
SURVIVED?
BLIMEY.
YOU'RE FLIERS, AREN'T YOU? FROM DOWN THE ROAD AT MANSTON?
NOT USUALLY.
OH NO, YOU'RE NAVY, NOT RAFF...
SORRY, I DON'T MEAN TO ASK SO MANY QUESTIONS. I MUST SOUND LIKE A JERRY SPY.
NO, NO...
CAN WE HAVE THE SAME AGAIN, LOVE?
THREE MORE DOUBLE SCOTCHES. RIGHT YOU ARE.

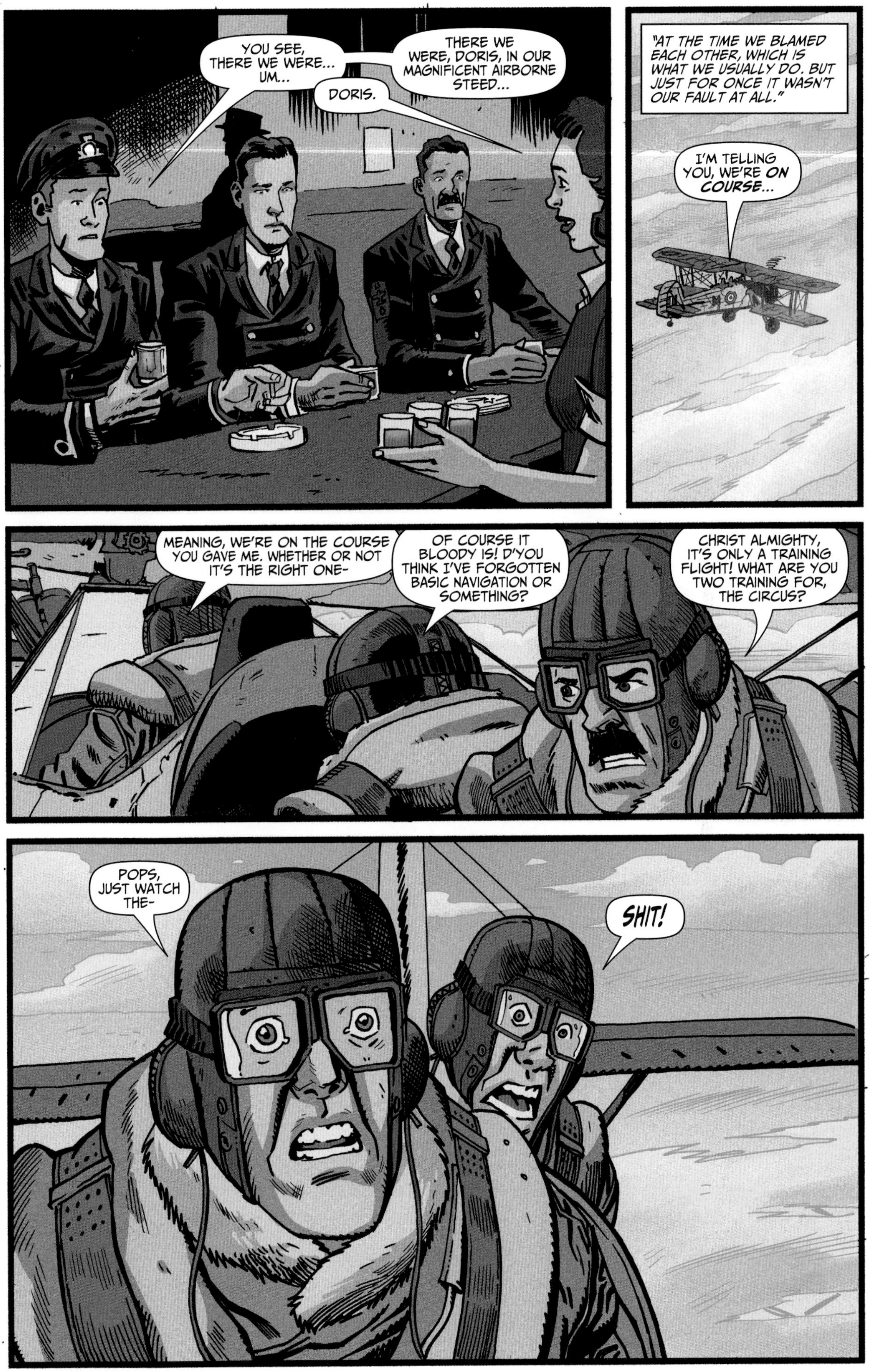
YOU SEE, THERE WE WERE... UM...
THERE WE WERE, DORIS, IN OUR MAGNIFICENT AIRBORNE STEED...
DORIS.
"AT THE TIME WE BLAMED EACH OTHER, WHICH IS WHAT WE USUALLY DO. BUT JUST FOR ONCE IT WASN'T OUR FAULT AT ALL."
I'M TELLING YOU, WE'RE ON COURSE...
MEANING, WE'RE ON THE COURSE YOU GAVE ME. WHETHER OR NOT IT'S THE RIGHT ONE-
OF COURSE IT BLOODY IS! D'YOU THINK I'VE FORGOTTEN BASIC NAVIGATION OR SOMETHING?
CHRIST ALMIGHTY, IT'S ONLY A TRAINING FLIGHT! WHAT ARE YOU TWO TRAINING FOR, THE CIRCUS?
POPS, JUST WATCH THE-
SHIT!

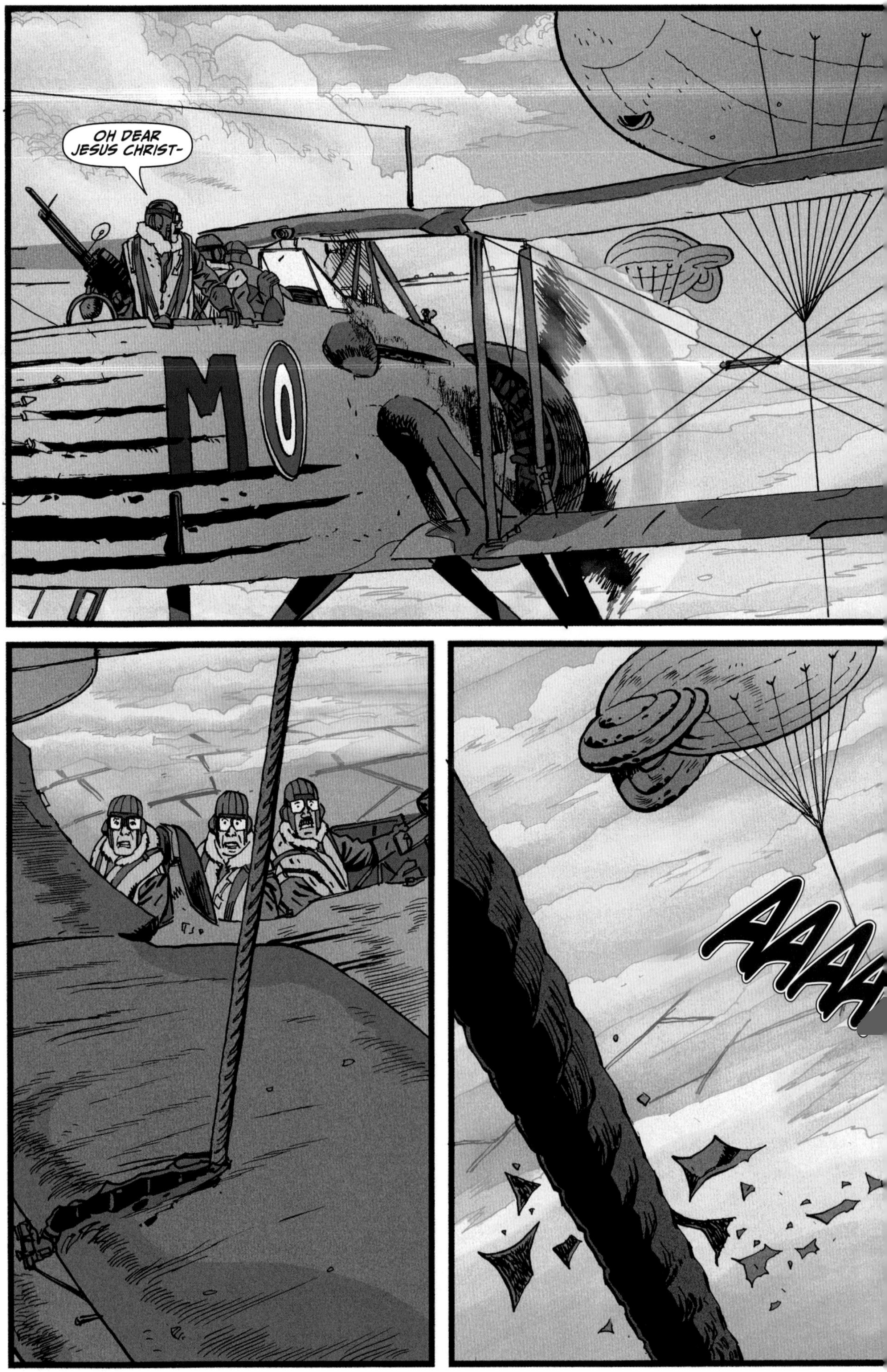
OH DEAR JESUS CHRIST-
AAAA

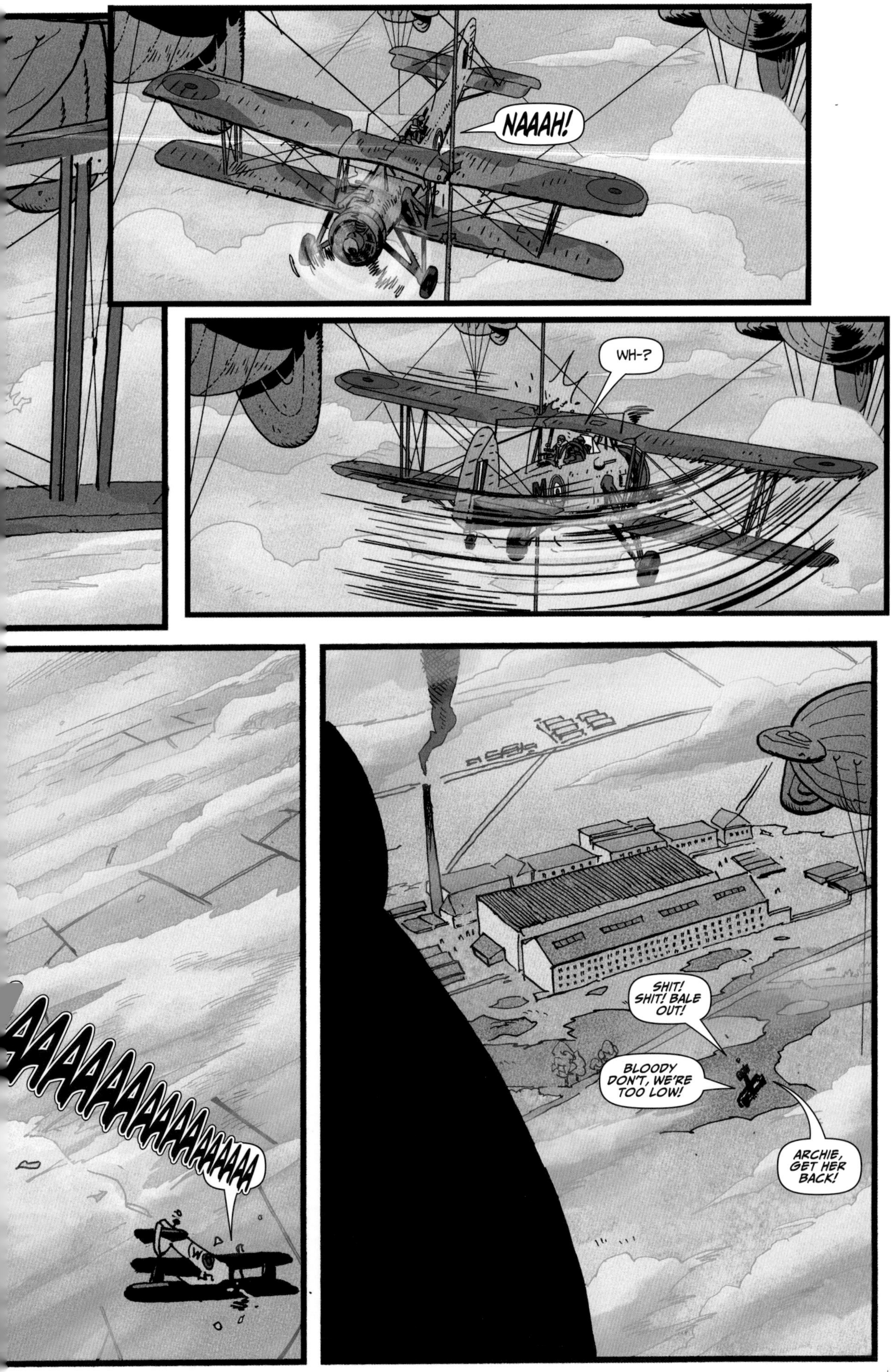
NAAAH!
WH-?
AAAAAAAAAAAAAAAAAA
SHIT! SHIT! BALE OUT!
BLOODY DON'T, WE'RE TOO LOW!
ARCHIE, GET HER BACK!

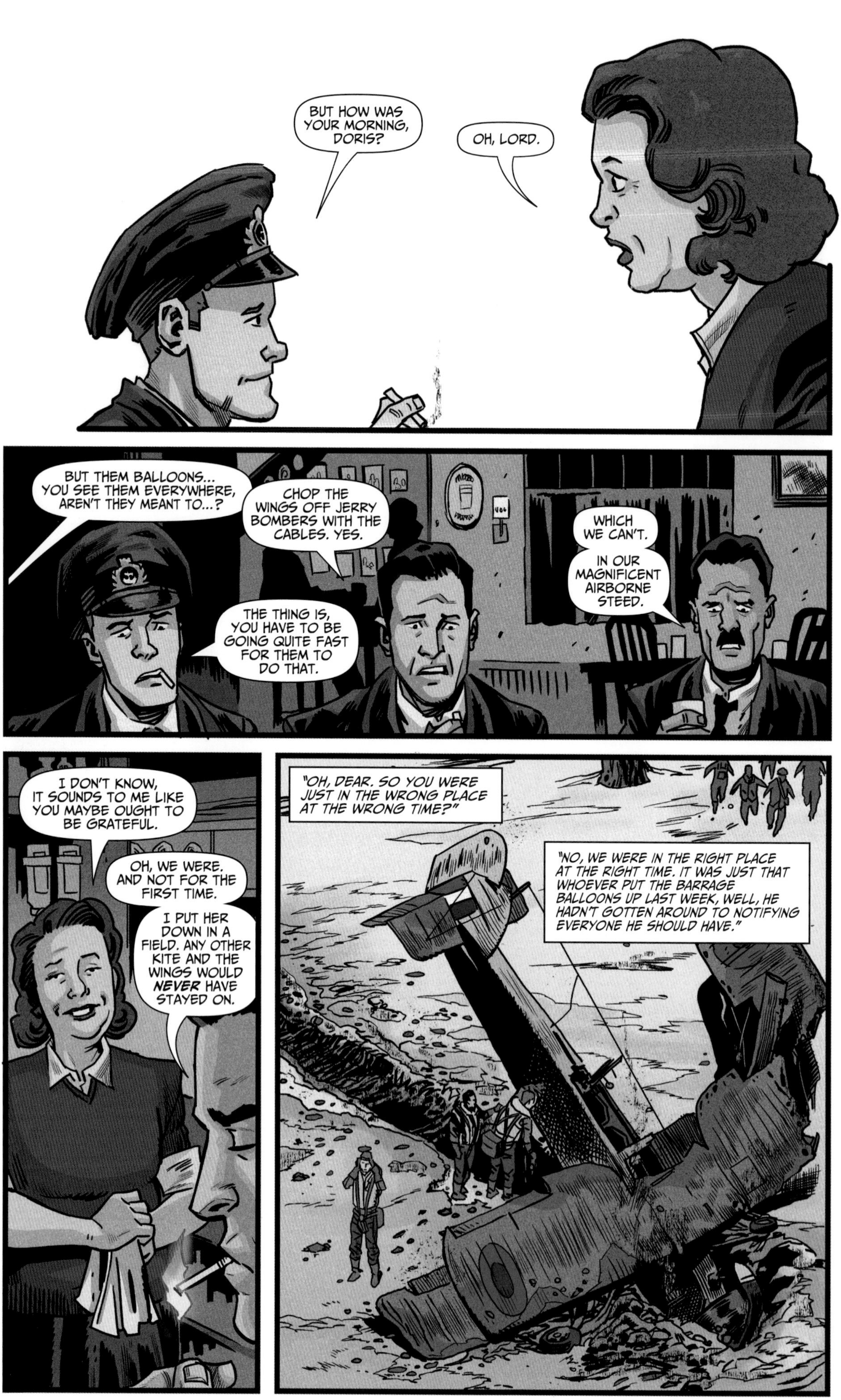

BUT HOW WAS YOUR MORNING, DORIS?
OH, LORD.
BUT THEM BALLOONS... YOU SEE THEM EVERYWHERE, AREN'T THEY MEANT TO...?
CHOP THE WINGS OFF JERRY BOMBERS WITH THE CABLES. YES.
THE THING IS, YOU HAVE TO BE GOING QUITE FAST FOR THEM TO DO THAT.
WHICH WE CAN'T.
IN OUR MAGNIFICENT AIRBORNE STEED.
I DON'T KNOW, IT SOUNDS TO ME LIKE YOU MAYBE OUGHT TO BE GRATEFUL.
OH, WE WERE. AND NOT FOR THE FIRST TIME.
I PUT HER DOWN IN A FIELD. ANY OTHER KITE AND THE WINGS WOULD NEVER HAVE STAYED ON.
"OH, DEAR. SO YOU WERE JUST IN THE WRONG PLACE AT THE WRONG TIME?"
"NO, WE WERE IN THE RIGHT PLACE AT THE RIGHT TIME. IT WAS JUST THAT WHOEVER PUT THE BARRAGE BALLOONS UP LAST WEEK, WELL, HE HADN'T GOTTEN AROUND TO NOTIFYING EVERYONE HE SHOULD HAVE."

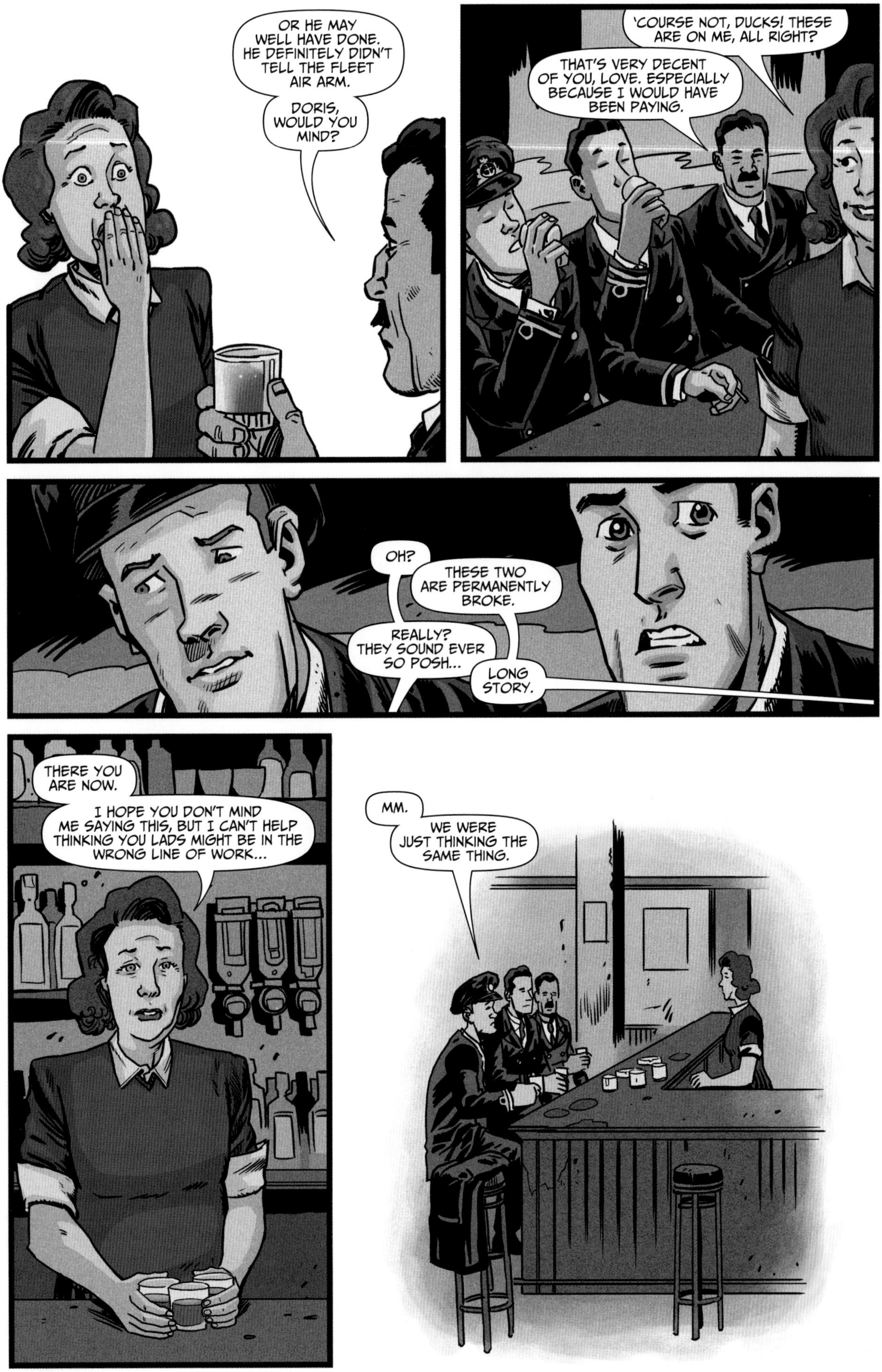
OR HE MAY WELL HAVE DONE. HE DEFINITELY DIDN'T TELL THE FLEET AIR ARM.
DORIS, WOULD YOU MIND?
'COURSE NOT, DUCKS! THESE ARE ON ME, ALL RIGHT?
THAT'S VERY DECENT OF YOU, LOVE. ESPECIALLY BECAUSE I WOULD HAVE BEEN PAYING.
OH?
THESE TWO ARE PERMANENTLY BROKE.
REALLY? THEY SOUND EVER SO POSH...
LONG STORY.
THERE YOU ARE NOW.
I HOPE YOU DON'T MIND ME SAYING THIS, BUT I CAN'T HELP THINKING YOU LADS MIGHT BE IN THE WRONG LINE OF WORK...
MM.
WE WERE JUST THINKING THE SAME THING.

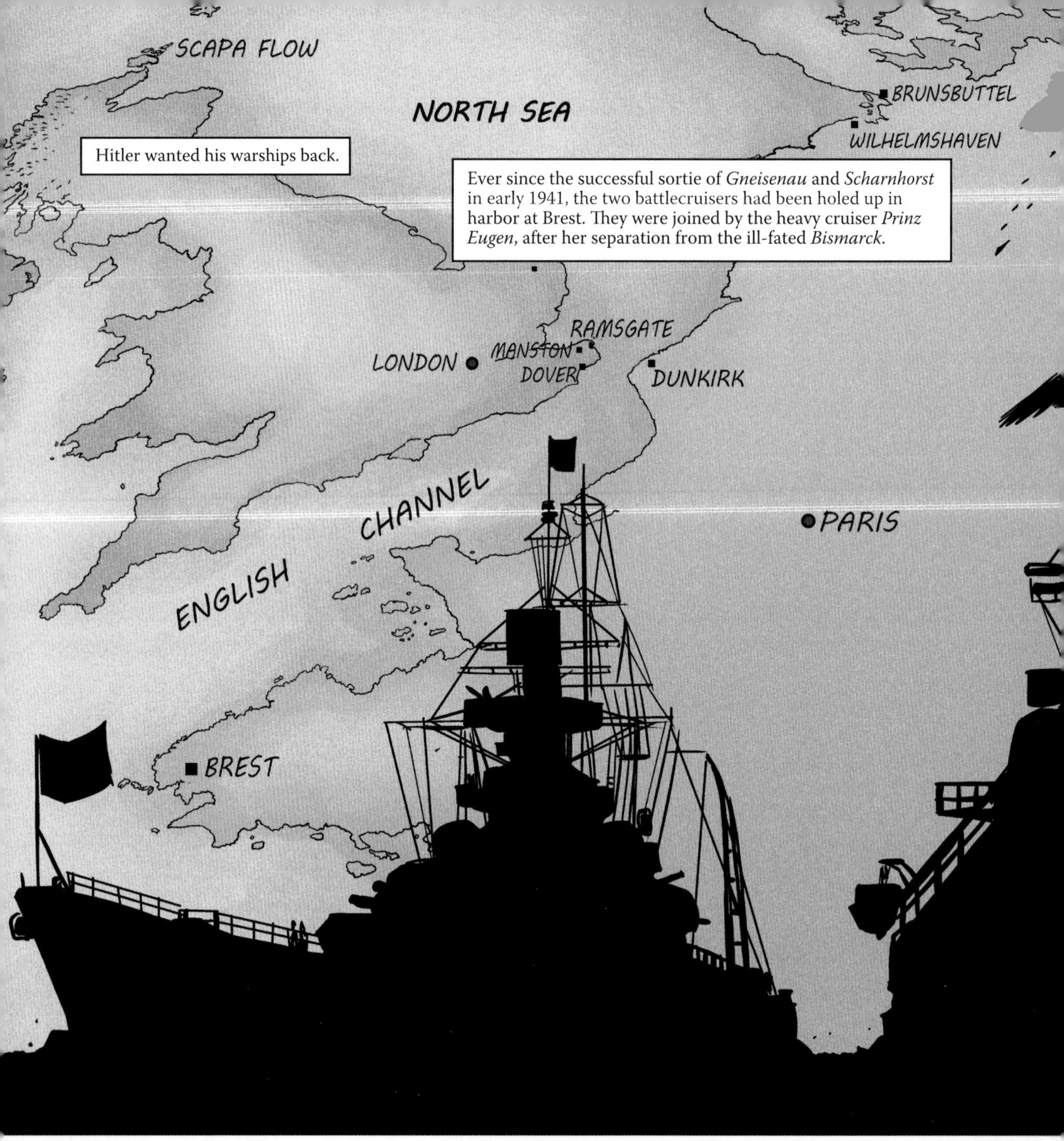
SCAPA FLOW
NORTH SEA
BRUNSBUTTEL
WILHELMSHAVEN
Hitler wanted his warships back.
Ever since the successful sortie of *Gneisenau* and *Scharnhorst* in early 1941, the two battlecruisers had been holed up in harbor at Brest. They were joined by the heavy cruiser *Prinz Eugen*, after her separation from the ill-fated *Bismarck*.
RAMSGATE
LONDON
MANSTON
DOVER
DUNKIRK
ENGLISH CHANNEL
PARIS
BREST

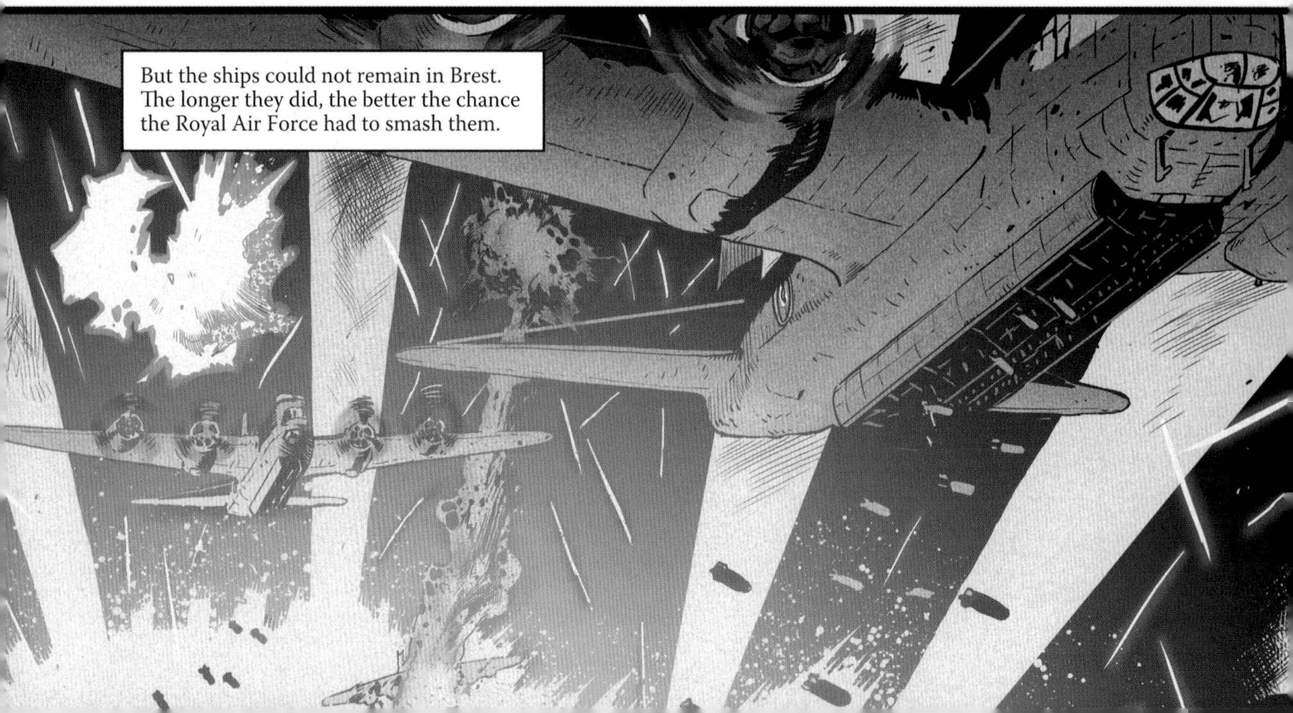
But the ships could not remain in Brest. The longer they did, the better the chance the Royal Air Force had to smash them.

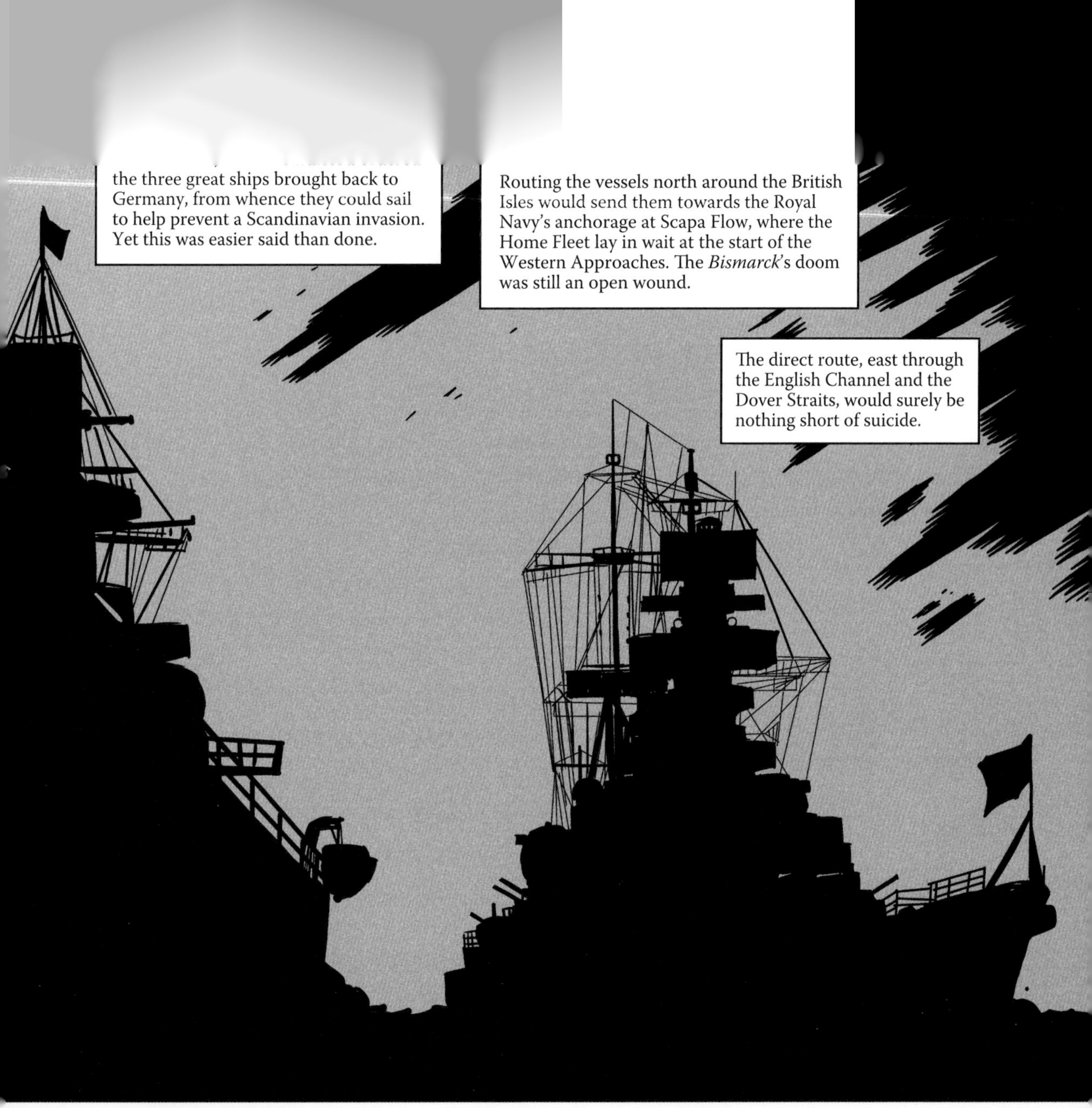
the three great ships brought back to Germany, from whence they could sail to help prevent a Scandinavian invasion. Yet this was easier said than done.
Routing the vessels north around the British Isles would send them towards the Royal Navy's anchorage at Scapa Flow, where the Home Fleet lay in wait at the start of the Western Approaches. The *Bismarck*'s doom was still an open wound.
The direct route, east through the English Channel and the Dover Straits, would surely be nothing short of suicide.

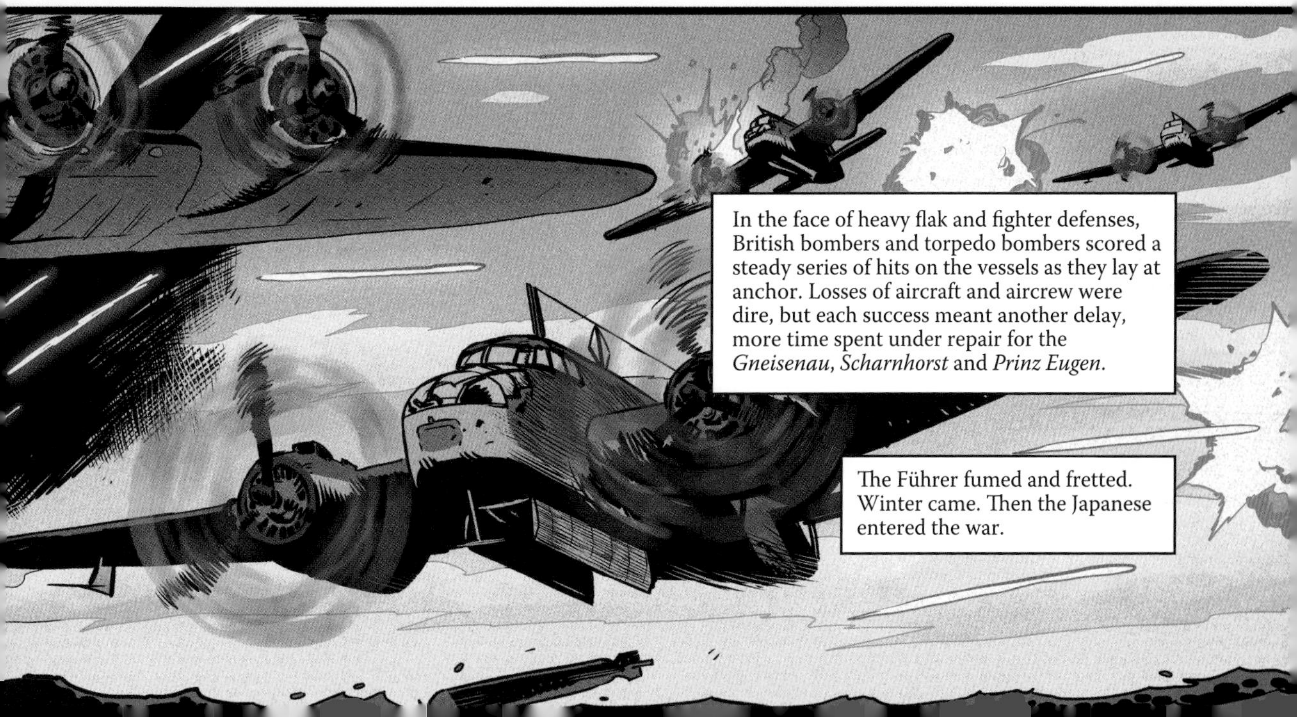
In the face of heavy flak and fighter defenses, British bombers and torpedo bombers scored a steady series of hits on the vessels as they lay at anchor. Losses of aircraft and aircrew were dire, but each success meant another delay, more time spent under repair for the *Gneisenau*, *Scharnhorst* and *Prinz Eugen*.
The Führer fumed and fretted. Winter came. Then the Japanese entered the war.

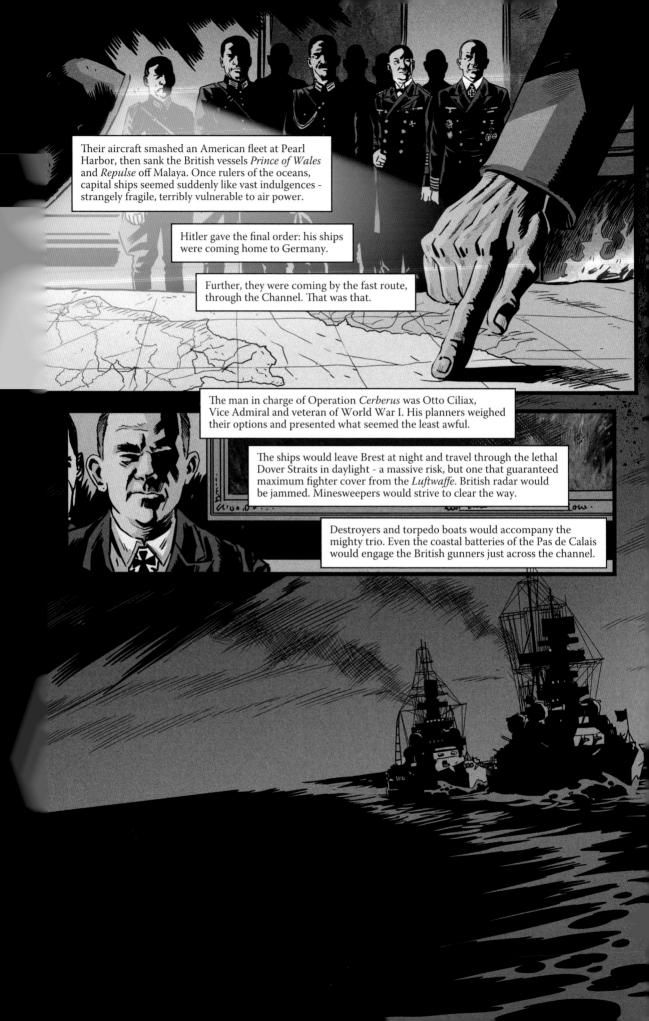

Their aircraft smashed an American fleet at Pearl Harbor, then sank the British vessels *Prince of Wales* and *Repulse* off Malaya. Once rulers of the oceans, capital ships seemed suddenly like vast indulgences - strangely fragile, terribly vulnerable to air power.

Hitler gave the final order: his ships were coming home to Germany.

Further, they were coming by the fast route, through the Channel. That was that.

The man in charge of Operation *Cerberus* was Otto Ciliax, Vice Admiral and veteran of World War I. His planners weighed their options and presented what seemed the least awful.

The ships would leave Brest at night and travel through the lethal Dover Straits in daylight - a massive risk, but one that guaranteed maximum fighter cover from the *Luftwaffe*. British radar would be jammed. Minesweepers would strive to clear the way.

Destroyers and torpedo boats would accompany the mighty trio. Even the coastal batteries of the Pas de Calais would engage the British gunners just across the channel.

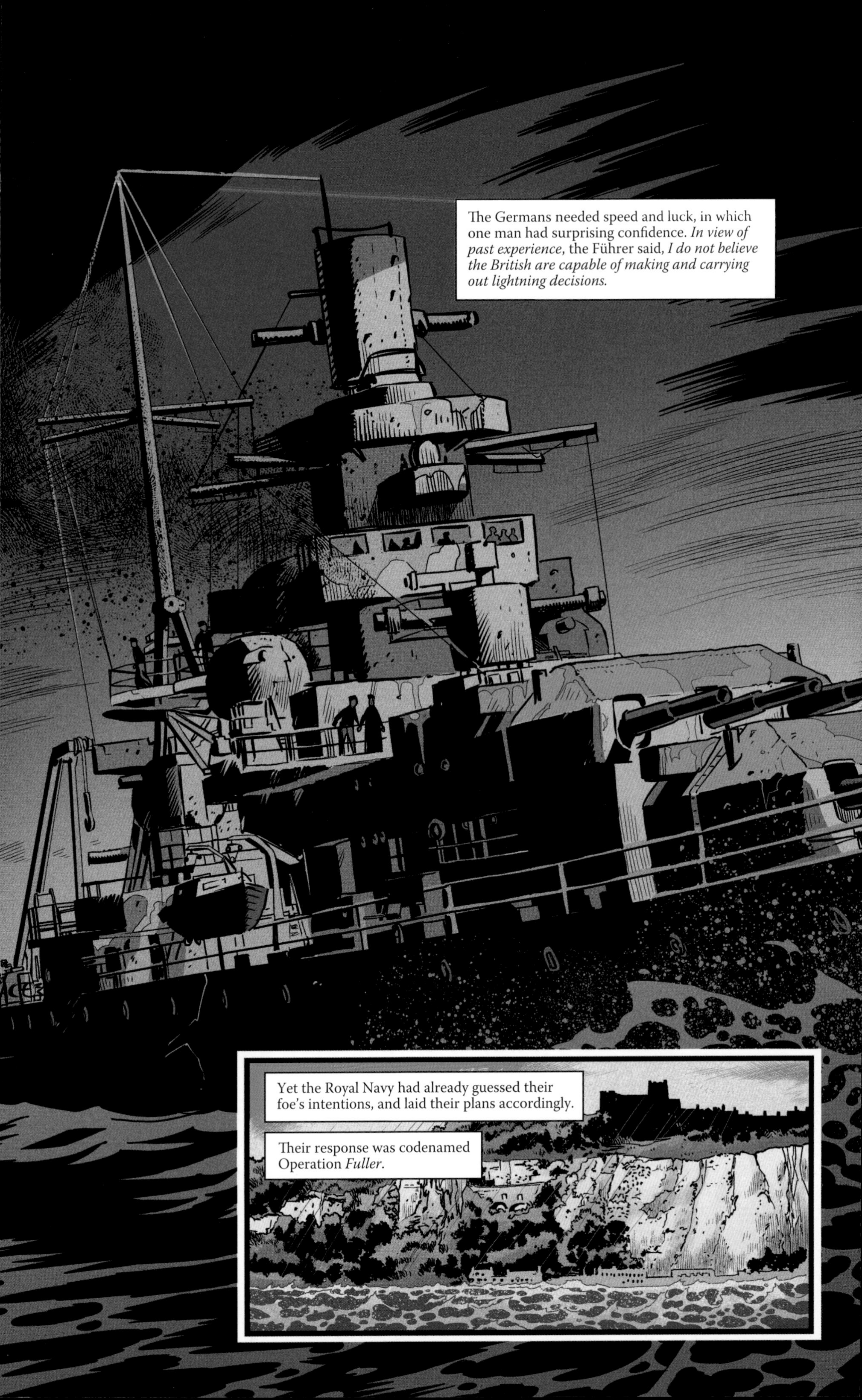
The Germans needed speed and luck, in which one man had surprising confidence. *In view of past experience*, the Führer said, *I do not believe the British are capable of making and carrying out lightning decisions.*
Yet the Royal Navy had already guessed their foe's intentions, and laid their plans accordingly.
Their response was codenamed Operation *Fuller*.

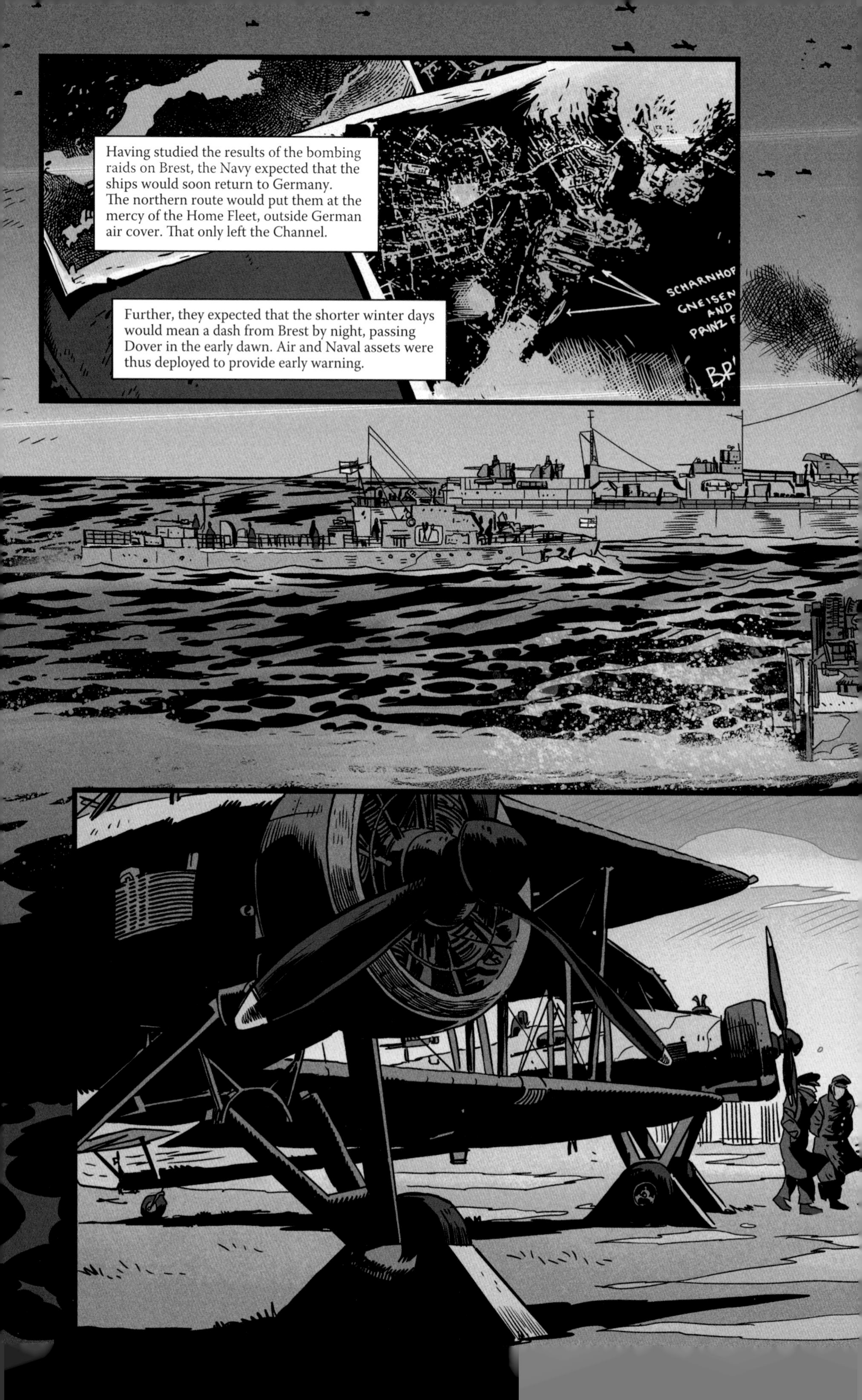
Having studied the results of the bombing raids on Brest, the Navy expected that the ships would soon return to Germany. The northern route would put them at the mercy of the Home Fleet, outside German air cover. That only left the Channel.
Further, they expected that the shorter winter days would mean a dash from Brest by night, passing Dover in the early dawn. Air and Naval assets were thus deployed to provide early warning.

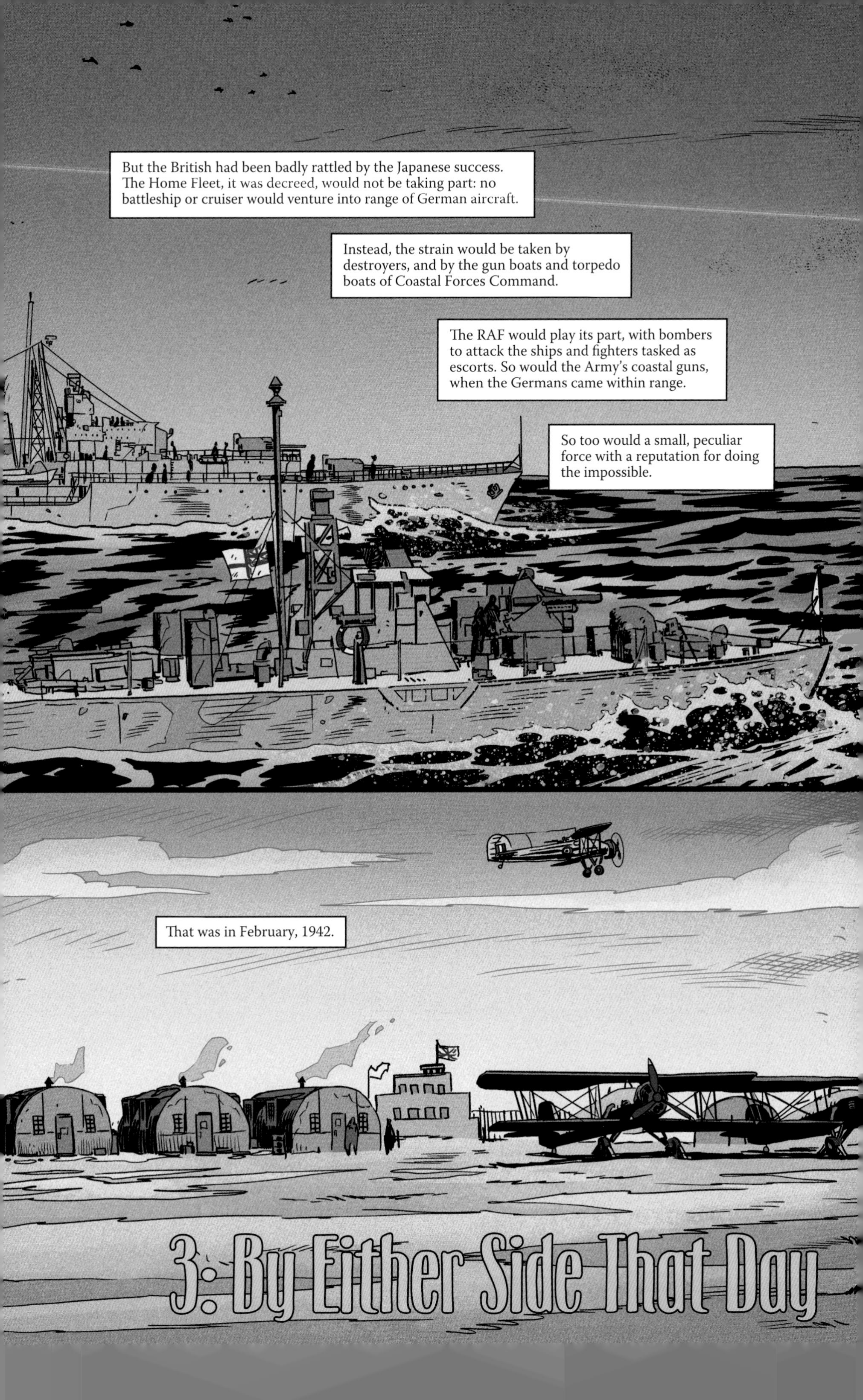
But the British had been badly rattled by the Japanese success. The Home Fleet, it was decreed, would not be taking part: no battleship or cruiser would venture into range of German aircraft.
Instead, the strain would be taken by destroyers, and by the gun boats and torpedo boats of Coastal Forces Command.
The RAF would play its part, with bombers to attack the ships and fighters tasked as escorts. So would the Army's coastal guns, when the Germans came within range.
So too would a small, peculiar force with a reputation for doing the impossible.
That was in February, 1942.
3: By Either Side That Day

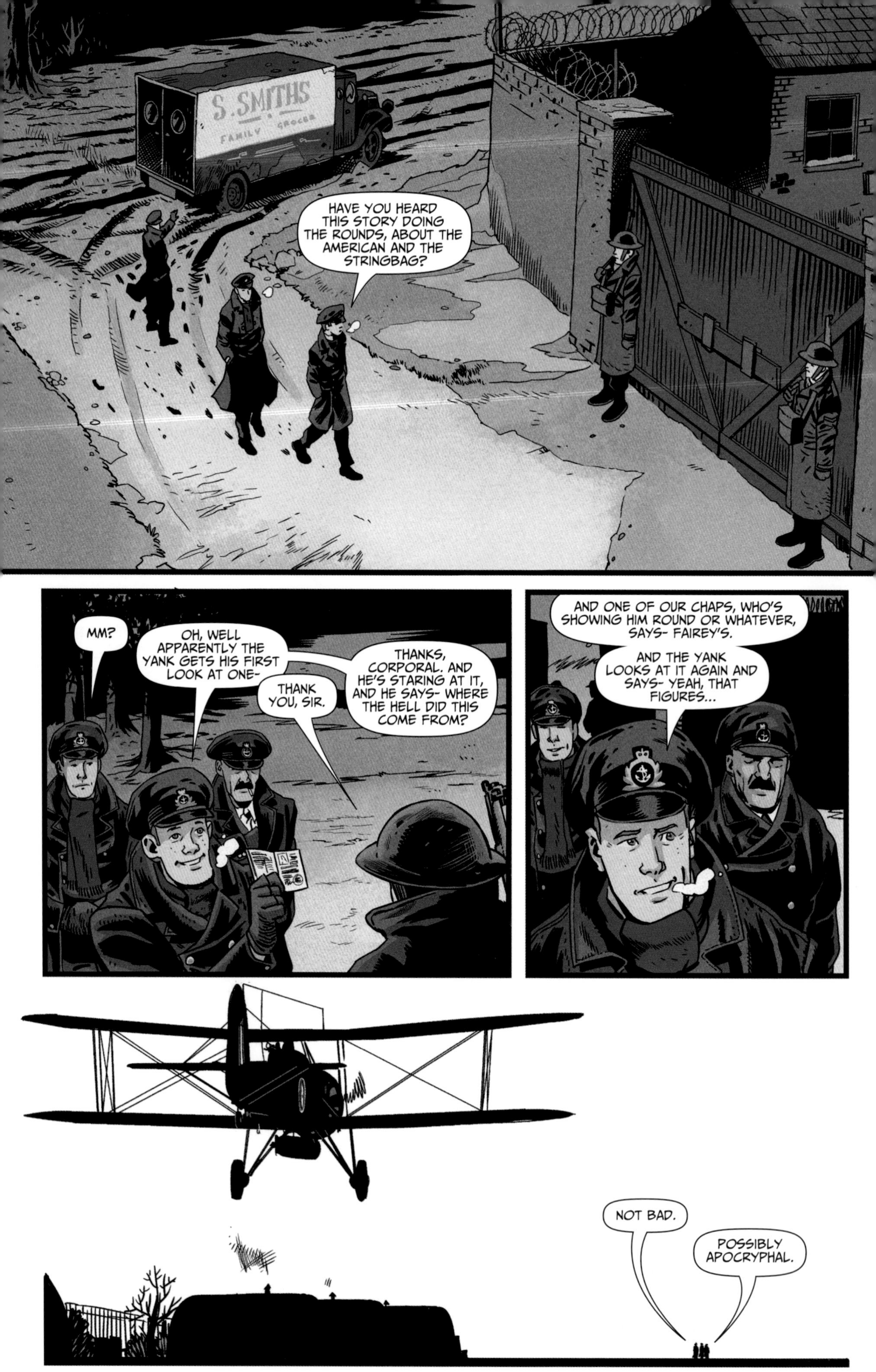
S. SMITHS
&
FAMILY GROCER
HAVE YOU HEARD THIS STORY DOING THE ROUNDS, ABOUT THE AMERICAN AND THE STRINGBAG?
MM?
OH, WELL APPARENTLY THE YANK GETS HIS FIRST LOOK AT ONE-
THANK YOU, SIR.
THANKS, CORPORAL. AND HE'S STARING AT IT, AND HE SAYS- WHERE THE HELL DID THIS COME FROM?
AND ONE OF OUR CHAPS, WHO'S SHOWING HIM ROUND OR WHATEVER, SAYS- FAIREY'S.
AND THE YANK LOOKS AT IT AGAIN AND SAYS- YEAH, THAT FIGURES...
NOT BAD.
POSSIBLY APOCRYPHAL.

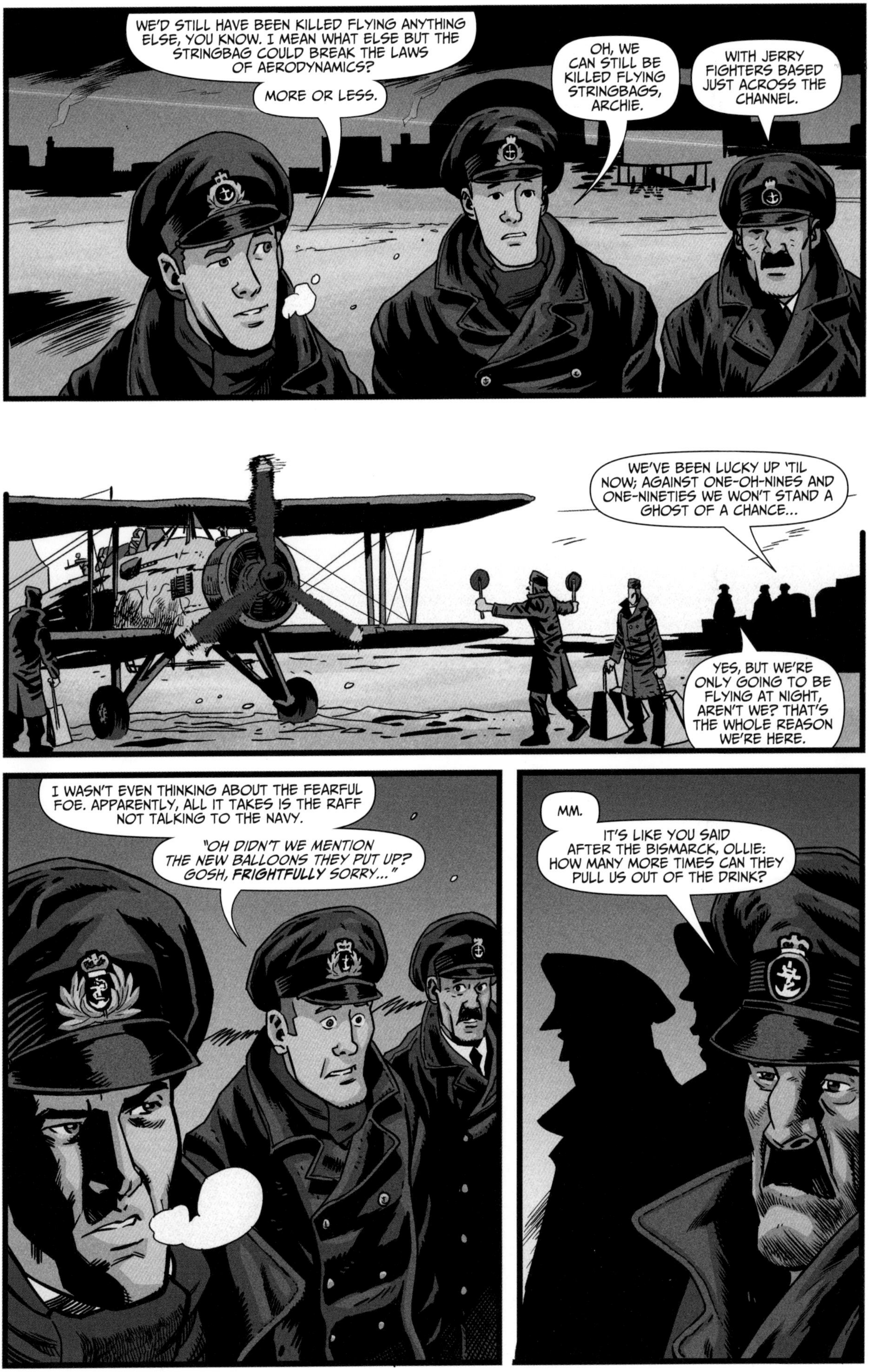
WE'D STILL HAVE BEEN KILLED FLYING ANYTHING ELSE, YOU KNOW. I MEAN WHAT ELSE BUT THE STRINGBAG COULD BREAK THE LAWS OF AERODYNAMICS?
MORE OR LESS.
OH, WE CAN STILL BE KILLED FLYING STRINGBAGS, ARCHIE.
WITH JERRY FIGHTERS BASED JUST ACROSS THE CHANNEL.
WE'VE BEEN LUCKY UP 'TIL NOW; AGAINST ONE-OH-NINES AND ONE-NINETIES WE WON'T STAND A GHOST OF A CHANCE...
YES, BUT WE'RE ONLY GOING TO BE FLYING AT NIGHT, AREN'T WE? THAT'S THE WHOLE REASON WE'RE HERE.
I WASN'T EVEN THINKING ABOUT THE FEARFUL FOE. APPARENTLY, ALL IT TAKES IS THE RAFF NOT TALKING TO THE NAVY.
"OH DIDN'T WE MENTION THE NEW BALLOONS THEY PUT UP? GOSH, FRIGHTFULLY SORRY..."
MM.
IT'S LIKE YOU SAID AFTER THE BISMARCK, OLLIE: HOW MANY MORE TIMES CAN THEY PULL US OUT OF THE DRINK?

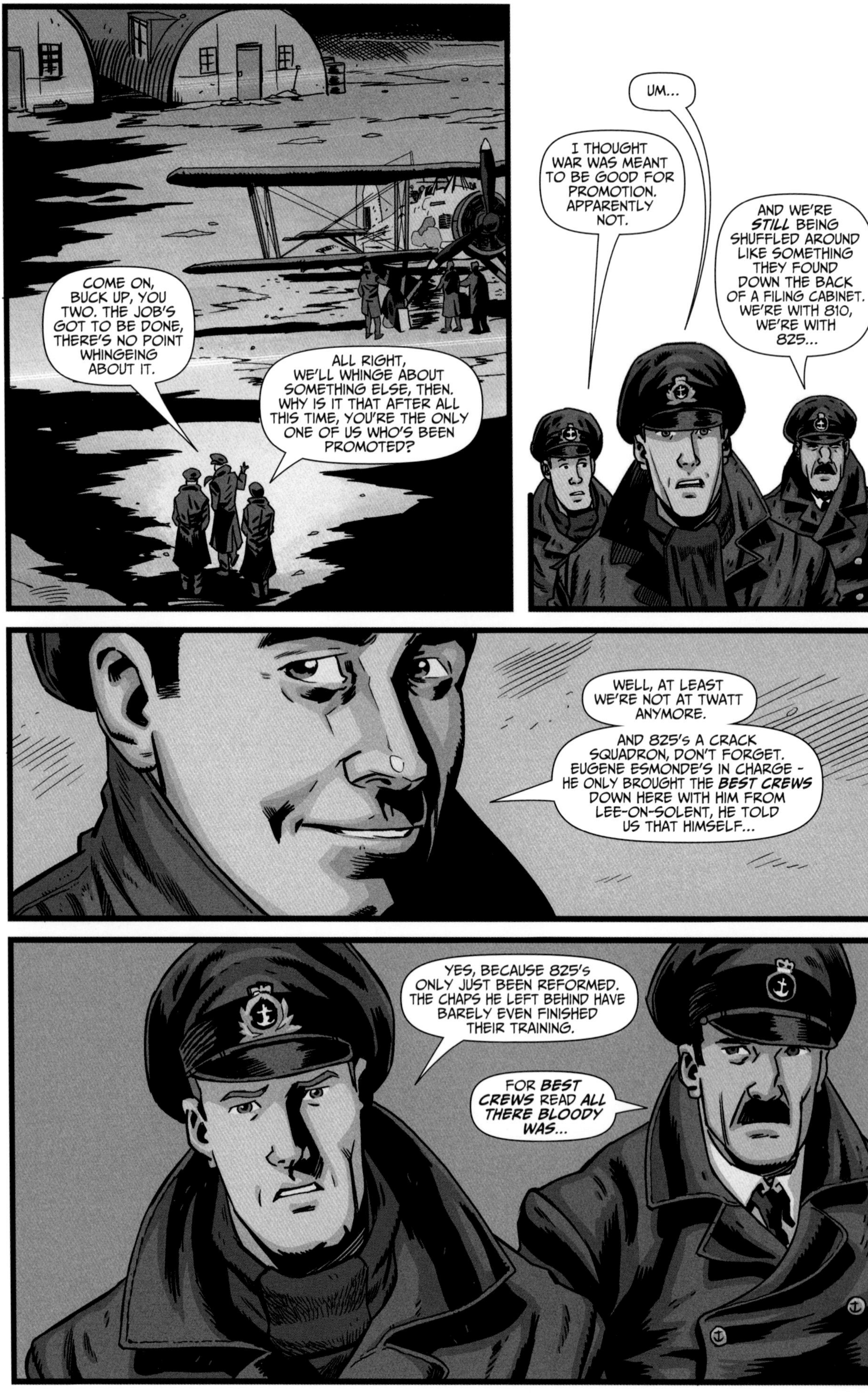
COME ON, BUCK UP, YOU TWO. THE JOB'S GOT TO BE DONE, THERE'S NO POINT WHINGEING ABOUT IT.
ALL RIGHT, WE'LL WHINGE ABOUT SOMETHING ELSE, THEN. WHY IS IT THAT AFTER ALL THIS TIME, YOU'RE THE ONLY ONE OF US WHO'S BEEN PROMOTED?
UM...
I THOUGHT WAR WAS MEANT TO BE GOOD FOR PROMOTION. APPARENTLY NOT.
AND WE'RE *STILL* BEING SHUFFLED AROUND LIKE SOMETHING THEY FOUND DOWN THE BACK OF A FILING CABINET. WE'RE WITH 810, WE'RE WITH 825...
WELL, AT LEAST WE'RE NOT AT TWATT ANYMORE.
AND 825'S A CRACK SQUADRON, DON'T FORGET. EUGENE ESMONDE'S IN CHARGE - HE ONLY BROUGHT THE *BEST CREWS* DOWN HERE WITH HIM FROM LEE-ON-SOLENT, HE TOLD US THAT HIMSELF...
YES, BECAUSE 825'S ONLY JUST BEEN REFORMED. THE CHAPS HE LEFT BEHIND HAVE BARELY EVEN FINISHED THEIR TRAINING.
FOR *BEST CREWS* READ *ALL THERE BLOODY WAS...*

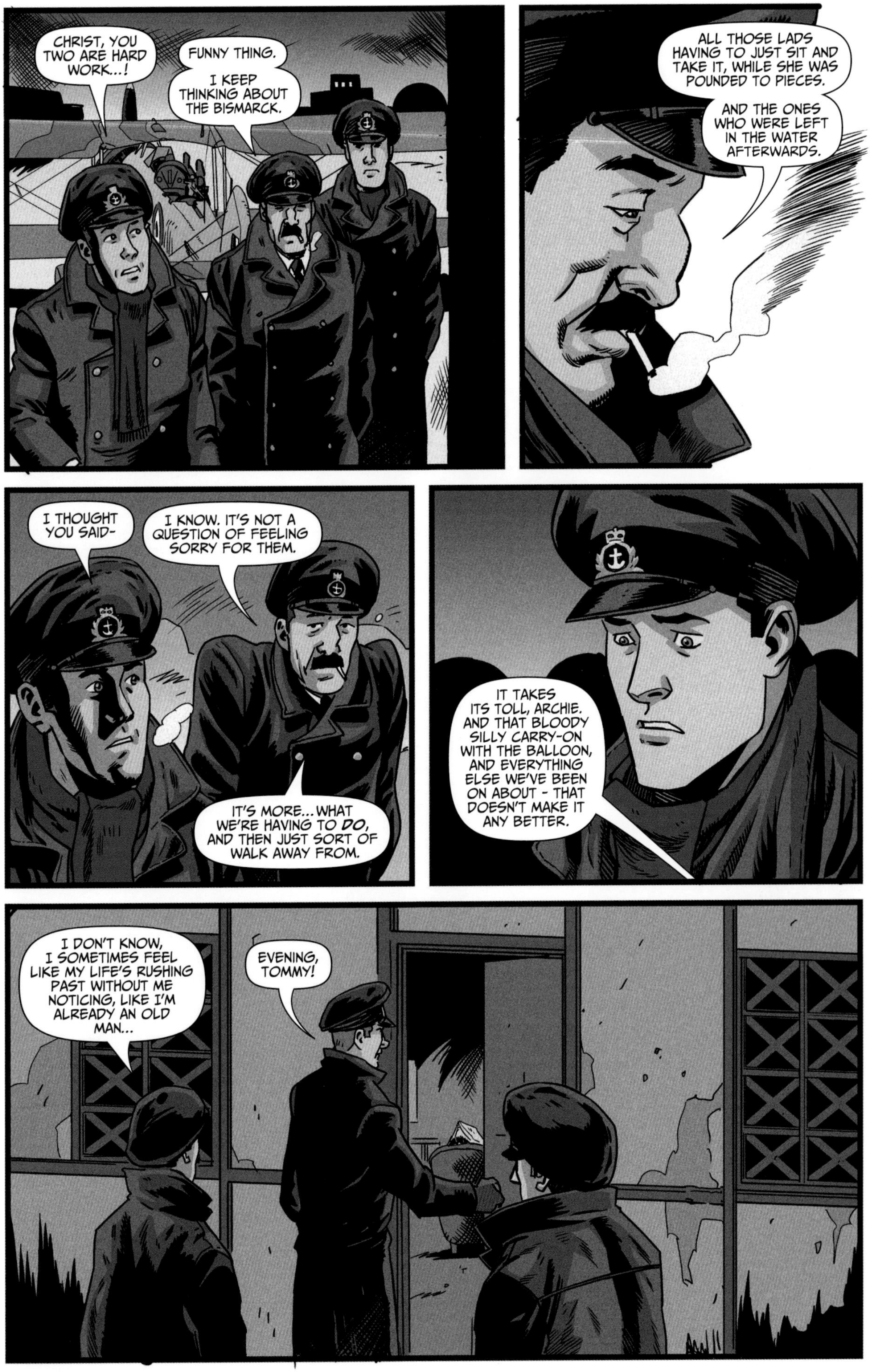
CHRIST, YOU TWO ARE HARD WORK...!
FUNNY THING.
I KEEP THINKING ABOUT THE BISMARCK.
ALL THOSE LADS HAVING TO JUST SIT AND TAKE IT, WHILE SHE WAS POUNDED TO PIECES.
AND THE ONES WHO WERE LEFT IN THE WATER AFTERWARDS.
I THOUGHT YOU SAID-
I KNOW. IT'S NOT A QUESTION OF FEELING SORRY FOR THEM.
IT'S MORE...WHAT WE'RE HAVING TO DO, AND THEN JUST SORT OF WALK AWAY FROM.
IT TAKES ITS TOLL, ARCHIE. AND THAT BLOODY SILLY CARRY-ON WITH THE BALLOON, AND EVERYTHING ELSE WE'VE BEEN ON ABOUT - THAT DOESN'T MAKE IT ANY BETTER.
I DON'T KNOW, I SOMETIMES FEEL LIKE MY LIFE'S RUSHING PAST WITHOUT ME NOTICING, LIKE I'M ALREADY AN OLD MAN...
EVENING, TOMMY!

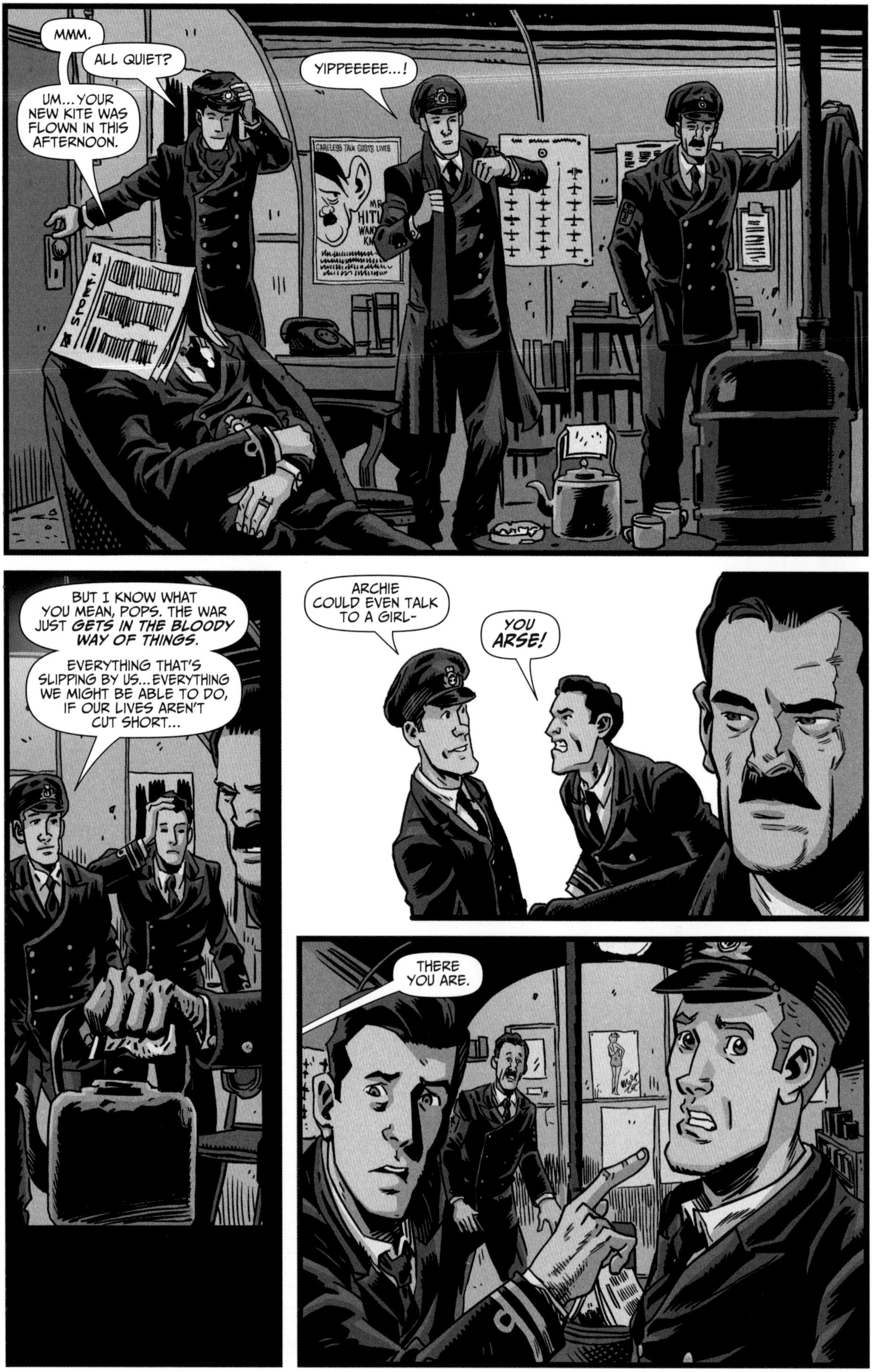
MMM.
ALL QUIET?
UM...YOUR NEW KITE WAS FLOWN IN THIS AFTERNOON.
YIPPEEEEE...!
CARELESS TALK COSTS LIVES
BUT I KNOW WHAT YOU MEAN, POPS. THE WAR JUST GETS IN THE BLOODY WAY OF THINGS.
EVERYTHING THAT'S SLIPPING BY US...EVERYTHING WE MIGHT BE ABLE TO DO, IF OUR LIVES AREN'T CUT SHORT...
ARCHIE COULD EVEN TALK TO A GIRL-
YOU ARSE!
THERE YOU ARE.

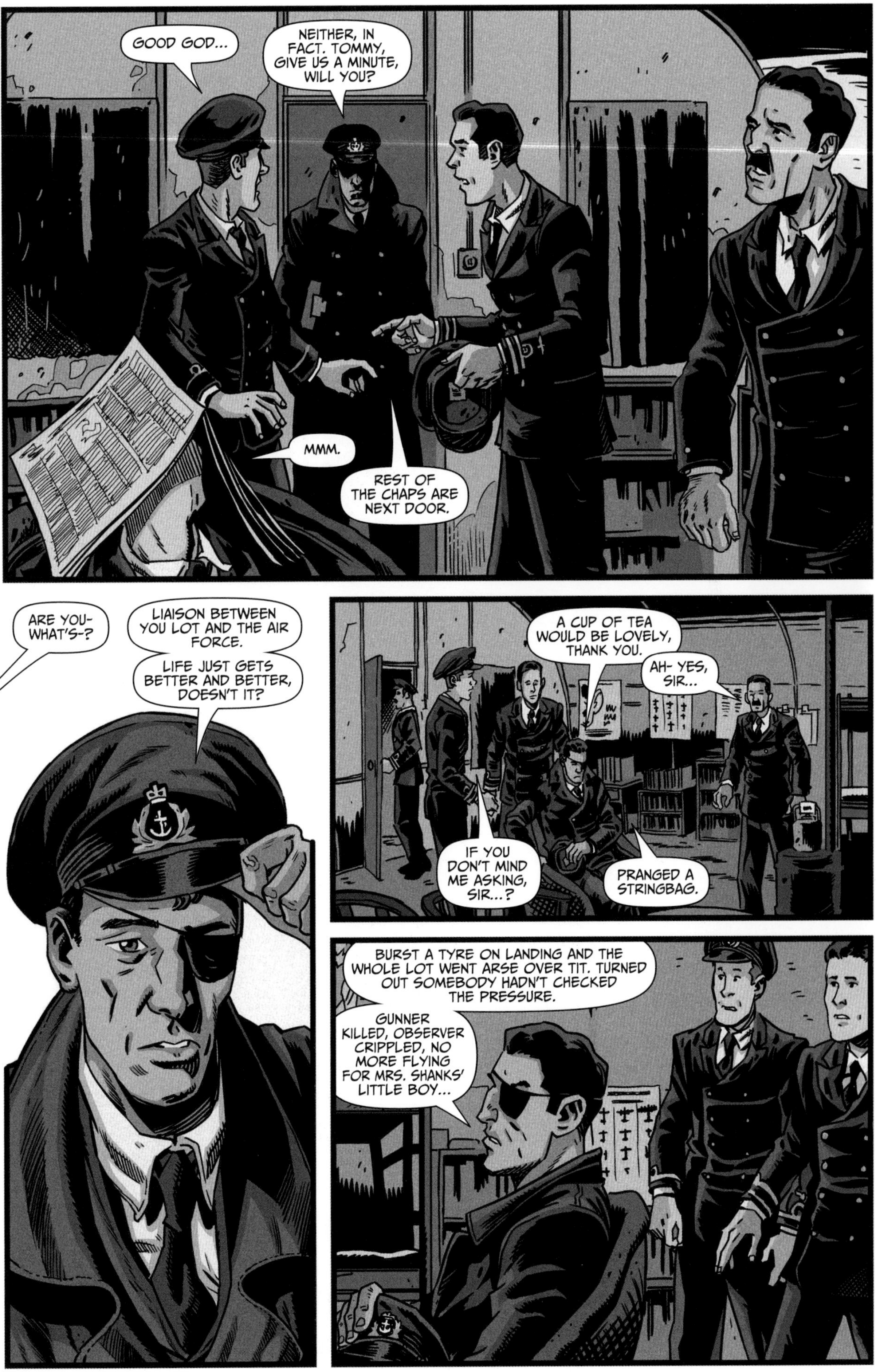
GOOD GOD...
NEITHER, IN FACT. TOMMY, GIVE US A MINUTE, WILL YOU?
MMM.
REST OF THE CHAPS ARE NEXT DOOR.
ARE YOU- WHAT'S-?
LIAISON BETWEEN YOU LOT AND THE AIR FORCE.
LIFE JUST GETS BETTER AND BETTER, DOESN'T IT?
A CUP OF TEA WOULD BE LOVELY, THANK YOU.
AH- YES, SIR...
IF YOU DON'T MIND ME ASKING, SIR...?
PRANGED A STRINGBAG.
BURST A TYRE ON LANDING AND THE WHOLE LOT WENT ARSE OVER TIT. TURNED OUT SOMEBODY HADN'T CHECKED THE PRESSURE.
GUNNER KILLED, OBSERVER CRIPPLED, NO MORE FLYING FOR MRS. SHANKS' LITTLE BOY...

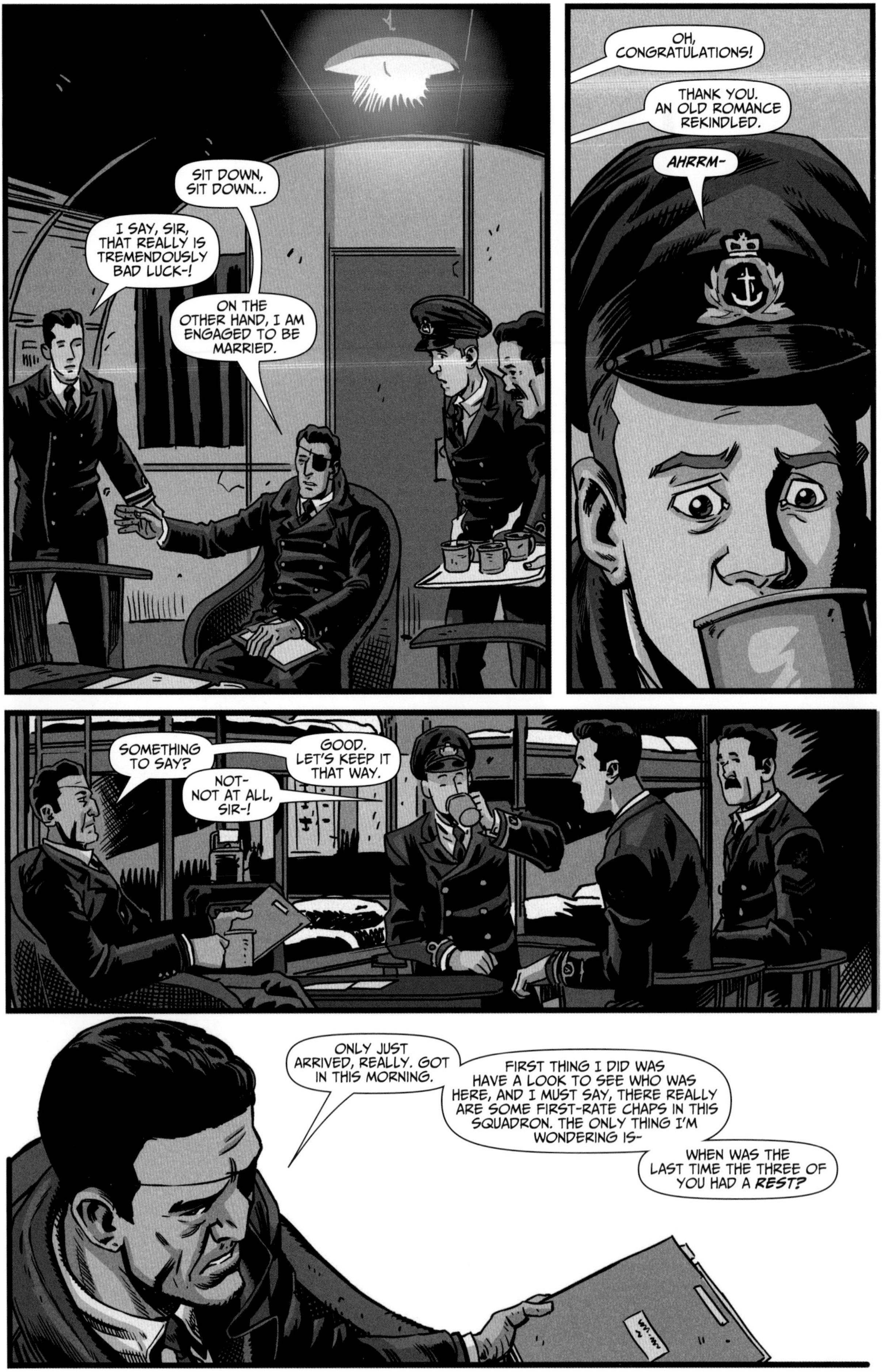
SIT DOWN, SIT DOWN...
I SAY, SIR, THAT REALLY IS TREMENDOUSLY BAD LUCK-!
ON THE OTHER HAND, I AM ENGAGED TO BE MARRIED.
OH, CONGRATULATIONS!
THANK YOU. AN OLD ROMANCE REKINDLED.
AHRRM-
SOMETHING TO SAY?
NOT- NOT AT ALL, SIR-!
GOOD. LET'S KEEP IT THAT WAY.
ONLY JUST ARRIVED, REALLY. GOT IN THIS MORNING.
FIRST THING I DID WAS HAVE A LOOK TO SEE WHO WAS HERE, AND I MUST SAY, THERE REALLY ARE SOME FIRST-RATE CHAPS IN THIS SQUADRON. THE ONLY THING I'M WONDERING IS-
WHEN WAS THE LAST TIME THE THREE OF YOU HAD A REST?

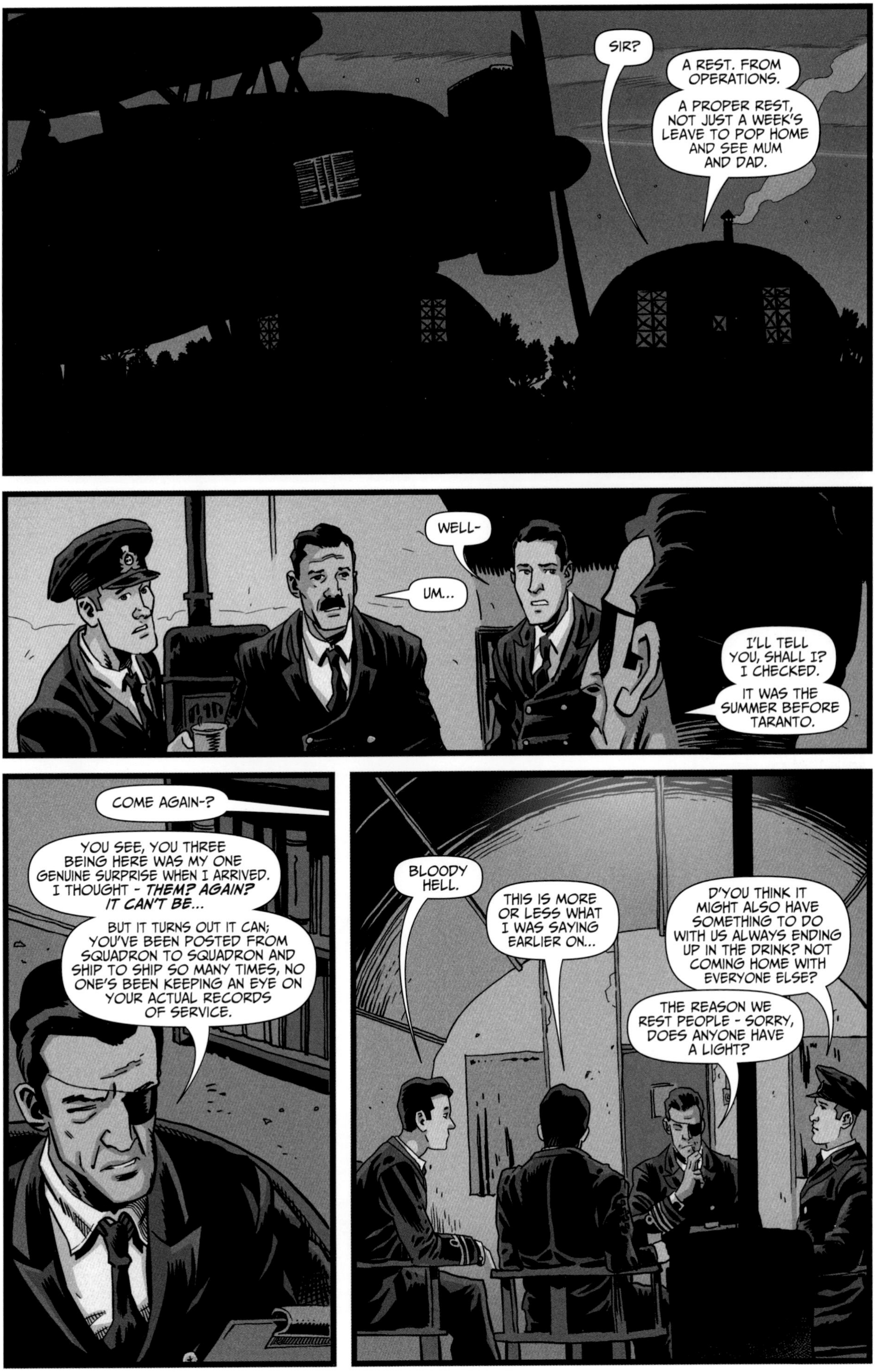
SIR?
A REST. FROM OPERATIONS.
A PROPER REST, NOT JUST A WEEK'S LEAVE TO POP HOME AND SEE MUM AND DAD.
WELL-
UM...
I'LL TELL YOU, SHALL I? I CHECKED.
IT WAS THE SUMMER BEFORE TARANTO.
COME AGAIN-?
YOU SEE, YOU THREE BEING HERE WAS MY ONE GENUINE SURPRISE WHEN I ARRIVED. I THOUGHT - *THEM? AGAIN? IT CAN'T BE...*
BUT IT TURNS OUT IT CAN; YOU'VE BEEN POSTED FROM SQUADRON TO SQUADRON AND SHIP TO SHIP SO MANY TIMES, NO ONE'S BEEN KEEPING AN EYE ON YOUR ACTUAL RECORDS OF SERVICE.
BLOODY HELL.
THIS IS MORE OR LESS WHAT I WAS SAYING EARLIER ON...
D'YOU THINK IT MIGHT ALSO HAVE SOMETHING TO DO WITH US ALWAYS ENDING UP IN THE DRINK? NOT COMING HOME WITH EVERYONE ELSE?
THE REASON WE REST PEOPLE - SORRY, DOES ANYONE HAVE A LIGHT?

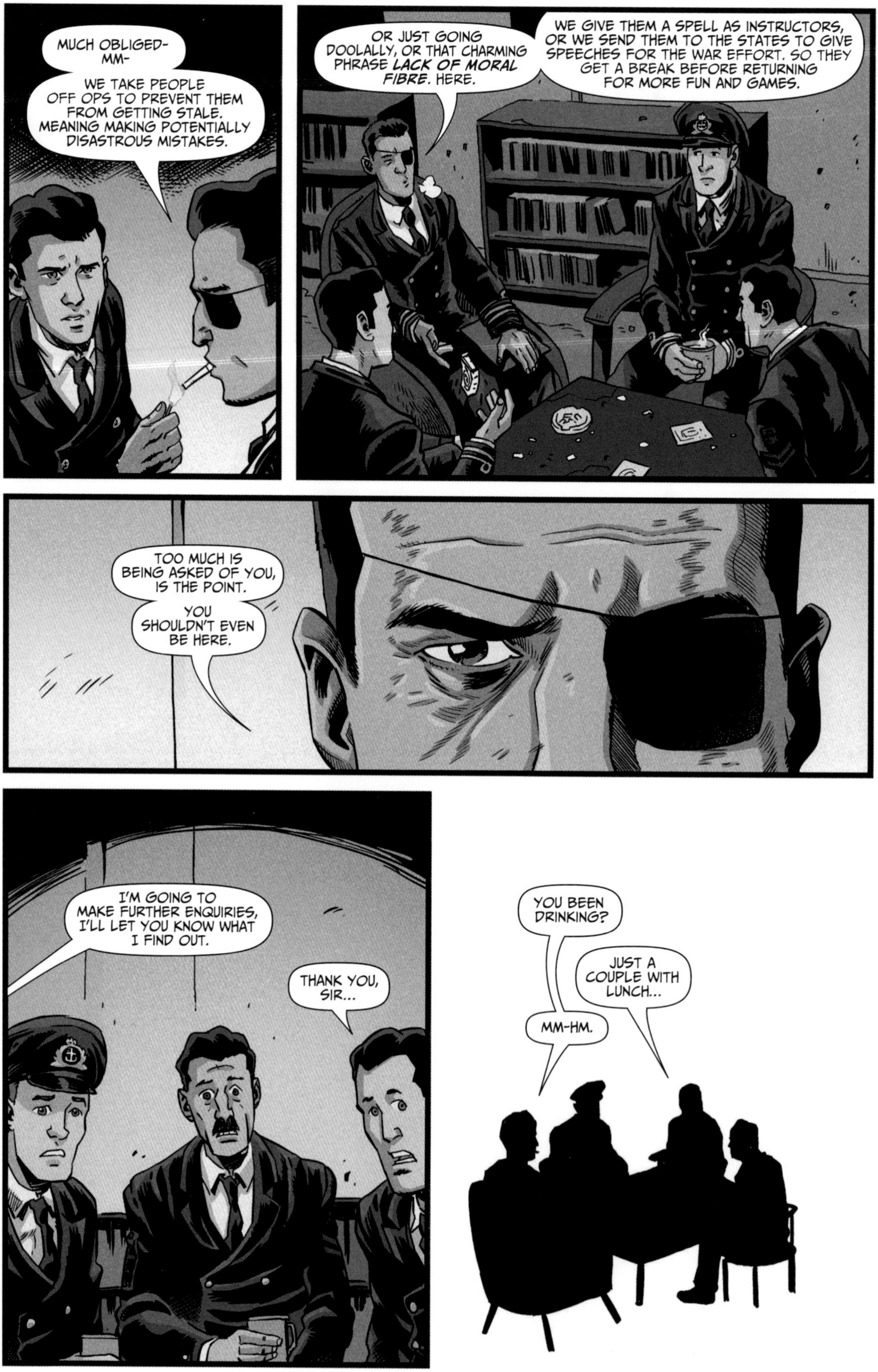
MUCH OBLIGED-
MM-
WE TAKE PEOPLE OFF OPS TO PREVENT THEM FROM GETTING STALE. MEANING MAKING POTENTIALLY DISASTROUS MISTAKES.
OR JUST GOING DOOLALLY, OR THAT CHARMING PHRASE *LACK OF MORAL FIBRE*. HERE.
WE GIVE THEM A SPELL AS INSTRUCTORS, OR WE SEND THEM TO THE STATES TO GIVE SPEECHES FOR THE WAR EFFORT. SO THEY GET A BREAK BEFORE RETURNING FOR MORE FUN AND GAMES.
TOO MUCH IS BEING ASKED OF YOU, IS THE POINT.
YOU SHOULDN'T EVEN BE HERE.
I'M GOING TO MAKE FURTHER ENQUIRIES, I'LL LET YOU KNOW WHAT I FIND OUT.
THANK YOU, SIR...
YOU BEEN DRINKING?
JUST A COUPLE WITH LUNCH...
MM-HM.

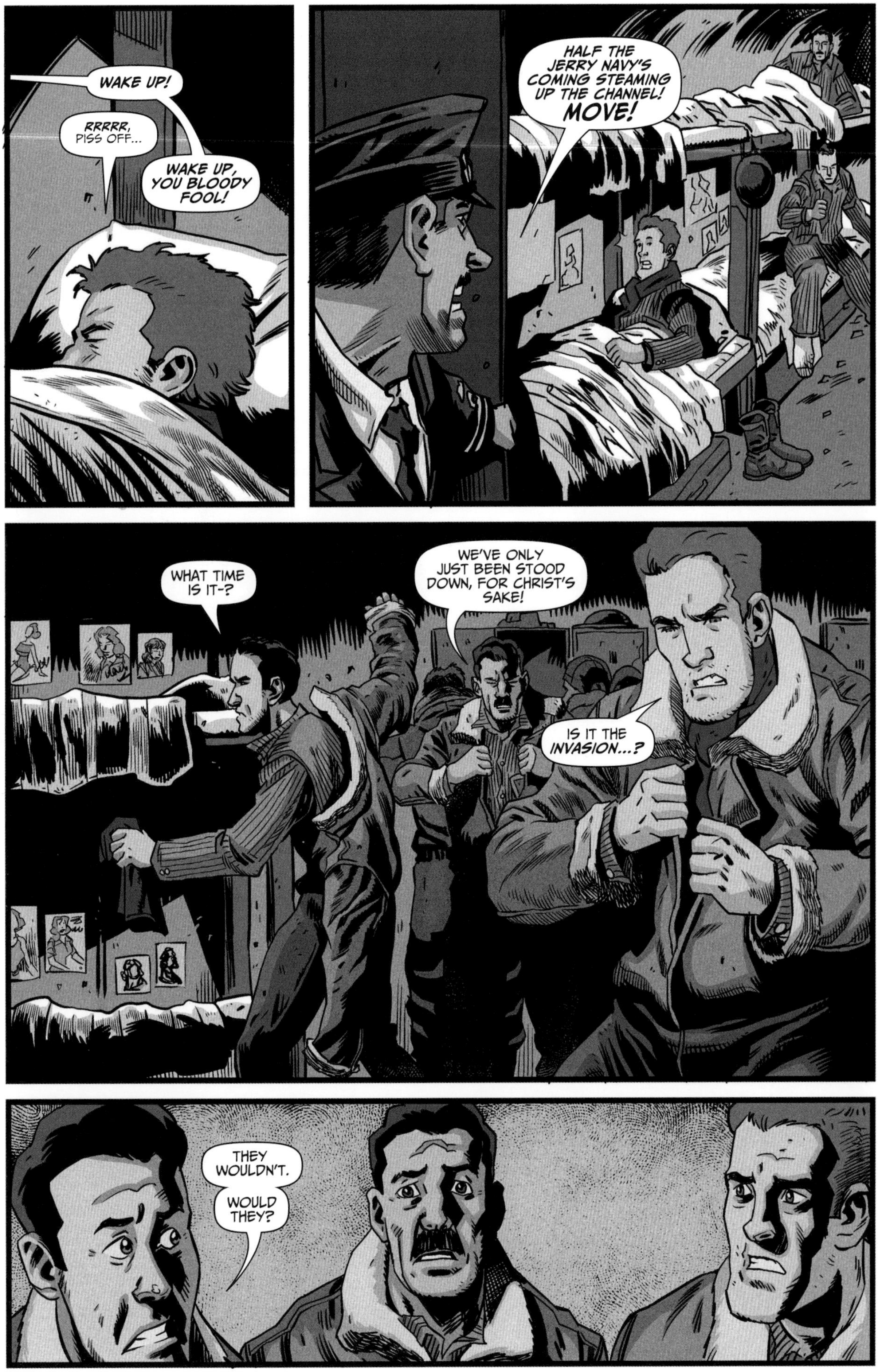
WAKE UP!
RRRRR, PISS OFF...
WAKE UP, YOU BLOODY FOOL!
HALF THE JERRY NAVY'S COMING STEAMING UP THE CHANNEL! MOVE!
WHAT TIME IS IT-?
WE'VE ONLY JUST BEEN STOOD DOWN, FOR CHRIST'S SAKE!
IS IT THE INVASION...?
THEY WOULDN'T.
WOULD THEY?

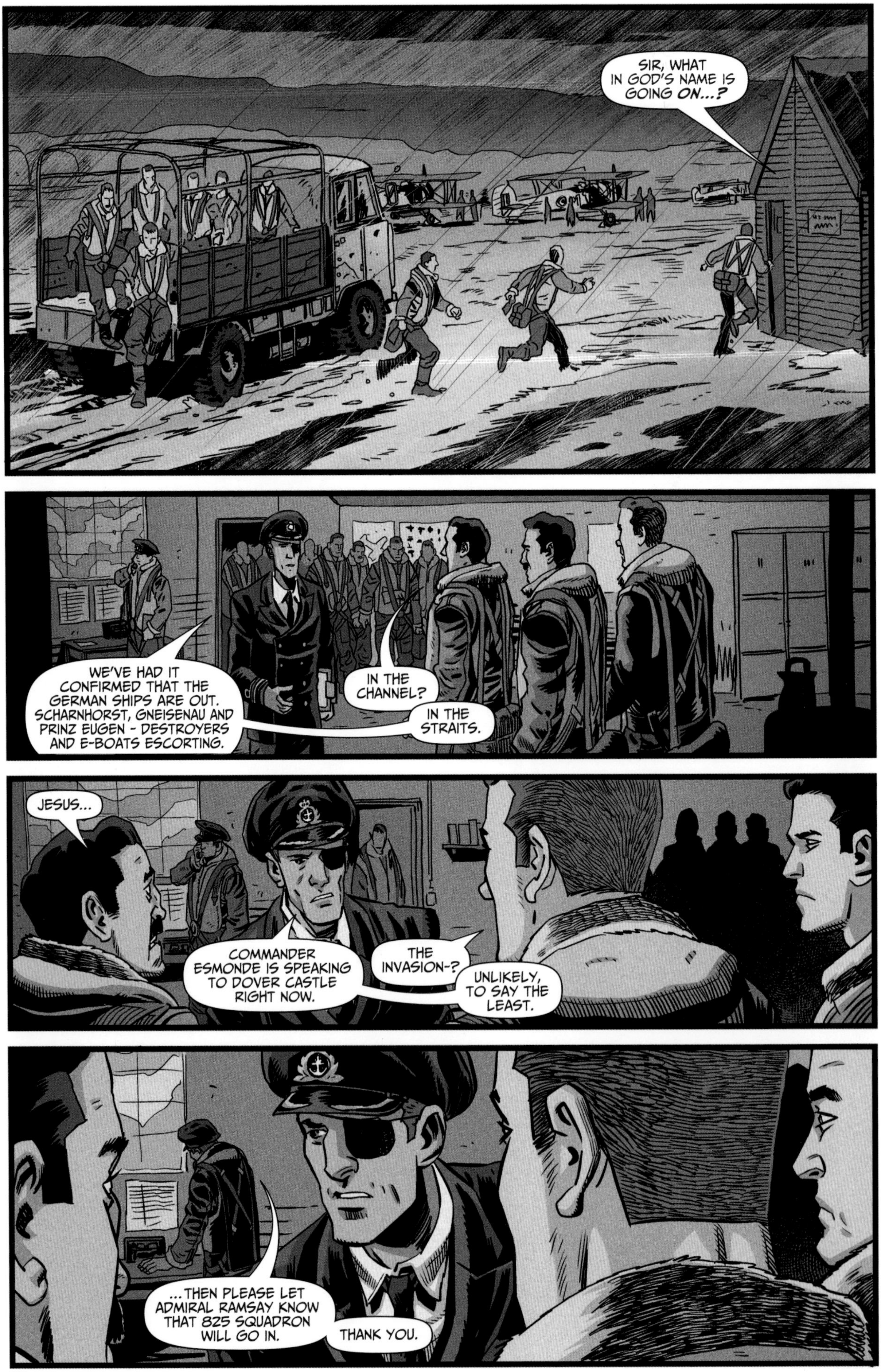
SIR, WHAT IN GOD'S NAME IS GOING ON...?
WE'VE HAD IT CONFIRMED THAT THE GERMAN SHIPS ARE OUT. SCHARNHORST, GNEISENAU AND PRINZ EUGEN - DESTROYERS AND E-BOATS ESCORTING.
IN THE CHANNEL?
IN THE STRAITS.
JESUS...
COMMANDER ESMONDE IS SPEAKING TO DOVER CASTLE RIGHT NOW.
THE INVASION-?
UNLIKELY, TO SAY THE LEAST.
...THEN PLEASE LET ADMIRAL RAMSAY KNOW THAT 825 SQUADRON WILL GO IN.
THANK YOU.

RIGHT THEN. THESE JERRY BATTLEWAGONS HAVE HAD THE CHEEK TO PUT THEIR NOSES INTO THE CHANNEL, SO WE'RE GOING OUT TO DEAL WITH THEM.

FLY AT FIFTY FEET IN LOOSE LINE ASTERN, MAKE INDIVIDUAL ATTACKS AND FIND YOUR OWN WAY HOME.

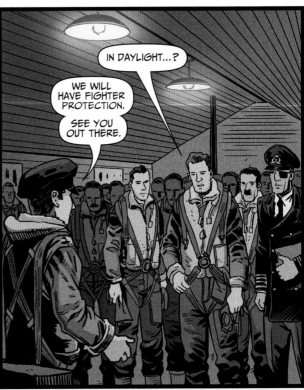

IN DAYLIGHT...?

WE WILL HAVE FIGHTER PROTECTION.

SEE YOU OUT THERE.

LET HIM KNOW YOU'LL GO IN, THAT ALMOST SOUNDS LIKE HE GAVE YOU A CHOICE...

WELL, HE DID, IN A MANNER OF SPEAKING.

THE CHAP I SPOKE TO SAID THE ADMIRAL ONLY WANTED ME TO GO AHEAD IF I WAS SATISFIED WITH OUR FIGHTER COVER. SAID HE'D BEEN IN TOUCH WITH THE ADMIRALTY, ASKING NOT TO HAVE TO SEND US IN.

BUT WE'RE ALL THERE IS UNTIL THE RAF GET THEIR ACT TOGETHER, APPARENTLY. SO THE ANSWER HE GOT WAS NO.

149

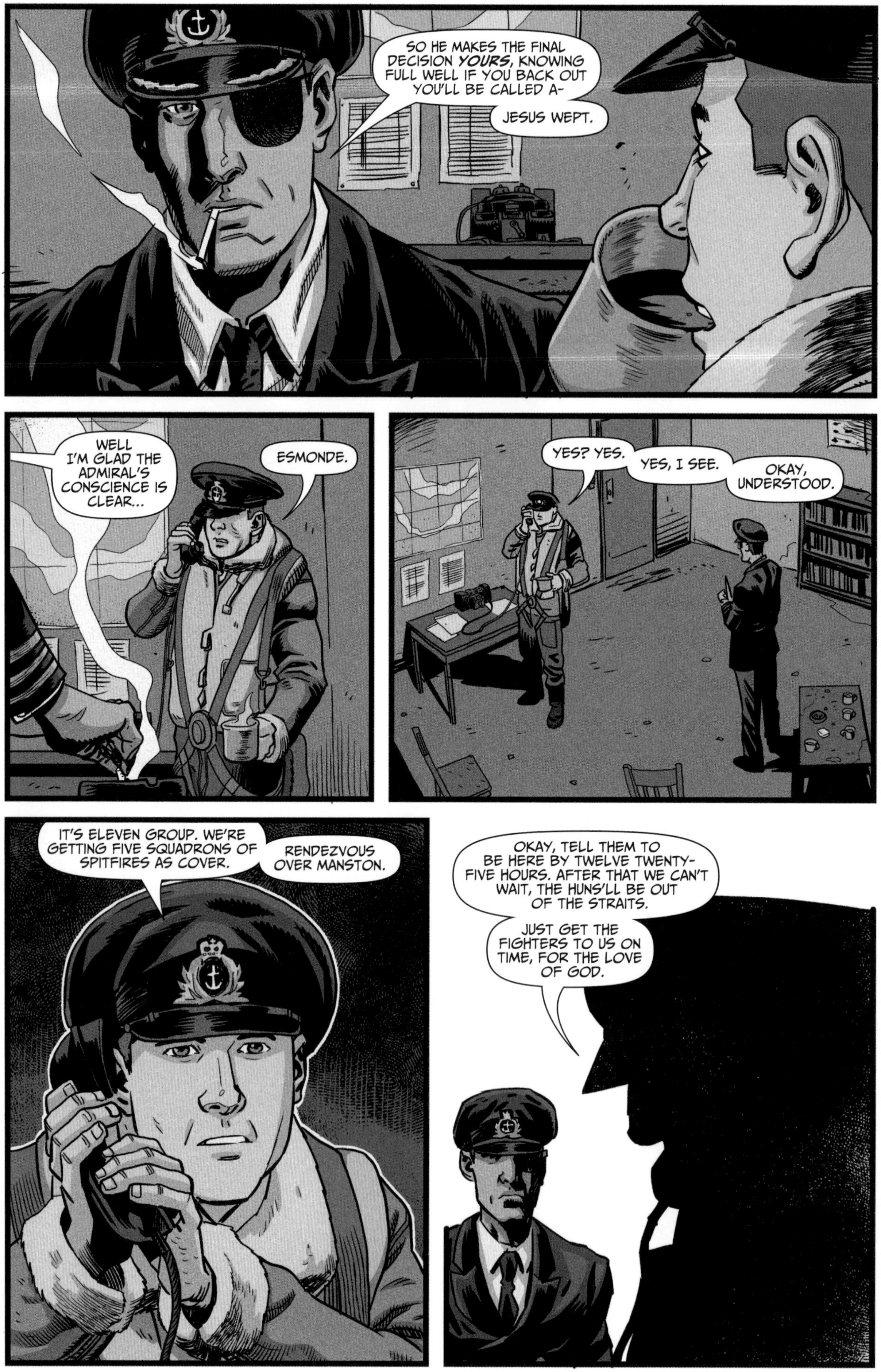
SO HE MAKES THE FINAL DECISION YOURS, KNOWING FULL WELL IF YOU BACK OUT YOU'LL BE CALLED A-
JESUS WEPT.
WELL I'M GLAD THE ADMIRAL'S CONSCIENCE IS CLEAR...
ESMONDE.
YES? YES.
YES, I SEE.
OKAY, UNDERSTOOD.
IT'S ELEVEN GROUP. WE'RE GETTING FIVE SQUADRONS OF SPITFIRES AS COVER.
RENDEZVOUS OVER MANSTON.
OKAY, TELL THEM TO BE HERE BY TWELVE TWENTY-FIVE HOURS. AFTER THAT WE CAN'T WAIT, THE HUNS'LL BE OUT OF THE STRAITS.
JUST GET THE FIGHTERS TO US ON TIME, FOR THE LOVE OF GOD.

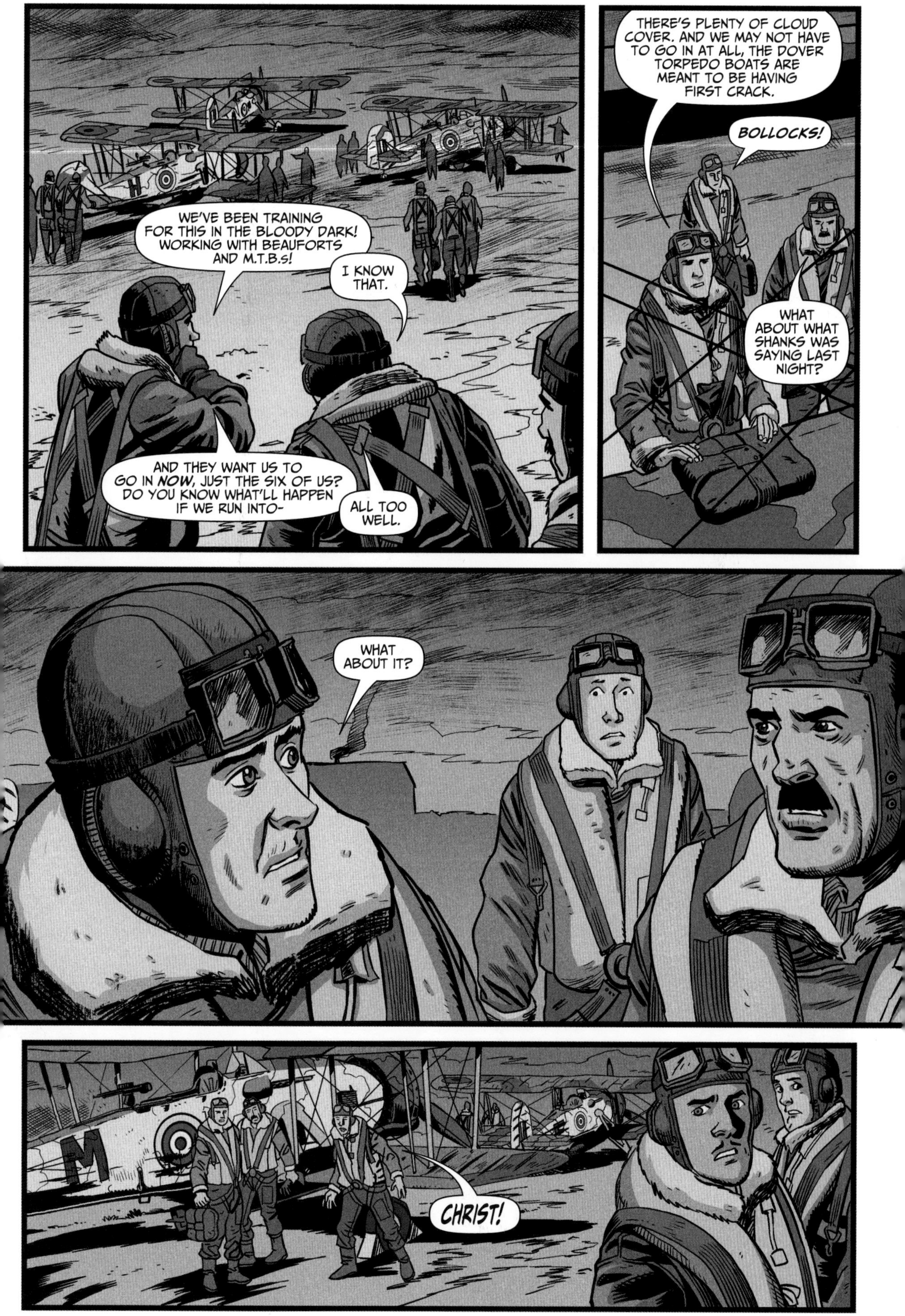
WE'VE BEEN TRAINING FOR THIS IN THE BLOODY DARK! WORKING WITH BEAUFORTS AND M.T.B.s!
I KNOW THAT.
AND THEY WANT US TO GO IN NOW, JUST THE SIX OF US? DO YOU KNOW WHAT'LL HAPPEN IF WE RUN INTO-
ALL TOO WELL.
THERE'S PLENTY OF CLOUD COVER. AND WE MAY NOT HAVE TO GO IN AT ALL, THE DOVER TORPEDO BOATS ARE MEANT TO BE HAVING FIRST CRACK.
BOLLOCKS!
WHAT ABOUT WHAT SHANKS WAS SAYING LAST NIGHT?
WHAT ABOUT IT?
CHRIST!

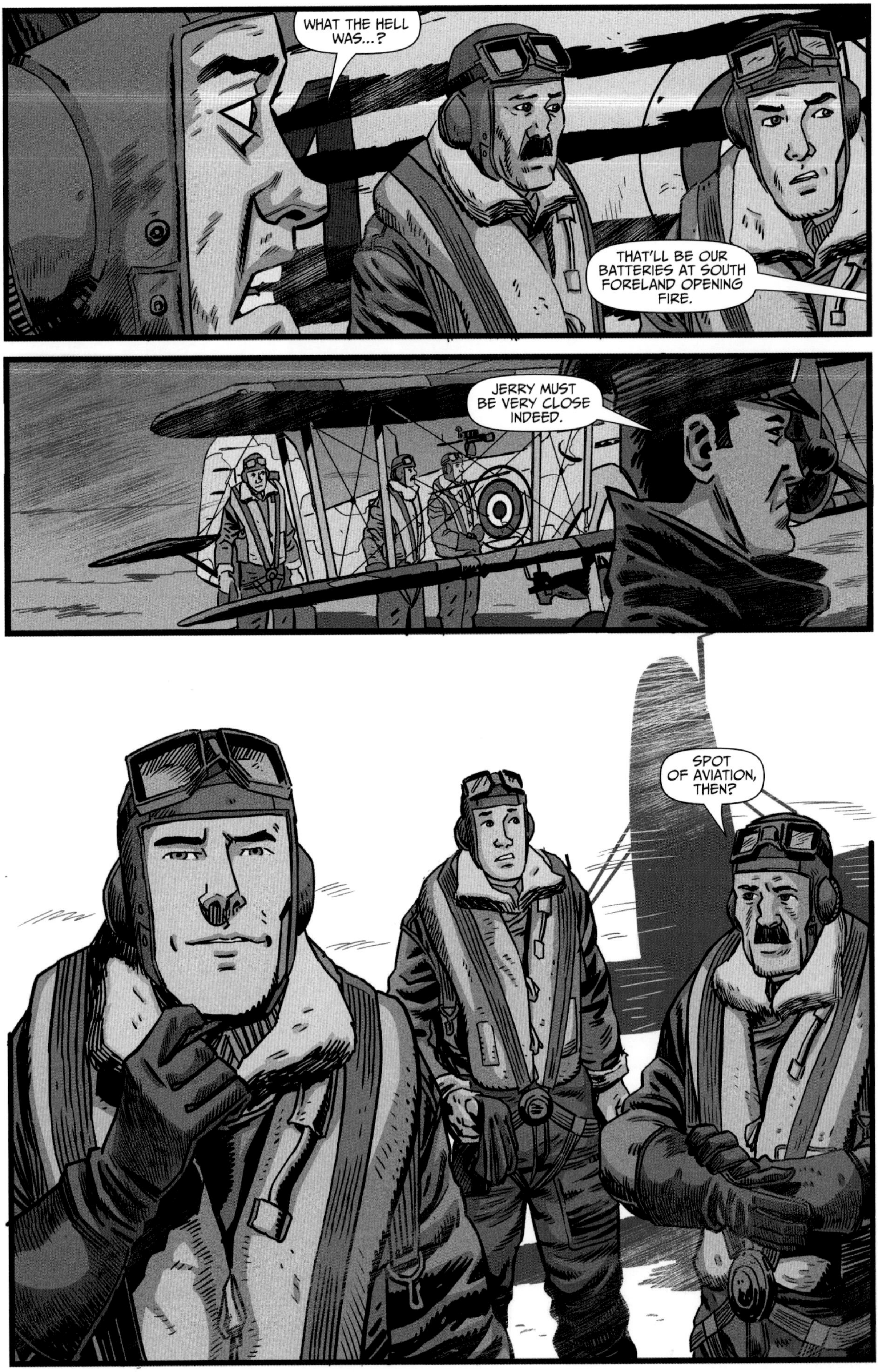
WHAT THE HELL WAS...?
THAT'LL BE OUR BATTERIES AT SOUTH FORELAND OPENING FIRE.
JERRY MUST BE VERY CLOSE INDEED.
SPOT OF AVIATION, THEN?

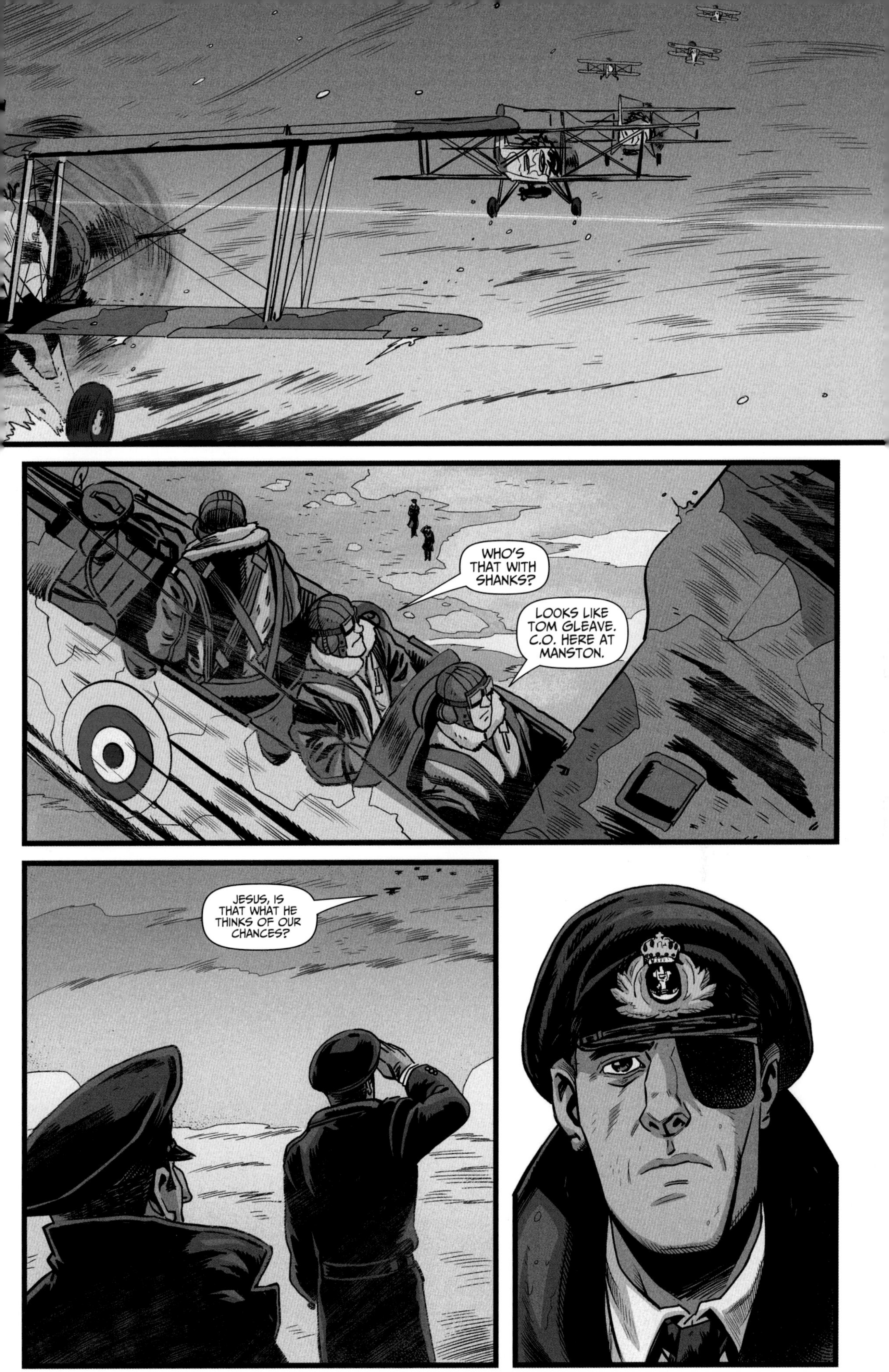
WHO'S THAT WITH SHANKS?
LOOKS LIKE TOM GLEAVE. C.O. HERE AT MANSTON.
JESUS, IS THAT WHAT HE THINKS OF OUR CHANCES?

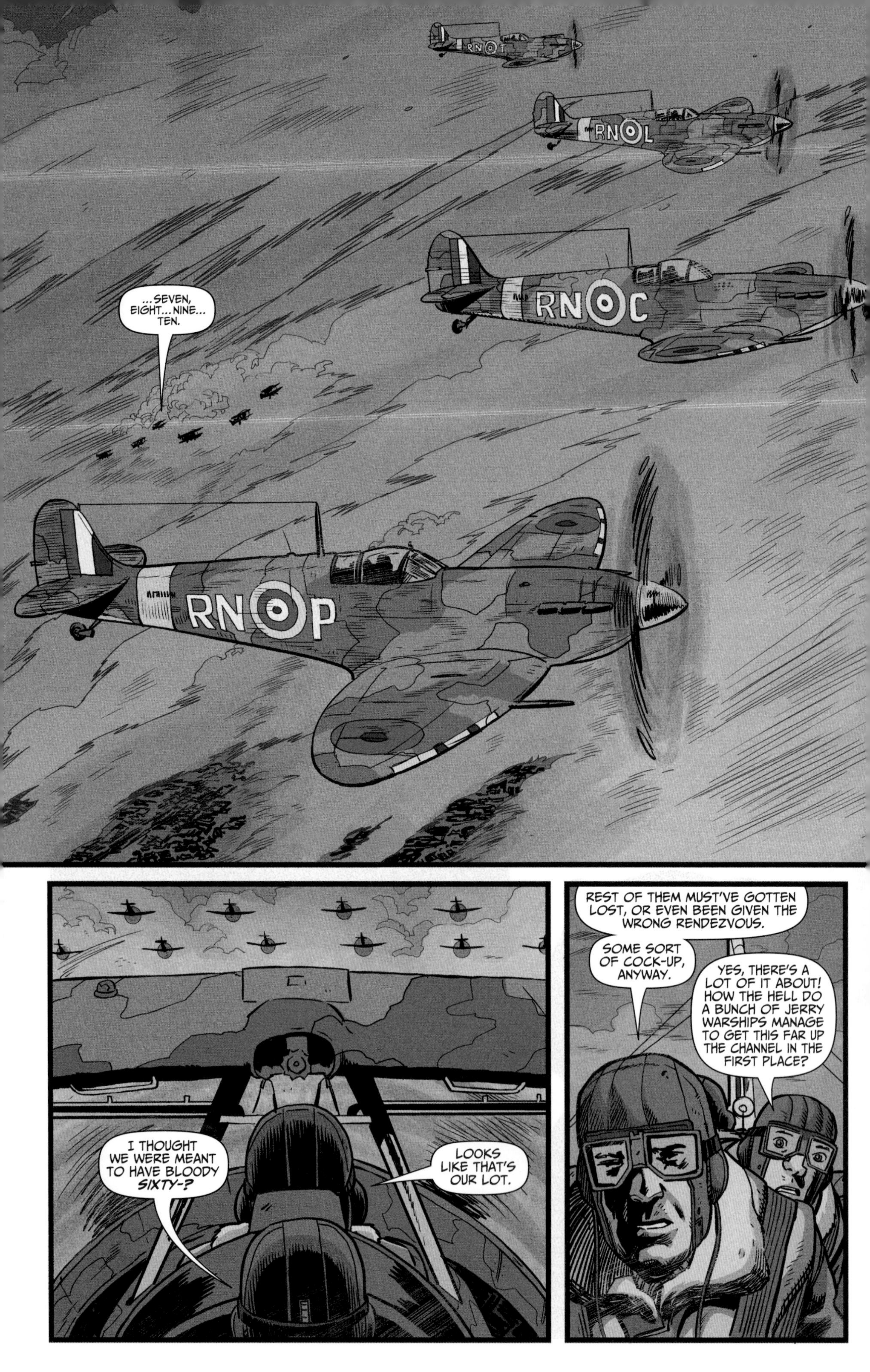
...SEVEN, EIGHT...NINE... TEN.
I THOUGHT WE WERE MEANT TO HAVE BLOODY *SIXTY-?*
LOOKS LIKE THAT'S OUR LOT.
REST OF THEM MUST'VE GOTTEN LOST, OR EVEN BEEN GIVEN THE WRONG RENDEZVOUS.
SOME SORT OF COCK-UP, ANYWAY.
YES, THERE'S A LOT OF IT ABOUT! HOW THE HELL DO A BUNCH OF JERRY WARSHIPS MANAGE TO GET THIS FAR UP THE CHANNEL IN THE FIRST PLACE?

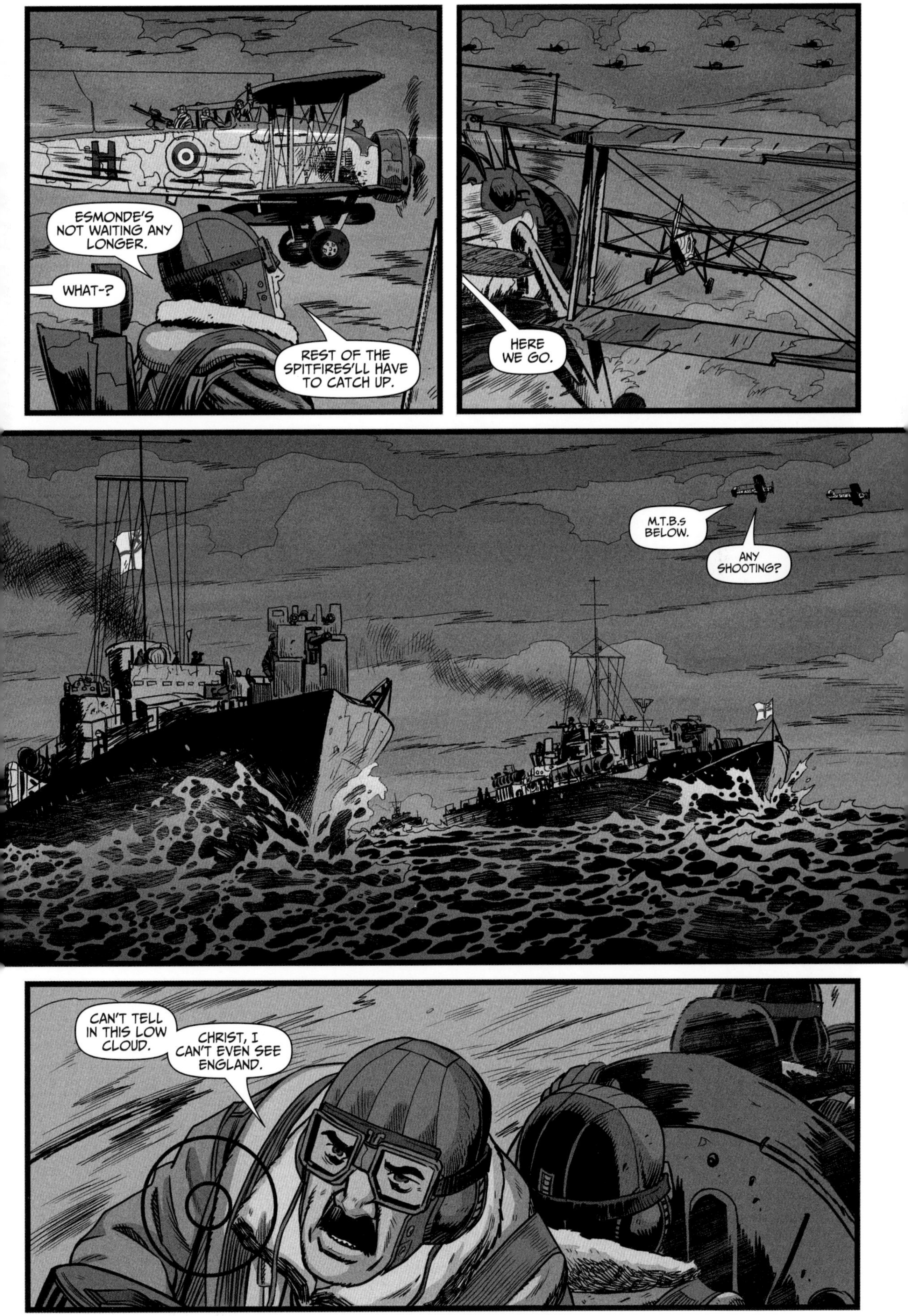
ESMONDE'S NOT WAITING ANY LONGER.
WHAT-?
REST OF THE SPITFIRES'LL HAVE TO CATCH UP.
HERE WE GO.
M.T.B.s BELOW.
ANY SHOOTING?
CAN'T TELL IN THIS LOW CLOUD.
CHRIST, I CAN'T EVEN SEE ENGLAND.

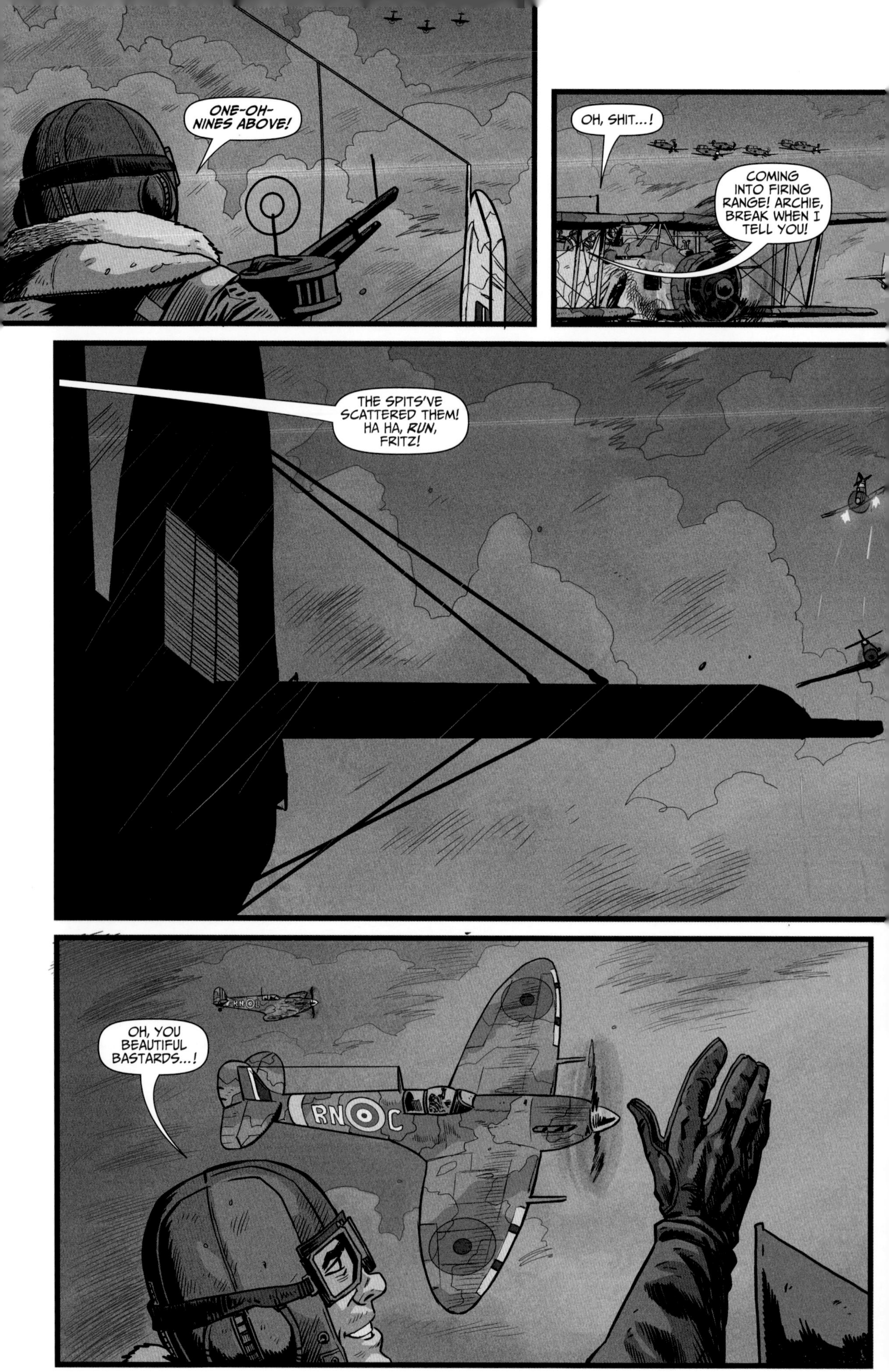
ONE-OH-NINES ABOVE!
OH, SHIT...!
COMING INTO FIRING RANGE! ARCHIE, BREAK WHEN I TELL YOU!
THE SPITS'VE SCATTERED THEM! HA HA, *RUN*, FRITZ!
OH, YOU BEAUTIFUL BASTARDS...!

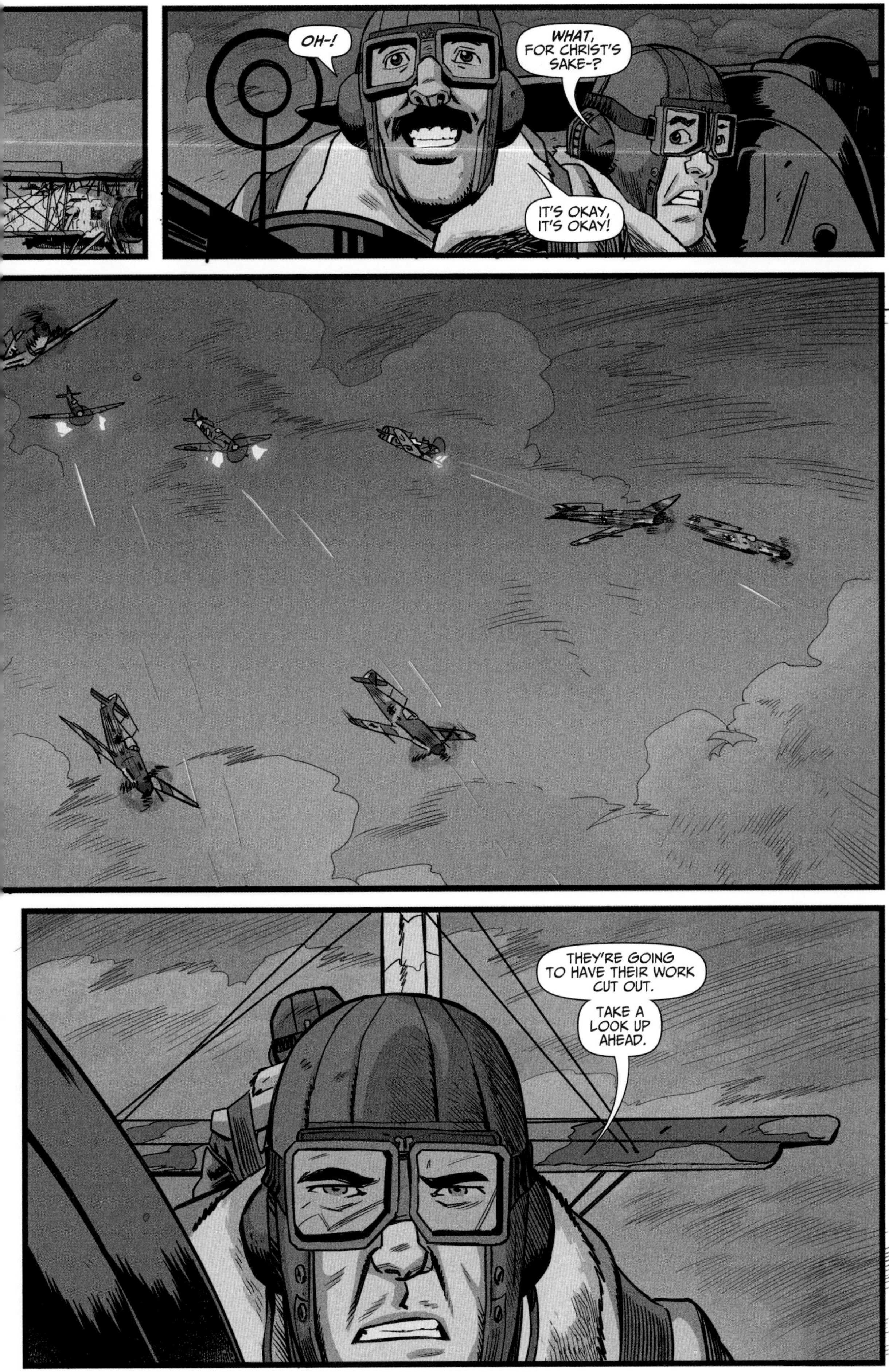
OH-!
WHAT, FOR CHRIST'S SAKE-?
IT'S OKAY, IT'S OKAY!
THEY'RE GOING TO HAVE THEIR WORK CUT OUT.
TAKE A LOOK UP AHEAD.

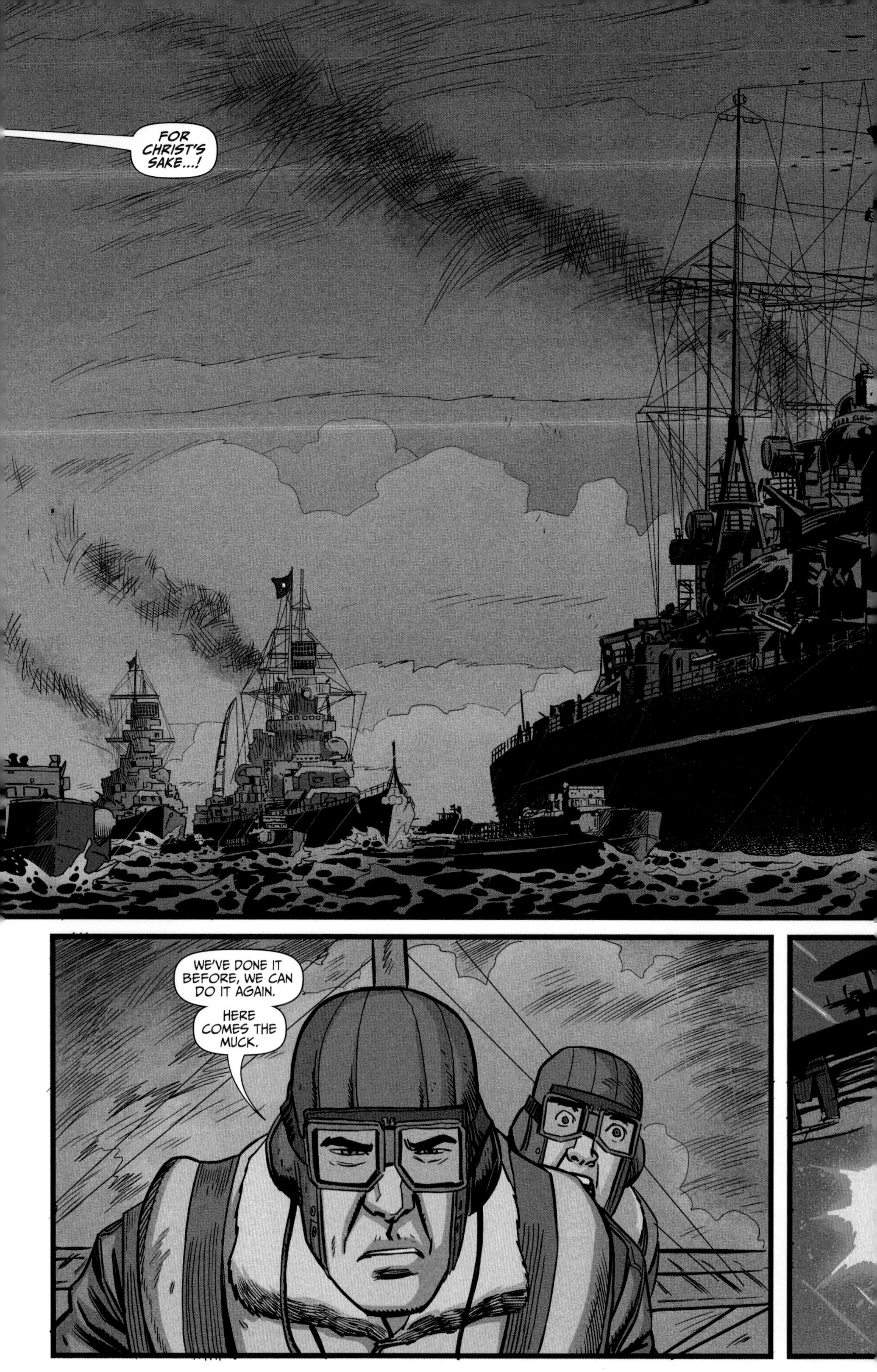
FOR CHRIST'S SAKE...!
WE'VE DONE IT BEFORE, WE CAN DO IT AGAIN.
HERE COMES THE MUCK.

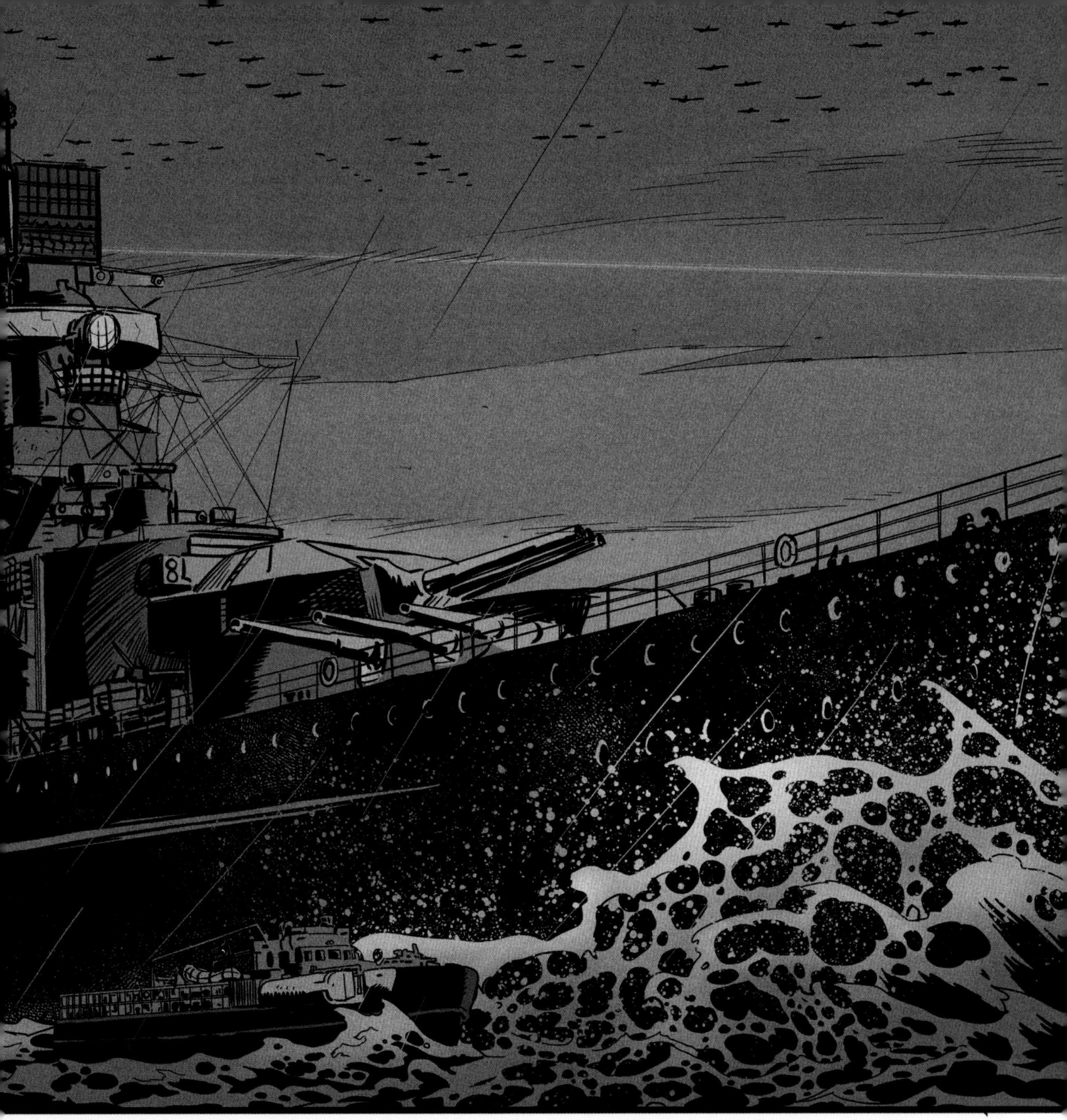

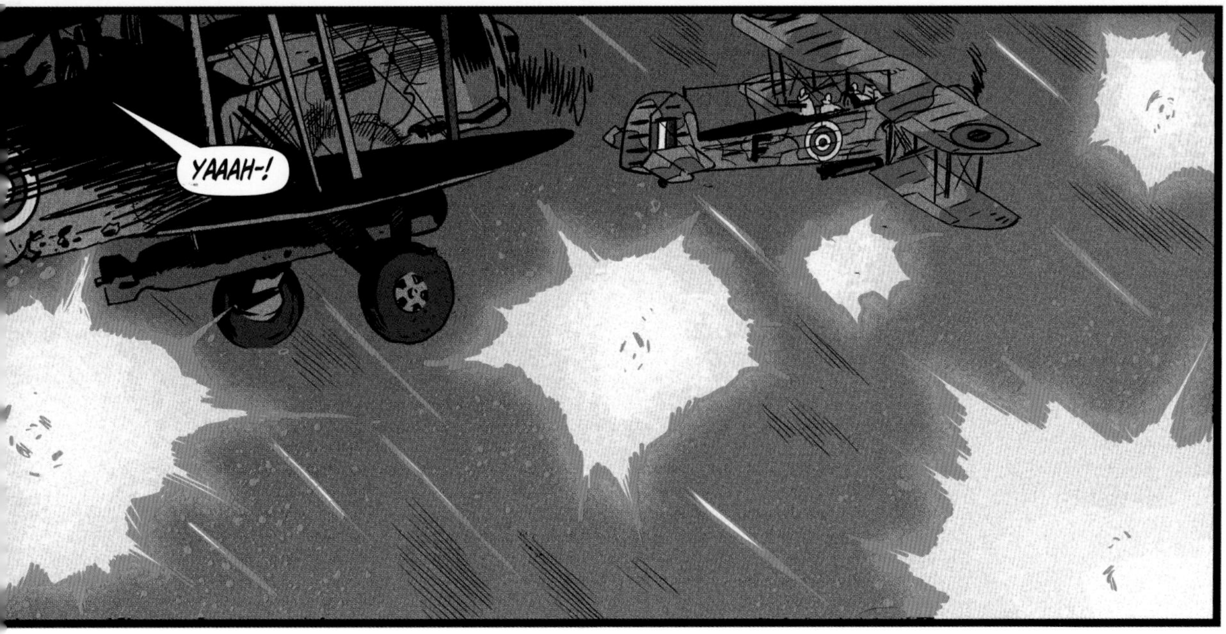
YAAAH-!

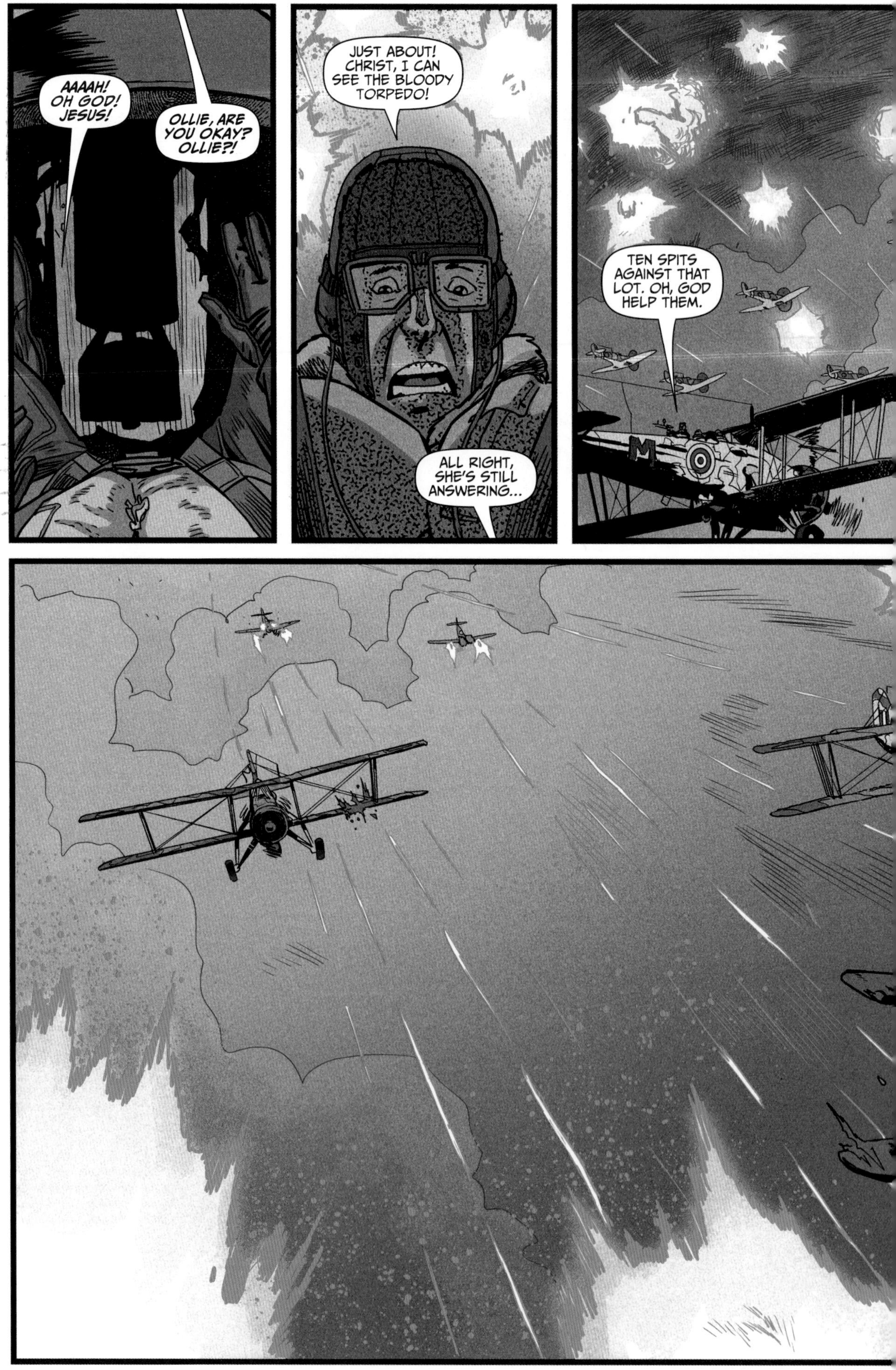
AAAAH! OH GOD! JESUS!
OLLIE, ARE YOU OKAY? OLLIE?!
JUST ABOUT! CHRIST, I CAN SEE THE BLOODY TORPEDO!
ALL RIGHT, SHE'S STILL ANSWERING...
TEN SPITS AGAINST THAT LOT. OH, GOD HELP THEM.

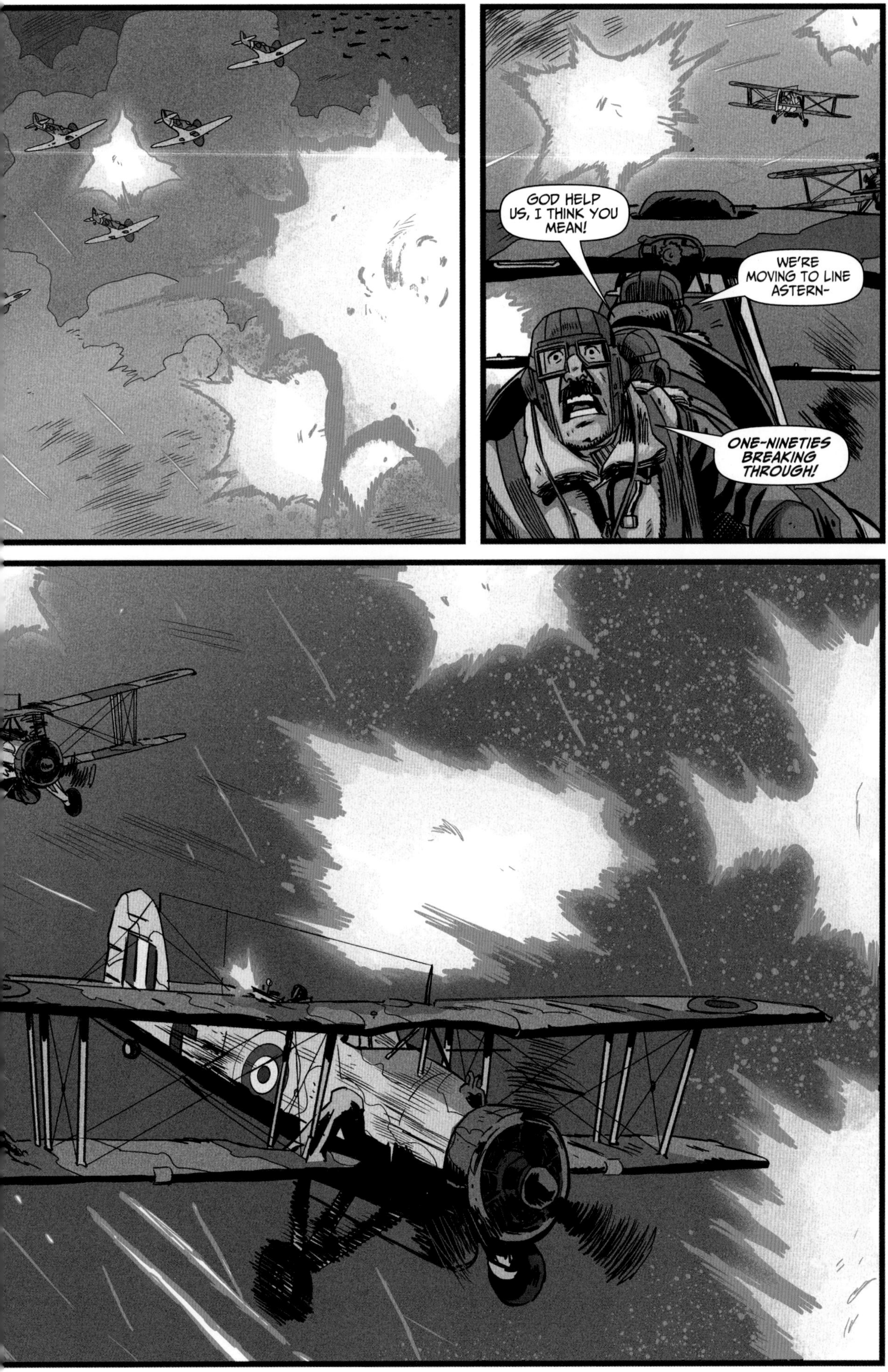
GOD HELP US, I THINK YOU MEAN!
WE'RE MOVING TO LINE ASTERN-
ONE-NINETIES BREAKING THROUGH!

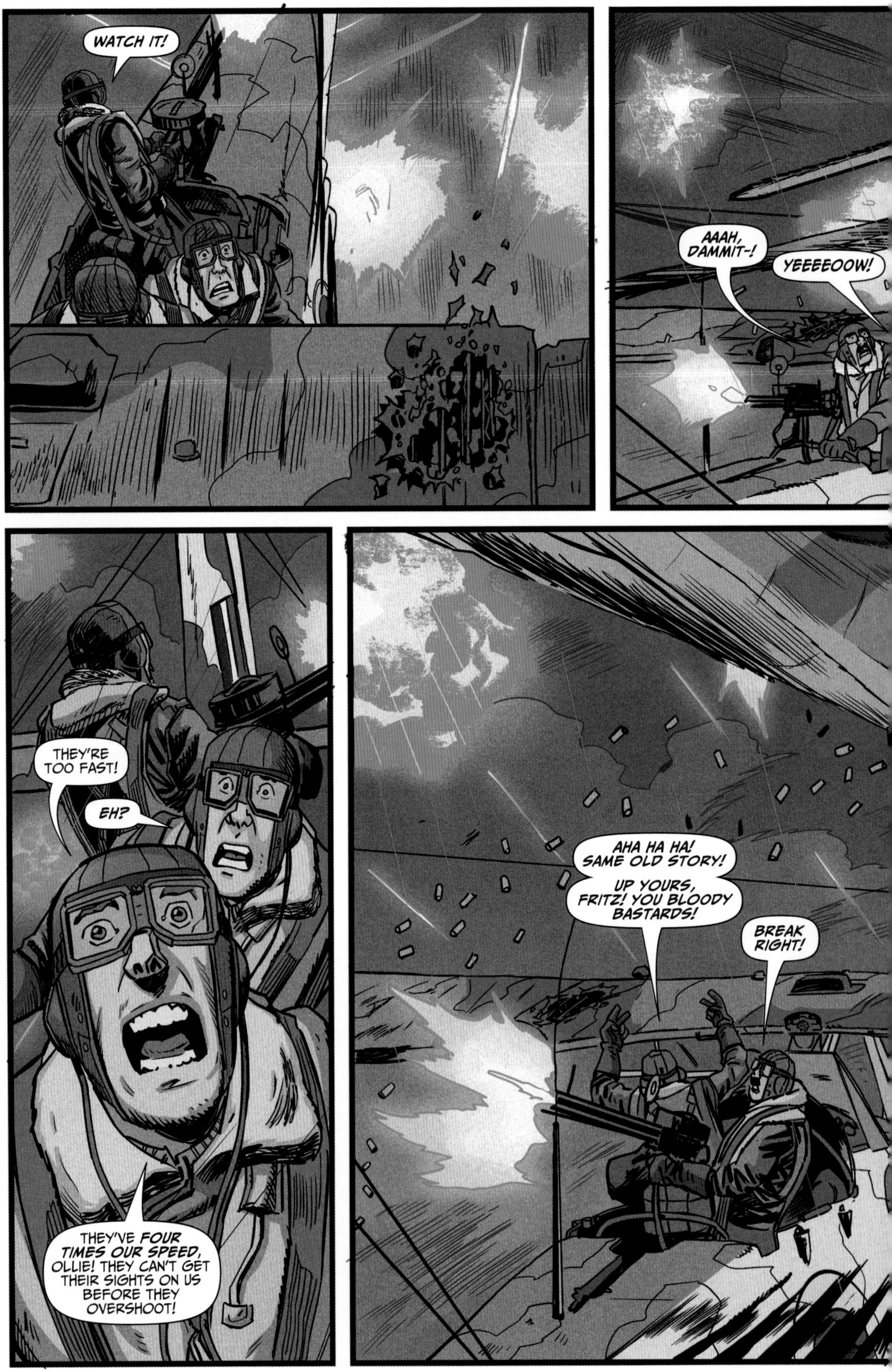
WATCH IT!
AAAH, DAMMIT-!
YEEEEOOW!
THEY'RE TOO FAST!
EH?
THEY'VE FOUR TIMES OUR SPEED, OLLIE! THEY CAN'T GET THEIR SIGHTS ON US BEFORE THEY OVERSHOOT!
AHA HA HA! SAME OLD STORY!
UP YOURS, FRITZ! YOU BLOODY BASTARDS!
BREAK RIGHT!

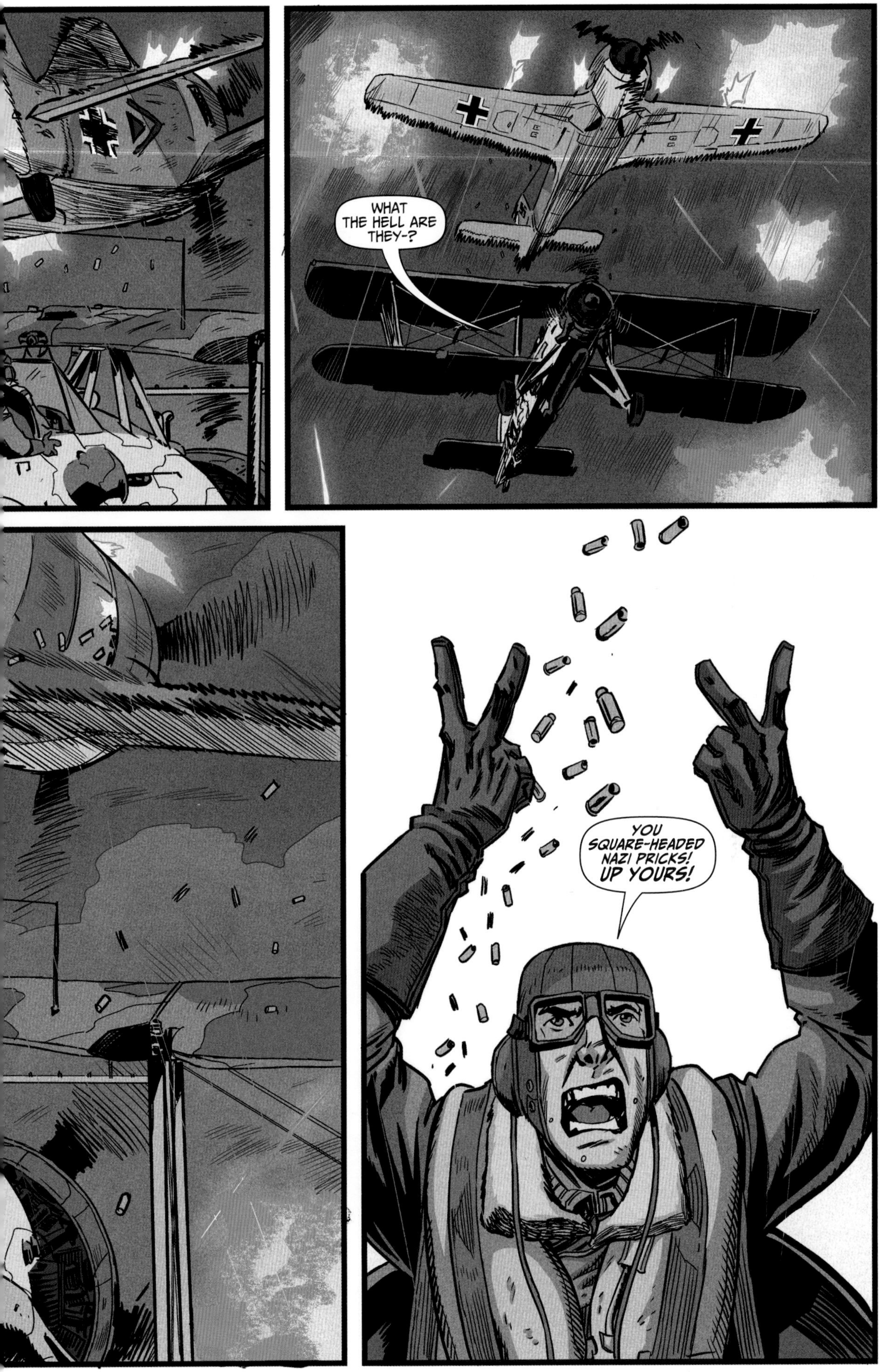
WHAT THE HELL ARE THEY-?
YOU SQUARE-HEADED NAZI PRICKS! UP YOURS!

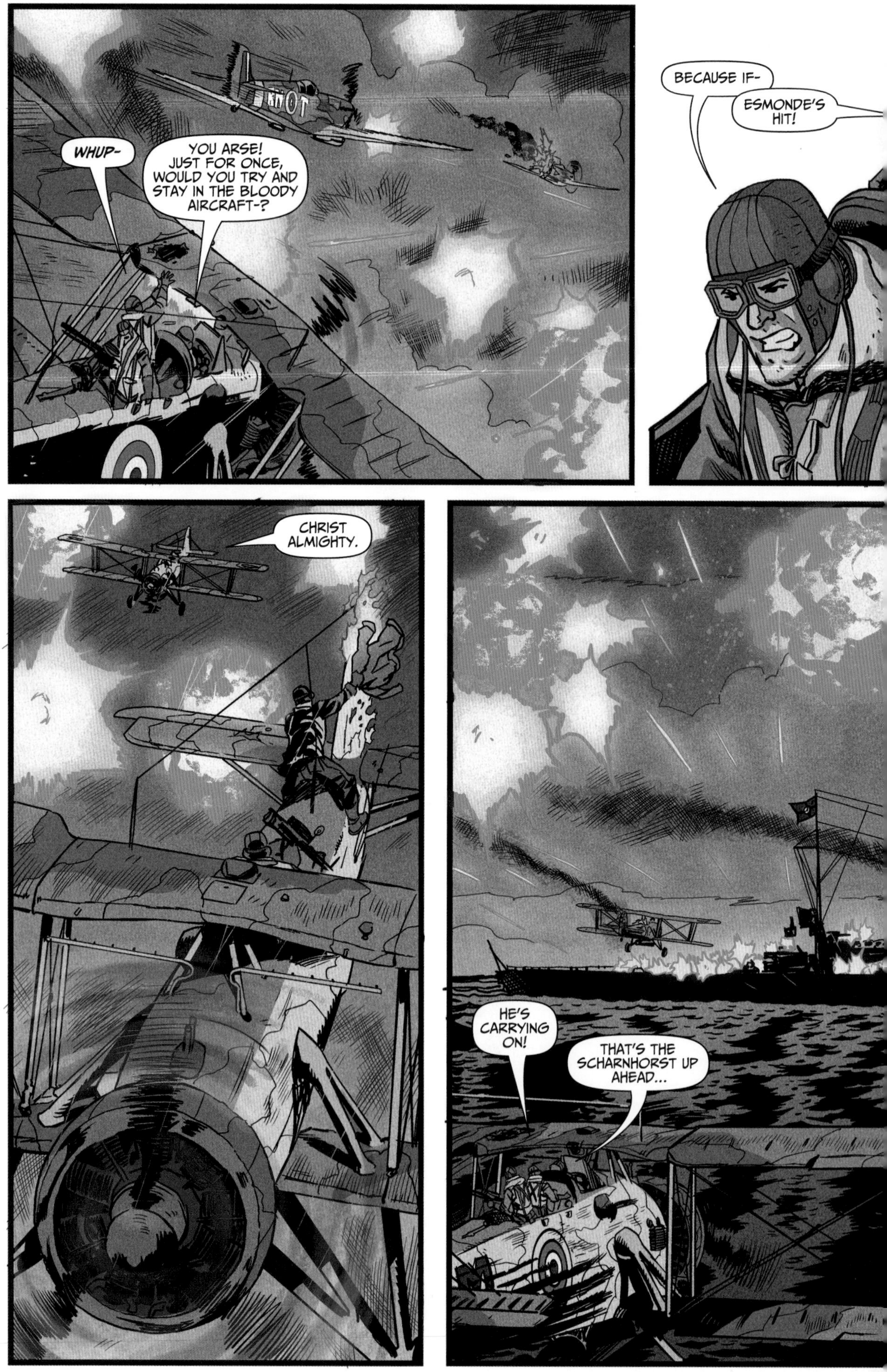

WHUP-
YOU ARSE! JUST FOR ONCE, WOULD YOU TRY AND STAY IN THE BLOODY AIRCRAFT-?
BECAUSE IF-
ESMONDE'S HIT!
CHRIST ALMIGHTY.
HE'S CARRYING ON!
THAT'S THE SCHARNHORST UP AHEAD...

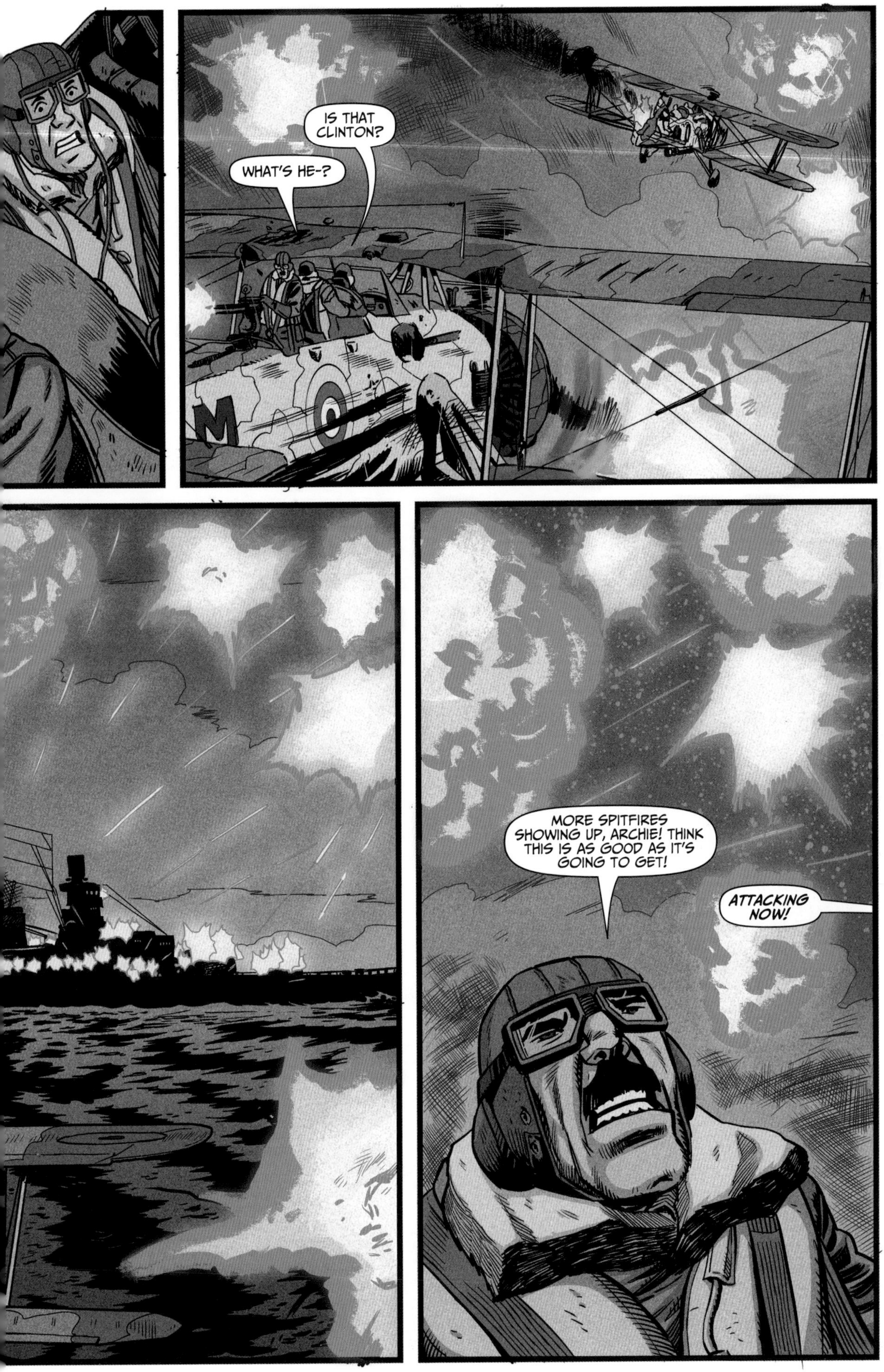
IS THAT CLINTON?
WHAT'S HE-?
MORE SPITFIRES SHOWING UP, ARCHIE! THINK THIS IS AS GOOD AS IT'S GOING TO GET!
ATTACKING NOW!

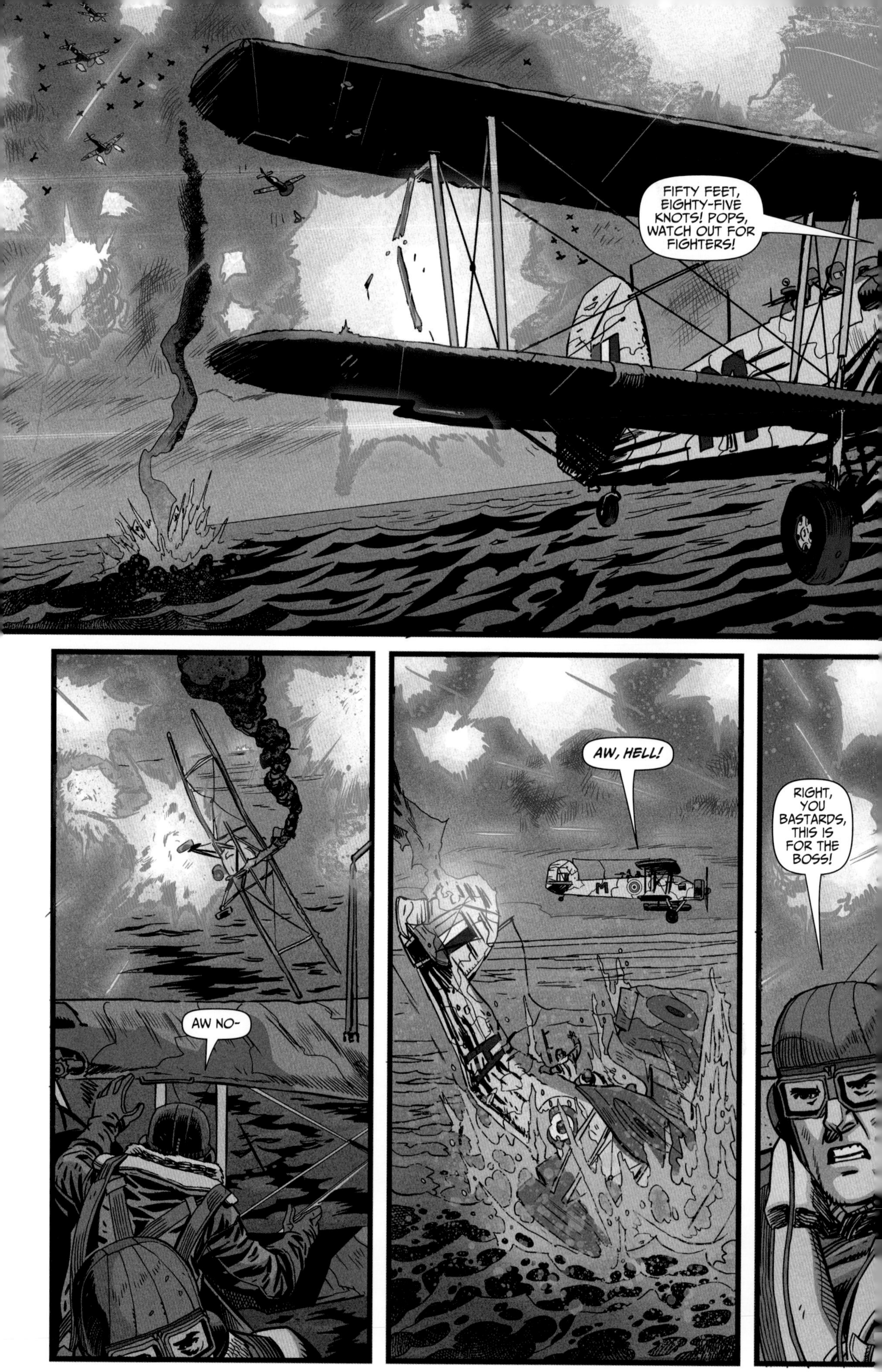
FIFTY FEET, EIGHTY-FIVE KNOTS! POPS, WATCH OUT FOR FIGHTERS!
AW NO-
AW, HELL!
RIGHT, YOU BASTARDS, THIS IS FOR THE BOSS!

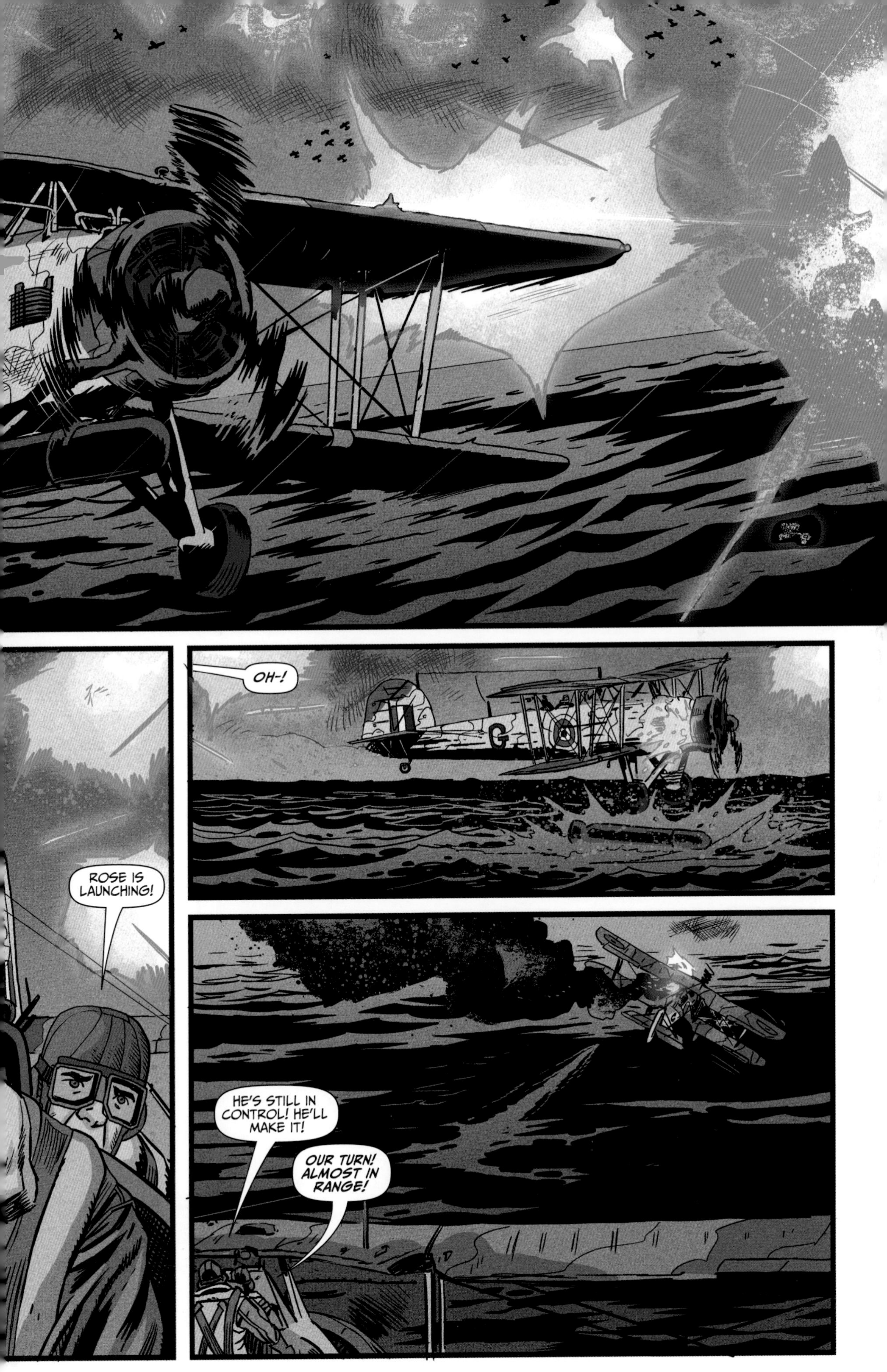
ROSE IS LAUNCHING!
OH-!
HE'S STILL IN CONTROL! HE'LL MAKE IT!
OUR TURN! ALMOST IN RANGE!

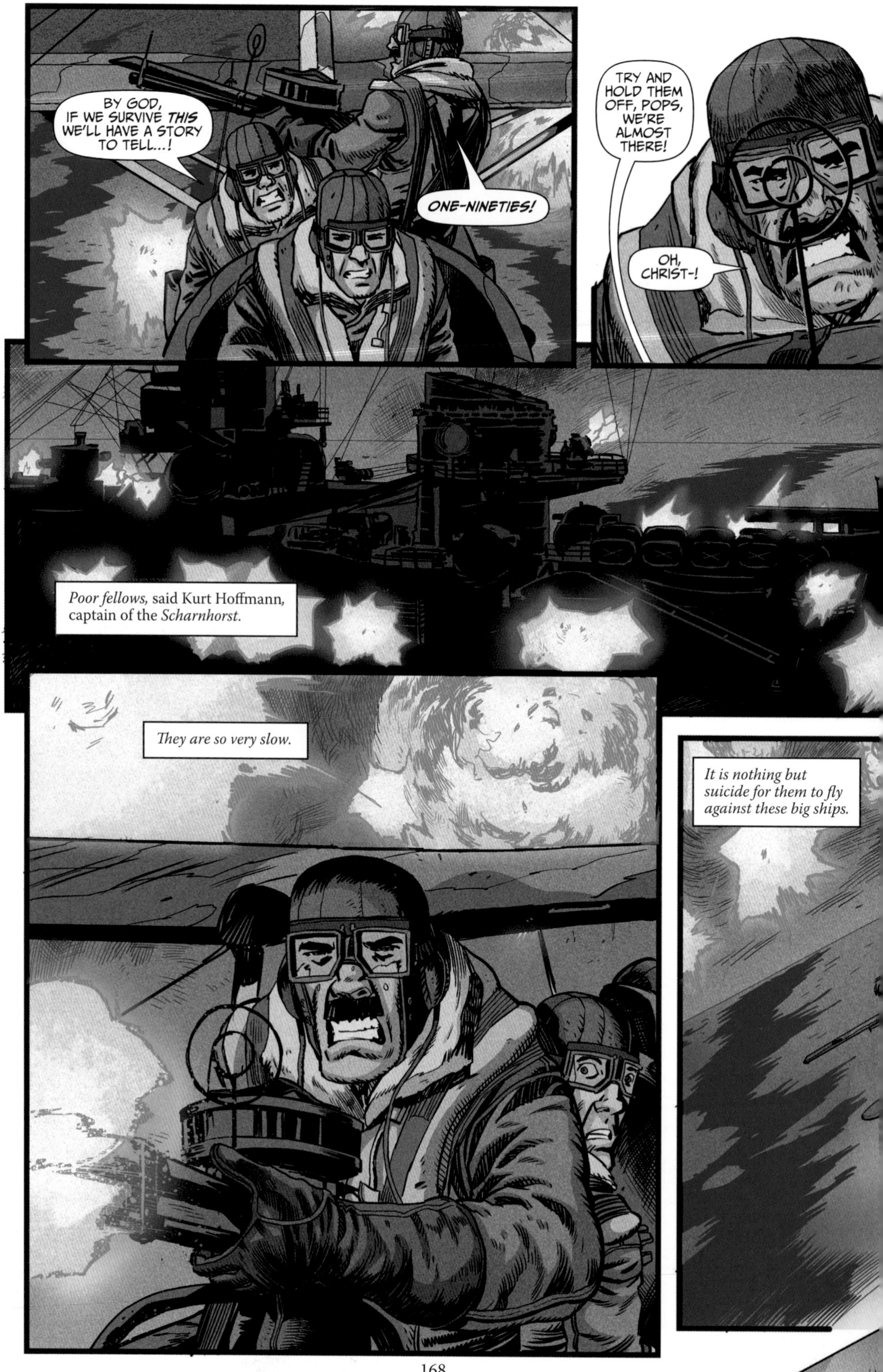
BY GOD, IF WE SURVIVE THIS WE'LL HAVE A STORY TO TELL...!
ONE-NINETIES!
TRY AND HOLD THEM OFF, POPS, WE'RE ALMOST THERE!
OH, CHRIST-!
Poor fellows, said Kurt Hoffmann, captain of the Scharnhorst.
They are so very slow.
It is nothing but suicide for them to fly against these big ships.

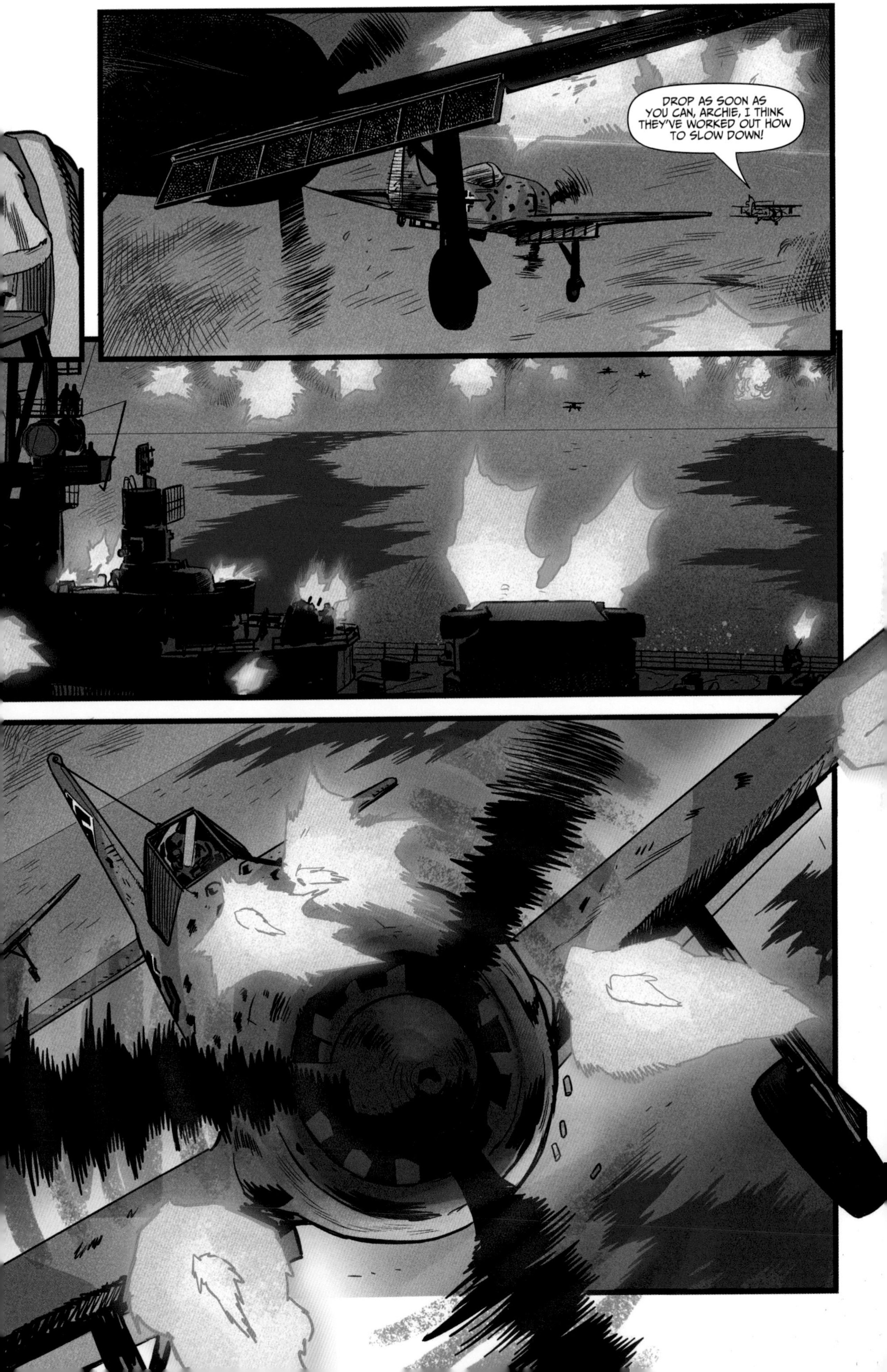
DROP AS SOON AS YOU CAN, ARCHIE, I THINK THEY'VE WORKED OUT HOW TO SLOW DOWN!

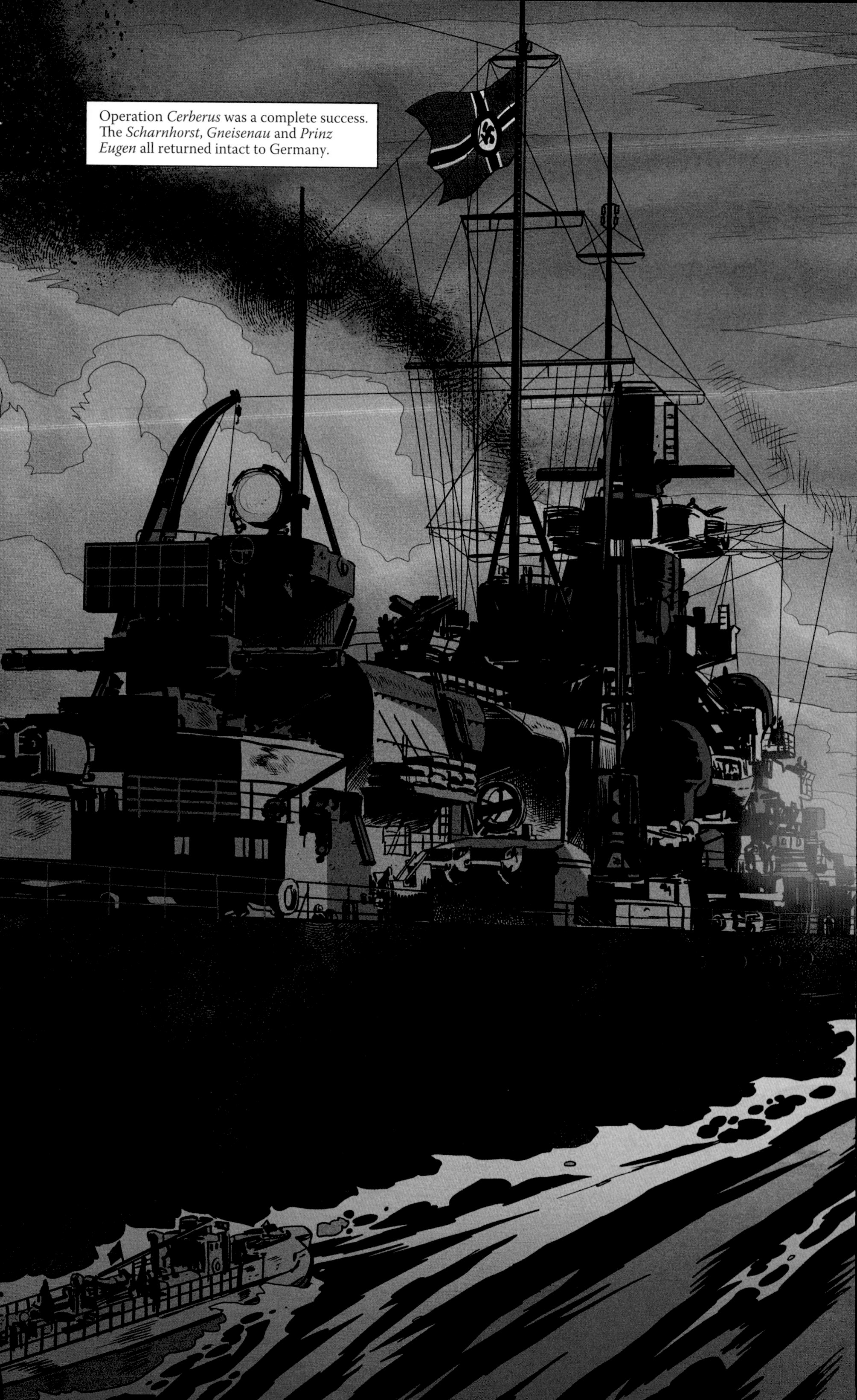
Operation *Cerberus* was a complete success. The *Scharnhorst*, *Gneisenau* and *Prinz Eugen* all returned intact to Germany.

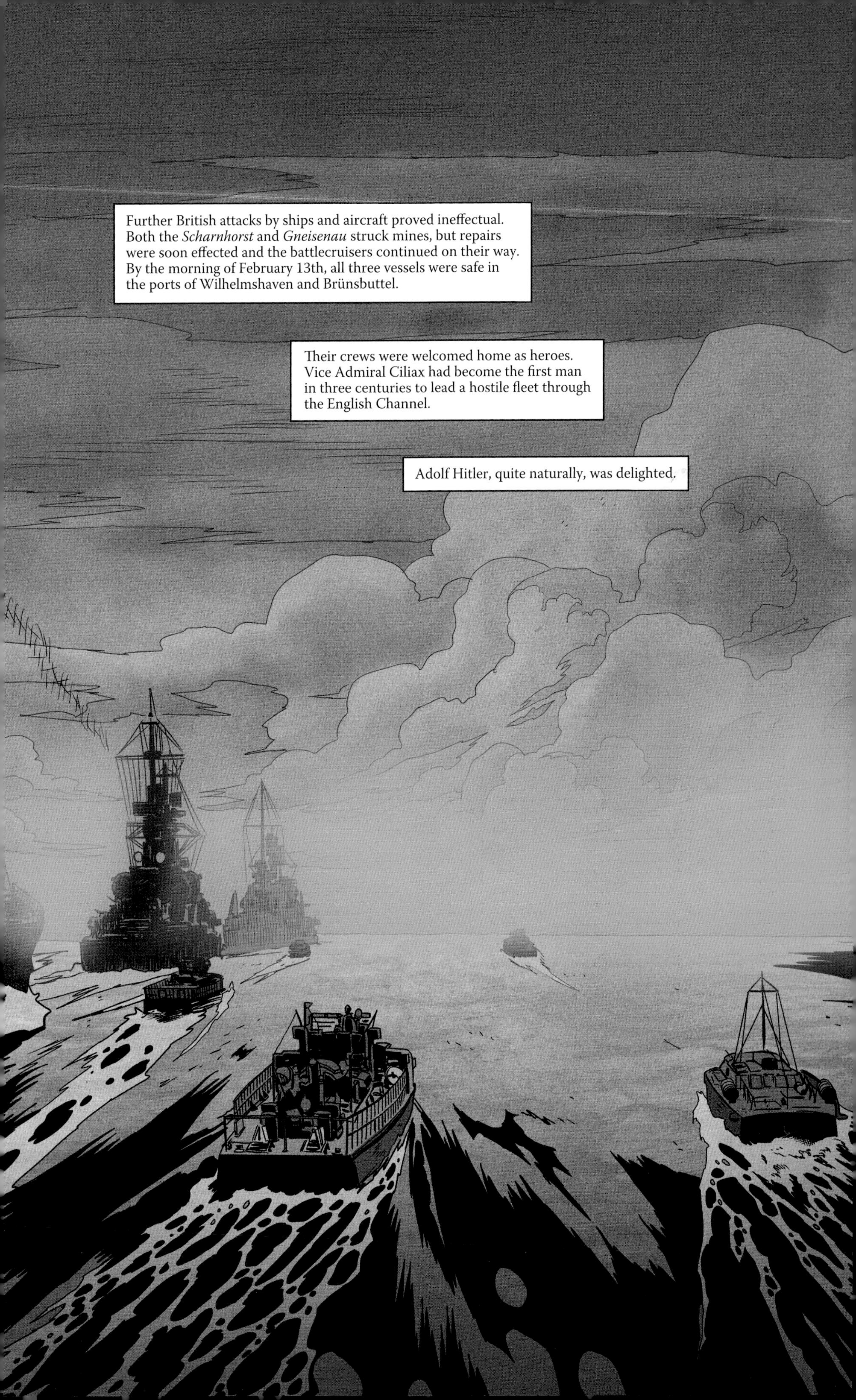
Further British attacks by ships and aircraft proved ineffectual. Both the *Scharnhorst* and *Gneisenau* struck mines, but repairs were soon effected and the battlecruisers continued on their way. By the morning of February 13th, all three vessels were safe in the ports of Wilhelmshaven and Brünsbuttel.
Their crews were welcomed home as heroes. Vice Admiral Ciliax had become the first man in three centuries to lead a hostile fleet through the English Channel.
Adolf Hitler, quite naturally, was delighted.

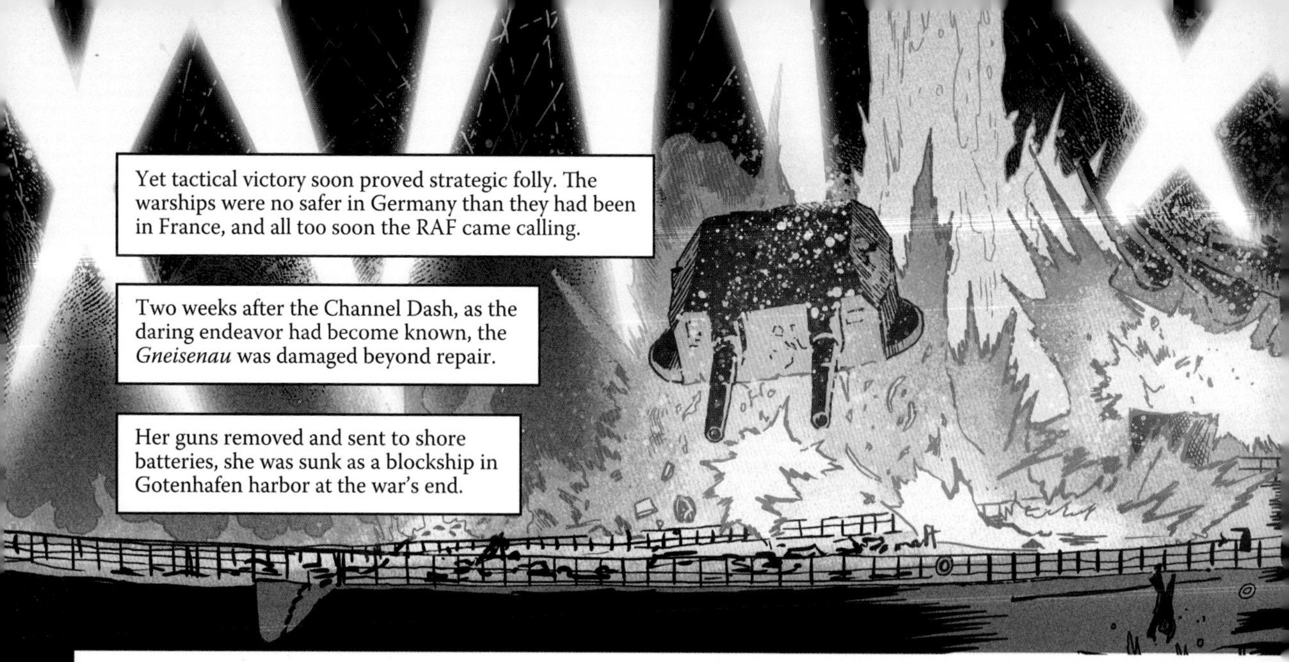
Yet tactical victory soon proved strategic folly. The warships were no safer in Germany than they had been in France, and all too soon the RAF came calling.
Two weeks after the Channel Dash, as the daring endeavor had become known, the *Gneisenau* was damaged beyond repair.
Her guns removed and sent to shore batteries, she was sunk as a blockship in Gotenhafen harbor at the war's end.

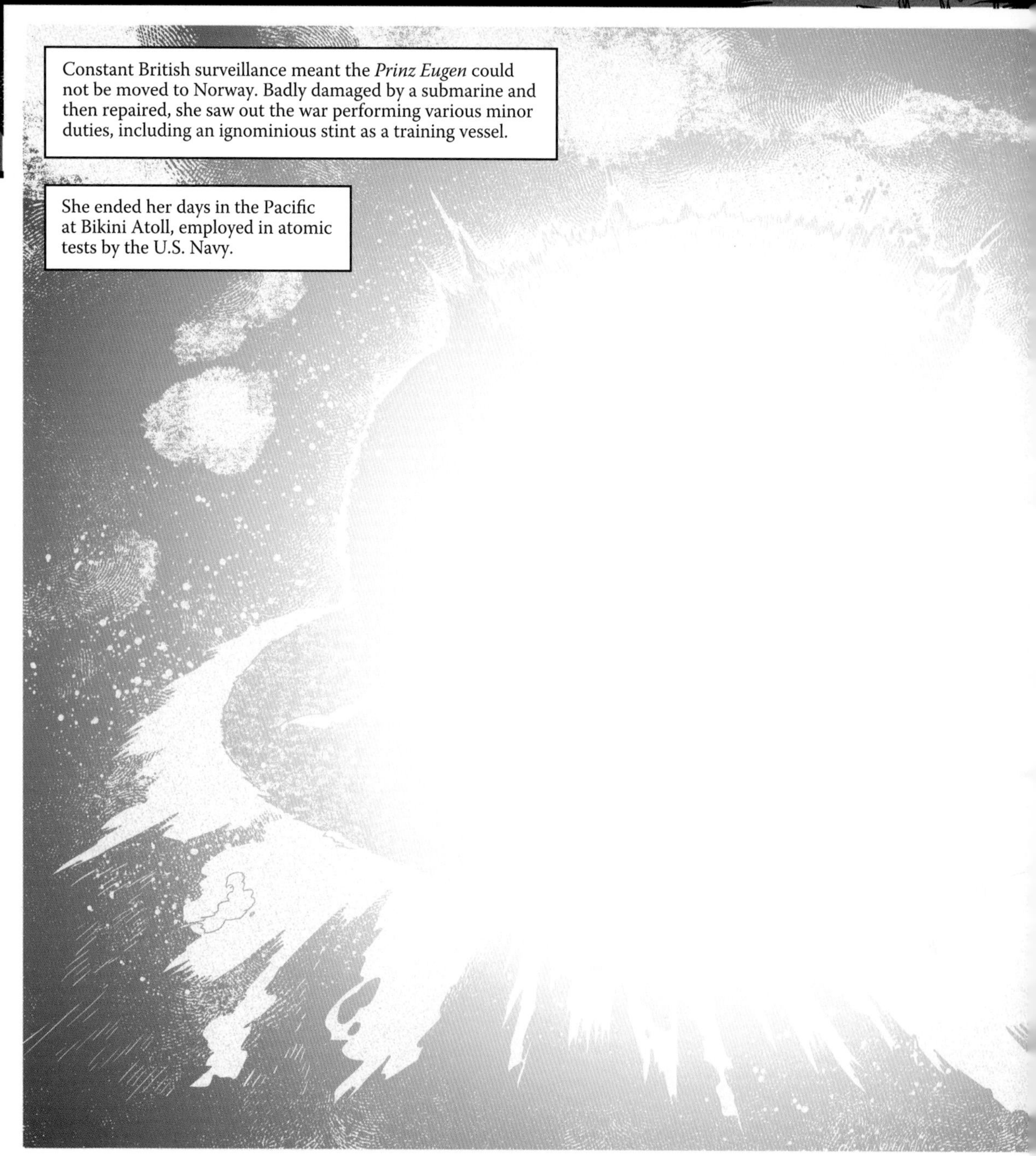
Constant British surveillance meant the *Prinz Eugen* could not be moved to Norway. Badly damaged by a submarine and then repaired, she saw out the war performing various minor duties, including an ignominious stint as a training vessel.
She ended her days in the Pacific at Bikini Atoll, employed in atomic tests by the U.S. Navy.

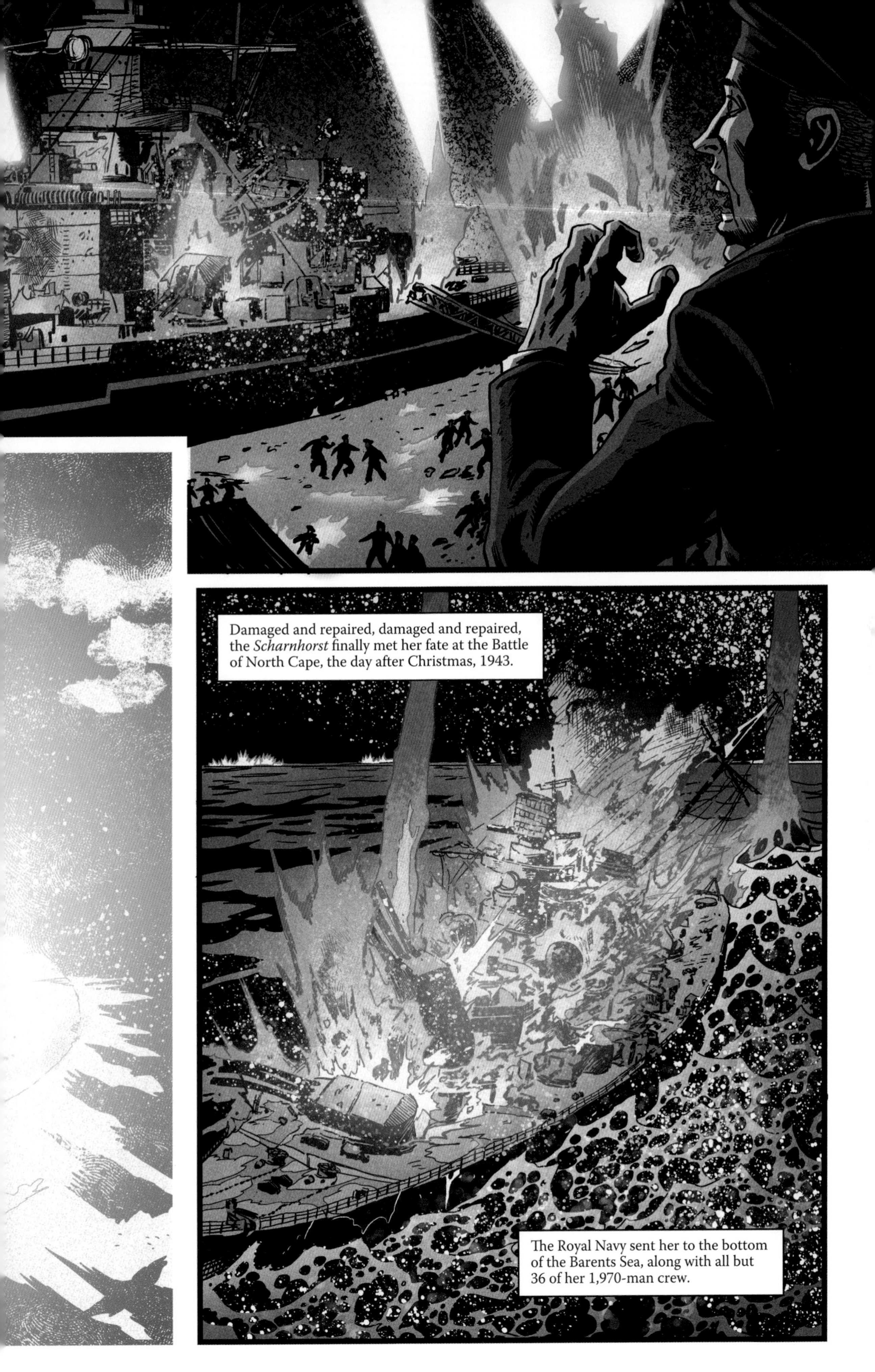
Damaged and repaired, damaged and repaired, the *Scharnhorst* finally met her fate at the Battle of North Cape, the day after Christmas, 1943.
The Royal Navy sent her to the bottom of the Barents Sea, along with all but 36 of her 1,970-man crew.

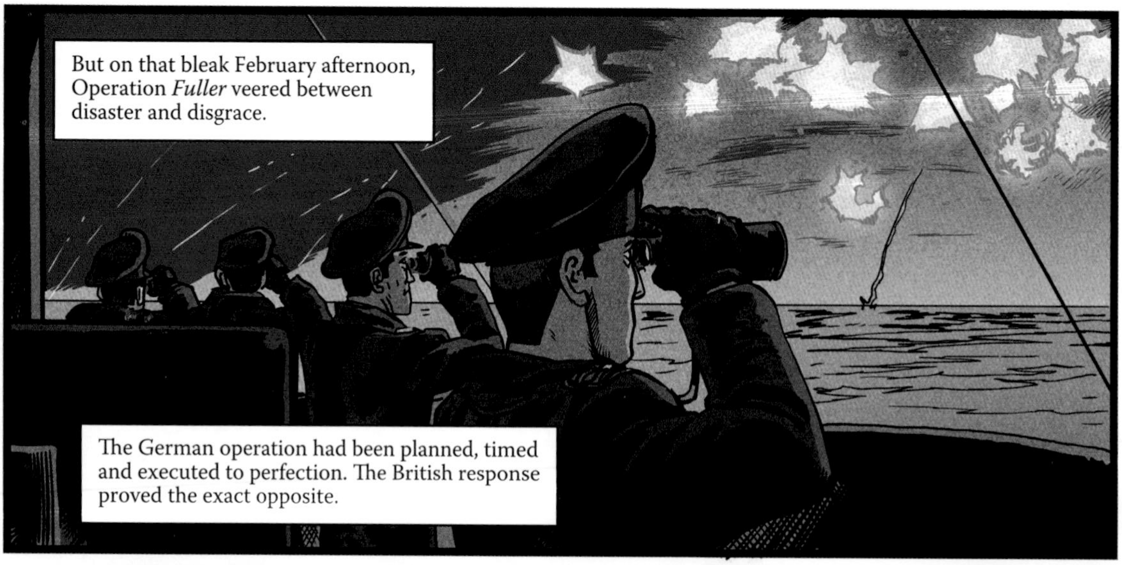
But on that bleak February afternoon, Operation *Fuller* veered between disaster and disgrace.
The German operation had been planned, timed and executed to perfection. The British response proved the exact opposite.

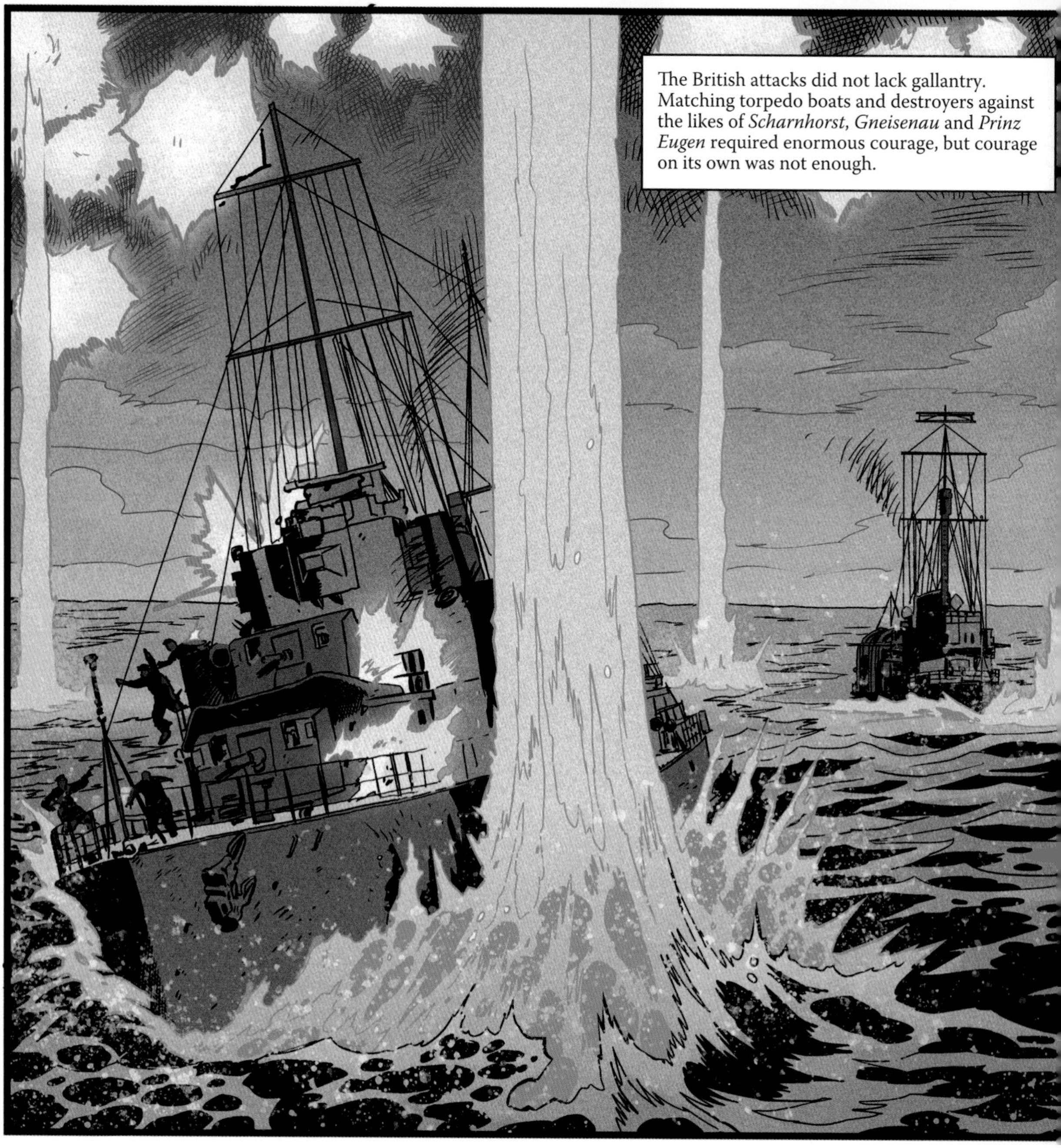
The British attacks did not lack gallantry. Matching torpedo boats and destroyers against the likes of *Scharnhorst*, *Gneisenau* and *Prinz Eugen* required enormous courage, but courage on its own was not enough.

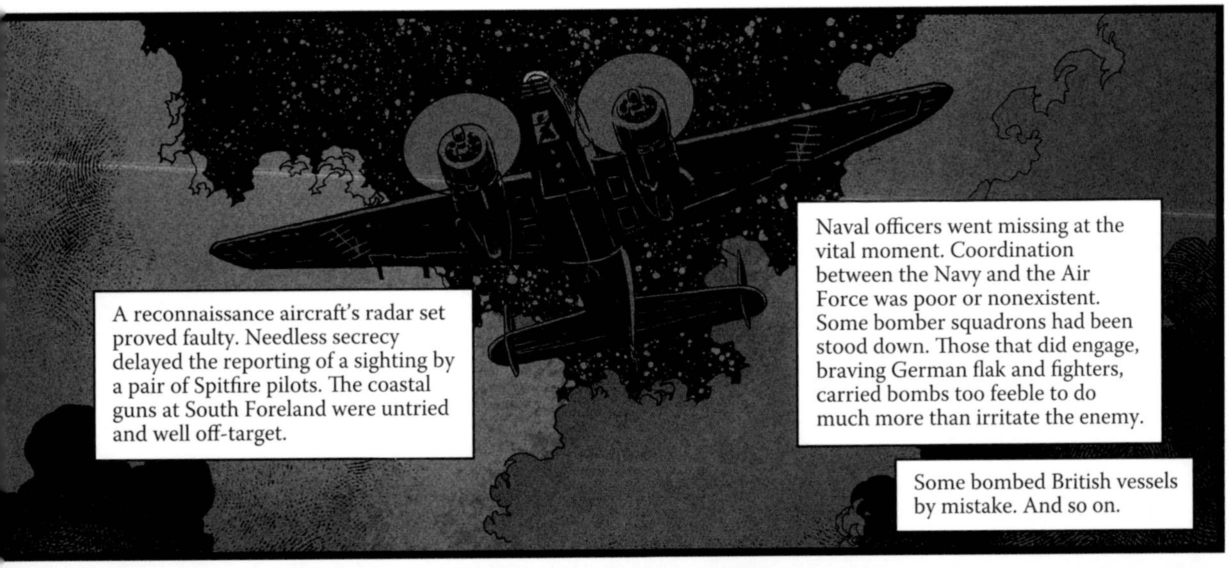
A reconnaissance aircraft's radar set proved faulty. Needless secrecy delayed the reporting of a sighting by a pair of Spitfire pilots. The coastal guns at South Foreland were untried and well off-target.
Naval officers went missing at the vital moment. Coordination between the Navy and the Air Force was poor or nonexistent. Some bomber squadrons had been stood down. Those that did engage, braving German flak and fighters, carried bombs too feeble to do much more than irritate the enemy.
Some bombed British vessels by mistake. And so on.

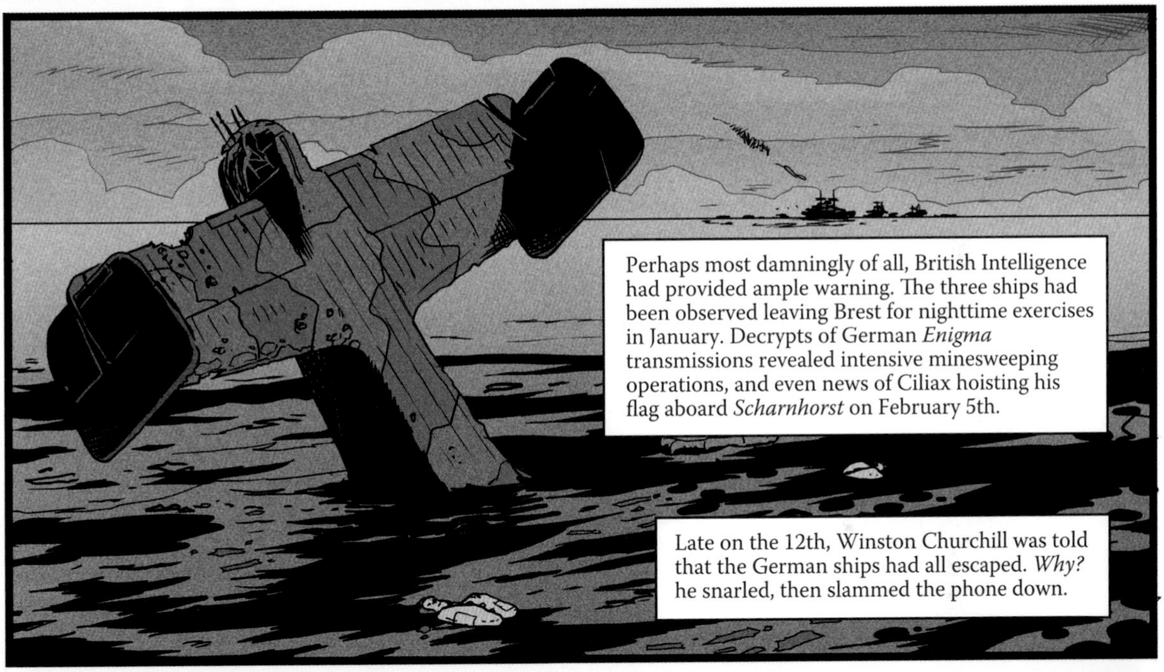
Perhaps most damningly of all, British Intelligence had provided ample warning. The three ships had been observed leaving Brest for nighttime exercises in January. Decrypts of German *Enigma* transmissions revealed intensive minesweeping operations, and even news of Ciliax hoisting his flag aboard *Scharnhorst* on February 5th.
Late on the 12th, Winston Churchill was told that the German ships had all escaped. *Why?* he snarled, then slammed the phone down.

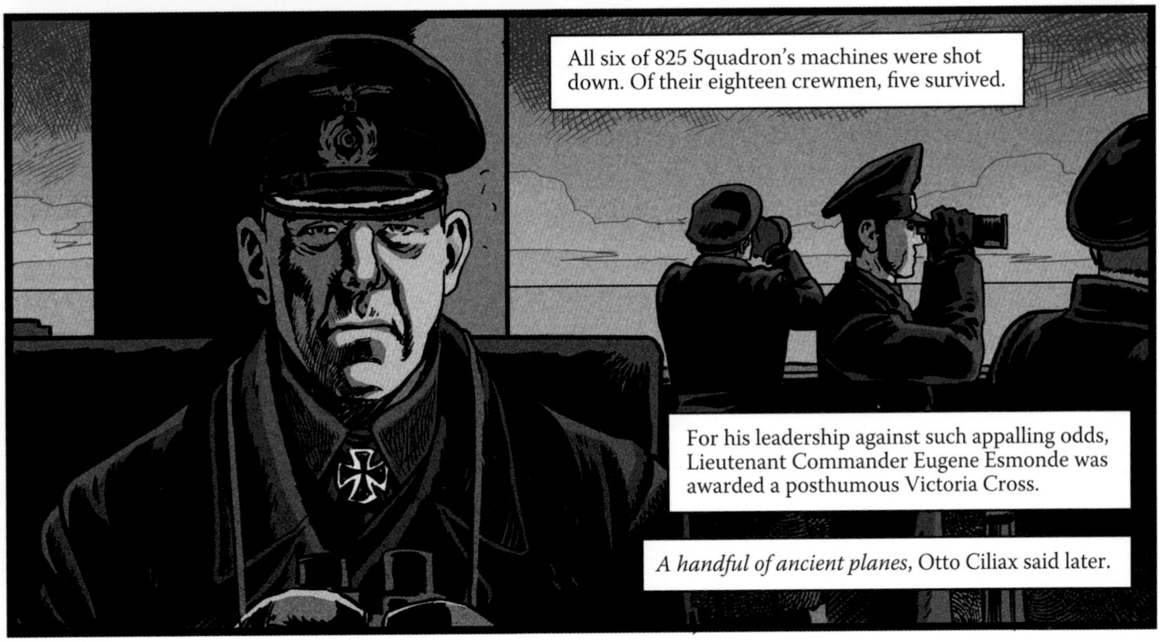
All six of 825 Squadron's machines were shot down. Of their eighteen crewmen, five survived.
For his leadership against such appalling odds, Lieutenant Commander Eugene Esmonde was awarded a posthumous Victoria Cross.
A handful of ancient planes, Otto Ciliax said later.

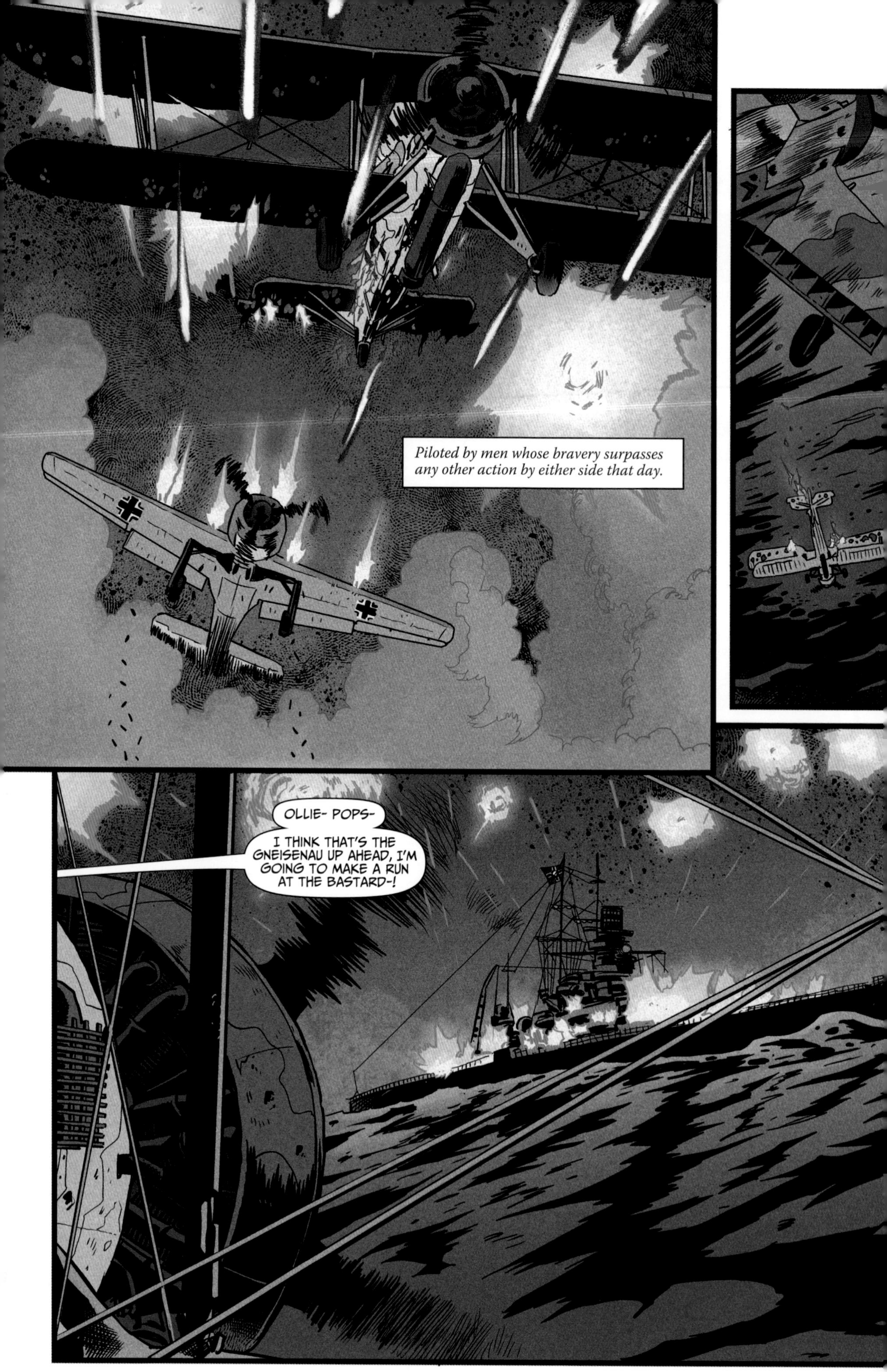
Piloted by men whose bravery surpasses any other action by either side that day.
OLLIE- POPS-
I THINK THAT'S THE GNEISENAU UP AHEAD, I'M GOING TO MAKE A RUN AT THE BASTARD-!

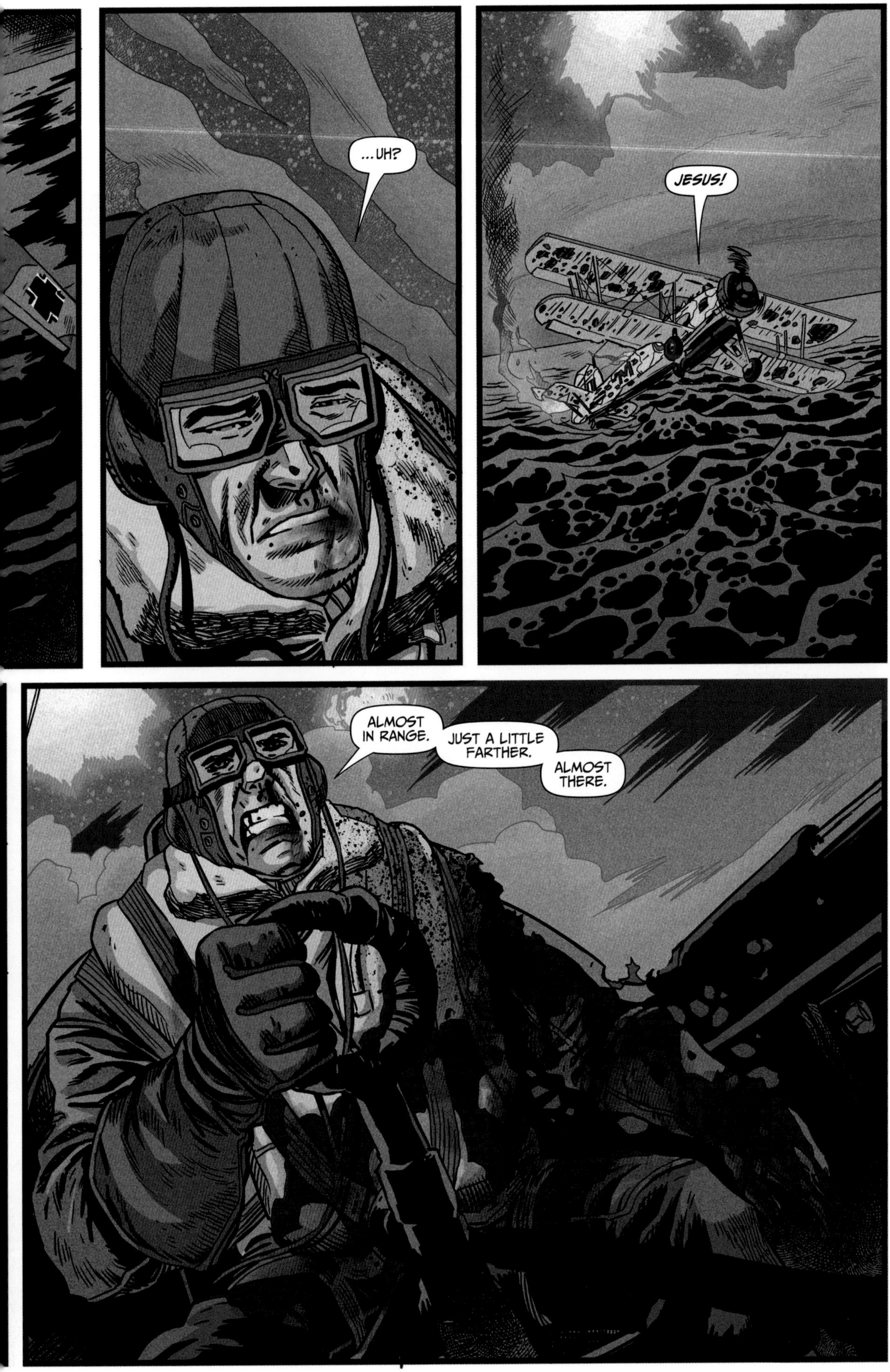
...UH?
JESUS!
ALMOST IN RANGE.
JUST A LITTLE FARTHER.
ALMOST THERE.

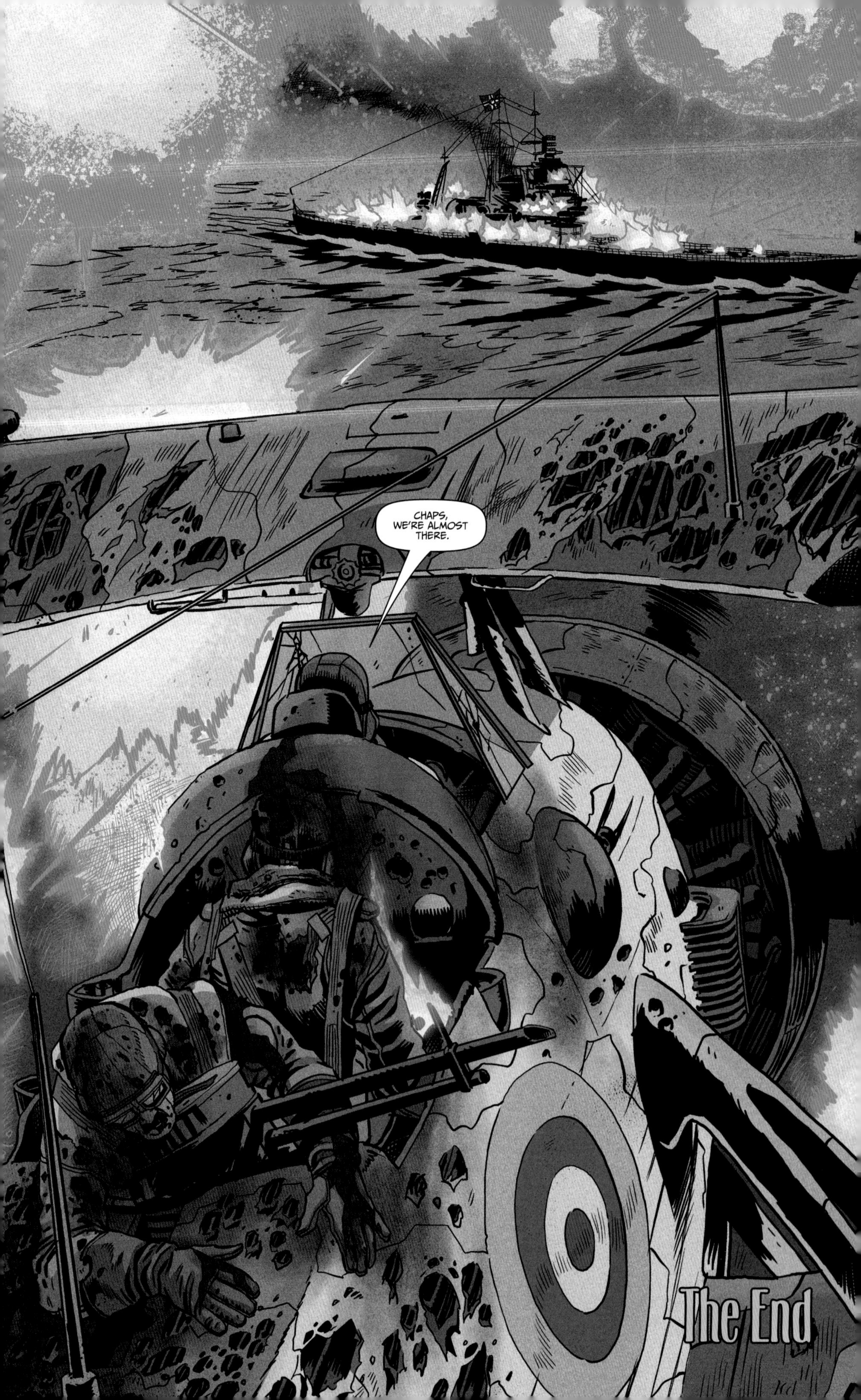
CHAPS, WE'RE ALMOST THERE.
The End

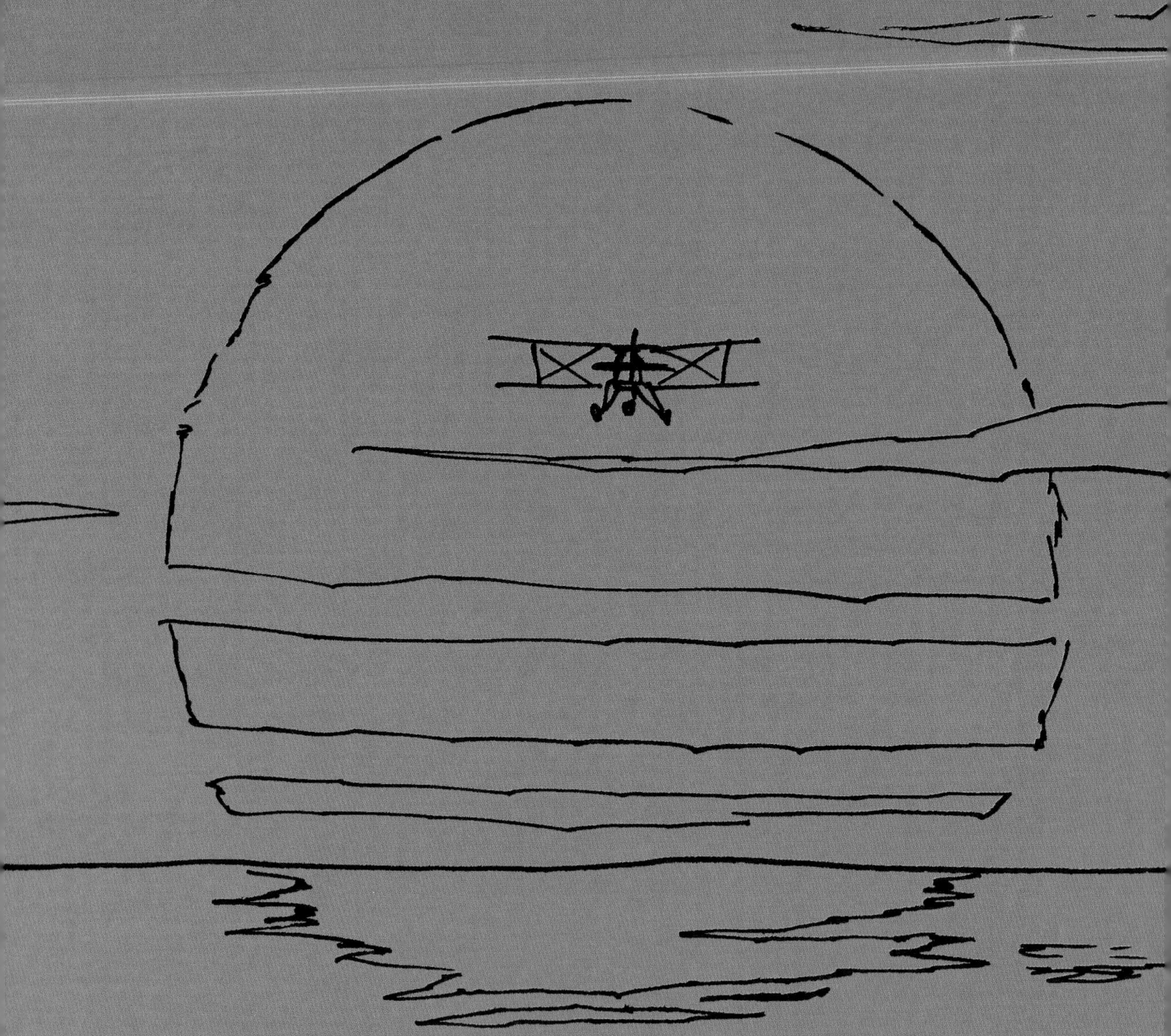

Afterword
FACT & FICTION

More than most of the war stories I've written, *The Stringbags* makes direct use of historical events and personalities, and it seems only proper to distinguish those elements from material invented for the narrative. So whereas the attack on Taranto, the sinking of the *Bismarck* and the Channel Dash all actually occurred, the three main characters are fictional creations. They are not thinly disguised versions of real individuals, nor even amalgamations of the same. Archie, Ollie and Pops are simply stand-ins for the men who crewed the Fairey Swordfish, and flew the aircraft on the operations our story depicts. The reasons for this creative choice were twofold.

First, and most practically, no single Swordfish crew took part in all three actions. The epic scope of the story—involving as it does the crippling of a fleet, the hunt for a Nazi battleship, and the death ride of heroes—seemed to me to be in danger of dwarfing all other elements, and without strong and consistent characters to inspire the reader's sympathy could easily reduce the narrative to dry documentary. The answer was obviously to follow one crew of three men throughout, which would mean creating a completely fictional trio. It would also require a little bit of historical tinkering.

Taranto was the stumbling block. As Ollie notes just after take-off, the other Swordfish on the raid each had only two men aboard, thus allowing for a large auxiliary fuel tank that would grant each aircraft the required range. (To be absolutely precise, the torpedo-carrying Stringbags had the tank placed in the cockpit in what was normally the observer's position, while the flare-droppers flew with it slung beneath the fuselage.) With our heroes assigned the latter task, it seemed to me not completely unreasonable that Archie's enthusiasm—combined with the confusion after Captain Shanks' collapse and the preoccupation of other personnel with the job at hand—might just be enough to get them airborne, before Ollie realized they'd bitten off more than they could chew. The loss of the tank itself made the whole thing a fait accompli, ensuring that the improbable would not become the impossible; they could go on the raid, but not make it back. To my mind, that was fair enough.

(The reader may be interested to note the experience of Lieutenants Clifford and Going, whose Swordfish was damaged on the flight deck of HMS *Illustrious*, and who subsequently took off almost half an hour after the rest of the first wave had departed. Having pleaded with their superiors to be allowed to join the raid, the two made their way to Taranto alone—well aware that the Italian defenses would be fully alert after the initial British attack. Guided to their target by the storm of antiaircraft fire over the distant harbor—"the biggest firework display we had ever seen," said Going—they survived the undivided attention of the Italian gunners during their attack, then escaped into the darkness. So individual acts of courage and initiative were not unheard of.)

This minor sleight of hand allowed me a couple of other indulgences, most obviously the night fighter attack and our heroes' subsequent ditching. Apart from the two Swordfish lost over Taranto itself, the British suffered no other losses, nor did they encounter any Italian aircraft during the operation. Yet fighters would certainly have been up that night, and a chance encounter wherein the trio picked up a few bullet holes in their already doomed aircraft (as opposed to some epic dogfight from which they emerged victorious) felt reasonably credible.

The second reason for creating three fictional heroes is a simple matter of respect for the men who did these things. I have usually shied away from using historical figures in stories like *The Stringbags*, just because it seems unfair to ascribe invented opinions and behaviors to people who in all likelihood never said or felt any such thing. Sometimes involving the genuine players is unavoidable, of course, or even desirable—having Rear Admiral Lyster express mild amusement at Admiral Cunningham's signal, for instance, or reproducing some of Lieutenant Commander Esmonde's actual dialogue in an otherwise invented conversation with the fictional Captain Shanks. But to go further and make, say, Launcelot Kiggell and Johnny Neale the heroes of the entire three-part story, to involve them in the *Bismarck* strike or the Channel Dash, to put words in their mouths that they never spoke but which suited my own purposes—that would betray a lack of respect. And respect, at the end of the day, is what this is all about.

Having created Archie, Ollie and Pops—and kept them moving between squadrons and aircraft carriers in unlikely but not impossible fashion—P. J. and I worked hard to depict the three operations concerned as accurately as possible. This includes the background pieces that introduce and conclude each of the episodes, as well as dialogue attributed to the likes of Günther Lütjens, Otto Ciliax, Adolf Hitler, and Winston Churchill. (With its mention at the end of part one, it is worth noting that the question of Taranto's influence on Pearl Harbor has always been slightly controversial; certainly the latter raid was already well into its planning stages when Japanese observers visited the site of the British strike. So while one certainly did not inspire the other, it seems reasonable to assume that some degree of influence was exerted.)

I was very careful to avoid the portrayal of any of our heroes' actions as having been decisive. For them to have launched the torpedo that disabled the *Bismarck*'s steering gear, or to have gained a direct hit on one of the Italian battleships, would once again have been unfair to the men who performed these feats in real life. Of course, determining who exactly accomplished what in such circumstances is not always easy; an attack made at night or in mid-Atlantic twilight is not exactly conducive to calm recollection

by eyewitnesses, particularly with heavy antiaircraft fire thrown into the mix. Yet what seems clear is that at Taranto, Kenneth Williamson and Norman Scarlett not only survived the disabling and ditching of their Swordfish after making the initial attack, but also scored a critical hit on the *Conti di Cavour.* Swordfish L4K crewed by Lieutenants Kemp and Bailey appears to have done the same to the *Littorio*, while Lea and Jones (of the second attack wave) put a torpedo into the *Caio Duillo.* As for the *Bismarck*, exactly who deserves credit for the crucial strike remains a matter of some conjecture, but the most likely candidates are the aircraft flown by Lieutenant Godfrey-Faussett and Sub-Lieutenant Moffat. Add to this roll of honor the names of those who caused further damage to vessels and installations at Taranto, or split the German defensive fire six months later, or flung themselves at Otto Ciliax's warships during the Channel Dash, and the folly of attributing their actions solely to fictional replacements should become clear.

Yet Archie, Ollie and Pops are involved in several more minor but specific incidents that did actually take place. Here my rationale was that a leavening of such details could enliven, humanize and even where necessary distract from the ongoing narrative, whose epic nature has, as I say, certain all-eclipsing qualities. A brief rundown on these—and their real-life origins—seems appropriate at this point, beginning with the dire Royal Naval Air Service station Twatt. There is an actual Twatt in the Orkney Isles, just to the north of Scotland—the Navy ended its presence at the airfield there in 1949. Deciding that the name was too good not to employ, I moved the location much closer to London, really to grant our heroes convenient access to the fleshpots of the big city. There is another Twatt even farther north in the Shetlands, this time sans airfield. In the original Norse it translates as "small parcel of land".

After their dunking in the Strait of Otranto the trio are rescued by the very real HMS *Nubian*, whose task force destroyed four Italian merchant ships and damaged two of their escorts. Later, Captain Shanks' account of the *Illustrious*' ghastly ordeal is based on accounts of survivors; the carrier was bombed again while undergoing temporary repairs at Malta, crossed the Mediterranean and transited to South Africa via the Suez Canal, then made her way to Norfolk, Virginia, for permanent repair work. It is a measure of the dreadful damage she sustained that—several months after the initial attack—American dock workers were still finding human remains trapped deep inside the great ship's superstructure.

The pursuit and destruction of the *Bismarck* is probably the most well-known aspect of *The Stringbags*; again, the saga of the *Hood*, the *Prince of Wales*, the Nazi battleship and the Home Fleet is portrayed as accurately as could be achieved. Ollie's magnificent moment of insanity was actually that of Sub-Lieutenant J. D. "Dusty" Miller, whose pilot, John Moffat, remembered:

Then I heard Dusty Miller shouting in my ear, "Not yet, not yet!" and I thought, "Has he gone mad? What is he doing?" I turned and realized that he was leaning out of the cockpit, looking down at the sea, trying to prevent me from dropping the torpedo on to the crest of the wave . . . the ship was getting bigger and bigger, and I thought. "Bloody hell, what are you waiting for?" Then he said, "Let her go, Jock," and I pressed the button on the throttle. Dusty yelled, "I think we have got a runner."

Most of *Ark Royal*'s Stringbags were damaged to some extent during the attack, but none were actually shot down. Yet considering the weight of lead being flung around the sky, it seemed not impossible for our heroes to end up in the drink. Likewise, despite the earlier (and real) blunder involving HMS *Sheffield*, I decided that Captain Larcom would have a big enough heart to fish them out.

Which brings me to the story's melancholy ending. No one in 825 Squadron or at RAF Manston was under any illusion about what a daylight attack would mean for the Swordfish crews, particularly in the face of German fighter opposition. The station commander, Tom Gleave, did indeed salute the aircraft as they took off—and Gleave was a man who knew something of sacrifice, having been shot down and horribly burned during the Battle of Britain. Squadron Leader Brian Kingcome led the ten Spitfires that did initially show up, and his recollection of the Stringbags' encounter with the mighty *Kriegsmarine* warships makes for grim reading:

The contrast between our lumbering patrol of Swordfish, wallowing sluggishly over the waves, and this magnificent floating fortress cruelly showed up the contrast between struggling museum relics and a sleek, deadly product of the latest technology . . . then the battleship raised her sights and let fly directly at the Swordfish with a fiery inferno. The brave "Stringbags" never faltered, but just kept driving steadily on at wave-top height, straight and level as though on a practice run. They made perfect targets as they held back from firing their missiles before closing to torpedo range. They were flying to unswerving destruction, and all we as their escort could do was sit helplessly in the air above them and watch them die.

Kingcome's squadron was soon fighting for its life in the face of terrible odds, and even when more Spitfires arrived there were not enough to protect the Swordfish from the swarms of Messerschmitts and Focke-Wulfs.

The man that Archie, Ollie and Pops watch trying to beat out the flames on his aircraft's fuselage is Petty Officer Clinton, Eugene Esmonde's gunner; both they and observer Lieutenant Williams died in the attack. So did all nine men in the second wave of three

Swordfish; they were last seen flying straight into the enemy guns, and to this day are listed as missing in action. One of the survivors of the first wave was Sub-Lieutenant R. M. Samples, whose fluent Anglo-Saxon and accompanying two-fingered gestures inspired Ollie's own defiance of the enemy. Samples was fortunate enough to have been rescued from the waters of the Channel, along with the rest of his crew.

The German pilot who figured out how to match his FW 190's speed to that of the Swordfish was Leutnant Egon Mayer of *Jagdgeschwader* 2. His boss, Adolf Galland, *General der Jagdflieger* and responsible for the aerial component of Operation *Cerberus*, regarded the Channel Dash as his finest hour. In this light, it may seem odd that the story should end with praise for the Swordfish crews from a man they were trying to kill, and who was, in turn, ultimately responsible for their deaths. All I can say is that, to my mind, Otto Ciliax was in a position to know.

The actual origin of the term "Stringbag" had less to do with the Swordfish itself and more with what it could carry. Torpedoes, bombs, mines, depth-charges, rockets, flares—there seemed no limit to what could be loaded aboard the aircraft, and its nickname was thus derived from the all-purpose string shopping bags in common use at the time. If that seems a mundane comparison for a machine that accomplished so much, what should perhaps be borne in mind is the illimitable British talent for understatement. Besides, when it entered service, the Swordfish did not seem like a world-beater. Its crews had yet to get down to work.

The incident with the barrage balloon happened; and if the tale of the American observer learning the aircraft's provenance is indeed apocryphal, that is perhaps a matter for some regret. Taranto, the *Bismarck* and the Channel Dash are the most famous moments by far in the Stringbag's history, but considering its service throughout the war they are perhaps only the tip of the iceberg. *The Stringbags*, then, is offered in tribute to the men who flew the Fairey Swordfish into battle. I hope it would not have displeased them.

—Garth Ennis
New York City, June 2019

About the Creators

Garth ENNIS has been writing comics since 1989. Credits include *Preacher*, *The Boys* (both adapted for TV), *Hitman*, and successful runs on *The Punisher* and *Fury* for Marvel Comics. He is particularly known for his war comics, including *War Stories*, *Battlefields*, *Out of the Blue*, *Sara*, and a recent revival of the classic British series *Johnny Red*. Originally from Northern Ireland, Ennis now lives in New York City with his wife, Ruth.

PJ HOLDEN is a Belfast-based comic artist. Best known for his work for *2000AD* on *Judge Dredd*, over the last twenty years he has also drawn *Rogue Trooper*, *Robocop/ Terminator*, *James Bond: M*, *World of Tanks*, and *Battlefields*. He is the co-creator of *Dept. of Monsterology* and *Numbercruncher*. He is married to Annette and has two kids, Thomas and Nathan.

Kelly FITZPATRICK is a Hugo-nominated comic book colorist and illustrator. She has worked on everything from Kickstarter and indie publications to DC graphic novels. Kelly spends all of her free time doting on her dog, Archie, as well as training dogs, doing yoga and aerial acrobatics, and self-publishing her own books.

Rob STEEN has lettered comics for all major comic book companies. He is also the illustrator of the children's book series *Flanimals*, written by Ricky Gervais, and *Erf*, written by Garth Ennis.